THE UNITED NATIONS PROGRAMME ON CRIME PREVENTION AND CRIMINAL JUSTICE

This book documents the evolution of the United Nations (UN) Crime Programme and its changing priorities, from the early focus on juvenile delinquency and correctional treatment, to the present preoccupation with transnational organized crime. It analyses what factors have contributed to this evolution, and to the shift from the original work on "soft law" resolutions and international standards, to "hard law" conventions, and to the expansion of technical assistance. It also examines the changing structure and working methods of the Programme, such as the UN Crime Commission and the UN Secretariat unit responsible for the Programme, the UN Crime Congresses, and the Programme Network Institutes. Drawing on almost 50 years of experience on the "inside" of the UN Crime Programme and his hands-on knowledge of the working of governmental and intergovernmental processes, Matti Joutsen explores the transitions that have taken place in the UN Crime Programme over the seven decades of its existence, assesses the changing impact of the Programme, and suggests possible future directions in international cooperation in crime prevention and criminal justice.

An accessible and compelling read, this book will appeal to students and scholars of criminology, sociology, politics, criminal justice, policy makers, and those interested in the evolution of the UN Crime Programme.

Matti Joutsen is the former Director of the European Institute for Crime Prevention and Control, affiliated with the United Nations.

THE UNITED NATIONS PROGRAMME ON CRIME PREVENTION AND CRIMINAL JUSTICE

Matti Joutsen

Routledge
Taylor & Francis Group

LONDON AND NEW YORK

Designed cover image: © Getty Images / JacobH

First published 2024
by Routledge
4 Park Square, Milton Park, Abingdon, Oxon OX14 4RN

and by Routledge
605 Third Avenue, New York, NY 10158

Routledge is an imprint of the Taylor & Francis Group, an informa business

© 2024 Matti Joutsen

British Library Cataloguing-in-Publication Data
A catalogue record for this book is available from the British Library

ISBN: 978-1-032-77024-6 (hbk)
ISBN: 978-1-032-77021-5 (pbk)
ISBN: 978-1-003-48090-7 (ebk)

DOI: 10.4324/9781003480907

Typeset in Sabon
by codeMantra

The UN Crime Programme has benefitted from the contributions of many persons around the world.

*This book is dedicated to three of them:
Inkeri Anttila, for her inspiration,
Gerhard Mueller, for his vision, and
Gary Hill, for his commitment.*

CONTENTS

TABLES

BOXES

ABOUT THE AUTHOR

For close to 50 years, Dr. Matti Joutsen has combined academic work, governmental work, and hands-on involvement in intergovernmental policy-making on criminal justice.

Dr. Joutsen has a degree in political science and a doctorate in law. He was drawn into criminology and international cooperation by the legendary Professor Inkeri Anttila, who was one of the pioneers in combining sociological research and criminal law, promoting international cooperation, and advocating for a rational, just, and humane criminal policy. He began as a criminologist at Finland's national Research Institute of Legal Policy, but soon moved to international work at the European Institute for Crime Prevention and Control, affiliated with the United Nations (HEUNI), the European regional institute in the United Nations (UN) Crime Programme, becoming in time its director. Along the way, he took leave of absence to serve as a lower court judge in Finland, and as Director of International Affairs at the Ministry of Justice of Finland. He spent extended periods as visiting professor, teaching comparative and transnational criminal justice, at the University of Illinois in Chicago and at John Jay College of Criminal Justice, City University of New York.

Dr. Joutsen contributed to the development of Europe-wide comparative analyses of crime trends and the operation of criminal justice systems, which served as the template for subsequent global analysis within the UN Crime Programme. He has also conducted research on a range of subjects, such as victim policy, prosecutorial decision-making, and non-custodial sanctions.

When the European Union (EU) expanded its activities to include crime and criminal justice in 1995, Dr. Joutsen became involved in the rapid evolution of European cooperation in this field. He had a hand in the drafting of many EU decisions, among them the European Arrest Warrant in the immediate aftermath of the 9/11 attacks, and was closely involved in the negotiation of EU–U.S. treaties on extradition and mutual legal assistance. He has also served as an expert for the Council of Europe.

Dr. Joutsen began attending UN Crime Programme meetings in 1975, at the Fifth UN Crime Congress (Milan). Thereafter he soon came to play an active role in many key UN Crime Programme negotiations. He was one of the architects of the restructuring of the UN Crime Programme, which culminated in 1991 with the replacement of a UN committee of experts by a commission consisting of Member States. A few years later, he played an instrumental role in the drafting of the UN Convention on Transnational Organized Crime. Dr. Joutsen's influence can be seen in his repeated election at global UN meetings to key positions, including Rapporteur-General at the Tenth UN Crime Congress (Vienna, 2000), and vice-chairperson of all subsequent UN Crime Congresses (Bangkok, 2005; Salvador de Bahia, Brazil, 2010; Doha, 2015; and Kyoto, 2021).

Among his UN Crime Programme colleagues, he is perhaps most noted for having been a tenacious negotiator on the mechanism for the review of the implementation of the UN Convention on Corruption, which for the first time in connection with any UN treaty, incorporated the concept of peer review. Subsequently, he has been at the forefront of the continuing UN debate on the involvement of civil society in crime prevention and criminal justice.

Dr. Joutsen has received the "Distinguished International Scholar" award from the Division of International Criminology of the American Society of Criminology, the Order of the White Rose by the Government of Finland, and the Order of the Rising Sun by the Government of Japan for his work in international criminal justice.

PREFACE

This book describes the emergence and development of the UN Crime Programme over the course of 75 years and its impact on international cooperation in criminal justice.

Traditionally, countries have rarely looked beyond their borders when deciding what conduct should be considered criminal, how to prevent crime, how to protect and assist victims, and how to punish offenders.

That has changed. First individual practitioners and academics, and then governments, realized that exchanging experiences with foreign colleagues on what works in crime prevention and criminal justice (and what does not) can help strengthen domestic policy and improve domestic practice. International cooperation has been further expanded in recent decades by the growing realization that, in a globalized world, unilateral action by individual countries is insufficient to prevent and respond to organized crime and terrorism.

This international cooperation has expanded on an *ad hoc* basis, through the work of individuals, and of various professional, academic, and other organizations. Governments, in turn, have entered into a dense network of bilateral and multilateral agreements and other arrangements.

When the UN was established in the aftermath of the Second World War, it created the possibility of bringing countries around the world to the same table to discuss and develop practice and policy, and to see if a global framework for cooperation could be established. The United Nations Crime Prevention and Criminal Justice Programme – the UN Crime Programme – was born.

The *UN Crime Programme* is the shorthand used when referring to the work that is conducted under the coordination of the United Nations Commission on Crime Prevention and Criminal Justice. Much of this work is carried out by the United Nations Office on Drugs and Crime (UNODC) in

Vienna, in UNODC field offices around the world, and by a number of institutes and other entities that work together with the UN Secretariat. The work also takes place within the framework of the Conferences of the States Parties to two UN Crime Conventions (on, respectively, transnational organized crime and corruption), the mammoth UN Crime Congresses which are held every five years, and a variety of UN *ad hoc* expert and intergovernmental meetings.

This book has been written to serve several different functions. It is a history, a guide, and an attempt to assess the impact of the UN Crime Programme.

As a *history of the UN Crime Programme*, it provides an overview of the evolution of the Programme. Although earlier authors (in particular Dr. Manuel López-Rey and Dr. Slawomir Redo) have provided good accounts of this history (and Dr. Redo considerable analysis), there is much that has been left unrecorded, or that is not readily accessible. The present book is the first to bring together the development not only of the main structural elements (such as the UN Crime Committee, the UN Crime Commission, and the Secretariat unit responsible for the Programme), but also of such parts of the Programme as the UN Crime Congresses and the Programme Network Institutes. I also describe the emergence of the two UN Crime Conventions (on transnational organized crime and corruption), and the work on their implementation, as well as the ongoing negotiations on a UN Cybercrime Convention.

Traces of this historical record can be found scattered in different documents, and as unrecorded oral lore. Many of the key persons involved (such as Ms. Irene Melup, Prof. Gerhard Mueller, Mr. Dimitri Vlassis, and Mr. Gary Hill) have sadly passed away in recent years. I have tried to record their contribution as best as I can, along with the contributions of many others who would otherwise remain unrecognized.

The second intended function of this book is to serve as a *guide to the UN Crime Programme*. The book is designed to help representatives who have been assigned by their Member State or organization to attend meetings and negotiations related to the Programme, academics studying international cooperation, as well as others who are interested in what the UN is doing in this important sector.

There are many elements of the UN Crime Programme. The complicated structure, the at times arcane language, and the occasionally almost ritual choreography of meetings can be bewildering. The UN being what it is, reference is constantly being made to earlier resolutions or to the work of different UN bodies. First-time participants may not understand what the purpose of certain procedural stages is, nor what the implications of certain words or phrases can be. As a result, they may miss opportunities to have an impact on decision-making in the UN Crime Programme.

For outsiders trying to make sense of this "black box" of a policy-making structure, it may be even more difficult to understand what kind of decisions are being made, who makes the decisions, where and when these decisions are made, and on what basis the decisions are made.

The third function is to look at *the impact of the UN Crime Programme*. This ties in with the history of the UN Crime Programme, since it requires looking at why the Programme was established, why it has evolved in the way it has, and in what direction(s) it appears to be heading. The book seeks to assess the extent to which the UN Crime Programme has succeeded in helping Member States prevent and respond to crime – and where it has fallen short. In this, I make use of the theoretical concepts of *international regimes* and *global governance*.

As I argue in this book, the UN has its own criminal policy, which is the result of a relatively intricate process. Representatives of the 193 Member States of the UN, several intergovernmental organizations, and a large number of non-governmental organizations, individual experts, and many other stakeholders are involved in defining what the priorities of UN criminal policy should be, and what should be done about them. One would like to think that the process is based on a careful weighing of the available criminological evidence by leading experts, a review by practitioners of local and national experience with "what works" in preventing and responding to crime, the development of a comprehensive and well-defined global agenda, as well as the allocation of sufficient resources to the UN so that it can assist Member States in the implementation of that agenda. However, the process often proves to be less rational and somewhat messier.

My intention is to show how the reality on the ground matches the grand visions in the conference halls.

ACKNOWLEDGEMENTS

I have spent some 50 years working within the framework of the UN Crime Programme, both as a representative of my own country (Finland), and as the Director of the European regional institute in the UN Programme Network (the European Institute for Crime Prevention and Control, affiliated with the UN, HEUNI). I have also served for a short stint as the UN Interregional Adviser on Crime Prevention and Criminal Justice, and for several years as special advisor to another UN-affiliated institute, the Thailand Institute of Justice.

Over the course of these 50 years, I have spent a considerable amount of time sitting in various UN Crime Programme meetings around the world, including nine UN Crime Congresses beginning in 1975 (at one of which I was general rapporteur, and at the four most recent Congresses, I was one of the chairpersons), negotiations on the two UN Crime Conventions and their implementation, over 30 annual sessions of the UN Crime Commission (and seven biannual sessions of its predecessor, the UN Crime Committee), various intergovernmental expert meetings, a large variety of expert meetings and seminars organized by the different entities in the UN Crime Programme network, as well as innumerable meetings organized by my own regional institute, HEUNI. All told (and allowing for weekends off), this adds up to a solid three or four years of my working life sitting in a meeting room, listening to my colleagues, trying to understand their arguments, concerns, and priorities, and seeking to find formulations that would work in six official UN languages and ultimately arrive at a consensus – and, I hope, still make a difference in how crime is prevented and how humane, effective, and rational criminal justice is promoted all around the world.

The experience has allowed me to see the inner workings of the UN Crime Programme, as well as chart the considerable changes that have taken place in its structure and priorities and in the way that it works.

It has also given me the privilege to work with and learn from many of the persons who have influenced the direction of the UN Crime Programme over the years, and who feature throughout this book. Among them (in rough chronological order) are Ms. Irene Melup (who was the first Secretariat member assigned to the UN Crime Programme, and widely considered its conscience), Dr. Manuel López-Rey (UN Secretariat/Bolivia),[1] Minoru Shikita-sama (UN Secretariat/Japan), Mr. Bill Clifford (UN Secretariat/Australia), Prof. Gerhard Mueller (UN Secretariat), Prof. Inkeri Anttila (Finland), Dr. Adolfo Beria di Argentine (Italy), Mr. Dusan Cotic (Yugoslavia), Ms. Simone Rozes (France), Chief Adedokun Adeyemi (Nigeria), Mr. Vasily Ignatov (the Russian Federation), Prof. Roger Clark (New Zealand), Ambassador Luigi Lauriola (Italy), Mr. Herman Woltring (UN Secretariat/Australia), Mr. Gary Hill (United States), and Mr. Dimitri Vlassis (UN Secretariat).

The experience has also allowed me the great pleasure of working alongside such experts as (and this time in alphabetical order) Prof. Rosemary Barberet (United States), Mr. John Brandolino (UN Secretariat), Mr. Ronald Gainer (United States), Ms. Junko Irie-san (Japan), Dr. Kittipong Kittayarak (Thailand), Mr. Taro Morinaga-san (Japan), Mr. Gioacchino Polimeni (Italy), Mr. Christopher Ram (Canada), Dr. Slawomir Redo (UN Secretariat), Dr. Phiset Sa-ardyen (Thailand), Mr. Eduardo Vetere (UN Secretariat), Mr. Emil Wandzilak (UN Secretariat), and Dr. Ugljesa Zvekic (UN Interregional Crime and Justice Research Institute/Serbia), many of whom have been very generous with their time in assisting me in assembling material for this book, and when needed, gently setting the record straight. I would like to thank Dr. Redo, Mr. Vetere, and Dr. Zvekic in particular for their unstinting help above and beyond the call of either duty or friendship. I would also like to thank Irie-san, Morinaga-san and Dr. Phiset very warmly not only for their friendship, but also for their generosity in providing the support of their respective UN-affiliated institutes at various stages of the preparation of this book. Any errors or omissions that remain here are my own.

I have also enjoyed befriending many persons around the world whose companionship, counsel, and good humour considerably brightened up those long, long days (and at times evenings and even nights) sitting in session. A partial list in alphabetical order would definitely include Prof. Jay Albanese (United States), Ms. Anna Alvazzi del Frate (Italy), Ms. Lucie Angers (Canada), Dr. Elias Carranza (Costa Rica), Mr. Arkadi Erokhine (UN Secretariat), Mr. David Faulkner (United Kingdom), Mr. Aarne Kinnunen (Finland), Mr. Don Piragoff (Canada), Prof. Rodrigo Paris-Steffans (UN Secretariat), Prof. Phil Reichel (United States), Mr. John Sandage (UN Secretariat), Mr. Bo Svensson (Sweden), and Ms. Terhi Viljanen (Finland).

I am very grateful for the continuous support that I have received from the Finnish Embassy in Vienna. Again and again, I have been impressed by the professionalism and dedication shown by the respective ambassadors, counsellors, and desk officers in their work. The UN Crime Programme was only a small part of their duties, and yet they have all been generous with their time and expertise.

I would also like to express my deepest appreciation to the huge number of persons in the UN Secretariat and in the institutes that constitute the UN Programme Network, the UN interpreters and translators, the document editors, the technicians, and all the others who service the different UN Crime Programme meetings and keep the Programme running. It is you, the yeomen and yeowomen, who make international cooperation possible and, even more than that, enjoyable.

Part of the presentation of the review of the implementation of the UN Crime Convention, in Chapter 3, is based on Joutsen, Matti and Adam Graycar (2012), When Experts and Diplomats Agree: Negotiating Peer Review of the UN Convention Against Corruption, in *Journal of Global Governance: A Review of Multilateralism and International Organizations*, October–December 2012, 18(4), 425–439.

The presentation on the proposed UN Convention on Cybercrime in Chapter 3 is based on Joutsen, Matti (2023), Negotiating United Nations Crime Conventions: Comparing the Negotiations on the Proposed UN Cybercrime Convention with Earlier Conventions, *PNI Newsletter*, issue 3, Bangkok 2023, pp. 18–22.

Chapter 10 is a condensed version of Joutsen, Matti (2021), *The Evolution of the United Nations Congress on Crime Prevention and Criminal Justice*, Thailand Institute of Justice, Bangkok.

Chapter 11 is a condensed version of Joutsen, Matti (2011), The Impact of United Nations Crime Conventions on International Cooperation, in Cindy Smith, Sheldon X. Shang, and Rosemary Barberet (eds.), *Routledge Handbook of International Criminology*, Routledge, London and New York, pp. 112–124.

Annex 4 is based on Joutsen, Matti (2012), Negotiating Conventions in the United Nations: Ten Rules to Follow, in Marc Groenhuijsen, Rianne Letschert, and Sylvia Hazenbroek (eds.), *KLO Van Dijk. Liber amicorum prof.dr,mr. J.J.M. van Dijk*, Wolf Legal Publishers, Nijmegen 2012, pp. 177–190.

I wish to express my appreciation to Mr. Thomas Sutton, at Routledge Books, for his encouragement throughout the long writing process, to Ms. Jessica Phillips and Ms. Sue Cope for their dedication, diligence, and expertise in copyediting, and to the five anonymous reviewers who provided helpful suggestions for elaboration of some of the themes.

Note

1 UN Secretariat staff members are international civil servants, and do not represent their Member State. However, many persons, such as Dr. López-Rey, have influenced the UN Crime Programme both as a member of the UN Secretariat, and (at a different time) as a national representative. In such cases, I have indicated both affiliations.

METHODOLOGY AND USE OF SOURCES

The primary source of data on the UN Crime Programme is the voluminous documentation that has been produced; not only the official documents and meeting records, but also various other publications. As noted in "Acknowledgements," I have had the privilege of representing my country, Finland, in UN Crime Programme meetings for half a century. Throughout that period, I made it a habit to read the various documents (I believe that I am one of the few who have actually done so over an extended period of time), take copious notes of the proceedings, and prepare end-of-mission reports for my colleagues. Over the years, I have also written and lectured extensively on different aspects of the UN Crime Programme. In the preparation of this book, I have revisited many of the key documents, and as many of those personal notes and reports as I could lay my hands on.

Only a few publications exist on the UN Crime Programme, but I have sought out what is available. Of the books and articles listed in the bibliography, I have found the following three to be particularly helpful:

- Manuel López-Rey (1985), *A Guide to United Nations Criminal Policy*,
- Roger Clark (1994), *The United Nations Crime Prevention and Criminal Justice Program. Formulation of Standards and Efforts at Their Implementation*,
- Slawomir Redo (2012), *Blue Criminology*.

Benedict Alper and Jerry Boren (1972) have written on the historical and ideological context in which the UN Crime Programme was established, and on its first twenty years. William Clifford (1979) has provided a personal account of his many years of service on the UN Crime Committee, and Christopher Ram (2012) has provided an insightful analysis of the first twenty years of the work of the UN Crime Commission.

In addition to Dr. Redo (and Mr. Ram in respect of the UN Crime Commission), others have sought to analyse *how* the UN Crime Programme works. As part of a wider analysis of the interplay between criminology, politics, and policy, Reese Walters describes in particular the scientific influences during the early years of the UN Crime Programme. In describing various elements of "global crime governance," Anja Jakobi provides a few references to the UN Crime Programme, and also to the UN Drug Control Programme.

More recent and much more comprehensive and analytical presentations of the evolution of UN crime policy are provided by Jarret Blaustein, Tom Chodor, and Nathan W. Pino, first in two articles, and then in a book published in 2022 that takes the story up to the present. Their work, taken together with that of Walters, Jakobi, and others, serves as a reminder that the same power politics that can be seen on the local and national level in governance, also extend to international affairs.

Trying to identify when and how Member State or other stakeholders are pushing their own agenda in the UN Crime Programme, however, is no easy task, since such fundamentally national interests are rarely expressed overtly in the UN. Instead, proposals will tend to be justified with more palatable arguments, such as principles of international law and institutionalized UN praxis ("this is how we have always done it"), or references to rationality and efficiency ("this is a much better way of doing it"). I would argue that identifying hidden agendas is made much more difficult by the reality of work in the UN. In my own experience, for example the members of national delegations come from a variety of different backgrounds, have their own personal understanding of how to prevent crime and operate the criminal justice system, and have different degrees of skill in the cut-and-thrust of diplomatic negotiations. Furthermore, at times the decision-making in the UN Crime Programme can be chaotic, and involve lengthy negotiation sessions extending far into the night, when it is difficult to keep track of how a constantly evolving draft resolution aligns with one's national position, and there may be no time to seek instructions from the capital city (which may be located several time zones away).

Because of this, I have used my own experience and understanding of what is going on to try to make sense of the whole. As a criminologist, I have a background in participatory observation, interviews, and the use of surveys (as well as other methodological tools used in the social sciences). The value of participatory observation was of special importance because I had the privilege of being directly involved in many of the key inflection points and transitions in the history of the UN Crime Programme, such as the restructuring of the Programme in 1989–1992, the drafting of the two UN Crime Conventions in 1998–2003, and the increasingly politicized debate during the past fifteen years (such as on the review of the implementation of the Conventions, on the role of non-governmental organizations, and on whether or not to begin work on a UN Cybercrime Convention). This is alongside those 50 years of attending different UN Crime Programme meetings, including almost every session of the UN Crime Commission, as well as nine of the quinquennial UN Crime Congresses.

A comment on my use of oral sources. I have participated in many formal negotiations among representatives of UN Member States, and in many confidential informal negotiations (UN usage refers to these as "informals"). UN Crime Programme documentation generally does not identify which delegation said what during formal meetings. Instead, the documents would include a reference along the lines of "Several delegations expressed view A, while others expressed view B."[1] (One notable exception is when a Member State presents a written proposal. In such cases, the Member State is generally identified.) No official records are kept of the informals. As a Finnish civil servant, I regard myself as bound to confidentiality with regard to who said what in such negotiations. Wherever possible, I have provided information in the endnotes on what is recorded in the official UN documentation on the meetings. In some cases, however, I have noted what views and concerns have been expressed orally in these negotiations, without identifying the delegation(s) in question.

Along the same lines, at an early stage in the writing of the book, I interviewed several of the key persons who have been involved in the UN Crime Programme regarding their experiences and perspectives. Some have preferred to remain anonymous, and I have respected their wishes.

Note

1 Occasionally, when the draft meeting report has been presented, there has been considerable discussion over exactly how the official record of what was said should be formulated. It is, apparently, one thing to say, "A few delegations argued X," and quite a different thing to say, "Several delegations argued Y."

References

Alper, Benedict S. and Jerry F. Boren (1972), *Crime: International Agenda, Concern and Action in the Prevention of Crime and Treatment of Offenders, 1846–1972*, Lexington Books

Blaustein Jarrett, Tom Chodor and Nathan W. Pino (2019), Development as a Historical Component of the UN Crime Policy Agenda: From Social Defence to the Millennium Development Goals, *Criminology and Criminal Justice* 21(2), https://doi.org/10.1177/1748895819877453

Blaustein, Jarrett, Tom Chondor and Nathan W. Pino (2021), Governing the Crime-Development Nexus: A Historical Perspective, in Jarrett Blaustein, Kate Fitz-Gibbon, Nathan W. Pino, and Rob White (eds.) (2021), *The Emerald Handbook of Crime, Justice and Social Development*, Emerald Publishing, pp. 25–41

Blaustein, Jarrett, Tom Chondor and Nathan W. Pino (2022), *Unravelling the Development – Crime Nexus*, Rowman & Littlefield

Clark, Roger S. (1994), *The United Nations Crime Prevention and Criminal Justice Program. Formulation of Standards and Efforts at Their Implementation*. University of Pennsylvania Press

Clifford, William (1979), *Echoes and Hopes. The United Nations Committee on Crime Prevention and Control*, Australian Institute of Criminology, Canberra, available at https://www.aic.gov.au/sites/default/files/2020-07/echoes-and-hopes.pdf

Jakobi, Anja P. (2013), *Common Goods & Evils? The Formation of Global Crime Governance*, Oxford University Press

López-Rey de Arroya, Manuel (1985) *A Guide to United Nations Criminal Policy*, Cambridge Studies in Criminology LIV

Ram, Christopher (2012a), *Meeting the Challenge of Crime in the Global Village: An Assessment of the Role and Future of the United Nations Commission on the Crime Prevention and Criminal Justice*, HEUNI publication no. 73, HEUNI

Redo, Slawomir (2012a), *Blue Criminology. The Power of United Nations Ideas to Counter Crime Globally – A Monographic Study*, HEUNI publication no. 72, available at https://www.heuni.fi/en/index/publications/heunireports/reportseriesno.72.bluecriminologythepowerofunitednationsideastocountercrimeglobally-amonographicstudy.html

Walters, Reese (2003), *Deviant Knowledge: Criminology, Politics and Public Policy*, Routledge

1

INTRODUCTION TO THE UNITED NATIONS CRIME PREVENTION AND CRIMINAL JUSTICE PROGRAMME

1.1 Crime prevention and criminal justice as an international concern

Countries around the world have long faced, and continue to face, severe problems in finding an effective response to national and transnational crime. Police, judicial, and correctional statistics provide a measure of the flow of cases coming to the attention of the authorities, and then being processed through the criminal justice system. International victimization surveys[1] have provided evidence of the prevalence and the impact of crime, much of it unreported to the authorities and thus not reflected in the statistics. Recent UN and other research have shown the prevalence and widespread harm caused by of such largely "hidden" crimes as domestic violence, corruption, trafficking in persons, trafficking in endangered species, and cybercrime.

Although informal social control still operates effectively in large parts of the developing world, many countries have undergone massive rural-urban migration, with new arrivals in the cities often faced with a lack of prospects for education and employment. In many countries, attempts at economic development have failed, leaving a legacy of a growing external debt. War, internal conflict, and natural disasters have not only had a disastrous effect on persons caught in their grip, they have also increased the number of internally displaced persons and the international flow of refugees. In some cases, dysfunctional economic development and internal conflicts have been so severe that a new concept has been coined to refer to countries on the verge of collapse: "failing nations." Given the scale of such problems, it is understandable that the criminal justice system in many countries, both developed and developing, in the global North as well as the global South, is under-resourced and overstrained.

DOI: 10.4324/9781003480907-1

The potential targets for crime and the number of likely and motivated offenders have proliferated, while the ability of formal and informal control to prevent potential offenders from committing crime has weakened. The widening economic disparity has increased absolute and relative deprivation, which can serve as an inducement to crime. The reality and perception of increased crime and of weakened control may also have contributed to an increased readiness by many persons to commit crime.

The number of likely and motivated offenders is also being expanded by the prison system. Because of economic difficulties and the low priority assigned to prisons, conditions in prisons are often poor, and they can thus do little to rehabilitate the offenders. On the contrary, the time spent in prison can provide the prisoners with information on new crime techniques and suitable targets, reinforce their self-identity as "criminals" unwanted by society, as well as supply them with willing future partners in crime, once they are released.

The weakened ability of many countries to respond to crime effectively has contributed to an increase in what is known as "ordinary crime" (for example theft, robbery, and assault), and in organized crime. Indeed, these developments have created an almost ideal climate for the growth of international organized crime. One of organized crime's greatest assets is its ability to adapt to change, including change resulting from global pandemics and climate change. Organized crime has also adapted to the improvements in communication and transportation, utilizing the increased ease of international travel, developments in technology such as computers, cellular telephones, and artificial intelligence to evade detection and apprehension, and has been using increasingly sophisticated money laundering techniques.

Crime and the prevention of crime are among the major concerns of both the individual citizen and the state. The terrible destruction caused by the Second World War heightened the need to find ways to restore and maintain stability in society. It is thus understandable that crime was one of the first topics that the United Nations (UN) included in its agenda when it was established in 1945.

Throughout this book, reference is made to the *UN Crime Programme*. Over the course of 75 years, the Programme has been known by different names. Initially, it was called the UN Programme on the Prevention of Crime and the Treatment of Offenders, and subsequently the UN Programme on Crime Prevention and Control.[2] The current formal name is the United Nations Programme on Crime Prevention and Criminal Justice. All three names are rather lengthy. For the sake of simplicity and brevity, I shall refer to it throughout as the UN Crime Programme. This is in line with the way in which the earlier United Nations Committee on Crime Prevention and Control was widely referred to as the UN Crime Committee, the United Nations Commission on Crime Prevention and Criminal Justice is referred to as the

UN Crime Commission, and the United Nations Congresses on Crime Prevention and Criminal Justice are referred to as UN Crime Congresses.[3]

The UN Crime Programme consists of the work carried out under the co-ordination of the *UN Crime Commission* in order to help Member States to prevent crime and improve the response to national and transnational crime, for example through data collection, the sharing of information and experience, and training.[4]

National crime in this context refers to crime, as defined by domestic law, which primarily affects the jurisdiction of only one country. Most "ordinary crime" (also referred to as "conventional crime") is local. Typical examples are youth crime, domestic violence, street crime, property crime (such as burglaries and shoplifting), and vandalism. *Transnational crime* is crime that involves the jurisdiction of more than one country, for example because the offender has crossed borders to commit the offence (as in the smuggling of migrants), the suspect has fled to another country, the offence has an impact across borders (as with extensive environmental crime), the same offence is directed at victims in more than one country (as in many cybercrimes), or the proceeds of crime are transferred abroad (as with many cases of economic crime and corruption).[5] The UN has an interest in helping Member States prevent and respond to both national and international crime. National (ordinary) crime constitutes the bulk of the workload of the criminal justice system in any country, and exchanging information and experiences in how to prevent such crime, assist the victims, and deal with the offenders is of help to developed and developing countries alike, in the Global North as well as in the Global South. Such sharing of approaches helps Member States also in addressing transnational crime, but there is the added element that preventing and responding to such crime generally requires cooperation between Member States in detecting the offences, identifying the offenders and bringing them to justice, assisting the victims, and recovering the proceeds of crime.

Over the past 70 plus years, the UN Crime Programme has produced two conventions on crime (with work currently underway on a third), an extensive set of UN standards and norms on crime prevention and criminal justice, considerable research, and a very active technical assistance programme. A network of institutes has been established or co-opted to provide Member States with training, research, and other assistance on request.

This book describes how the UN Crime Programme has evolved, and assesses its impact on domestic and international criminal policy. Member States adopt and change their policy in response to many different, and predominantly domestic, factors. It would be difficult to trace a cause-and-effect relationship between proposals and recommendations made within the framework of the UN Crime Programme, and changes in local or national law, policy, and practice. However, I shall try to show how the UN has contributed to changes around the world in how crime and justice are understood, and in how Member States respond to crime. The UN Crime Programme brings representatives of different Member States as well as many other stakeholders around the same table to exchange their experiences and insights, and in this way fosters debate and helps to disseminate new approaches and ideas. The UN Crime Programme helps to identify and share experience with "good practice" (best practice),[6] and certainly has been encouraging international cooperation in crime prevention and criminal justice, ranging from police and judicial cooperation to technical assistance.

1.2   Structure of the book

Chapter 2 deals with the creation and evolution of the UN Crime Programme. Section 2.1 describes how the Programme was established largely on the basis of a series of international conferences spanning almost a century, the work of the International Penal and Penitentiary Commission (IPPC), and the League of Nations. Section 2.2 covers the discussions that led to the creation of the Programme, noting for example how the main elements – the experts, the staff, and the quinquennial UN Crime Congresses – were inherited from the IPPC. Section 2.3 takes the story through the first 40 years, the time of the UN Crime Committee, when the Programme was served by a miniscule and poorly resourced Secretariat unit. This period produced many "soft law" resolutions, standards, and norms, but towards the end there was increasing criticism of its lack of effectiveness.

Chapter 3 takes the story through the last three decades. A major transition took place at the beginning of the 1990s, when the UN Crime Programme was restructured. This is covered in section 3.1. The restructuring involved replacing the expert-driven UN Crime Committee by the government-driven UN Crime Commission. The major consequence of this was an increasing focus on the negotiation and implementation of two hard-law crime conventions, the UN Convention on Transnational Organized Crime and the UN Convention against Corruption (with work underway at the time of writing on a UN convention on cybercrime). These developments are covered in section 3.2. Section 3.3 examines the impact of the 2030 Sustainable Development Goals (adopted by the General Assembly (GA) in 2015), and suggests that this is not only restoring attention to so-called "ordinary crime" and the operation of the domestic criminal justice system, but also increasing cooperation between the UN Crime Programme and other entities in the UN organization.

Chapter 4 deals with the main structures in the UN Crime Programme. These structures include the United Nations Office on Drugs and Crime (section 4.2), the UN Crime Commission (section 4.3) and the Conferences of the States Parties to the two UN Crime Conventions (section 4.4). (A fourth structure, the UN Crime Congresses, is covered in Chapter 10.)

The actors are dealt with in turn in Chapters 5, 6, and 7. The main actors are the Member States, represented by the permanent missions and the national experts (5.1). Other actors include the regional coordination mechanisms, specialized UN agencies (5.2), intergovernmental organizations (5.3) and individual experts (5.4).

Separate chapters deal with two further sets of actors. The role of the non-governmental organizations (Chapter 6) has been very influential in the UN Crime Programme, but over the past decade has become a particularly sensitive issue, with some Member States actively seeking to limit the participation of such organizations in the Programme. Chapter 7 deals with the UN Crime Programme Network Institutes, which have in several senses become the unrecognized workhorses of the Programme, often overlooked by the UN Crime Commission, but providing extensive technical assistance, research, and advisory services to Member States on request.

The UN Crime Programme has been in existence for 75 years, and as with the criminal policy of any Member State, the criminal policy reflected in the Programme has evolved over time. Chapter 8 looks in particular at how three major topics have changed over the years: corrections (section 8.2), youth crime (section 8.3), and development, social defence, and crime (section 8.4). Section 8.5 looks at how gender issues have been dealt with in the UN Crime Programme. Chapter 8.6 gives a briefer overview of the evolution of three topics, access to justice, victims, and computer systems and cybercrime.

The main tools of the UN Crime Programme, the instruments used to influence the criminal policy of Member States and to implement UN criminal policy, are covered in Chapters 9–11.

Chapter 9 deals with the growing body of UN standards and norms on crime prevention and criminal justice.

Chapter 10 covers the UN Crime Congresses, which have been held every five years since 1955, and seeks to show how these Congresses have contributed to the conceptualization of crime (i.e., what conduct should be criminalized), the dissemination of innovations in crime prevention and criminal justice around the world, and a better understanding of how Member States and other stakeholders can prevent and respond to crime more effectively.

Whereas Chapter 3 described the emergence of the two UN Crime Conventions, Chapter 11 examines these Conventions from another perspective: how they have changed and continue to change international cooperation in criminal justice, as well as the domestic crime policy of States Parties.

Chapter 12 describes how the United Nations Office on Drugs and Crime, together with the UN Crime Programme Network, provide technical assistance to Member States on request, produce a rapidly expanding amount of research, and are involved in UN peace-keeping and peace-building.

The final chapter, Chapter 13, seeks to bring the narrative together, taking a look back at the major successes and missed opportunities in the UN

Crime Programme, and hazarding some predictions as to how the UN Crime Programme could evolve – at least in the near future.

Specialized fields tend to develop their own terms and abbreviations which may not be familiar to many readers. This is also true of the UN Crime Programme. Annex 1 provides brief definitions of the main terms and abbreviations.

Annex 2 describes some of the currently sensitive issues in the UN Crime Programme.

Annex 3 lists the themes, agenda items and workshop topics of the different UN Crime Congresses.

People may have quite different ideas of how the UN works, and how it is possible to find consensus among 193 Member States. Some may assume that the so-called major powers dominate the proceedings, unless a significant consortium of medium and smaller-sized Member States can carry the day. Others may imagine that debates are decorous affairs, with experts on crime prevention and criminal justice using rational arguments to promote what they consider promising practice in crime prevention and criminal justice. My own experience is that, perhaps surprisingly often, a decision may be the result of misunderstandings, random occurrences, and above all tactical manoeuvring. Annex 4, "Ten rules for success in negotiation at UN Crime Programme meetings," is not intended as dogma or a distillation of scientific truth, but seeks to suggest what factors may come into play when representatives from different legal systems, cultures, language groups, and other backgrounds try to reach agreement on how to prevent crime and improve the operation of the criminal justice system.

1.3 The UN Crime Programme and the UN Drug Control Programme

Although in many jurisdictions a considerable proportion of crime is influenced by, or otherwise directly involves, narcotic drugs and psychotropic substances (Tonry and Wilson, 1990), this book does not cover the UN Drug Control Programme. This Programme emerged quite separately from the UN Crime Programme, and was based largely on international agreements from the outset. The two Programmes are overseen by different bodies. The main issues involved in the UN Drug Control Programme, such as treatment versus control, drug eradication, alternative development, harm reduction, border management, and so on, have taken on specific connotations and dynamics that differ markedly from their counterparts in the UN Crime Programme.

The UN Commission on Narcotic Drugs was created in 1946 to oversee the application of international instruments on narcotic drugs, advise the Economic and Social Council (ECOSOC) on the control of such drugs, and prepare draft conventions as necessary (ECOSOC resolution 9(1) of 16 February 1946). These earlier instruments included the first Opium Convention of 1908, the Hague Opium Conventions of 1912 and 1925, the Convention for Limiting the Manufacture and Regulating the Distribution of Narcotic Drugs of 1931, and the Convention on Illicit Drug Trafficking of 1936.[7]

Following the establishment of the UN, these early multilateral drug conventions were updated by a protocol signed in Lake Success, New York in 1946, and then essentially replaced by the 1961 Single Convention on Narcotic Drugs. The 1961 Convention provided for new mechanisms and obligations. The International Narcotics Control Board was created as a body of experts to oversee the list of precursor chemicals; decisions on these are made by the Commission on Narcotic Drugs. The 1961 Convention required States Parties to provide annual estimates of drugs used for various purposes, to abide by restrictions on manufacture, production, and import, to criminalize the possession, supply, and transport of drugs, and to make these extraditable offences.

The 1961 Single Convention was amended by a protocol in 1972. This protocol did not change the substantive scope of the Convention, which continued to encompass cannabis, coca leaf, and opium, and drugs with similar effects. Developments during the 1950s and, especially, the emergence of a drug "counter-culture" during the 1960s focused attention on a new form of drugs, psychotropics, perhaps first and foremost psychedelics (such as LSD), but also amphetamines and barbiturates. A separate Convention on Psychotropic Substances was adopted in 1971.

Calling upon States that were parties to these agreements to criminalize drugs proved to be insufficient, as long as there were no parallel agreements on various forms of procedural cooperation, such as police cooperation, extradition, and mutual legal assistance. When work began on a convention that would expand the substantive scope of the 1961 Single Convention to include psychotropics, the negotiations were for the first time extended to include such procedural provisions. The result was the 1988 United Nations Convention against Illicit Traffic in Narcotic Drugs and Psychotropic Substances (*UN 1988 Drug Convention*), which still remains the basic international agreement on drugs.

Although this book does not deal with the UN Drug Control Programme, several references will be made to work carried out within its mandate. The UN Secretariat has sought to increase the integration of these two UN programmes. Most significantly, since 1997 the two have been dealt with by the same Secretariat unit, the UN Office on Drugs and Crime, located in Vienna. There are no longer clear lines separating staff working on "crime issues" from those working on "drug issues." Particularly since the GA adopted the Sustainable Development Goals in 2015 (A/RES/70/1), increasing effort has been made to work across the divide and learn from one another. The concept of alternative development, for example, has been given greater attention also in the UN Crime Programme.

Moreover, as noted, in many jurisdictions much crime involves narcotics and psychotropic substances. Many crimes around the world are committed under the influence of drugs, or in order to obtain drugs. Trafficking in drugs is one of the major forms of international organized crime, and is often closely linked to many other forms of international organized crime, and can be used to fund terrorism. Drug use is a factor considered in deciding on the treatment of suspects, defendants, and convicted offenders, and thus an essential element in correctional programmes around the world.

1.4   Crime and criminal justice on the agenda of other UN agencies

Several other UN bodies, entities, and specialized agencies deal with crime-related issues as part of their specific mandate.

The United Nations Development Programme (UNDP) was established to coordinate economic and development assistance to developing countries. It seeks to promote economic growth and human development, the reduction of inequalities and exclusion, the eradication of poverty, and the building of resilience. It has increasingly been involved in helping developing countries to increase their capacity for good governance. In many of its country programmes, it cooperates with the United Nations Office on Drugs and Crime (UNODC) on a broad range of issues, ranging from urban crime to corruption, from financial crime to wildlife crime, and from police-community partnerships to AIDS and Covid-19 in prisons.

The International Labour Organization (ILO) also deals with such crime-related issues as forced labour, migrant workers, and prison labour. It has cooperated with the UN Crime Programme from the outset. For example, it submitted a report on juvenile delinquency to the First UN Crime Congress (1955), a report on vocational guidance, training, and placement of prisoners to the Second UN Crime Congress (1960), and a paper on employment opportunities and work in youth adjustment to the Third UN Crime Congress (1965) (López-Rey, 1985, 32). With the increased attention given by the UN Crime Programme since the turn of the millennium to trafficking in persons and the smuggling of migrants – very much "labour" issues – this cooperation has remained extensive.

Other UN agencies and entities that cooperate with the UNODC in preventing and responding to trafficking in persons and the smuggling of migrants include the International Organization for Migration, the UN High Commissioner for Refugees, and the UN Special Rapporteur on Trafficking in Persons, Especially Women and Children.

The World Health Organization deals with drugs and counterfeit medicines, and even in the early years of the UN submitted reports to UN Crime Congresses on such subjects as the prevention of juvenile delinquency, the causes and prevention of crime, abnormal offenders, criminal statistics and psychosocial indexes, deprivation of material care, delinquency in Africa, health and social defence planning, the juvenile justice system, and ethical issues in respect of the provision of medical attention to prisoners and detainees (López-Rey, 1985, 32–33).

Initially the UN Crime Programme cooperated with the United Nations Entity for Gender Equality and the Empowerment of Women (UN Women), which deals with gender issues, largely in the prevention of and response to violence against women, but the cooperation has expanded to include several other issues, such as the treatment of women in prison, and the integration of a gendered perspective into the treatment of victims, witnesses, survivors, suspects, and offenders in the criminal justice system more broadly.

The United Nations Educational, Scientific, and Cultural Organization (UNESCO) submitted papers at the Second and Third UN Crime Congresses on juvenile delinquency and the role of youth centres and schools (López-Rey, 1985, 32). More recently, UNESCO and the UNODC have worked together, for example, on the prevention of trafficking in cultural property, and on educational initiatives related to the promotion of the rule of law.

Further areas in which the UN Crime Programme has an overlap with the mandate of other UN bodies, entities, and specialized agencies include:

- the strengthening of airport security against terrorist and other criminal threats; the International Civil Aviation Organization (ICAO);
- the protection of human rights in law enforcement and in criminal proceedings; the Office of the UN High Commissioner for Human Rights;[8]
- implementation of the UN standards and norms related to extra-legal executions; the UN Special Rapporteur on Extrajudicial, Summary or Arbitrary Executions;
- environmental crime; the UN Environment Programme.

1.5   The UN Crime Programme as an international regime

Criminal policy is closely tied to the values of a society, and national governments have jealously sought to retain their sovereignty over issues related to crime prevention and criminal justice. However, the Member States of the UN are not the only actors which are active in international cooperation in this field.

The UN Crime Programme can be seen as part of an *international regime* for crime prevention and criminal justice. The concept of "international regimes" has been developed in the discipline of international relations to refer to a set of implicit or explicit principles, norms, rules, and decision-making procedures that have emerged to deal with specific international problems (Krasner 1983; Levy et al., 2014). The concept is thus a theoretical construct, and should not be confused with the concepts of international organizations (organizations that have members from different countries) or intergovernmental organizations (organizations that have individual governments as its members; the UN itself is perhaps the best-known example).

International regimes have developed, for example, in respect of the protection of human rights (Follesdal et al., 2014), health care (Jin, 2021), and the protection of the environment (Levy et al., 1995). They can help to mobilize different actors, deepen a shared understanding of the nature and cause of the global challenges in question, and promote a collective and coordinated response to these challenges. The framework of international regimes can involve international agreements, recommendations, guidelines, and protocols for action, and the work of international organizations. The actors, in turn, can include states, intergovernmental and non-governmental organizations, professional associations, businesses, religious communities and individual experts.

A central feature of international regimes is their perceived *legitimacy*. Different approaches to the analysis of international regimes regard legitimacy differently. The *realist* approach regards legitimacy as a tool that states exploit to advance their interests, but does not constrain their actions. The *liberal* approach argues that legitimacy has a functional utility in the international regime. The *constructivist* approach goes even further, suggesting that the more an international regime is accepted by key actors as legitimate, the greater their willingness to comply with the underlying principles and norms, and the greater their commitment to following the rules and procedures (Fioretos and Tallberg, 2021).

The concept of international regimes is related to another concept, "*global governance.*" This can be understood as the *process* through which various actors (states as well as non-state actors) seek to promote cooperation within an international regime. This process involves the setting of the agenda ("what are our priorities?"), the formulation of policy ("how shall we meet the challenges?"), implementation, and assessment of the impact of the policy.

Global governance also examines how policy is diffused, and how this leads to convergence, in that the policies adopted by states becomes more similar over time. To take the specific example of the UN Crime Programme, what is of interest is the way in which it can help disseminate ideas and "promising practice," set standards and norms to be followed by practitioners and policy-makers, coordinate policy development and implementation, and provide technical assistance (Jakobi, 2013).

The concepts of an international regime and global governance are useful when examining the UN Crime Programme. The concepts implicitly assume that international cooperation is not the sole prerogative of Member States, but that non-state actors can also have a role to play. As will be shown in this book, the UN Crime Programme began with extensive cooperation among a range of actors, in particular non-governmental organizations and individual experts. Especially over the past two decades, some Member States have increasingly questioned the involvement of non-state actors, arguing in essence that, since the UN is an intergovernmental organization, decisions in the UN Crime Programme (to the extent that these are made by the UN Crime Commission, the Conferences of the States Parties to the two UN Crime Conventions, and the UN Crime Congresses) should be made only by duly accredited representatives of Member States.

The difficulty with this argument is that the international regime of which the UN Crime Programme is a part constitutes a complex network of interdependencies. Truly effective crime prevention and criminal justice on the local and national level requires the cooperation of a variety of professional organizations, civil society organizations, the private sector, academia, religious communities, educators, and the media. The same is true on the regional and interregional level. Non-state actors should be provided incentives for cooperation, and procedures should be developed to minimize and diffuse conflict in the strengthening, implementation, and assessment of the UN Crime Programme.

1.6   The UN Crime Programme and other international structures for cooperation in crime prevention and criminal justice

If Member States disagree on criminal policy and on priorities within the UN Crime Programme – as they often do – they will continue to explore other arrangements for cooperating with other countries, including through alternative structures. Because of this, any presentation of the UN Crime Programme should be read in the context of what other global governance structures have emerged to promote bilateral, multilateral, and even global cooperation in preventing and responding to crime.

There is a considerable variety in these other structures. They vary as to what stakeholders are involved (intergovernmental, non-governmental organizations, professional organizations, the private sector, academia, the media, and religious communities), their subject matter (in particular, which type of crime is being dealt with), their purpose (such as criminalization of conduct, greater efficiency in bringing offenders to justice, helping victims of crime, and strengthening crime prevention), their scope (bilateral and multilateral), and the means selected (for example international agreements, "soft law" recommendations, exchange of information, and technical assistance).

Intergovernmental organizations can be and often are very active in promoting cooperation in crime prevention and criminal justice. Examples are (in alphabetical order) the African Union, the Association of Southeast Asian Nations (ASEAN), the Commonwealth Secretariat, the Council of Europe, the European Union, the Group of Seven, the League of Arab States, the Organization of American States (OAS), the Organization for Economic Development and Cooperation, the Organization for Security and Cooperation in Europe, and the Shanghai Cooperation Organization. Many of these have adopted multilateral treaties, and some have developed advanced forms of cooperative structures (such as Europol, Frontex, Eurojust, the European Public Prosecutor's Office, the European Anti-Fraud Office, and the Schengen Area, all within the European Union (EU), Aseanapol within ASEAN, and the Southern Africa Regional Police Chiefs Cooperation Organization.

In law enforcement, the International Criminal Police Organization (Interpol) is the pre-eminent global structure for cooperation (Deflem, 2005; Haberfeld and MacDonald, 2005; Mesko and Furman, 2014). Its perhaps most widely known function is the circulation of information internationally on wanted persons (so-called red notices). Interpol maintains several databases, for example, on stolen property, stolen works of art, and child sexual abuse images. It also seeks to improve the professional capacity of law enforcement agencies through training and other forms of technical assistance.[9]

Other structures seek to strengthen procedural cooperation in investigating and prosecuting offences, assisting victims, and recovering the proceeds of crime. These structures may operate on the informal and formal levels, and on bilateral as well as multilateral levels. Informal structures have developed for the exchange of information between law enforcement authorities. Formal procedures are used in mutual legal assistance (for example, the serving of summonses, the questioning of witnesses, the obtaining of records and various documents from another country, and the return of stolen assets), the extradition of suspects or convicted persons, and the transfer of proceedings.

The diversity in international structures can be illustrated by taking the example of trafficking in persons (Ollus and Joutsen, 2021). Action to prevent and respond to trafficking in persons originated in campaigns against slavery in the late eighteenth century, and even today work on trafficking in persons is closely related to work on slavery, forced labour, human rights, prostitution, migration, the rights of children, and transnational organized crime.

Several agreements were formulated during the early 1900s on "white slavery" (essentially, trafficking in women and children for the purposes of sexual exploitation). One of the first conventions adopted by the UN was the 1949 Convention for the Suppression of the Traffic in Persons and of the Exploitation of the Prostitution of Others. The League of Nations adopted the first international agreement on slavery in 1926. Several of the conventions on human rights that were adopted following the Second World War, in turn, contain specific provisions prohibiting slavery. A number of conventions prepared within the framework of the ILO deal with forced labour, migrant labour, and child labour. The 1989 Convention on the Rights of the Child calls upon States Parties to protect children from all forms of sexual exploitation and sexual abuse. The Council of Europe and the EU have adopted regional instruments on this same topic.

The UN Convention against Transnational Organized Crime includes a protocol on trafficking in persons, adopted in 2000. This protocol did not have the last word on the subject. It was soon followed by several regional instruments: a South Asian Association for Regional Cooperation convention in 2002, an EU Council Framework in 2002 (updated as a Directive in 2011), a Council of Europe convention in 2005, a Commonwealth of Independent States agreement in 2005, a League of Arab States Framework Act in 2008, and an ASEAN convention in 2015.

In addition to these international agreements, several political declarations, action plans, and recommendations have been adopted on trafficking in persons, and in principle guide the criminal policy of the countries in question. On the global level, these have been adopted, for example, by the UN, the United Nations International Children's Emergency Fund (UNICEF), the Office of the United Nations High Commissioner on Refugees (UNHCR), and the UN Commission on Human Rights. The main global soft law framework is the UN Global Plan of Action to Combat Trafficking in Persons (A/RES/64/293, annex), which was adopted by the GA in 2010, and which builds on several earlier GA resolutions.

Virtually every region around the world has developed action plans designed to enhance the prevention of trafficking in persons, improve the protection of and assistance to victims, increase the efficiency of prosecution (including identification and interdiction of trafficking, and bringing the offenders to justice), and strengthen partnerships. These have been adopted, for example, by the Economic Community of Western African States (2001), the Organization of American States (2003), the Organization for Security and Co-operation in Europe (2003), ASEAN (2004 and 2010), the Middle East and North African states (2006), the African Union (2006), the Southern African Development Community (2009), Arab countries (2010), and, separately, the Council of Arab Ministers of Justice (2012).

Separate reference should also be made to the 2014 Declaration by the major leaders of many different religions (Anglican, Buddhist, Catholic, Hindu, Jewish, Muslim, and Orthodox Christian), which calls for the elimination of slavery and human trafficking by the year 2020.

As noted, the above overview of initiatives by different actors to prevent and respond to trafficking in persons is presented only as an example. Corresponding overviews can be prepared on, for example, initiatives against money laundering, corruption, trafficking in endangered species, trafficking in cultural heritage, and the smuggling of migrants. The work of the UN Crime Programme is only one part of the kaleidoscope of action – but it nonetheless calls for analysis in its own right.

Notes

1 See, for example, van Dijk (2008, pp. 45–88). On crime statistics, see S. Harrendorf, M. Heiskanen, and S. Malby (eds.), 2010.
2 During the early years, it was also referred to as the UN Programme for Social Defence.
3 Although the title of Clark's (1994) extensive presentation of the programme is "The United Nations Crime Prevention and Criminal Justice Program," he often shortens the reference to the "UN Crime Prevention Program."
4 See A/46/152 on the creation of an effective UN Crime Prevention and Criminal Justice Programme, para. 14.
5 The term *international crime* refers to conduct that is deemed a crime under international law. Examples are genocide, war crimes, crimes against humanity, and piracy. Within the UN system, the more serious international crimes are dealt with largely by the Security Council, and not by the UN Crime Programme, the subject of this book.

   The International Criminal Court is the most important institution dealing with international crimes. Its mandate is based on an international treaty, the Statute of Rome, signed in 1998. It is not a UN body.

   For a recent dissection of the concepts of international criminal law and transnational criminal law, see Clark (2022, esp. pp. 112–119).
6 This is an example of a term that time and again has given rise to hours of discussion at UN meetings. Practitioners often want to know what works, and what doesn't. However, if the term "good practice" or "best practice" is used at a UN meeting, someone will usually be quick to point out that what works in one connection or in one legal and administrative system may not work as well elsewhere. Furthermore, they may object to suggestions that the UN is able to determine what is "best practice," which all Member States should promote.
7 The 1925 Convention has subsequently been amended several times with protocols. This series of amendments was extended in 1953 by the Protocol Limiting and Regulating the Cultivation of the Poppy Plant, the Production of, International and Wholesale Trade in, and Use of Opium.
8 The interrelationship between the two may at times seem confusing to some. The author was present at one informal negotiating session at the UN Crime Commission in Vienna on the text of a relatively standard draft resolution. The representative of one Member State, which was opposed in general to the entire draft, kept questioning the appropriateness of various passages, apparently in an effort to encourage other representatives to join in the opposition. At one point, the representative (who was not speaking his native language), questioned the propriety of several references to universally recognized human rights instruments. (His point, apparently, was that such matters should be dealt with by UN human rights bodies in Geneva.) He ended his impassioned intervention with a blunt "There are no human rights in criminal justice."

   The chairperson, after an astonished silence during which other representatives were apparently wondering if they had heard the speaker correctly, finally observed that these passages were standard "agreed language," which had been used in similar resolutions adopted by the GA.

The representatives proceeded with their work, and the references to human rights remained in the text. The draft was finalized and ultimately submitted to the GA, which adopted it by consensus.

9 Interpol has cooperated with the UN Crime Programme from the outset, for example by submitting reports to UN Crime Congresses (López-Rey, 1985, p. 35).

References

Clark, Roger S. (2022), The Concept of International Criminal Law and Its Relationship with Transnational Criminal Law and Conflict of Laws, *Transnational Criminal Law Review*, 1(2), 100–122

Clark, Roger S. (1994), *The United Nations Crime Prevention and Criminal Justice Program. Formulation of Standards and Efforts at Their Implementation.* University of Pennsylvania Press

Deflem, Matthieu (2005), "Wild Beasts Without Nationality": The Uncertain Origins of Interpol, 1989–1910, in Philip Reichel (ed.), *Handbook of Transnational Crime & Justice*, Sage Publications, pp. 275–285

Fioretos, Orfeo and Jonas Tallberg (2021), Politics and Theory of Global Governance. *International Theory*, 13(1), 99–111. doi:10.1017/S1752971920000408

Follesdal, Andreas, Johan Karlson Schaffer and Geir Ulfstein (2014), *The Legitimacy of International Human Rights Regimes*, Cambridge University Press

Haberfeld, Maria (Maki) and William H. MacDonald (2005), International Cooperation in Policing, in Philip Reichel (ed.), *Handbook of Transnational Crime & Justice*, Sage Publications, pp. 286–309

Harrendorf, S., M. Heiskanen and S. Malby (eds.) (2010), *International Statistics on Crime and Justice*, HEUNI/UNODC

Jakobi, Anja P. (2013), *Common Goods & Evils? The Formation of Global Crime Governance*, Oxford University Press

Jin, Jiyong (2021), *International Regimes in Global Health Governance*, Routledge

Krasner, Stephen (ed.) (1983), *International Regimes*, Cornell University Press

Levy, Mark A., Oran R. Young and Michael Zürn (1995), *European Journal of International Relations*, 1(3), 267–330

López-Rey de Arroya, Manuel (1985), *A Guide to United Nations Criminal Policy*, Cambridge Studies in Criminology LIV

Mesko, Gorazd and Robert Furman (2014), Police and Prosecutorial Cooperation in Responding to Transnational Crime, in Philip Reichel and Jay Albanese (eds.), *Handbook of Transnational Crime & Justice*, second edition, Sage Publications, pp. 323–352

Ollus, Natalia and Matti Joutsen (2021), International Policies to Combat Human Trafficking, in Rochelle L. Dalla and Donna Sabella (eds.), *Routledge International Handbook of Human Trafficking: A Multi-Disciplinary and Applied Approach*, Routledge/Taylor & Francis, pp. 71–102

Tonry, Michael and James Q. Wilson (eds.) 1990, *Drugs and Crime*. Vol. 13 of *Crime and Justice: A Review of Research*, University of Chicago Press the representatives proceeded with their work, and the reference to human rights remained in the revised headnote as hortatory subject to the ...

... intergral, has cooperated with the UN ... ing from the outset, for example in submitting reports to UN Charter bodies: see López ..., 1998, p. 315.

References

Clark, Roger S. (2013), 'The Concept of International Obligations and the Relationship with Renunciation of Original Law', in *Journal of Laws Management
International* ..., 25(1), 100–127.

Ehret, Klaus S. (2001), *The Future Subject: Online Regulation and Current Initiative Boundaries* (Stanford) and [Ithaca at their Single international laters],
... at Cambridge University Press.

Poillot, Madeline (2016), 'World Peace Without Sovereignty', *The Universal Origins
of the great 1945–1975*, in John K. Joint (ed.), *Handbook of International Juris-
prudence* (Singapore, Faithen Group), pp. 2–354.

Florianis, Orion and Fattee Gilbert (2012), 'Politics and the Role of Colonial Governance and National Theory', 45(1), 99–117. Doi: 10.1017/S1235791500008520

Fullenden, Arthur, John W. Karharu-Tarnier and Otto Hart Jr. (2019), 'The Trade-off
... International Human Rights Re-Post Constitution Development', in
Maguire III, Jeane (ed.), and William T. MacDonald (2006), *International Polit-
ical ...: Politics*, in Philip R. Gardner (ed.), *Handbook of International Course
Process State Publications*, pp. 254–272.

Friedman, Scott Timothy and J. Walter and Zhi ... Berne, ... International Sources of
... ations and ...: Illustrations 164 ...

Jakobi, Anja P. (2013), 'Crime as a ... Issue?', in *The International Politics of Crime
Governance* (Oxford University Press).

..., Joe Joseph (2023), 'International Response to Global ... and Interstate Violence ...',
Transitions Symposium' (2019 ...: International Governance Council Institutes), Vol.
2033, Article 4; Otto ... Comparative Soviet Societies (2019 ...), *The Journal of International and Relations* ..., 2(3), 255–270.

..., Jacques A, Alejo, Rezael (2016), 'Soft Law as ... Law, Hard ... Voting, Normative ...',
Compliance and Power Communication HR ...

..., Jacques and Jacques Forest ... (2011), 'Reference to the International Organisation
... to provide in the Context of International Criminal Law and its Relevance',
Journal of ... International ..., ... of Human Rights ... Regime, ... since 2006,
... 171.

..., Monde, Michael and ... ... Zengarity (2009), ... in ..., The ... of ... International Law International Law International ... and ... and ... the ... for ..., for ...
Scholarly ..., 1938, pp. 4–5 ... by ... 1994.

PART I

The development

2

THE CREATION AND FIRST YEARS OF THE UN CRIME PROGRAMME

2.1 The prehistory of the UN Crime Programme: international conferences and the League of Nations

The roots of the UN Crime Programme can be traced back to two main sources: the early work of international scientific and professional organizations and the work of the League of Nations.

At the end of the 1800s and the beginning of the 1900s, discussions on crime and criminal policy began to become international. Practitioners, reformers, and academics from different countries started to exchange their experiences and theories and organize international conferences. In 1846, the International Congress of Penitentiary Science was held in Frankfurt am Main, Germany.[1] It attracted 75 participants from twelve European countries and from the United States to discuss such matters as the purpose of imprisonment and the merits of different prison regimes in the "betterment of the prisoners, the decrease of recidivism and convictions in general."[2] The first International Congress on the Prevention and Repression of Crime, including Penal and Reformatory Treatment, was held in London in 1872, bringing together not only practitioners, reformers, and academics but also governmental representatives. The London Congress led to the establishment of the International Penal and Penitentiary Commission (IPPC), which undertook to organize similar international congresses every five years.[3]

The themes considered during these first international conferences were heavily oriented towards what today would be called institutional corrections, in other words the treatment of offenders in closed institutions. Among the topics discussed were the training of prison staff, the registration and classification of prisoners, the benefits of solitary cells versus "congregate

DOI: 10.4324/9781003480907-3

imprisonment" (in which the prisoners live and work together with other inmates, under supervision), large prisons versus small ones, indeterminate sentences vs. fixed-term sentences, the progressive system,[4] different forms of prison labour, abolition of corporal punishment, pre-trial detention, commutation of sentences for good behaviour, the use of probation, and prison statistics.

A theme that was closely intertwined with correction in the 1880s was juvenile justice, and this remains the case today. Among the issues considered at the international congress in London in 1872 was juvenile reformatories and, more broadly, how society should deal with delinquent children. Ten years later, juvenile justice was addressed in its own right at the international level. In 1882, the first International Congress on Child Welfare was held in Paris, followed by the International Congress for the Welfare and Protection of Children in 1896 in Florence, Italy. The Third International Congress for the Welfare and Protection of Children (London, 1902) considered the problem of neglected children, and the probability (not "possibility") that such children would turn to delinquency if due care was not taken. By the beginning of the 1900s, there was wide agreement at these conferences that children should be kept separated from adults in correctional treatment and institutional care of children should be avoided if at all possible. The concept of separate courts for young offenders was widely welcomed.

When the League of Nations was established in the aftermath of the First World War, criminal justice became not only an international issue but also an intergovernmental one. The League of Nations organized discussions among experts on crime-related issues and produced a few reports on such subjects as trafficking in women and children, counterfeiting, and correction. In general, however, it did not have a very high profile in international discussions on crime and justice (López-Rey, 1985, pp. 8 and 93–95; Redo, 2012, p. 68).

The one exception to this low profile was in respect of juvenile delinquency and child welfare. The League of Nations had a Child Welfare Bureau, which was quite active in considering juvenile delinquency, the rights of children, juvenile courts vs. administrative child welfare boards, street children, slavery, child labour, child trafficking, and the prostitution of minors (Alper and Boren, pp. 55–69).

The League of Nations did not have staff to deal with crime prevention and criminal justice issues (other than child welfare), and much of its work was delegated to pre-existing international organizations, all of which were European (López-Rey, 1985, pp. 2–3 and p. 9, fn. 3).[5] Nonetheless, in 1934 the League of Nations endorsed an early text prepared by the IPPC of the Standard Minimum Rules for the Treatment of Prisoners. It also prepared an inquiry into prison populations, a draft set of rules on the treatment of witnesses and suspects, and several draft treaties. Furthermore, it served as depositary for a series of treaties dealing with trafficking in women and children (Alper and Boren, 1972, pp. 61–63; López-Rey, 1985, pp. 2–3; Clark, 1994, pp. 10 and 12).

During the 1930s, the League of Nations worked particularly closely with the IPPC. The experts involved in the work of both the League of Nations and the IPPC often knew one another personally and shared many basic assumptions about the causes of crime and the treatment of offenders. The League of Nations even worked with the IPPC in organizing the last three quinquennial conferences before the Second World War, in London in 1925, Prague in 1930, and Berlin in 1935 (Alper and Boren, 1972, pp. 65–74).

2.2 Getting crime and justice onto the UN agenda

At the time that the UN was established a few months after the end of the Second World War, the general view seemed to be that in respect of crime and criminal justice it should continue where the League of Nations had left off. After all, one of the main purposes of the UN, as grandly expressed by Article 55 of the UN Charter, is to create the "conditions of stability and well-being which are necessary for peaceful and friendly relations among nations," based on mutual respect, equality, and self-determination. The UN is also specifically charged with the promotion of universal respect for, and observance of, human rights and fundamental freedoms.[6] Surely crime and criminal justice fit somewhere in here.

Resolution 10(III)1948 of ECOSOC established the Temporary Social Commission, which was charged with considering how effective machinery could be developed "for studying on a wide international basis, the means of the prevention of crime and the treatment of offenders."[7]

The Temporary Social Commission started by identifying what crime and justice topics it would deal with. The Secretariat prepared a draft list of topics, primarily revolving around juvenile delinquency and correctional treatment, which were the Western European and North American criminological and penological preoccupations at that time and holdovers from the work of the League of Nations.

When the draft list was debated in the Temporary Social Commission, the U.S.S.R. and a few of its allies opposed the inclusion within the framework of UN social policy of any of the proposed items, on the grounds that, given article 2(7) of the UN Charter, they were domestic issues which should be outside the UN mandate. Their view was that the UN should only deal with international issues, either those on which "relevant decisions by international organizations already existed" (such as incitement to war, which had already been dealt with in GA resolutions), or "questions on which relevant international conventions existed, such as slavery, narcotic drugs and the suppression of the traffic in women and children and of obscene publications" (United Nations, 1948, pp. 613–614; *International Review of Criminal Policy*, July 1952, p. 12; Redo, 2012, p. 110).

The U.S.S.R. proposal to delete domestic crime concerns was rejected by the Temporary Social Commission. Somewhat modifying the list of topics suggested by the Secretariat, the Commission approved the following list:

(a) the problem of juvenile delinquency in all its phases, including the study of advanced legislation on the subject;
(b) medical, psychiatric and social examination of adult offenders before sentence is passed;
(c) probation;
(d) fines, also in connection with short-term imprisonment;
(e) open penitentiary institutions;
(f) habitual offenders;
(g) a general inquiry into the functions of the medical, psychological and social sciences in dealing with the problems of delinquency and crime;
(h) the training of staff for penal institutions; and
(i) criminal statistics, with a view to a report on the state of crime.

The matter was referred to ECOSOC, where the U.S.S.R. again proposed restricting the list to international concerns. The U.S.S.R. proposal was rejected by a vote of 14 votes to 3, with 1 abstention. In adopting resolution 155(VII) C, ECOSOC endorsed the list submitted to it. The same resolution, setting out the framework for the future work of the UN in crime prevention and criminal justice, reads in full as follows:

The Economic and Social Council

Endorses the opinion of the Social Commission that, in view of the importance of the study, on an international basis, of the problem of the prevention of crime and treatment of offenders, the United Nations should assume leadership in promoting this activity, having regard to international and national organizations which have interests and competence in this field, and making the fullest use of their knowledge and experience;

Requests the Secretary-General, subject to budgetary limitations, to convene in 1949 a group of internationally recognized experts not to exceed seven in number and selected by him in such a way that the constitution of the group maintains an international character, to act in an honorary capacity as an advisory body and to advise the Secretary-General and the Social Commission in devising and formulating policies and programmes appropriate to:

(a) the study on an international basis of the problem of prevention of crime and the treatment of offenders; and
(b) international action in this field.

The next step for the UN was to determine how to go about getting this nascent UN Crime Programme into operation. The IPPC, which had actively sought to promote international cooperation in crime prevention and criminal justice, would have been a suitable partner. It had staff, it had a structure, and it organized regular international conferences. The IPPC was interested in following the model that the newly established UN was using in other fields. The Postal Union, the World Health Organization, the Food and Agricultural Organization, the International Labour Organization, and the UN Educational, Scientific and Cultural Organization had all started out on the basis of international conferences and an international structure, and had become UN agencies. Perhaps that same model could be followed with crime prevention and criminal justice (Clifford, 1979, pp. 4–5).

However, those plans for a UN "Crime Control" agency were not to be, for various reasons. One reason was the perceived lack of a need for international oversight. When it came to issues such as postal delivery, health care, and food and agriculture, there was a broad consensus that international cooperation, and perhaps even some international oversight, was needed. This was not necessarily the case with crime and justice, issues that were generally considered to be closely tied to the fundamental value systems of individual Member States.

A second reason was the relative absence of an emerging global consensus on the scientific foundation for crime prevention and criminal justice. Subjects such as medicine and agriculture had long scientific pedigrees, and in general it was relatively easy to reach agreement on what was known and what was not. In comparison, criminology was a relatively new field of research. Cesare Lombroso, who is widely regarded as the "father of criminology," did not publish his *L'uomo delinquent* (The Criminal Man) until 1878.[8] At the time of the establishment of the UN, there were few experts in criminology, or in what could be called criminal justice studies. Moreover, there were key differences between Member States in their approach to criminology. The U.S.S.R. and its allies followed a Marxist theory of crime, which was fundamentally different from the more sociologically oriented theories that were evolving in Western academia.

These differences in criminological theories had a political dimension. Blaustein et al. argue that at the time of its establishment the UN was a "First World" organization that took on the task of using knowledge and skill developed in the capitalist West to relieve the suffering of people in underdeveloped areas, and its early work "directly contributed to the universalization of the idea that Western, social scientific approaches to theorizing crime were essential for understanding and addressing the criminological effects of economic development (Blaustein et al., 2022, p. 103).[9] :

A fourth reason lay in questions regarding the acceptability of the IPPC as a partner in setting up a UN agency. The last IPPC conference before the

Second World War was held in Berlin in 1935. The international forum provided by the Berlin conference was used by German participants to expound on the principles behind the new national socialist penal law and its application, including the adoption of *ex post facto* laws. (Among the featured speakers was Joseph Goebbels, Germany's Minister for Propaganda.) During the war years, the primary source of funds for the IPPC, which was based in Switzerland, was the Axis powers, which used IPPC as a channel for propagating and justifying their repressive laws and regulations.[10]

The result was that instead of a separate UN agency, the responsibility for the new programme was given to a small Secretariat unit, the Social Defence Section, within the Social Affairs Division of the UN. Furthermore, the UN did not want there to be any overlap with IPPC activities, much less cede any control of the international crime prevention and criminal justice agenda to the IPPC (Clifford, 1979, p. 5).

On 1 December 1950, the GA adopted resolution 414(v), *Transfer of functions of the International Penal and Penitentiary Commission.*[11] In doing so, the UN received the following from the IPPC:

- two IPPC staff members who formed the nucleus for the new Social Defence Section;[12]
- a pool of experts who had been active in the IPPC, from among whom the experts were often found during the first years to serve on an ad hoc Advisory Committee assisting the Secretariat; and
- the model for the future UN Crime Congresses.[13]

The mandate of the IPPC had focused on penal and penitentiary matters. The Temporary Social Commission suggested that the functions of the League of Nations concerning the traffic of women and children, prostitution, and related matters should be transferred to the UN and become part of the activities enumerated (López-Rey, 1985, p. 2).

2.3   The UN Crime Committee years

Formally speaking, the principal policy-making body in the UN in crime and justice-related matters is the *Economic and Social Council (ECOSOC)*, which may submit what it considers high-profile matters to the GA for approval. Many politically sensitive crime issues, such as war crimes, genocide, and terrorism, are occasionally debated in the GA of the UN. In addition, the GA has sometimes appointed ad hoc intergovernmental committees or other special bodies to deal with specific issues, such as the drafting of new international agreements.

However, ECOSOC has a rather large mandate and its members cannot be expected to have sufficient substantive knowledge of crime prevention and criminal justice issues to formulate policy. In 1949, ECOSOC established an *ad hoc advisory body of experts* to advise it and the UN Secretariat on such issues, a body which evolved to become (in 1965) the UN Committee on the Prevention of Crime and the Treatment of Offenders, and in 1992 the UN Commission on Crime Prevention and Criminal Justice.

According to *GA resolution 415(V),* adopted on 1 December 1950, the mandate of the experts was to advise the Secretary-General and the Social Commission in

> devising and formulating programmes for study on an international basis and policies for international action in the field of the prevention of crime and the treatment of offenders and also to advise on the co-ordination of the work of the United Nations consultative groups.

The original intention was that the experts would meet once a year (Clifford, 1979, p. 7). However, for the first twenty years, the ad hoc body was convened on average twice every five years, a schedule that enabled it to help the Secretariat plan the quinquennial UN Crime Congresses.

The members of this expert body were appointed initially in their personal capacity by the Secretariat, and selected to provide a sounding board in developing and implementing the programme of activities and in planning the Congresses. They did not represent their government or their organization. The experts selected by the UN were generally senior officials working in the criminal justice system of their respective countries, or (in a few cases) academics. Since there was relatively little turnover, they tended to be familiar not only with criminal justice in general but also with the working of the UN Crime Programme.[14]

The expert body was convened twice before the GA adopted resolution 415(V). The experts attending the first meeting of the advisory group, held in August 1949, were Henri Donnedieu de Vabres (France, chairman), Thorsten Sellin (United States, rapporteur), Stanford Bates (United States), Dennis Carroll (United Kingdom), José Augustin Martinez (Cuba), and J.M. Kumarappa (India) (Clifford, 1979, p. 8). The second meeting, in December 1950, was chaired by Margery Fry (United Kingdom), with Marc Ancel (France) as rapporteur. The membership of the expert body was augmented with Ronald Beattie (United States), Veli Verkko (Finland), and Sebastian Soler (Argentina) (Clifford, 1979, p. 8).

Unsurprisingly, these first experts were predominantly Western European and North American criminologists and criminal justice practitioners, many of whom had been active in the IPPC.

In 1965, the membership of the ad hoc Committee was increased to ten (López-Rey, 1985, pp. 15 and 44, n.5; Clark, 1994, pp. 19–20). In 1971, the Advisory Committee became a permanent subsidiary organ of ECOSOC, the

TABLE 2.1 UN expert bodies on crime prevention and criminal justice; meetings and participants

Meetings of the International Group of Experts on the Prevention of Crime and the Treatment of Offenders

Date, location and signum of the meeting report	Participants, 1949–1972	Comments regarding the agenda
1–8 August 1949 Lake Success, New York E/CN.5/154	Henri Donnedieu de Vabres (France, chairperson) Thorsten Sellin (U.S., rapporteur) Sanford Bates (U.S.) Denis Carroll (U.K.) J.M. Kumarappa (India) José Augustin Martinez (Cuba)	
December 1950 New York E/CN.5/231	Margery Fry (U.K., chairperson) Marc Ancel (France, rapporteur) Ronald Beattie (U.S.) Sebastian Soler (Argentina) Veli Verkko (Finland)	

Meetings of the ad hoc Advisory Committee of Experts on the Prevention of Crime and the Treatment of Offenders

15–24 June 1953 Geneva E/CN.5/298	Thorsten Sellin (U.S., chairperson) Paul Cornil (Belgium, rapporteur) Samuel T. Barnett (New Zealand) Behram H. Mehta (India) Sebastian Soler (Argentina)	Preparations for the First UN Crime Congress Prison labour Prevention of types of criminality resulting from social changes and accompanying economic development in less developed countries
8–17 August 1955 Geneva (just before the First UN Crime Congress) E/CN.5/319	Thorsten Sellin (U.S., chairperson) Charles Germain (France, rapporteur) Israel Drapkin (Chile) Ernest Lamers (Netherlands)	Preparations for the First UN Crime Congress
5–15 May 1958 New York E/CN.5/329	Lionel Fox (U.K., chairperson) Thorsten Sellin (U.S., rapporteur) James Bennett (U.S.) Alfredo M. Bunye (the Philippines) Paul Cornil (Belgium) J.A. César Salgado (Brazil)	Preparations for the Second UN Crime Congress

Date / Document	Members	Notes
25 July–3 August 1960 (just before the Second UN Crime Congress) E/CN.5/345	Nikola Srzentich (Yugoslavia, chairperson) V.N. Pillai (Ceylon, rapporteur) Juan Carlos Garcia Basalo (Argentina) Francois Clerc (Switzerland) Ato Yohannes Wolde Gerima (Ethiopia) Francis Graham-Harrison (U.K.) Paul Tappan (U.S.)	Preparations for the Third UN Crime Congress
7-16 January 1963 Geneva E/CN.5/371	Torsten Eriksson (Sweden, chairperson) Edward Moore (Liberia, rapporteur) Murad bin Ahmad (Malaysia) Juan Carlos Garcia Basalo (Argentina) James Bennett (U.S.) Arthur W. Peterson (U.K.) Hafez Abdel-Hade Sabek (U.A.R.) L.N. Smirnov (U.S.S.R.)	

Sessions of the Advisory UN Committee on Crime Prevention and Control

Date / Document	Members
13–22 December 1965 Geneva first session E/CN.5/398	Thomas Lambo (Nigeria, chairperson) Norval Morris (Australia, rapporteur) Myrl Alexander (U.S.) Yoshitsuga Baba (Japan) Louis Damour (France) Durgabai Deshmukh (India) Torsten Eriksson (Sweden) Ahmad M. Khalifa (U.A.R.) Alfonso Quiroz-Cuarón (Mexico) L.N. Smirnov (U.S.S.R.)
12–16 December 1966 New York second session E/CN.5/408	Torsten Eriksson (Sweden, chairperson) T.A. Lambo (Nigeria, rapporteur) H.G. Moeller (U.S.) Atsushi Nagashima (Japan) Alfonso Quiroz-Cuarón (Mexico) L.N. Smirnov (U.S.S.R.)

TABLE 2.1 (Continued)

24–30 June 1969, Rome third session E/CN.5/443	Norval Morris (Australia, chairperson) T.A. Lambo (Nigeria, rapporteur) Yoshitsugu Baba (Japan) Thorsten Eriksson (Sweden) Pierre Frank (France) Ahmad M. Khalifa (U.A.R.) Pietro Manca (Italy) H.G. Moeller (U.S.) Alfonso Quiroz-Cuarón (Mexico) L.N. Smirnov (U.S.S.R.)	Main topic: preparations for the Fourth UN Crime Congress The meeting was preceded by a meeting of the *ad hoc* meeting of experts on social defence policies in relation to development planning, E/CN.5/C.3/R.4/Rev.1
27–31 August 1970 Kyoto fourth session E/CN.5/457	Myrl Alexander (U.S., chairperson) Norval Morris (U.S., rapporteur) Yoshitsugu Baba (Japan) Thorsten Eriksson (Sweden) Duncan Fairn (U.K.) Ahmad M. Khalifa (U.A.R.) K.A. Naqvi (India) José Arthur Alves da Cruz Rics (Brazil) Boris Alekseevich Victorov (U.S.S.R.)	Meeting held after the Fourth UN Crime Congress to turn Congress resolutions into proposals which went through the Commission for Social Development and on to ECOSOC
19–26 July 1971 New York fifth (and last) session E/CN.5/474	Myrl Alexander (U.S., chairperson) Norval Morris (U.S., rapporteur) Yoshitsugu Baba (Japan) Thorsten Eriksson (Sweden) Duncan Fairn (U.K.) Ahmad M. Khalifa (U.A.R.) K.A. Naqvi (India) José Arthur Alves da Cruz Rics (Brazil) Boris Alekseevich Victorov (U.S.S.R.)	

Sessions of the UN Committee on Crime Prevention and Control

8–17 May 1972 first session E/AC.57/7	First members of the UN Crime Committee: Ahmed Khalifa (Egypt, chairperson) José Arthur Alves Da Cruz Ríos (Brazil, rapporteur) Inkeri Anttila (Finland) Maurice Aydalot (France) Alphonse Boni (Ivory Coast) Norman A. Carlson (U.S.) William Robert Cox (U.K.) Taslim Olawale Elias (Nigeria) József Gödöny (Hungary) Pietro Manca (Italy) Khaleeq Ahmed Naqvi (India) Hamood'ur Rahman (Pakistan) Boris Alekseevich Viktorov (U.S.S.R.)	
14–25 May 1973 second session E/AC.57/14		ECOSOC resolution 1768 (LIV), section VIII: Committee would meet every second year
23 September–3 October 1974 third session E/AC.57/21/rev.1		Discussion of transnational crime and violence: consumer fraud, extortion, new forms of extortion, trafficking in cultural property, etc.
21 June–2 July 1976 fourth session E/CN.5/536		
5–16 June 1978 fifth session E/CN.5/558		Discussion of need for greater coordination in UN -> GA resolution 1979/19
8–12 September 1980 sixth session Caracas E/1980/112		
15–24 March 1982 seventh session E/CN.5/1983/2		

TABLE 2.1 (Continued)

21–30 March 1984 eighth session E/AC.57/1984/18	
5–14 March 1986 ninth session E/AC.57/1986/9	
22–31 August 1988 tenth session E/1988/20	Establishment of a sub-committee to review the functioning and programme of work of the UN Crime Programme
5–16 February 1990 eleventh session E/1990/31	Last (full) session of the Committee

UN Committee on Crime Prevention and Control. Its membership was expanded to fifteen. From then on, the experts were proposed by governments and elected by ECOSOC (ECOSOC 1584 (L) of 21 May 1971). In 1977, the GA decided that the seats were to be distributed according to "equitable geographical representation" (A/RES/32/60)[15] and thus, the composition of the policy-making body also began to reflect the global nature of the UN Crime Programme. The formal and practical dominance of Western Europe and North American experts on the Committee had come to an end.[16]

In 1979, membership on the Committee was almost doubled to 27, with seven seats assigned to Africa, six to Asia, three to Eastern Europe, five to Latin America, and six to "Western Europe and other states" (ECOSOC 1979/30 of 9 May 1979). The new functions of the Committee were to include:

- preparing UN Crime Congresses;
- preparing and submitting to competent UN bodies and the UN Crime Congresses proposals related to the prevention of crime and the treatment of offenders;
- assisting ECOSOC in the coordination of the activities of UN bodies in matters concerning the prevention of crime and the treatment of offenders, and preparing and submitting findings and recommendations to the Secretary-General and the appropriate UN bodies;
- promoting the exchange of experience gained by states in the prevention of crime and the treatment of offenders; and
- discussing major issues of professional interest as a basis for international cooperation in this field, particularly those related to the prevention and reduction of crime.

At first, the Committee reported to ECOSOC through the Commission on Social Development. However, since the Commission met only every second year, and there was little time on its agenda for crime-related issues, the GA decided in 1983 that the Committee would report directly to ECOSOC (A/RES/1983/25).

Other UN Crime Programme structures during the early years

GA resolution 415(V) provided the UN Secretariat with a small Social Defence Section, and the mandate to organize congresses every five years. Later incarnations of these remain key elements of the UN Crime Programme even today.

The resolution also provided for other elements some of which have evolved considerably, and some of which have disappeared: national correspondents to be appointed by each Member State, regional "consultative groups" of national correspondents which would meet every other year (or more often if required), and the publication of an international review.

The national correspondents and their regional consultative groups were designed to provide the Secretary-General and the UN Crime Programme with global reach, as well a channel for Member States to provide the Secretary-General with information and comments.[17] The national correspondents were to be appointed by their respective government.

Many Member States did initially appoint one or more *national correspondents*, and some national correspondents were quite active in providing the Secretariat with information (on request, or on their own initiative) and responding to requests for comments.[18] Many national correspondents attended the regional preparatory meetings for the UN Crime Congresses. For the Second (1955), Third (1965), Fourth (1970), and Fifth (1975) UN Crime Congresses, separate invitations were sent to national correspondents to attend, in the capacity of individual experts.[19]

In addition, the list of national correspondents maintained by the Secretariat provided a roster of persons who could be called on as experts or advisors in initiating, planning, and conducting technical assistance projects (Alper and Boren, 1972, pp. 71–72).

However, the system of national correspondents proved somewhat cumbersome to administer. There were considerable differences in the extent to which the national correspondents were willing or able to respond to requests for comment or convey information. There was also the practical difficulty that at times a national correspondent would move on to other duties, and the government in question did not notify the Secretariat of the name of their replacement. At the Fifth UN Crime Congress (1975), Prof. Ahmad Khalifa, Chairman of the National Centre for Social and Criminological Research, Cairo, presented a paper on the role of the national correspondents (Report of the Fifth UN Crime Congress, paras. 423–431). He concluded that despite efforts to ensure the effectiveness of the system, it had never proved satisfactory, and the functions entrusted to the national correspondents "remained, to a great extent, unfulfilled."

A meeting of national correspondents was organized at the Eighth (1990) UN Crime Congress, and a resolution was adopted to consolidate the role of the national correspondents (Report of the Ninth UN Crime Congress (1990), p. 133–134).[20] Among other actions, the resolution called for defining the specific tasks of the national correspondents, "including the quantity and quality of the data and information to be transferred to the United Nations according to pre-determined time-tables and methods"; and recommended that Member States review and update the list of national correspondents on an annual basis.

When the UN Crime Programme was restructured in 1991, the system of national correspondents was retained (A/RES/46/152, annex, paras. 39–40).

Each Member State was to appoint one or more national correspondents as focal points for maintaining communication with the Secretariat and with other elements of the UN Crime Programme. However, in practice few Member States have done so, and this element in the UN Crime Programme has largely fallen into disuse.

Not only were the national correspondents supposed to provide the Secretary-General with information, as well as disseminate information from the Secretary-General among the relevant agencies in their government, they were also to liaise on a regional level in the form of *regional consultative groups*. The original intention had been that these regional consultative groups would also make nominations for membership on the *ad hoc* Advisory Committee of Experts (Clifford, 1979, p. 7).

The system of regional consultative groups presented even more difficulties than did the national correspondents. Clifford (1979, pp. 7–8) provides a succinct analysis of the difficulties encountered, both in respect of the regional consultative groups and the national correspondents themselves:

> In practice it proved financially and administratively difficult for a number of consultative groups of national correspondents to be formed and convened at regular intervals. ... In fact, the maintenance of regular correspondence in all the different languages proved difficult and, as governments changed, the lists of national correspondents grew dated; and not infrequently nominees were held on the lists long after they had died or retired – or perhaps after they had been imprisoned by the new governments of different political complexions!"[21]

Although regional consultative groups were established, only one, the European Consultative Group, proved at least modestly viable. Its membership consisted to a large extent of former members of the IPPC, and it was convened four times during the 1950s. Perhaps unsurprisingly, the agenda of its meetings also reflected the focus of the general UN Crime Programme at the time on corrections and young offenders.[22] In 1959, perhaps as a tacit admission that the other regional consultative groups no longer functioned, the European group was redesignated – with membership also including representatives of a few Member States from outside the European region – as the UN Consultative Group on the Prevention of Crime and the Treatment of Offenders. This group held two further meetings, in 1961 and 1968.[23]

At the 1970 session of the Advisory Committee of Experts, the experts noted that there had been excessive overlap between the agenda of the (European) Consultative Group, and the quinquennial UN Crime Congresses. That same year ECOSOC decided to disband the Consultative Group. Its utility as a European regional forum had more or less disappeared along with the initiation, in 1958, of the work of the European Committee on Crime

Problems, which is part of the Council of Europe (E/CN.5/457, 1979; Alper and Boren, 1972, p. 99, and López-Rey, 1985, p. 37).[24]

The final structural element cited in GA resolution 415(V) is the publication of an international review. Between 1951 and 1999, the UN Secretariat published a total of 50 issues of the *International Review of Criminal Policy* (some of which were combined). The *International Review* generally appeared in English, with later issues also appearing in French and Spanish. As of 2001, the name of the journal was changed to "Forum on Crime and Society." In principle, this has been published annually, in all six official UN languages. The most recent issue, volume 10, numbers 1 and 2 (a combined issue), appeared in 2019, and dealt with the smuggling of migrants.

Notes

1 In 1848, Frankfurt am Main was a city state. It became part of Prussia in 1866.
2 Alper and Boren (1972, pp. 11–20) put the first international conferences on penitentiary matters in their historical context and provide details on the proceedings. The 1846 conference came out in support of solitary confinement combined with "useful" labour, education, and religious instruction, daily exercise, and open air (Alper and Boren, 1972, p. 14). Subsequent conferences during the 1800s took a more nuanced view. The 1872 conference in London favoured reformation over deterrence, and leniency over severity. Ibid., pp. 25–27.
3 The IPPC was originally called the International Prison Commission. Its mandate was to collect penitentiary statistics, promote penal reform, and organize international conferences. In 1935, the name of the Commission was changed to the International Penal and Penitentiary Commission to indicate that its field of interest was not limited to penitentiaries, but extended to penal matters in general. https://www.unodc.org/congress/en/previous/previous-ippc.html
    Subsequent IPC/IPPC conferences were held in Stockholm (1878), Rome (1885), St. Petersburg (1890), Paris (1895), Brussels (1900), Budapest (1905), and Washington (1910). Following the break caused by the First World War, the last IPC/IPPC conferences were held in London (1925), Prague (1930), Berlin (1935), and the Hague (1950). Alper and Boren, 1972, pp. 30–46, 65–74, and 124–125, summarize the proceedings of these individual conferences.
4 The progressive system, which was initially often connected with indeterminate sentences, seeks to promote rehabilitation and motivate prisoners by granting them increasing privileges and improved conditions as long as they remain well behaved. The last stage of the progression is often release on supervised parole.
5 These European-based international organizations included the IPPF and the Howard League for Penal Reform, the International Association of Penal Law (founded in 1924), the International Association of Children's Court Judges, and the International Bureau for the Unification of Penal Law. A fuller list is provided in *International Review of Criminal Policy*, no. 1 (January 1952), pp. 28–39.
6 Clark, 1994, pp. 10–13, lays particular emphasis on the human rights context of the fledgling UN Crime Programme. At the time that the UN was established, there were international agreements not only on drugs but also on trafficking in women and children and the circulation of obscene publications. When the UN was established, custody of these agreements was transferred to the Legal Office of the UN.

7 ECOSOC established two subsidiary bodies, the Temporary Economic Commission and the Temporary Social Commission.

   The Temporary Economic Commission morphed over time into the network of regional economic commissions.

   The Temporary Social Commission eventually became the Commission for Social Development, a functional commission of ECOSOC. As of 1984, the UN Crime Committee (and then the UN Crime Commission) reported directly to ECOSOC, thus bypassing the Commission for Social Development. López-Rey, 1985, pp. 12 and 19.

8 "L'uomo delinquent," which hypothesized a link between body structure and crime, was translated into several European languages towards the end of the 1800s. The most recent translation in English is Lombroso, 2006.

   Redo, 2012, p. 51, notes that the concept of "criminology" appeared even later, around 1885.

   The argument can also be made that the philosophical roots of UN criminal policy can be traced back to the work of John Howard and Cesare Beccaria during the second half of the 1700s. See Redo, 2012, pp. 43 and 49.

9 Blaustein et al., 2022, pp. 78 and 99, refer to the concern of the United States and its allies that the instabilities caused by free market liberalism might increase the appeal of communism.

   On development and crime in the UN Crime Programme, see section 8.4.

10 The UN website (https://www.unodc.org/congress/en/previous/previous-ippc.html) notes that during the 1930s and the war years of the 1940s, the Axis powers used the IPPC as a forum for their theories on the "racial and biological roots of crime and on draconian measures for its control." See also Alper and Boren, 1972, pp. 69–72 (on the proceedings of the IPPC conference held in Berlin in 1935) and pp. 79–80 (on IPPC activities during the Second World War).

   However, it should be noted there had also been interest in other countries in the possible racial and biological roots of crime. Perhaps the leading researcher and theorist in the eugenics approach in criminology ("crime is the result of defective genes") was the Harvard anthropologist Earnest A. Hooten in the United States, who argued, especially during the 1930s, that criminality is a biological trait found more frequently in some ethnic and national groups than in others.

11 Clifford, 1979, p. 6, notes that the GA resolution was based on resolutions 262B(ix) and 333H(xi) of ECOSOC, and a "dovetailing" resolution adopted by the IPPC on 12 August 1950.

   López-Rey, 1985, p. 5, stresses that even before assuming responsibility for the task that had been taken care of by the IPPC, the UN already had its "own" criminal policy as of 1946.

   The IPPC did not completely disappear. It retained its financial assets, and re-emerged as the International Penal and Penitentiary Foundation, which as a non-governmental organization continued to be actively involved in the work of the UN Crime Programme. (Adler and Mueller, 1995, p. 5, refer to its status as a "quasi-intergovernmental body rather than a non-governmental organization.")

12 According to subparagraph (h) of GA resolution 415(V), two IPPC "professional officers" were detached to the Secretariat, and one Secretariat staff member "specialized in the field of the prevention of crime and the treatment of offenders" was assigned to work with them. This Secretariat staff member was Irene Melup, who continued to serve as a staff member until 1990, and remained a key person in the UN Crime Programme well beyond that date.

13 Paragraph (d) of GA resolution 415(V) stated that "The United Nations shall convene every five years an international congress similar to those previously

organized by the IPPC (International Penal and Penitentiary Commission). Resolutions adopted at such international Congresses shall be communicated to the Secretary-General and, if necessary, to the policy-making bodies."

Alper and Boren, 1972, pp. 125–129, note that the UN also received the library and archives of the IPPC and that the IPPC reconstituted itself as the IPPF, which has remained a major non-governmental organization in international cooperation on crime prevention and criminal justice.

14 López-Rey, 1985, pp. 14–20, and Clifford, 1979, *passim*, provide background on the Committee.

15 The "other states" in this last regional grouping include Australia, Canada, New Zealand, and the United States. Thus, the "Western Europe and other states" group was essentially the one that had previously dominated the debates and had set the agenda.

16 Alper and Boren, 1972, pp. 48–49, provide interesting examples of how, before the time of the UN, international cooperation beyond Europe and North America produced major contributions to global crime prevention and criminal justice. They note, for example, how persons working in China, Japan, India, and Argentina contributed to the innovation of fingerprinting.

17 According to Redo, 2012, p. 68, this mechanism was originally operationalized by López-Rey, the then head of the Social Defence Section, when he enlisted fifteen "social defence observers … mostly drawn from the ranks of the International Penal and Penitentiary Commission."

18 As of 25 November 1951, 37 national correspondents had been appointed from 21 Member States. *International Review of Criminal Policy*, no. 1 (January 1951), pp. 24–25.

As of 31 March 1953, the number had expanded to 78 national correspondents from 34 Member States and six non-member states. *International Review of Criminal Policy*, no. 5 (January 1954), pp. 75–77.

By 1 December 1967, there were 178 national correspondents from 61 Member States and two non-Member States. *International Review of Criminal Policy*, no. 25 (1967), pp. 83–90.

19 *Report of the Second UN Crime Congress* (1960), para. 12, *Report of the Third UN Crime Congress* (1965), para. 10, *Report of the Fourth UN Crime Congress* (1970), para. 11, and *Report of the Fifth UN Crime Congress* (1975), para. 445. The reports of the subsequent UN Crime Congresses, from 1980 onwards, do not mention such separate invitations to national correspondents.

20 This could be seen as follow-up to ECOSOC resolution 1989/58 adopted the previous year, entitled United Nations network of government-appointed national correspondents in the field of crime prevention and control. The primary purpose of this resolution was to encourage Member States to appoint national correspondents.

21 López-Rey, 1985, p. 6, notes the difficulties in getting Member States to appoint national correspondents.

22 The first meeting, from 8–16 December 1952, dealt with the draft rules for the treatment of prisoners, the recruitment, training, and status of the staff of penal and correctional institutions, open penal and correctional institutions, study on criminality, technical assistance, the treatment of juvenile delinquents, and the extension of such treatment to young adults. *International Review of Criminal Policy*, no. 2 (July 1952), p. 83.

The second meeting was from 23 August–2 September 1954, and dealt with prison labour, indeterminate sentence, probation, parole, and after-care, and the organization of technical assistance seminars. *International Review of Criminal Policy*, no. 9, (January 1956), pp. 85–88.

The third meeting was from 13–23 August 1956, and dealt with habitual offenders, abnormal offenders, and the treatment of young offenders. *International Review of Criminal Policy*, no. 10 (July 1956), pp. 68–72.

The fourth meeting was from 11–21 August 1958, and dealt with prison labour, young delinquents, habitual and abnormal offenders, and sexual offenders. *International Review of Criminal Policy*, no. 14 (April 1959), pp. 59–69.

23 The first meeting of the reconstituted group was from 5–15 December 1961. On the agenda were the planning and construction of institutions for the treatment of juvenile delinquents and adult offenders, the prevention of juvenile delinquency, pre-trial detention of adults and juveniles, evaluation of group therapy and related therapeutic methods in penal and correctional treatment. *International Review of Criminal Policy*, no. 19 (June 1962), pp. 65–69.

The second (and last) meeting was from 6–16 August 1968. The agenda consisted of prevention of delinquency in the context of national development, the economics of training in the social defence field, and implementation of the Standard Minimum Rules on the Treatment of Prisoners. *International Review of Criminal Policy*, no. 26 (1968), pp. 104–110.

E/CN.5/C.2/R.2, 1966, para. 77. López-Rey, 1985, p. 6, notes that the European Consultative Group "did good work."

24 The membership of the Council of Europe grew to include almost all European countries. According to the website of the Council of Europe (https://www.coe.int/en/web/cdpc#), the Committee on Crime Problems oversees and coordinates the work of the Council of Europe on crime prevention and crime control. Among its functions are the identification of priorities for legal cooperation, the elaboration of conventions, recommendations, and reports, and the organization of criminological research conferences and conferences of directors of prison administration.

References

Adler, Freda and Gerhard Mueller (1995), A Very Personal and Family History of the United Nations Crime Prevention and Criminal Justice Branch, in M. Cherif Bassiouni (ed.), *The Contributions of Specialized Institutes and Non-Governmental Organizations to the United Nations Criminal Justice Programme. In Honour of Adolfo Beria di Argentine*, Brill Publishers, pp. 3–13

Alper, Benedict S. and Jerry F. Boren (1972), *Crime: International Agenda. Concern and Action in the Prevention of Crime and Treatment of Offenders, 1846–1972*, Lexington Books

Blaustein, Jarrett, Tom Chondor and Nathan W. Pino (2022), *Unravelling the Development – Crime Nexus*, Rowman & Littlefield

Clark, Roger S. (1994), *The United Nations Crime Prevention and Criminal Justice Program. Formulation of Standards and Efforts at Their Implementation*, University of Pennsylvania Press

Clifford, William (1979), *Echoes and Hopes. The United Nations Committee on Crime Prevention and Control*, Australian Institute of Criminology, Canberra, available at https://www.aic.gov.au/sites/default/files/2020-07/echoes-and-hopes.pdf

International Review of Criminal Policy (1952, July), United Nations

Joutsen, Matti (2017), *Four Transitions in the United Nations Crime Programme*, HEUNI, available at https://www.unodc.org/documents/commissions/CCPCJ/CCPCJ_Sessions/CCPCJ_26/E_CN15_2017_CRP4_e_V1703636.pdf

Lombroso, Cesare (2006), *Criminal Man*, translated by Mary Gibson and Nicole Hahn Rafter, Duke University Press

López-Rey de Arroya, Manuel (1985), *A Guide to United Nations Criminal Policy*, Cambridge Studies in Criminology LIV

Redo, Slawomir (2012), *Blue Criminology. The Power of United Nations Ideas to Counter Crime Globally – A Monographic Study*, HEUNI publication no. 72, available at https://www.heuni.fi/en/index/publications/heunireports/reports-eriesno.72.bluecriminologythepowerofunitednationsideastocountercrimeglob-ally-amonographicstudy.html

Redo, Slawomir (2011), The United Nations and Criminology, in Cindy J. Smith, Sheldon X. Zhang and Rosemary Barberet (eds.), *Routledge Handbook of International Criminology*, Routledge, pp. 125–133

Report of the [xx] UN Crime Congress: the reports of, as well as other background documents relating to, the different UN Crime Congresses are available at www.unodc.org/congress/en/previous-congresses.html

United Nations (1948), *Yearbook of the United Nations 1947–48*, New York, available at unhcr.org/4e1ee75f0.pdf and https://www.unmultimedia.org/searchers/yearbook/page.jsp?bookpage=613&volume=1947-48

3

RESTRUCTURING, THE SHIFT TO HARD LAW, AND THE IMPACT OF THE SOCIAL DEVELOPMENT GOALS

3.1   The restructuring of the UN Crime Programme

During the first decades of work on the UN Crime Programme, the forms of work consisted primarily of the collection and exchange of information, a limited amount of technical assistance and research, and work on the development of international standards and norms (*"soft law"*).[1] Among the major achievements was the adoption of the first ever UN standard and norm, the Standard Minimum Rules on the Treatment of Prisoners, at the First UN Crime Congress in 1955.[2]

In those early years, the members of the ad hoc group of experts, and subsequently of the UN Crime Committee, repeatedly sought to draw the attention of ECOSOC to the need to expand the capacity of the Secretariat to carry out the work that was deemed necessary.[3] Various plans had been developed for the collection and analysis of information and for the provision of technical assistance, for example. However, the size of the Secretariat unit devoted to crime prevention and criminal justice remained small (less than ten professionals), and was clearly out of proportion to the amount of work that the experts regarded as necessary.

Towards the end of the 1980s, some Member States began to raise a different type of criticism. In their view, too much time was being devoted to the adoption of resolutions and to the formulation of soft law standards and norms. They argued that the growth of organized and international crime, including terrorism, trafficking in persons, money laundering and corruption required a more action-oriented UN Crime Programme.

In 1985, the Seventh UN Crime Congress, in adopting the Milan Plan of Action, requested that the Secretary-General, in consultation with the

DOI: 10.4324/9781003480907-4

UN Crime Committee, review the UN Crime Programme "in order to establish priorities and to ensure the continuing relevance and responsiveness of the United Nations to emerging needs" (*Report of the Seventh UN Crime Congress*, Milan Plan of Action, para. 5 (f)). The GA approved the Milan Plan of Action and ordered that such a review be conducted, with the Secretary-General to present the results to ECOSOC in 1987 (A/RES/32, paras. 3 and 13). This review process soon led to a fundamental restructuring of the UN Crime Programme.

In May 1986, ECOSOC received an initial report from the Secretary-General. ECOSOC reaffirmed the importance of the UN Crime Congresses, requested that the Secretary-General "ensure the optimal functioning" of the UN Crime Committee (albeit "without additional cost to the United Nations"), and urged the Secretary-General to "look critically at the existing structure and level of management of the Crime Prevention and Criminal Justice Branch ... with a view to strengthening its capacity and status commensurate with its responsibilities" (ECOSOC resolution 1986/11).

The initial report by the Secretary-General to ECOSOC indicated that any changes would be modest. He was apparently focusing on fine-tuning the existing structures, particularly the Secretariat unit and the UN Crime Committee. The bottom line was that the Secretary-General recognized the need for a strengthened UN Crime Programme, but the financial reality was that no significant increase in funding would be available for this purpose. This did not seem to be the fundamental reassessment of the UN Crime Programme that some had called for.[4]

Meanwhile, Prof. Inkeri Anttila, Director of the European UN regional institute HEUNI, took matters into her own hands. In 1986 in Helsinki, she organized what may have been the first meeting in the review process to produce truly new elements. She was aware that much of the criticism of the work of the UN Crime Committee came from Western European countries, as well as the United States. For this reason, she brought together senior governmental officials responsible for criminal justice: Erich Corves and Konrad Hobe (Germany), Gioacchino Polimeni (Italy), Julian Schutte (the Netherlands), Bo Svensson (Sweden), David Faulkner (United Kingdom), Ronald Gainer (United States) and Dusan Cotic (Yugoslavia). This group highlighted that the mandate of the UN Crime Programme had been constantly expanding but that its infrastructure and resources remained small. The UN Crime Committee met every second year. The respective UN Secretariat unit (at the time the Crime Prevention and Criminal Justice Branch) had only seven professional staff members, and its technical assistance capacity was provided by one interregional advisor. The group discussed, inter alia, placing the Committee on a par with the Commissions that dealt with other areas of UN action (narcotic drugs, social development, the status of women, and human rights) and that the Committee meet annually. They also discussed upgrading the Secretariat unit, as well as ways of expanding technical assistance and research activities, for example, through the resources of the interregional and regional institutes.[5]

At the following session of the UN Crime Committee, held two years later in 1988, these ideas were shared with other Committee members.[6] There was a growing conviction that the UN Crime Committee itself should take action. Accordingly, the Committee adopted resolution 10/1, in which it requested that its chairperson,

> on the basis of informal consultations with committee members, appoint a sub-committee composed of the bureau and other designated members, with due regard to the principles of geographical distribution, working in collaboration with the directors of the regional and interregional institutes. The sub-committee would provide an overview of the problem of crime; assess the most efficient means of stimulating practical action in support of Member States; and make recommendations to the ... Committee concerning the most effective mechanisms for the implementation of the overview.

The subcommittee, which included several persons who had participated in the informal meeting in Helsinki, met in Riyadh on 18–19 January 1989, at the invitation of the Arab Security Studies and Training Centre (later to become known as the Naif Arab University for Security Sciences). On the basis of the proceedings of this subcommittee, three co-rapporteurs, Ronald Gainer (the U.S.), Vasily Ignatov (the U.S.S.R.), and Matti Joutsen (Finland), submitted their report and recommendations to the 1990 session of the UN Crime Committee.[7] The report described the problem of contemporary crime at the national and the international level, emphasizing its social and monetary costs. It also described (E/1990/31/Add.1, para. 51) the inadequacy of present bilateral, regional, and interregional cooperation, noting inter alia in respect of UN assistance,

> The United Nations crime and justice programme has been embarrassingly inadequate for years. Over and over, countries that have recognized their need for outside assistance in meeting problems of crime have requested urgent assistance from the United Nations. Often they have obtained only heartfelt expressions of sympathy and formal regret.

The report contained a number of substantive recommendations, such as the development of a process for prioritizing issues (with several examples provided), designing programmes for each issue, assembling and deploying the needed resources, and evaluating the results. Regarding the organizational structure, the report proposed either a new UN agency, or a new, major unit of the Secretariat. The restructured programme should be responsible to a policy-directing body capable of reflecting the practical needs of Member States. The report also outlined the mechanism for restructuring the programme: the convening of a summit meeting or ministerial meeting, as well as the adoption of an international instrument such as an international convention (E/1990/31/Add.1, paras. 57–72).[8]

The Committee, which met the following month, was very much in agreement with the recommendations. In view of the fact that the Eighth UN Crime Congress was to be held six months later, the Committee forwarded a draft resolution to the Congress for action. The intention was that this would be directed to the GA, and lead to the establishment of an expert working group to further elaborate the proposed UN Crime Programme and the mechanisms required to implement this programme. The results of whatever emerged would go to a "high-level meeting" (E/1990/31, pp.169–170).

The Congress acted very much as requested, with a few amendments. One was to change the reference to an "expert working group" to an "intergovernmental group," and another was to change the reference to a "high-level meeting" to a "ministerial meeting" (Report of the Eighth UN Crime Congress, pp. 9–11; Clark, 1994, pp. 27–29).

Acting on cue, the GA adopted the result, as resolution 45/108 (Clark, 1994, pp. 53–57).

The 1990 UN Crime Congress was itself to provide added grounds for criticism of the UN Crime Programme. In addition to considering the draft resolution on the restructuring of the UN Crime Programme, the Eighth UN Crime Congress submitted 12 other new draft instruments or resolutions for adoption by the GA, as well as 33 other resolutions, for a grand total of 45 resolutions. For some participants, this torrent of paper was emblematic of growing problems in the UN Crime Programme.[9]

The large number of draft resolutions, all dealing with issues which were undeniably important, gave rise to considerable concern. Some governmental representatives complained that many of the draft standards and norms had been prepared without sufficient government input. Others were of the view that soft law instruments (standards and norms, as well as resolutions) were an ineffective response to the growing problems of crime and criminal justice and that the UN Crime Congresses should be prioritizing practical and effective action over words on paper. It was also pointed out by many participants that 24 – over half – of the draft resolutions had not been submitted until the Congress itself, and therefore there had been insufficient time to study these drafts. There was also wide agreement that it was simply not possible for any delegation to follow and contribute to, at more or less the same time, the negotiations on 47 separate draft resolutions (Clark, 1994, pp. 126–132; Clark, 1990).

Up to this point, the growing assumption had been that the UN Crime Committee would continue its work, perhaps with annual (as opposed to biannual) sessions. There were also proposals to base the work of the UN Crime Programme on an international convention. What such a convention would actually contain remained a subject for debate.[10] Others suggested different ways of placing the UN Crime Programme on a firmer footing; one suggestion was for a world foundation on crime control and assistance for victims (*Report of the Eighth UN Crime Congress*, 1990, para. 84).

The Intergovernmental Working Group established by the GA met in August 1991. It had before it several quite new elements, contained in a discussion paper dated 10 June 1991, and circulated by HEUNI: a "Plan for the Restructuring of the United Nations Crime Prevention and Criminal Justice System." This had been prepared by a second group sitting informally at HEUNI, with Polimeni, Schutte, and the present author, who had attended the first informal meeting at HEUNI in 1986, augmented by General Vasily Ignatov (U.S.S.R.) and Prof. Roger Clark (New Zealand). The main structural change proposed in the discussion paper was the replacement of the UN Crime Committee, which consisted of individual experts, by a Commission of Member States, under ECOSOC.[11]

This "Plan" was reflected in many ways in the final product that was subsequently worked out at an Intergovernmental Working Group meeting in Vienna on 5–9 August 1991 (A/CONF.156/2)[12] and approved under the chandeliers of Versailles at a grand ministerial conference on 21–23 November 1991, to be formally adopted by the GA at the end of 1991 with resolution 46/152 of 18 December 1991. The result was the *restructuring of the UN Crime Programme.*

The GA resolution contains an annex outlining the elements and method of work of the restructured UN Crime Programme:

- the goals (paras. 15–16);
- the scope of the UN Crime Programme (paras. 17–20);
- the Programme priorities (paras. 21–22);
- the structure and management of the Programme (paras. 23–34; the Crime Commission, the UN Crime Congresses and the Secretariat);
- Programme support (paras. 35–43; the institutes, the national correspondents, the Global Crime and Criminal Justice Information Network, and IGOs and NGOs);[13] and
- Programme funding (para. 44).

The most notable and ultimately far-reaching change was that the expert-driven Crime Committee was replaced by a government-driven Commission on Crime Prevention and Criminal Justice (the *UN Crime Commission*).[14]

The new UN Crime Commission consists of forty Member States elected by ECOSOC for a term of three years: twelve from the African region, nine from the Asian region, eight from the Latin American and Caribbean region, four from the Eastern European region, and seven from the "Western Europe and others" regional group.

Whereas the UN Crime Committee had been convened (during the last years of its existence) for a leisurely two weeks every second year, the UN Crime Commission began by holding annual sessions of one week, and gradually added annual "*reconvened*" sessions as well as "*intersessional*" meetings.[15]

Once the UN Crime Commission was established in 1991, this body began to identify priority themes and priority issues. (During the time of the UN Crime Committee, there had been little evidence of an overall strategy. Although the Committee dealt with a large number of important issues, this was almost invariably done on a piecemeal basis.) At its second session in 1993, the Commission established the following as priority themes for the UN Programme:

  (i)   national and transnational crime, including organized crime, economic crime (including money-laundering), and the role of the criminal law in the protection of the environment;
 (ii)   crime prevention in urban areas, juvenile and violent crime; and
(iii)   efficiency, fairness and improvement in the management and administration of criminal justice and related systems with due emphasis on the strengthening of national capacities in developing countries for the regular collection, collation, analysis and utilization of data in the development and implementation of appropriate policies.

The Commission also noted the need to make provision for special operational activities and advisory services in situations of urgent need and for programme organization, evaluation, and reporting obligations.

The three priority *themes* noted above offer considerable scope for activity and can be understood as setting out the broad outlines of the UN Crime Programme in the long term.[16] At its third and fourth sessions in 1994 and 1995, the Commission singled out some more specific topics as priority *issues* at least in the short term:[17]

(a)   organized transnational crime;
(b)   the control of the proceeds of crime;
(c)   the organized smuggling of illegal migrants across national boundaries;
(d)   violence against women and children;
(e)   the regulation of firearms; and
(f)   the role of criminal law in the protection of the environment.

These six priority *issues* suggest that one consequence of the shift from an expert-driven to a Member State-driven UN Crime Programme has been that the debates, and the output of the debates, have increasingly focused on transnational organized crime, with correspondingly less attention paid, for example, to crime prevention or the day-to-day operation of the criminal justice system.[18]

Attempts to develop a more coherent approach for the UN Crime Programme were taken one step further in late 1994 and the spring of 1995, when work began on the drafting of "action plans" on such issues as transnational organized crime, the regulation of firearms, juvenile justice, violence against women, and international cooperation in computerization and statistical applications in the management of the criminal justice system.

Such action plans recommend both short-term and long-term action to be undertaken by the Secretariat, governments, intergovernmental and nongovernmental organizations, and other entities. In so doing, they provide more detailed guidance on how to approach at least some of the priority issues identified by the UN Crime Commission.

Following the Ninth UN Crime Congress (1995), a (lengthy) resolution embodying the results of the Congress was submitted to the UN Crime Commission. This draft occasioned heated discussion both inside and outside the meeting room: should all of the resolutions and recommendations reached by consensus among a hundred delegations from Member States attending the Congress be adopted as such, or should the Commission, with its substantive responsibility for the UN Crime Programme, identify a few issues among them to become priorities or, at the very least, amend the terms of reference of some of the issues? A group of Member States (primarily from the "Western Europe and others" regional group) questioned whether the UN Crime Programme can effectively deal with all the different activities proposed.

The arguments of the other Member States, which supported adoption of the Ninth UN Congress resolutions and recommendations *en bloc*, ultimately carried the day. The terms of references were modified slightly (and, even then, primarily for stylistic reasons). However, the first group of Member States kept returning in other connections to the same theme: the UN Crime Commission must set priorities and must determine exactly what it is that the UN Crime Programme should do.

3.2 Moving from soft law to hard law: negotiating the UN Crime Conventions

While the UN Committee on Crime Prevention and Control was producing soft law, the UN Drug Control Programme continued work on hard law (international conventions) that had begun during the early 1900s.[19] As noted in the introduction, this work resulted, for example, in the 1961 Single Convention on Narcotic Drugs (amended by a protocol in 1972) and the Convention on Psychotropic Substances in 1971. In 1988, at the same time as criticism of the UN Crime Programme was growing, work was completed on the UN Convention against Illicit Traffic in Narcotic Drugs and Psycho-tropic Substances (the *1988 UN Drug Convention*). This remains the basic international agreement on drugs and marked a considerable improvement in several respects. It consolidated and brought international hard law up to date on the definition of drug-related crime. It also included, for the first time in a multilateral treaty, provisions on international law enforcement coop-eration, mutual legal assistance, and extradition.

Perhaps inevitably, the 1988 Drug Convention became a template for those who wanted a more vigorous and effective UN Crime Programme.[20] They ar-gued that domestic law and practice on responding to *organized crime* should be updated and strengthened and that a UN Crime Convention would in-crease political support for measures in this field. There were, however, very different visions of what such a convention would look like: a consolidation of existing conventions on international law enforcement and judicial coopera-tion, the establishment of a world foundation on crime control and assistance to victims, a convention focusing on some form of crime (such as organized crime), or perhaps even the establishment of an international criminal court.[21]

There were some early signs of this push for a UN Crime Convention. At the Seventh and Eighth UN Crime Congresses (in 1985 and 1990), be-fore the UN Crime Commission had been established, it was argued that conventional methods of cooperation between countries in combating crime were no longer sufficient in the face of the internationalization of criminal activities. It was therefore regarded as imperative to adopt new international instruments specially designed for this purpose.[22]

Although the United States did not send a delegation to the Eighth UN Crime Congress, which was held in Havana, Cuba, it had shown an interest in promoting international cooperation in criminal justice (primarily through the signing of bilateral agreements with a number of countries). Over a hun-dred years after England promoted anti-slavery around the world as part of its foreign policy, in the 1960s the United States injected a clear foreign policy aspect into its "war on drugs". The rash of skyjackings soon after, in the 1970s, by its very nature required a transnational response (Andreas and Nadelmann, 2006, esp. pp. 106–107).

A year after the Ninth UN Crime Congress, in 1991, General Vasily Igna-tov (U.S.S.R.), a member of the UN Crime Committee, circulated a proposal for a UN "Convention On Crime Control," and at the Versailles Ministerial Meeting, Costa Rica submitted a draft convention on international coopera-tion in crime prevention and criminal justice. Both proposals focused largely on procedural cooperation (Clark, 1994, p. 49; Redo, 2012, p. 118).[23]

With its long experience in trying to respond to organized crime, Italy was active in lobbying for a convention that would contain both procedural and substantive provisions on preventing and responding to this form of crimi-nality. Only a few years after the 1988 Drug Convention entered into force, and just after the restructuring of the UN Crime Programme, Italy hosted the World Ministerial Conference on Organized Transnational Crime in 1994, in Naples (21–23 November 1994). After this conference, which was attended by representatives of 124 Member States, the GA adopted the Naples Political Declaration and Global Action Plan. The action plan calls for a number of measures that were designed to promote the prevention and control of organized transnational crime on both the national and international level.

However, there remained considerable resistance to the idea of a UN convention on organized crime, particularly among the Western Europe and others group of countries. This could be seen in the careful way in which the Declaration of the 1994 conference and the resolution of the GA referred to the issue. There was no direct statement to the effect that a convention would be drafted. Instead, the Secretary-General was asked to consult with governments on the "opportunity of elaborating new international instruments such as a convention or conventions and on the issues and elements that could be covered therein."

There were various reasons for this hesitancy. Those who were sceptical of the need for a new convention argued that the concept of organized transnational crime is too vague, that it appears in too many forms to be dealt with other than on a high level of generality, and that existing instruments on extradition and mutual assistance (if promoted and properly implemented) could already provide an adequate basis for international cooperation. The focus, in their view, should be on the development and strengthening of practical measures. The sceptics also noted that negotiating a convention is an expensive process, for both the countries involved and for the UN. The resources needed for this would inevitably be taken away from other projects, which were perhaps just as deserving.

At the Ninth UN Crime Congress, held in 1995, the subject inevitably arose, with the same arguments for and against. Again, the resolution was carefully worded: the Secretary-General should "continue his consultations with Governments on the possibility of elaborating a convention or conventions against organized transnational crime and on the elements that could be included therein." He should analyse the views of governments on this issue, and "make proposals on the action that would be appropriate." The matter was due to come up at the sixth (1997) session of the Commission, where it would be dealt with in a working group.

During the autumn of 1996, however, Poland submitted a proposal for a draft convention on transnational organized crime to the GA (A/C.3/51/7, annex).[24] The matter was referred to the UN Crime Commission by General Assembly resolution 51/120, which was adopted by consensus.

This resulted in considerable political pressure to start work on the proposed convention. Organized crime is something that constantly makes the headlines and people know where they stand on this issue: they are against it. Individual criminal justice practitioners and victims are doubtless earnest in their conviction that not enough is being done on the local, national, or international level to prevent and control organized crime. Consequently, the idea that the UN should develop an international convention on this subject soon took on a life of its own. Many of the Member States that had initially strongly opposed the idea of a convention, concluded that if energy and resources were going to be expended on the process, it would be better to join in and seek to ensure that the end result is as useful as possible.

At the sixth (1997) session of the UN Crime Commission, a number of participants noted that several somewhat related conventions had also been proposed, such as on money laundering, trafficking in children, the regulation of firearms, the smuggling of migrants, corruption, terrorism, and trafficking in nuclear waste. Although some delegations supported continued work on one or another of these conventions separately, a number of delegations were of the view that the need for at least some of these conventions could be met by supplementing existing international instruments, by combining some or all of these proposed conventions into one new convention, or by adding protocols to a convention.[25]

Getting the focus on transnational organized crime

Following extensive discussion in a working group, the UN Crime Commission decided to submit a draft resolution entitled *Follow-up to the Naples Political Declaration and Global Action Plan against Organized Transnational Crime* to the GA. This draft sought the establishment of an intergovernmental group of experts that would consider the elaboration of a "preliminary draft of a possible comprehensive convention against organized transnational crime." This was accordingly done by the GA (A/RES/52/85 of 12 December 1997), which charged the intergovernmental group with taking into account existing instruments, the Polish draft, and a number of other proposals.

The intergovernmental group of experts met three times, in Warsaw on 2–6 February 1998, in Vienna on 21–30 April 1998, and in Buenos Aires on 31 August–4 September 1998.

When the experts in the intergovernmental group first convened in Warsaw in February 1998, they found before them not one, but two drafts for the new convention. As noted, Poland had submitted a preliminary draft directly to the GA. The Polish draft was loosely based on the 1988 UN Convention against Illicit Traffic in Narcotic Drugs and Psychotropic Substances, but with several points of difference. The United States had also submitted a "discussion draft" in advance of the Warsaw meeting. The U.S. draft incorporated many elements that the United States includes in its many mutual legal assistance treaties.[26] At the request of the UN Secretariat, the Max Planck

Institute for Foreign and International Criminal Law had prepared a paper that summarized the various proposals on the different issues for Warsaw.

When the work began in Warsaw, the general view was that both the Polish draft and the U.S. draft contained many good elements, but neither was suitable as it stood as the basic text on which to proceed. Several delegations stated their preference for using the 1988 Drug Convention as the starting point, arguing that this was a relatively recent and widely ratified Convention that dealt with one aspect of organized crime. In addition, some delegations made proposals regarding various parts of the draft Convention.[27]

Working overnight at the meeting in Warsaw, the Finnish delegation produced a single composite text that more or less followed the structure of the 1988 Drug Convention for the use of a drafting group set up by the meeting. The various proposals (Polish, U.S., and others) were inserted into this text. Where the 1988 Drug Convention and the various proposals differed, the texts were offered as "options." This "options document" became the basis for the work that was done over the next two years, with the major focus being on eliminating options, leaving just one – which was almost always extensively amended – with various words or passages "bracketed" to denote that they remained subject to negotiation. The document was constantly being updated by the Secretariat to reflect the discussions at the different sessions, and became known as the "rolling text."

As for the three protocols, the basic drafts for each had different origins. The United States (A/AC.254/4/Add.3) and Argentina (A/AC.254/8) had both prepared drafts for the proposed protocol on trafficking in persons, and these were combined.[28] Austria and Italy had submitted a draft for the protocol on the smuggling of migrants (A/AC.254/4/Add.1).[29] The basic draft for the protocol on trafficking in firearms had been submitted by Canada (A/AC.254/4/Add.2).[30]

Establishment of the intergovernmental Ad Hoc Committee on the negotiation of the UN Convention against Transnational Organized Crime (UNTOC) and its protocols

At the end of 1998, the GA took note of the work done by the experts and established an open-ended intergovernmental Ad Hoc Committee to carry on the work (A/RES 53/111). The members of the Ad Hoc Committee were to spend much of the following two years in the confines of the Vienna International Centre seeking to define the vague concept of "transnational organized crime," bridging the gap between different legal systems in defining offences such as "participation in an organized criminal group," working out myriad technical questions (ranging from what travel documents should be required at borders to the marking of ammunition), and confronting a host of political problems, large and small.[31]

The negotiations were difficult for a variety of reasons. One was the sheer scope of the issues to be covered: transnational organized crime, trafficking in persons, the smuggling of migrants, and trafficking in firearms. This required not only the participation of the diplomats based in Vienna, who were familiar with the UN context, but also of a rotating cast of negotiators and experts "from the capitals" on the specialist and technical issues. It required working out a strategy for simultaneously negotiating the main Convention (on transnational organized crime) and the three protocols. At the outset, it was not clear what the relationship would be between these: to what extent would each protocol echo provisions also found in the main Convention, and to what extent would provisions in the main Convention be applied *mutatis mutandis* to one or more protocols? Also, to what extent would their scope of application need to be based on that of the main Convention, or could they have a different scope of application?

A second difficulty was the relative absence of earlier conventions to use as a point of reference. The 1988 Drug Convention became an important source, in particular in respect of the general provisions (such as on jurisdiction and on signature and ratification of the Convention) and the provisions on law enforcement and judicial cooperation.[32] Some regional conventions prepared within the scope of regional bodies such as the Organization of American States and the Council of Europe were also examined.

A third difficulty arose towards the end of the negotiations, in 2000, when the cast of negotiators began to change quite substantially from one session to the next. New negotiators would come in with fresh ideas and fresh energy, submitting (at times lengthy) proposals that would require re-opening provisions that had already been negotiated at length and "gavelled," i.e., the chairperson had concluded that there was a consensus on the wording of the provision in question and had banged his gavel to end the debate and move on to the next issue. Although over the course of the negotiations, the number of options in the text were reduced, the remaining text remained littered with brackets to indicate that certain provisions or certain phrases in these provisions were still subject to debate. As the negotiators kept reminding one another, "Nothing is approved until everything is approved."

A fourth difficulty arose because of the multilingual environment of the UN, the use of six official UN languages (Arabic, Chinese, English, French, Russian, and Spanish).[33] The UN interpretation at the Vienna International Centre was as usual excellent and allowed speakers from all language groups to take a full part in the proceedings. The necessity for full interpretation, however, meant that "break-out groups" could not be set up to deal with specific vexing issues (although the chairperson often requested that certain delegations would get together informally to deal with an issue and report back to the plenary). Towards the end of the process, when informal sessions became necessary, these could only be arranged to the extent that they had full interpretation.

The multilingual environment also required constant translation of different written proposals into all UN languages. Often, when a delegation made a somewhat lengthy or complicated oral proposal, some other delegations would request that it be circulated in writing and in all languages before being discussed in the plenary.[34]

Particular issues arising in the negotiation of UNTOC

Among the difficulties encountered during the negotiations were the following:

- the *scope of application* of the main Convention (art. 3). For example, should it be limited to a list of serious crimes (as proposed by Latin American countries) or should it be generic? Should it be limited to offences in which an organized criminal group is involved? Should it be limited to offences that are transnational and, if so, how would "transnationality" be defined?

  Much of this discussion was repeated at almost all the first sessions, with essentially the same arguments put forward by the different sides. Time and again, the negotiators reluctantly agreed to postpone a decision on this question until the substantive provisions in the text had been finalized – only for the discussion on these substantive provisions to become bogged down when some exasperated negotiators would argue that they could not agree to any substantive provision until they had clarity on the scope of the Convention.

  It was ultimately agreed to provide a generic definition of transnational organized crime and that a list of typical offences to which the Convention applied would be included in both the *travaux préparatoires* and in the resolution by which the Convention was adopted by the GA. In addition, the Convention requires that the States Parties criminalize four specific offences, participation in an organized criminal group, corruption, money laundering, and obstruction of justice. Each of the three protocols (trafficking in persons, the smuggling of migrants, and trafficking in firearms) contained further criminalizations.

- *how should organized crime and an organized criminal group be defined* (art. 2)? This fundamental question when negotiating a convention on (transnational) organized crime proved difficult, and the negotiations continued for quite some time. One key issue was whether or not to limit the scope to crimes that were committed for a "financial or other material benefit." Several Member States were of the view that terrorism was a particularly dangerous form of organized crime which should be covered. The definition of terrorism, however, raises difficult political questions. Ultimately terrorism as such was not included in the scope of the negotiations, on the grounds that work was proceeding elsewhere in the UN on a draft comprehensive treaty on terrorism. However, it was recognized that terrorist groups may commit offences for a financial or material benefit (such as extortion and robbery) to fund their activity, and the Convention would apply to these crimes.[35]

- *how should the offence of "participation in a criminal group" be defined* (art. 5)? The approach ultimately adopted was to offer a choice between two different definitions, one based largely on statutory law and the other based on the common law concept of conspiracy.
- *how should the offence of laundering of the proceeds of crime be defined* (art. 6)? The main issue here was the scope of predicate offences (art. 6(b)). As was the case with corruption (art. 8) and obstruction of justice (art. 23), the definition does not require that the offence be committed by an organized criminal group.
- *how should the offence of corruption be defined* (art. 8)? The solution here was to have a very brief provision on corruption, together with a commitment to work on a new instrument, the UN Convention against Corruption.
- the *funding of technical assistance* (art. 30). During the negotiations, the representatives of several developing Member States repeatedly expressed their concerns about the obligations that they would be undertaking in ratifying the Convention. Their States would require extensive technical assistance to meet these obligations.
- *review of implementation of the convention* (art. 32). Proposals by, among others, many Western countries to include provisions on the monitoring of implementation met with resistance. Various options were proposed, such as review by the UN Crime Commission and review by a special body, and detailed proposals were made for how this review would be undertaken. Ultimately, it was decided that this discussion could be deferred to the Conference of the States Parties which, in agreeing on its rules of procedure, could conceivably agree on the terms of reference for such a review. (The Conference of States Parties was not able to reach agreement on the review of implementation for almost two decades.)[36]
- the *possibility that the EU could accede to the convention*, something which had not happened before (art. 36 provides that the convention and its protocols are open for signature by regional economic integration organizations).

Each of the protocols raised issues of their own, such as:

- should the protocol on *trafficking in persons* only cover trafficking in women and children, or all trafficking? In view of the fact that parallel work in Geneva was underway on a draft optional protocol to the Convention on the Rights of the Child, on the sale of children, child prostitution and child pornography, and this had been opened for signature in 2000, the Ad Hoc Committee decided on the wider approach.

- should the protocol require States Parties to criminalize prostitution and pornography? (Such a provision was ultimately not included.)
- what should the scope of the provisions on victims be? (Art. 6; the compromise language was taken largely from the 1985 UN Victim Declaration.)
- how should the provision on the repatriation of victims be formulated? (Art. 8; this led to a lengthy article, with one key point being that the repatriation "shall preferably be voluntary.")
- should the protocol on the *smuggling of migrants* shield them from criminal liability in respect of the offence of trafficking? (Art. 5; this was answered in the affirmative.)
- the wording of the provision on the return of migrants to the State Party of which they are nationals or where they have the right of permanent residence (art. 18).
- in respect of the protocol on *trafficking in firearms*, the major political question was whether explosives should be included in the scope of the protocol (as is the case with the Inter-American Convention Against the Illicit Manufacturing of and Trafficking in Firearms, Ammunition, Explosives, and Other Related Materials, which entered into force in 1998). After extensive discussions in which it was pointed out that the original mandate from the GA did not include explosives, this was left outside the scope of the protocol.
- among the many difficult technical questions regarding the firearms protocol were those dealing with the marking of firearms (art. 8), deactivation of firearms (art. 9), export, import, transit licensing, or authorisation (art. 10), and the role of brokers and brokering (art. 15).

Throughout the two years that the Ad Hoc Committee worked on the convention, an exceptionally large number of delegations took an active part in the process. For example, at the tenth session, 121 national delegations attended. Almost all of the delegations contributed substantively to the discussions, often with well-reasoned submissions. One delegation quite appropriately pointed out at the tenth session that all the delegations had participated in practice on an equal basis in the negotiations.

After less than two years and a total of eleven sessions in Vienna,[37] the Ad Hoc Committee was able to finalise the text for the Convention and the protocols. Following its approval by the Millennium Session of the GA on 15 November 2000, it, together with separate protocols on trafficking in persons, the smuggling of migrants, and trafficking in firearms, was opened for signing amidst much pomp and ceremony in Palermo on 12 December 2000. UNTOC and the trafficking in persons protocol entered into force in 2003. The protocol on the smuggling of migrants entered into force in 2004, followed by the trafficking in firearms protocol in 2005.

Those who have been involved in the negotiation of multilateral conventions know that the process tends to be a long and arduous one. Getting States interested in an idea takes time, agreement has to be reached on the general outline of the convention and on the basic concepts, legal differences have to be worked out, political difficulties may bog the discussion down for years, and even the practical issues take time.

For the UNTOC process to go from start to finish in six years – and for the actual negotiations to only take two years (1999 and 2000) – is highly unusual. Including the various informal sessions held during the negotiations, a total of some 80 working days were devoted to the Convention (an average of only two days per article). This speed cannot be explained by the simplicity of the task, the clarity of the concepts, or the lack of political disagreements. On the contrary, as noted, there were a large number of substantive, technical, and procedural problems to be overcome. It was clear that there was a political will in the negotiating hall at the Vienna International Centre to achieve the goal: the opening of the Convention and the protocols in time for the signing conference in Palermo.

The evolution of the UN Convention against Corruption (UNCAC)

The dust had barely settled on the negotiating tables where the UNTOC Convention had been hammered out, when work began on a *UN Convention against Corruption* (UNCAC). Whereas UNTOC had one primary source of inspiration (the 1988 Drug Convention), UNCAC had several.[38]

The first attempts to develop a global response to corruption within the UN system were made in the mid-1970s and had to do with corrupt practices and illicit payments in international business transactions, the goal was the formulation of a code of conduct for transnational corporations.[39]

Within the UN Crime Programme, corruption was referred to in passing at the Fourth and Fifth UN Crime Congresses (1970 and 1975), in the context of "white collar crime" and economic crime. At the Sixth, Seventh, and Eighth UN Crime Congresses (1980, 1985, and 1990), the context was more of corruption as a challenge to development.[40] The Eighth UN Crime Congress adopted a resolution dealing specifically with corruption; "Corruption in Government." In it, the Congress requested that the UN Secretariat develop a draft international code of conduct for public officials and submit it to the next Congress, in 1995.

While these discussions were going on, progress was being made in another area. In 1979, the GA adopted the final text of the Code of Conduct for Law Enforcement Officials (A/RES/34/169). Article 7 of the Code of Conduct reads as follows: "Law enforcement officials shall not commit any act of corruption. They shall also rigorously oppose and combat all such acts." Subparagraph (b) of the commentary to this article even contains a definition of corruption, the first time such a definition has been formulated within the UN:

> While the definition of corruption must be subject to national law, it should be understood to encompass the commission or omission of an

act in the performance of or in connection with one's duties, in response to gifts, promises or incentives demanded or accepted, or the wrongful receipt of these once the act has been committed or omitted.

As has been noted above, the Eighth UN Crime Congress (1990) took place whilst intense work was being done on the restructuring of the UN Crime Programme. This work led to the establishment of the UN Crime Commission in 1991. The Commission, in turn, showed a strong interest in transnational organized crime generally and also in corruption. In recommending to ECOSOC the agenda for the Ninth UN Crime Congress in 1995, the Commission proposed that one day of the plenary debate be devoted to corruption, and that one of the Congress workshops deal with corruption. In addition, the draft code of conduct for public officials was to be prepared for submission to this next Congress (UNCAC, 2010, p. xx).

Accordingly, corruption figured prominently in the discussions at the Ninth UN Crime Congress. The draft code of conduct for public officials was duly considered, and submitted back to the UN Crime Commission for action. From the Commission, the draft code went on to ECOSOC and the GA, which adopted the International Code of Conduct for Public Officials in its resolution A/RES/51/59. Furthermore, on 16 December 1996, in resolution A/RES/51/191, the GA adopted the UN Declaration against Corruption and Bribery in International Commercial Transactions.

Between 1996 and 2003, seven different international conventions were negotiated on corruption, beginning with the 1996 Inter-American Convention against Corruption of the Organization of American States:

- the 1996 Inter-American Convention against Corruption of the Organization of American States;
- the 1997 Convention on Combating Bribery of Foreign Public Officials in International Business Transactions of the Organization for Economic Cooperation and Development (OECD);
- the 1998 Convention on the Fight against Corruption Involving Officials of the European Communities or Officials of Member States of the European Union;
- the 1999 Criminal Law Convention on Corruption of the Council of Europe;
- the 1999 Civil Law Convention on Corruption, of the Council of Europe;
- the 2001 Southern African Development Community Protocol against Corruption; and
- the 2003 African Union Convention on Preventing and Combating Corruption.

All of these conventions, UNCAC included, emerged within a relatively short period of time, the seven years from 1996 to 2003. A tipping point seems to have been reached sometime during the 1990s, when Member States realized that corruption cannot be dealt with solely on a national basis. International conventions were seen to be the necessary next step in dealing with the problem. It is likely that when work began in some forums on the drafting of a convention (the Inter-American Convention and the OECD Convention),[41] this gave the impetus for work to begin elsewhere (the EU, the Council of Europe, Southern Africa and Africa, as well as within the framework of the UN).

Indeed, soon after the Inter-American Convention on Corruption was adopted, and at the time that the OECD Convention was being finalized, a UN Expert Group Meeting on Corruption was held in Buenos Aires (17–21 March 1997). That meeting recommended that the UN Crime Commission should prepare an "international convention against corruption and bribery in international commercial transactions" (UNCAC, 2010, pp. xxviii–xxix). A second meeting, the Expert Group Meeting on Corruption and Its Financial Channels (Paris, 30 March–1 April 1999) was able to take into consideration the ongoing work on the UN Convention against Transnational Organized Crime. In view of the fact that UNTOC would only include a few provisions on corruption, this second expert group meeting repeated the call for a global international instrument specifically on corruption (UNCAC, 2010, pp. xxix–xxx).[42]

This initiative led in early 2000 to GA resolution 54/128, entitled "Action against Corruption." The resolution asked the Ad Hoc Committee drafting UNTOC *inter alia* to consider whether an international instrument against corruption should be prepared, after UNTOC had been finalized. The Ad Hoc Committee was of this opinion and that the Secretariat should start the preparations for such work (UNCAC, 2010, p. xxxi).[43]

The Tenth UN Crime Congress (2000) emphasized the importance of drafting such a new international instrument. The Congress adopted "the Vienna Declaration on Crime and Justice: Meeting the Challenges of the Twenty-first Century." In endorsing the Vienna Declaration (resolution 55/59), the GA asked the Secretariat to prepare plans of action for its implementation and for consideration and action by the UN Crime Commission. The resulting final text of the plans of action was annexed to GA resolution 56/261.

Section II of these plans of action was directly relevant to the proposed work on an international instrument against corruption. In it, Member States undertook to support the work of the Ad Hoc Committee for the negotiation of such a convention, with a view to finalizing it by the end of 2003.

On the same day as the GA adopted resolution 55/59 referred to immediately above, it adopted resolution 55/61, which inter alia established an ad hoc committee for the negotiation of the convention against corruption.

The next step was the preparation of draft terms of reference for such a convention. This was done by an intergovernmental, open-ended expert group, which met in Vienna from 30 July to 3 August 2001. Its work was simplified by being able to use the terms of reference of UNTOC as a point of departure. By this time it was clear that different Member States (and other stakeholders) had somewhat different priorities. Presumably amongst the primary concerns of all of them were the prevention of corruption and the strengthening of international cooperation in bringing corrupt offenders to justice. Some Member States envisaged a broad convention that would encompass not just the bribery of public officials (as was already achieved in article 8 of UNTOC) but also bribery in the private sector, trafficking in influence, unlawful enrichment, and abuse of power. Moreover, in their view, it should cover not just domestic, foreign, and international civil servants but also politicians. Other Member States were more cautious and wanted to focus on key corruption offences.

But for many countries, particularly developing countries, perhaps the greatest priority was to trace transfers of "funds of illicit origin" and expedite the return of these funds to their country of origin. Kleptocratic officials have siphoned off billions of dollars from developing countries and large sums of money have been transferred to bank accounts abroad.[44]

A few months after the intergovernmental, open-ended expert group meeting, an informal preparatory meeting of the Ad Hoc Committee for the Negotiation of a Convention against Corruption was held in Buenos Aires (4–7 December 2001). The UN Secretariat had invited Member States to submit proposals for the content of the draft convention and had prepared a draft consolidated text based on them. The outcome of the meeting in Buenos Aires essentially provided the first "rolling text" for the consideration of the Ad Hoc Committee (A/AC.261/3).[45]

On 21 January 2002, only a few weeks later, the Ad Hoc Committee began its work, which was to extend to seven sessions.[46] At its seventh session (29 September–1 October 2003), the Ad Hoc Committee was able to finalize and approve the draft convention and decided to submit it to the GA for consideration and action at its fifty-eighth session, in accordance with GA resolution 56/260 (UNCAC, 2010, p. vii).

Particular issues arising in the negotiation of UNCAC

UNTOC provided a template for many of the provisions that ultimately found their way into UNCAC, and corruption as a concept is arguably not as complex as transnational organized crime. Even so, there were a number of issues that led to extensive debate in the negotiation of UNCAC. The following are some of the difficulties encountered during the negotiations:

- There was a constant search for *balance between flexibility and precision*. Some delegations wanted more precise language, while others wanted flexibility.

- As with the scope of UNTOC, the scope of UNCAC was subjected to much debate. For example, some delegations wanted to include *integrity and good governance* among the objectives of the draft Convention. Others objected, inter alia on the grounds that dealing with the subject of integrity and good governance in the draft Convention would in their view allow for intervention in the affairs of States, and thus to potential violation of national sovereignty (UNCAC, 2010, p. 16, fn. 7).
- As had correspondingly been the case with the negotiation of UNTOC, the *definition of the basic concepts* used in UNCAC (art. 2) as well as the *scope of application* (art. 3) caused considerable debate. Much of the discussion was deferred until the end of the negotiations, when the substantive provisions had been agreed.
- Attempts to incorporate a *definition of corruption* into the Convention did not result in consensus. The chairperson sought to resolve the issue by suggesting that the following generic definition be included in the *travaux préparatoires:* "The use of the term 'corruption' in this Convention shall refer to the acts criminalized in Chapter III, as well as to such acts as States Parties may criminalize or have already criminalized." However, the Ad Hoc Committee could not agree on this (UNCAC, 2010, p. 51, fn. 122). As a result, the implicit definition is that the offences to be criminalized under UNCAC constitute the Ad Hoc Committee's understanding of "corruption."
- The *protection of personal data* was raised by Germany, which was concerned about the proliferation of computer-generated personal data files. Germany wanted provisions on this included in connection with article 10 of the Convention. However, there were no globally applicable standards to which reference could be made. Ultimately, Germany proposed that a reference be made in the *travaux préparatoires* stating that "States Parties should be inspired by principles laid down in the guidelines for the regulation of computerized personal data files, adopted by the General Assembly in its resolution 45/95 of 14 December 1990." The final (and rather odd and inelegant) formulation replaced "should" with a much weaker "may": "Regarding the protection of personal information, the use of which is addressed in the Convention, States Parties may be inspired by principles laid down in the guidelines for the regulation of computerized personal data files adopted by the General Assembly in its resolution 45/95 of 14 December 1990."
- Attempts to include a separate article on the *funding of political parties* failed, largely on the argument that there were extensive differences between political systems. The compromise was to include a paragraph in article 7, which dealt with the public sector in general. According to paragraph 3 of this article, "Each State Party shall also consider taking appropriate legislative and administrative measures, consistent with the

objectives of this Convention and in accordance with the fundamental principles of its domestic law, to enhance transparency in the funding of candidatures for elected public office and, where applicable, the funding of political parties." [47]

- Signs that some Member States were viewing with concern the activity of (in particular foreign-based) *civil society* groups could be seen in several aspects of the deliberations. The original heading of what is now article 13 was "civil society," and the draft provision called, for example, for the promotion of an active civil society and for including civil society in decision-making. The final version of the article is headed "Participation of Society," but references to the involvement of civil society in decision-making were deleted. An interpretative note in the *travaux préparatoires* has this to say: "Reference to non-governmental organizations and community-based organizations relates to such organizations established or located in the country. This note is intended as an explanation and not as an amendment to paragraph 1" (UNCAC, 2010, p. 145).
- Reference to the *Financial Action Task Force* (FATF). One aspect of the response to organized crime that has caused tensions between Member States in UN Crime Programme deliberations has been the efforts of some international organizations (such as the Financial Action Task Force) to establish standards and to promote their wider application within the UN framework. The response by at least some Member States has been that, since they had not been involved in the drafting of these standards, they do not want to be assessed on the basis of these standards, much less be bound by them. Even a reference in a draft resolution to the FATF as an organization often led to lengthy negotiations over whether it can be mentioned, or whether one should refer (for example) rather generically to "regional and interregional organizations." The compromise reached in the negotiation of UNCAC was that article 14, on measures to prevent money-laundering, contains a reference to "relevant initiatives of regional, interregional and multilateral organizations." A comment was inserted into the *travaux préparatoires* to the effect that this was understood to refer "in particular to the Forty Recommendations and the Eight Special Recommendations of the Financial Action Task Force on Money Laundering, as revised in 2003 and 2001, respectively, and, in addition, to other existing initiatives of regional, interregional and multilateral organizations against money-laundering, such as the Caribbean Financial Action Task Force, the Commonwealth, the Council of Europe, the Eastern and Southern African Anti-Money-Laundering Group, the European Union, the Financial Action Task Force of South America against Money Laundering and the Organization of American States" (UNCAC, 2010, p. 154).
- Criminalization of *bribery* or *corruption*? (art. 15). The heading of article 8 of UNTOC refers to the criminalization of *corruption*, although the

conduct described is *bribery* of a public official. This caused some difficulties in the negotiation of UNCAC, in that some Member States wanted to maintain consistency between the two UN Crime Conventions. The final version refers to "bribery of national public officials."

- Criminalization of *trading in influence* (art. 18). Despite some misgivings among some Member States regarding the term, the concept was retained. Much of the debate regarding this provision had to do with whether or not such a provision should be included, and whether or not it should be mandatory. The non-mandatory "shall consider adopting ..." was ultimately adopted.
- There was even more disagreement over the proposal for the criminalization of *unlawful enrichment* (art. 20), especially in view of the necessity to construct the provision so that it reverses the traditional approach to the burden of proof: instead of the prosecutor having to prove criminal conduct, in the case of unlawful enrichment, the prosecutor need only prove that the defendant has unexplained wealth, and it is for the defendant to prove that their assets had a legitimate source. Once again, consensus was achieved by using a number of qualifiers, including "subject to its constitution and the fundamental principles of its legal system" as well as the non-mandatory "each State Party shall consider adopting ...."
- The provision on the criminalization of *bribery in the private sector* (art. 21) also led to considerable debate. Some Member States argued that the Convention would be incomplete without a provision on corruption in the private sector, while others were concerned about efforts to introduce an international obligation for criminalization in this area on the grounds that normal economic activity could be hampered through the application of criminal law. Again, the inclusion of the provision was made possible by using the non-mandatory formulation "each State Party shall consider adopting ...."
- As noted above, representatives of many (in particular developing) Member States strongly advocated including a number of provisions designed to facilitate and expedite international cooperation in the recovery of assets and their return to the country of origin. The structural solution adopted was to include a *separate chapter on asset recovery* (Chapter V). An attempt was made by these Member States to refer, in this chapter, to recovery of assets by the affected States Parties of origin as an "inalienable" right. This, however, led to extensive debate. Consensus was reached by referring to the return of assets as "a fundamental principle of this Convention, and States Parties shall afford one another the widest measure of cooperation and assistance in this regard."
- Another debate was occasioned by the views of some Member States that it would not necessarily be the State Party of origin that would receive the returned assets; in some cases it would be the victim of the original offence.

Many delegations objected to such a reference, on the grounds that in their view it ran contrary to the notion that assets should be returned to the State. They argued that it would be up to that State to receive and process claims of natural or legal persons, or of other States that claimed a right in respect of the assets in question. Consensus was ultimately reached on the following formulation of art. 57(3)(c): States Parties are to "give priority consideration to returning confiscated property to the requesting State Party, returning such property to its prior legitimate owners or compensating the victims of the crime."

- The chapter on implementation (Chapter VII) was originally headed "Mechanisms for monitoring of implementation," and again resulted in extensive debate. The background to this is that many Member States involved in the negotiations were already parties to the OECD convention and/or to regional conventions on corruption, many of which had a robust peer review mechanism for monitoring implementation. (As will be noted in the following section, on the review of implementation of the UN Crime Conventions, the representatives of some Member States were unfamiliar with the peer-review process and had serious concerns that such peer review could constitute a violation of sovereignty.) It soon became apparent that consensus could not be reached in the allotted time. It was decided to follow the same approach as had been done with UNTOC, whereby the Conference of the States Parties would be mandated to develop mechanisms for the review of implementation. According to the final formulation of article 63(5),

For the purpose of paragraph 4 of this article, the Conference of the States Parties shall acquire the necessary knowledge of the measures taken by States Parties in implementing this Convention and the difficulties encountered by them in doing so through information provided by them and through such supplemental review mechanisms as may be established by the Conference of the States Parties.

UNCAC contains both mandatory and non-mandatory provisions. Among the mandatory provisions ("each State Party shall . . .") are those requiring the criminalization of active and passive bribery, embezzlement by a public official, and money laundering. There are also several mandatory provisions on extradition and mutual legal assistance. States Parties are obliged, for example, to "afford one another the widest measure of mutual legal assistance in investigations, prosecutions and judicial proceedings in relation to the offences" covered by UNCAC (art. 46(1)).

UNCAC was adopted by the GA by its resolution 58/4 of 31 October 2003. It was opened for signature by Member States at a high-level political conference convened for that purpose in Merida, Mexico, 9–11 December 2003.

The Convention entered into force on 14 December 2005 (A/RES/58/4). As of February 2024, it had been ratified by 190 States Parties, making it the only truly global convention on the prevention and control of corruption (www.unodc.org/unodc/en/treaties/CAC/index.html). As such, it allows for cooperation between industrialized and developing Member States as well as South–South cooperation. It can therefore assist States Parties that have extensive corruption by showing them what is needed to create a solid basis for preventing and responding to corruption. It also offers a comprehensive framework that may help them to receive targeted technical assistance. Additionally, UNCAC can provide a framework for bringing pressure to bear on States Parties that have so far chosen to retain a hands-off policy towards corrupt practices in international trade and development.[48]

The proposed UN Convention on Cybercrime[49]

In 1999, the Russian Federation introduced a draft resolution on cybercrime in the GA. This resulted in the adoption of GA resolution 53/70 (1999). Ten years later in 2010, in a resolution on the outcome of the Twelfth UN Crime Congress, the GA requested that the UN Crime Commission establish an open-ended intergovernmental expert group to study the problem of cybercrime and how Member States, the international community, and the private sector should respond to it, "with a view to examining options to strengthen existing and to propose new national and international legal or other responses to cybercrime" (GA resolution 65/230). A further ten years later, on 27 December 2019, the GA established an ad hoc intergovernmental committee of experts to elaborate a comprehensive international convention on countering the use of information and communications technologies for criminal purposes ("UN Cybercrime Convention"; GA resolution 74/247).

By March 2024, the Ad Hoc Committee had held one organizational and seven formal sessions, alternately in Vienna and New York, with a further session scheduled for July 2024. (Each session lasted for ten days.) Alongside these sessions, five sets of intersessional consultations have been held. Progress has been made but considerable difficulties remain. Some of those participating in the negotiations have become frustrated with the slow process and the sheer number of disagreements that remain on the table.

To put this into perspective, the negotiators on the cybercrime convention have been working on the draft for less than three years. The organizational session of the Ad Hoc Committee was held in May 2021. It is possible that the negotiators will be able, in the session in July 2024, to make a breakthrough and reach consensus, with perhaps an additional session later on.

However, when compared to the UN cybercrime convention negotiations, neither UNTOC nor UNCAC had as long a gestation period, from the first formal calls for their negotiation to their adoption by the GA. With transnational organized crime, this period was less than a decade. The roots of UNTOC can be traced to the Eighth UN Crime Congress in 1990 and, more clearly, to the World Ministerial Conference on Organized Crime hosted by Italy in Naples in 1994. With corruption, the roots can be traced to seven different international conventions on corruption that were negotiated between 1996 and 2003, starting with the 1996 Inter-American Convention against Corruption of the Organization of American States.

The reason for the slower progress on cybercrime is to be found, as so often, in a combination of factors. Among these factors are whether or not Member States are in agreement on the *need for a convention* and the anticipated *substantive scope of such a convention.* There have also been changes in the *negotiating atmosphere* in general in the UN Crime Programme over the past twenty years.

Is there a need for the convention? Disagreement over the proposed UN cybercrime convention dates back at least to the Twelfth UN Crime Congress in 2010, where there were protracted and, at times, heated negotiations even on how this issue should be reflected in the wording of the Congress Declaration. The meetings of the Intergovernmental Expert Group on Cybercrime saw considerable disagreement, starting with the first in January 2011. In comparison, the discussion during the 1990s on the need for a global convention on transnational organized crime and, a few years later, on the need for a convention against corruption was considerably less intense and less politicized.

The main disagreement regarding the need for the proposed UN cybercrime convention was between a large number of Member States which argued that existing conventions (particularly the Council of Europe Convention on Cybercrime of 2001) provided a sufficient, recent, and relatively comprehensive basis for international cooperation.[50] Several other Member States argued that the Council of Europe Convention was a regional convention and what was needed was a global convention that would meet what they saw as the broader concerns of other parts of the world.

This disagreement over the need for the proposed convention was reflected in the fact that the GA resolution setting up the Ad Hoc Intergovernmental Committee came after a close vote, with several abstentions.

What should the scope of the convention be? With UNTOC and UNCAC, there were some disagreements over the scope of the convention, but by and large the disagreements were relatively minor. In the case of UNTOC, everyone seemed to be satisfied at the outset that they understood what is meant by "transnational organized crime," even though it soon became apparent that these various perspectives were not always aligned. Different Member States had different priorities. Nonetheless, this did not appear to be a serious source of discord in the negotiations. Among the disagreements in respect of UNTOC was whether there should be extensive provisions on corruption. It was ultimately decided to include only relatively brief articles and to begin the drafting of a separate convention against corruption after UNTOC was completed. In the case of UNCAC, there was some disagreement over which criminalizations should be mandatory and how these should be drafted, but these were dealt with fairly expediently on the basis of consensus.

In respect of the proposed cybercrime convention, several substantive disagreements have arisen, including the following:

- What criminalizations should be included in the convention, and should these include criminalization of certain criminal content?
- Should the scope of international law enforcement and judicial cooperation be limited to the offences specified in the convention or should it be wider?
- How should the question of transborder access to data be addressed?
- What are the rights and responsibilities of information and telecommunications companies and service providers?
- What legal safeguards should be included (for example, on privacy and data protection) to protect the data subject and how strong should these be?

In contrast to the negotiations on UNTOC and UNCAC, these disagreements seem to be becoming intractable.

Has the negotiating atmosphere in the UN Crime Programme changed? At times, negotiations in the UN Crime Programme today seem to have become more politicized than they were twenty years ago, when UNTOC and UNCAC were negotiated. This shift became quite notable in connection with negotiations over the review of the implementation of UNCAC, when two issues in particular became divisive: the rigour of the review process itself and the extent to which civil society should be involved. Both are complex issues.[51] The shift can arguably be traced to changes in the respective roles of substantive experts and diplomats at negotiations within the framework of the UN Crime Programme. Negotiations require both experts and diplomats. The experts can set out the substantive issues and identify the options. The diplomatic representatives, in turn, can identify the political sensitivities, thus showing where compromises might be needed.

Technology also played a role. Mobile telephones were becoming more prevalent during the 1990s. At first the Vienna International Centre, where the negotiations were conducted, tried to dissuade participants from using their mobiles during meetings. When mobile telephones became not just a luxury but seemingly a necessity, it became much more common to see representatives placing calls while in meetings (or in the corridor outside while a meeting was taking place), presumably at times to ask for instructions on how to deal with a specific issue that had suddenly arisen.[52]

The global Covid-19 epidemic forced another technological shift in UN Crime Programme meetings, the impact of which still needs to be assessed: more participants are attending meetings remotely, by teleconference. This has the potential to allow on-site diplomatic representatives to consult with their technical experts "back in the capitals" almost as soon as new substantive issues arise. Hybrid meetings, with both in-person and on-line participants, have already been used extensively in the cybercrime convention negotiations.

Neither UNTOC nor UNCAC were easy to negotiate. However, once ratified and implemented, they have stood the test of time. Each has contributed to a more uniform and streamlined regime of international cooperation in criminal matters. As global conventions, they have considerably expanded the geographical scope of cooperation. They provide common definitions of certain key offences and require (or, in some cases, at least encourage) States Parties to criminalize these acts. They have standardized and contributed to the development of procedural forms of cooperation.

The UN cybercrime convention has proved more difficult to negotiate. Nonetheless, given that so much time and energy have been invested in the process, the negotiations will probably lead in time to the adoption of the third convention negotiated within the framework of the UN Crime Programme. If so, it can serve to expand the geographical scope of cooperation, provide common definitions of certain key offences, and help to standardize procedural forms of cooperation in the digital sphere. International cooperation can be improved further if the UNODC, the Programme Network Institutes, and other potential actors are given the necessary funding to provide technical assistance on request to States Parties in the implementation of the provisions of this new convention.

There are, however, concerns that the convention, once adopted, will not have the same impact on international cooperation as has been the case with UNTOC and UNCAC. Given that there are still major differences of approach among Member States on several key questions, reaching consensus on the content of the text may mean that there are fewer mandatory provisions in the text, and even these have had to be framed in a rather general manner. It is also possible that all the disagreements cannot be overcome, and some Member States will remain reluctant to ratify the convention.

Even if Member States decide to become States Parties to the convention, those that are already parties to other international instruments on cybercrime may prefer to continue to apply these, as their practitioners are more familiar with the procedures involved.

A UN cybercrime convention appears to be on the horizon but it may not be the one imagined at the outset.

3.3 Taking the next step: negotiating the review of implementation of the UN Crime Conventions

In the world of international treaties, there is no standard model for reviewing how each State Party implements a treaty. A treaty may be self-executing in that upon ratification its provisions may be directly applied in domestic courts.[53] Most treaties, however, generally require that the States Parties adopt legislation to implement – i.e., give force to – the provisions in question. Often, the States Parties to a particular treaty may deem the treaty itself sufficient and assume that all states that have ratified it will implement it appropriately. All that may be needed in such cases is agreement on what State or entity serves as the depositary that is responsible for keeping custody of the original text of the treaty, and maintaining records of signatures, ratification, entry into force, and denunciation.[54]

However, in other cases the States Parties in question may wish to create a mechanism to review implementation, identify problems that have been encountered, encourage States Parties that are apparently in non-compliance to amend their law, policy, and practice, and consider whether amendments to the treaty in question might be needed.

Even within the framework of the UN, a variety of models have been developed. Some are based on provisions to be found in the individual treaty itself, while others (in particular in the human rights area) are based on the UN Charter.[55] These models vary in regard to their form and their powers. The form may be a conference of all the States Parties, a smaller body of States Parties elected for this purpose, a pre-existing entity (such as in the case of the Human Rights Council mentioned above), or a committee of experts serving in their personal capacity. The powers may range from collection of information on implementation provided on a voluntary basis by States Parties, to fact-finding missions, to a robust peer review process.

Neither of the two UN Crime Conventions – UNTOC or UNCAC – are self-executing. Each State Party has to take domestic action (legislation, policy formulation, allocation of resources, training of practitioners) in order to implement the provisions of the Conventions, both mandatory and non-mandatory. Although the negotiators reached consensus on the objectives of the Conventions, agreement could not be reached (with one exception) on how to review this implementation, on how the States Parties could ascertain that implementation in their own country and elsewhere was on track and in line with the objectives, and whether in fact the Conventions were fulfilling their objectives.

The one exception is a provision in both Conventions (Article 32 of UNTOC and Article 63 of UNCAC), which provides simply for a Conference of the Parties (COP, for UNTOC) and a Conference of the States Parties (CoSP, for UNCAC) that is to "promote and review" implementation of the

Convention in question. However, COP and CoSP only meet for five days every other year. This does not provide them with sufficient time and capacity to analyse and act on information on implementation. Both Conventions (plus the three protocols to UNTOC) cover extensive ground, such as criminalization, law enforcement and judicial cooperation, preventive measures, and technical assistance. Furthermore, both Conventions currently have some 190 States Parties.

During the negotiation of the two Conventions, some Member States made proposals for a review mechanism. Among the suggestions made for UNTOC was that the UN Crime Commission could review implementation or that a special review body could be set up. In respect of UNCAC, some Member States supported a peer review model. The review of the implementation of the recent anticorruption treaties prepared within the framework of the Council of Europe and the OECD has shown that direct consultation among experts doing an on-the-ground review provides an effective learning experience.[56] Talking with experts from other systems often helps experts understand their own system better and realize that there are other – and perhaps more effective –ways of dealing with an issue. The problem, however, was that peer review had not previously been used in connection with the implementation of any UN treaty and, consequently, there was no UN precedent.[57]

UNTOC was the first of the two UN Crime Conventions to enter into force, and COP undertook to collect information by having the UN Secretariat send out questionnaires to States Parties on how the different provisions had been implemented. Although the Secretariat sought to keep the questionnaire as simple and easy to complete as possible, it remained lengthy, contained many open-ended questions, and required extensive coordination among different authorities in individual States Parties. The response rate remained low, and the questionnaire approach was gradually abandoned (CTOC/COP/2008/2, 2008). In its place, the Secretariat shifted to a computer-based self-assessment checklist, the structure of which was largely based on the earlier questionnaires. During sessions of COP and the UN Crime Commission, the Secretariat sought to provide representatives of States Parties with hands-on guidance to on how to input information. However, yet again the response rate remained low (CTOC/COP/2012.CRP.2, 2012).

The UN Secretariat also undertook to send reminders to States Parties that were apparently in non-compliance with some provisions of UNTOC and/or its protocols. However, these too were abandoned after a few years (CTOC/COP/2008/3, 2008, paras. 8 and 9).

It became clear to most States Parties that a supplementary mechanism for review of implementation of UNTOC and its protocols was needed and the question was discussed at length at all the subsequent sessions of COP but without any appreciable progress. UNTOC entered into force in 2003: but it took fifteen years before agreement was reached on a review mechanism.

The focus of negotiations on a supplementary review mechanism for a UN Crime Convention – in whatever form it took – shifted from UNTOC to UNCAC.[58]

UNCAC entered into force in December 2005 and discussions on a supplementary review mechanism began in earnest just one year later in Amman, Jordan, at the first session of CoSP. The discussions in Amman were protracted and convoluted. The crucial political agreement was reached that the CoSP itself was not enough and that something more was needed.

The difficulties lay in pinning down exactly what that "more" would be. States Parties that were already parties to other recently adopted conventions on corruption (such as within the framework, respectively, of the Organization of American States, the OECD, and the Council of Europe) proposed a peer-review approach, in which each State Party would be reviewed by two other States Parties. The representatives of several States Parties, however, were not familiar with how peer review works. Some of those States Parties were concerned that the confidentiality of ongoing investigations into individual cases of suspected corruption could be breached. (However, this concern seems unfounded. Peer review is focused on the legislation and policy of States Parties. Practice will also be considered, but this is largely limited to cases which have already been decided in court.) Other concerns were more understandable, such as that a peer-review model would be complex when applied to a global treaty and would be expensive to operate. Other concerns hinted at the essentially political difficulties to come in the negotiations. The main political concerns had to do with the proposal to have outside experts review implementation within a Member State of the UN. The objection to this was that it would allegedly be an intervention in the domestic affairs of a sovereign State. Furthermore, there were concerns about the proposal to involve elements of civil society in the review process. The main objection here was based on the argument that UNCAC was an agreement between sovereign States and consequently any review of implementation should be a purely "intergovernmental" process.[59]

At the first session of the UNCAC Conference of the States Parties, the States Parties agreed on some of the key features of the review mechanism: it should be transparent, efficient, non-intrusive, inclusive, and impartial; it should not produce any form of ranking; it should provide opportunities to share good practices and challenges; and it should complement existing international and regional review mechanisms in order to avoid duplication of effort.

Even though at first glance these would seem to be rather bland and universally acceptable characteristics, there was vigorous debate over them in Amman, which revealed that in some key respects different States Parties seemed to understand these concepts in divergent ways. For example, *transparency* was understood by some to mean that all the States Parties would have the right to be involved throughout the process. In effect, the review was to be carried out by a plenary body, as opposed to a smaller body, let alone a body of independent experts. Others understood transparency to refer to the ability of all stakeholders (including, for example, representatives of civil society) to follow and possibly even provide input to the review process. Still others understood transparency to refer to whether or not the reports that are produced as a result of the review process are available to all States Parties or, even, made public.

A second example was the concept of *non-intrusiveness*. Article 2(7) of the UN Charter stipulates that the UN may not "intervene in matters which are essentially within the domestic jurisdiction of any state." The concept is generally understood in international law to mean that the UN has no authority with respect to disputes that are essentially within domestic jurisdiction. There appeared to be different views as to what constitutes such intervention. At various stages in the negotiations, arguments based on non-intrusiveness and the protection of sovereignty were used to oppose proposals for, inter alia, the use of independent experts, the arrangement of country visits, the use of any information not provided by the government of the State Party under review, and the publication of the full report – all elements which other negotiators regarded as part and parcel of the peer-review process.[60]

At the second session of CoSP in Bali at the beginning of 2008, two opposing positions emerged regarding the contours of the prospective review mechanism. These two positions could be called the open review and the controlled review positions.

The *open review* position incorporated many elements found in peer review within the framework of the OECD and the Council of Europe:

- a team of experts collects information from a variety of sources;
- the team then visits the country under review in order to meet a wide range of stakeholders;
- the team prepares a country report that contains recommendations;
- the team submits this draft report to the country under review for comment;
- the amended country report together with recommendations is sent to a plenary body for discussion and adoption;
- the report is published; and
- there is some mechanism for follow-up by the plenary body to see whether the recommendations have been implemented.

Many proponents of the open review position tended to take a technocratic view of implementation, and many delegations at Bali and the subsequent meetings espousing this view included technical experts in addition to career diplomats. To these proponents, the review was a technical exercise in reporting and accountability, and the results should be transparent and available immediately for the world to see. The experts conducting the review should be free to gather information on implementation from a variety of sources in order to familiarize themselves with the situation and engage in discussions with a number of different stakeholders. Armed with this knowledge, they would be able to suggest best practice to the experts of the State Party under review.

According to the *controlled review* position:

- a team of experts (according to some who espouse this position, the team would also include experts representing the State Party under review) uses information received from the government to prepare a country report;
- the report is finalized on the basis of a dialogue between the experts and the representatives of the State Party under review;
- the secretariat prepares a general report for the plenary body that does not contain references to individual States Parties;
- the plenary body decides by consensus on the publication of the general report; and
- whether or not the full country report is published is decided by the State Party under review.

The proponents of the controlled review position tended to see the process as involving a number of serious political risks that had to be identified and defused. Since in their view outside experts lack local understanding, reliance on non-governmental sources might give them a distorted view of how the legal and administrative system actually operates in the State Party under review. Information obtained during the review process could be misused for political purposes, and thus there was a need to keep tight governmental control on what and how information is used. Non-governmental actors could in fact be hostile to government policy and might use involvement in the review process for their own ends. If the reports produced as a result of the review process became construed as "UN-endorsed" assessments of the extent of corruption in a certain State Party, this could have a negative impact on foreign investments in that country, and potential donors might seek to attach a variety of conditions on any offers of technical assistance. There were also considerable concerns about the expense of country visits and other aspects of peer review and that the necessary funds would not then be available for direct technical assistance.

Due to the deadlock between the open review and controlled review positions, little progress could be achieved at Bali. The resolution that emerged essentially repeated the general characteristics that had been identified two years earlier. The resolution continued with a number of general statements about effective implementation, a balanced geographical approach, the need to be non-adversarial and non-punitive, and that implementation should be of a technical nature and promote constructive collaboration (CAC/COSP/2008/15, par. 29).

It is clear that there was a great gulf between the two positions. It seemed as if the two sides were in fact speaking different languages and represented quite different concerns that were not being openly addressed. Integral to the open review position seemed to be the view that any efforts to oppose such openness were nothing less than a wish to avoid scrutiny and that the controlled review group was not really committed to the objectives of the UN-CAC. The controlled review position seemed to regard proposals to conduct country visits, contact local civil society organizations, publish the reports, and so on as politically based violations of sovereignty and as attempts to force States Parties to change their policies through "naming and shaming."

In the course of the ensuing negotiations over the next two years, which took place in an open-ended intergovernmental working group, the two rigid positions gradually softened. Many Latin American countries in the closed review group were using peer review in connection with the implementation of the 1996 Inter-American Convention Against Corruption. In addition, several developing countries were familiar with peer review in the context of the Financial Action Task Force. As a result, the debate could not be painted as a North-South one, in which the Western industrialized countries were opposed to the more numerous developing countries. Those supporting the controlled review position gradually realized that holding out against any form of peer review was not a sustainable position and that some workable format had to be found so that the long negotiations on UNCAC itself would not prove to be a waste of time and effort.

There was a growing awareness among the proponents of the open review that this was not simply a technical exercise (on how to collect and analyse information most effectively and encourage Member States to take the necessary implementation steps), it had obviously become imbued with political sensitivities. While some delegations (primarily some of the delegations that included technical experts) wanted to go to the wire, others (usually career diplomats) argued that the only way to reach the necessary consensus was by stepping back from the hard-line technocratic position. The talk shifted to the potential for compromise with the closed review proponents and to red lines that should not be crossed.

The key negotiations at the third session of the CoSP in Doha, in November 2009, took place not so much in the plenary room, but in a small room where about a dozen participants (primarily diplomats)[61] representing the two views worked their way through the issues. Their focus was on finding options that would allow various elements of peer review (thus satisfying the concerns of the open review proponents) while defusing the political risks raised by peer review (thus satisfying the concerns of the controlled review proponents).

The outcome at Doha can be considered a delicate balance between the two views (www.unodc.org/unodc/en/treaties/CAC/CAC-COSP-session3.html).The following elements were proposed for the mechanism:

- an implementation review group is set up for the review process. This body is, to use the UN parlance, intergovernmental and open, which means that any and all States Parties may participate;
- each State Party is to be reviewed by two other States Parties, which each appoint a governmental expert for this purpose;[62]
- the review process begins with the State Party under review preparing a self-assessment on the basis of a checklist prepared by the Secretariat. In doing so, the State Party should seek to engage in wide consultations with relevant individuals and groups outside the public sector;
- a country visit may be arranged with the consent of the State Party under review. However, the costs of this must be covered by extra-budgetary funding, not the regular UN budget (in practice, such country visits have been arranged in the majority of the reviews);
- in connection with such a country visit, the State Party under review is encouraged to promote discussions with all relevant national stakeholders;
- on the basis of their self-assessment, the country visit, and any information produced by other corresponding evaluation mechanisms, the experts prepare a country report and an executive summary. The report and its executive summary require the approval of the State Party under review;
- the Secretariat prepares thematic and supplementary regional geographical reports for the Implementation Review Group;
- these thematic and regional reports will serve as the basis for the analytical work of the Implementation Review Group. The executive summaries of the country reports are submitted to the Implementation Review Group for informational purposes only and not for discussion; and
- the country reports themselves are confidential and thus are not submitted as such to the Implementation Review Group. However, the States Parties in question are encouraged to publish these reports themselves. In addition, "States Parties shall, upon request, endeavour to make country review reports accessible to any other State Party. The requesting State Party shall fully respect the confidentiality of such reports.[63]

The CoSP also decided that the review would be conducted in two five-year cycles. The first cycle, which began in 2010, covered the chapters in UNCAC on criminalization, law enforcement, and international cooperation. Each year, 40 States Parties were to be reviewed, with the assumption that all current States Parties would be reviewed by the end of 2014.

This ambitious schedule for the first cycle did not work out in practice. By the end of the cycle, roughly half of the reviews were still in process (CAC/

COSP/2015/6, para. 6). Nonetheless, the second cycle, covering the chapters on preventive measures and asset recovery, was launched in 2015. The CoSP decided at its 2019 session to extend the second cycle to 2024.

UNCAC has been in force for almost two decades, and the review of implementation has lasted over a decade. UNCAC, with its 190 States Parties, is one of the few treaties which have almost full global coverage. Some tentative assessments can be made of the impact of UNCAC and of the peer-review model.

On the institutional level, a peer review model has been applied to a UN treaty for the first time. The model may not be as robust as some would have wanted but the concept has been accepted by consensus.

On the substantive level, the creation of the UNCAC review mechanism has had one major negative and two major positive impacts on the UN Crime Programme.

The major *negative impact* of the negotiation on the implementation review mechanism has brought to the fore within the UN Crime Programme clear disagreements over the *role of non-governmental organizations* (and more generally of civil society). Within the UNCAC context, non-governmental organizations have not been granted the usual observer status that they would seem to be entitled to, since the Intergovernmental Review Group is a body of the CoSP. However, the review process has allowed country visits (with the consent of the State Party under review) to incorporate input from non-governmental organizations, the private sector, academia, and other stakeholders. Such country visits by the reviewing experts have generally been arranged as have, in the large majority of country reviews, consultations with other stakeholders.[64]

Separately from the UNCAC context, the "non-governmental organization problem" appears to have sparked debates in connection with various draft resolutions at sessions of the UN Crime Commission and other UN Crime Programme fora; attempts have often been made to delete or significantly soften language that refers to the role of civil society more widely in crime prevention or in the operation of the criminal justice system.

The *first significant positive impact* of the adoption of the UNCAC review mechanism (based largely on anecdotal evidence) is that the process of review has encouraged many States Parties to actively amend their legislation, policy, and practice in respect of the prevention of and response to corruption (Rose, 2020, p. 66). This are presumably several reasons for this. Preparing the self-assessment may help policy-makers (and practitioners) in a State Party under review to identify areas in which such amendment is needed. When such self-assessments are prepared by bringing representatives of different governmental agencies (and perhaps also of other stakeholders) together to discuss their response, this can generate greater mutual understanding of what needs to be done and who needs to take responsibility.

During the country visit stage (and subsequently also when the draft country report is discussed), the dialogue between the reviewing experts and the representatives of the State Party under review can identify models from other countries that could be considered.

The *second positive impact* is that the creation of the UNCAC review mechanism resulted in an expansion of the number of UNODC staff members[65] and in the involvement of the UNODC not just in the individual country reviews, but more generally in providing technical assistance on request to States Parties (and other Member States) around the world with the implementation of UNCAC.

Developing an implementation review mechanism for UNTOC

Although the "Doha compromise" resulted in the adoption of a review mechanism for UNCAC, this did not lead to a quick breakthrough in developing a review mechanism for UNTOC. There was general (although not complete) agreement that a review mechanism was needed also for UNTOC and that a peer review model somewhat like that created for UNCAC would be appropriate. Even so, almost a decade passed before agreement was reached on the UNTOC review mechanism. There were three key reasons for this delay: *cost*, *complexity*, and the *continuing suspicion* on the part of some States Parties regarding the involvement of civil society.

Cost. As the number of States Parties countries signing or ratifying UNCAC expanded rapidly, the costs of the review of implementation were considerably higher than anticipated, some USD 5,000,000 each year.[66] At the same time, the worldwide financial crisis made the major donors to the UN Crime Programme averse to anything that would lead to an expansion of the regular UN budget. In discussions on creating a review mechanism for UNTOC, worried negotiators pointed out that if one basically replicated the UNCAC model, the cost would presumably be even greater, since the mechanism would be extended not just to UNTOC but also to its three protocols, all of which have different constellations of States Parties.

Complexity. A second reason picked up on what has just been noted, that UNTOC, with its three protocols, was more complex than UNCAC, and presumably any UNTOC peer review would require even more time and resources.

Continuing suspicion on the part of some States Parties. The debate over the involvement of non-governmental organizations (and more generally civil society) in the review of implementation of UNTOC was essentially a continuation of the debate that raged over the proposed UNCAC review mechanism. This time, some States Parties added the argument that articles 6(3) and 9(3) of the UNTOC protocol on trafficking in persons specifically refer to the role of civil society in implementing these protocols.

Because of these difficulties, the decade-long work on designing an UN-TOC review mechanism proceeded in fits and starts.[67] However, consensus was finally reached at the 2018 session of the COP. The elements of the UN-TOC mechanism are as follows:

- the States Parties are allocated into three groups (of roughly 60 each), with each group to be reviewed over the course of a two-year period. Group 1 began the review process in 2020; Group 2 in 2021; and Group 3 in 2022;
- the provisions of UNTOC and the three protocols have been divided into four clusters, with each cluster to be reviewed over the course of eight years. The first cluster deals with criminalization and jurisdiction; the second with international cooperation, mutual legal assistance, and confiscation; the third with law enforcement and the judicial system; and the fourth with prevention, technical assistance, protection measures, and other measures;
- each State Party is to be reviewed by two other States Parties, which each appoint one or more governmental experts for this purpose;
- the review process begins with the State Party under review preparing a self-assessment on the basis of a checklist prepared by the Secretariat. In doing so, the State Party is encouraged to engage in wide consultations with relevant individuals and groups outside the public sector;
- on the basis of the self-assessment, the experts prepare (as a desk review) written feedback, which may include requests for further clarification or additional information.
- each reviewing State Party, in close cooperation with the State Party under review, prepares a list of observations, based on the information provided by the State Party in question and the subsequent dialogue; this is shared with the appropriate working groups of the Conference of the Parties;
- a summary is prepared and made available for the Conference of the Parties and its working groups.

In the UNTOC review process, there is no Implementation Review Group, as there is with UNCAC. Much of the same functions are fulfilled by the five working groups that had already earlier been established under the CoSP. These deal, respectively, with technical assistance, international cooperation, trafficking in persons, smuggling of migrants, and trafficking in firearms.

3.4   The impact of the restructuring and the two UN Crime Conventions on the UN Crime Programme

The 1990s marked a massive change in the structure and orientation of the UN Crime Programme. The decade was bookmarked by two events that are symbolic of this change. The 1990s began with the *expert-driven UN Crime*

TABLE 3.1. Comparison of the review mechanisms for UNCAC and UNTOC

	UNCAC	UNTOC
Reviewing body	Implementation Review Group	Thematic Working Groups
Who reviews	Governmental experts from two States Parties	Governmental experts from two States Parties
Cycles	Two clusters of provisions, five years each, roughly 40 countries per year	Four clusters of provisions, three staggered groups of roughly 60 States Parties for two-year review cycles
Basic input	Self-assessment	Self-assessment
Initial output	Draft country report	Written feedback to State Party under review; possible request for clarification or additional information
Additional input	Reviewers may use information produced by other corresponding evaluation mechanisms Country visit with consent of State Party under review (in practice, generally organized)	Desk-based; no country visit
Final output	Finalization of country report and summary; text to be approved by State Party under review Discussion at the IRG on basis of consolidated thematic and regional reports prepared by the Secretariat The IRG receives executive summaries of country reports, but for information only; no reference may be made in the discussion to individual reports	Preparation of list of observations in close cooperation with the State Party under review The appropriate Working Groups receive the list of observations
Publication	Country reports remain confidential but may be published with consent of State Party under review	
Civil society involvement	In connection with country visit, State Party under review encouraged to promote discussions with all relevant national stakeholders (in practice, generally organized) "Constructive dialogue" in margins of IRG meeting	"Constructive dialogue" following meetings of thematic review groups

Committee in place, and with the Eighth UN Crime Congress producing a flow of *soft law*: new standards and norms as well as dozens of other resolutions. The decade ended with the *government-driven UN Crime Commission* setting policy and with the adoption by the GA of *hard law*, the first UN Crime Convention: the UN Convention on Transnational Organized Crime.

That is a remarkable shift and needs to be placed into its historical context. It seems we have always been interested in knowing why people commit crime. Over the centuries, we have gone from a largely religious understanding of crime ("crime is a sin against God") to (at first) a largely philosophical understanding ("crime shows a lack of honesty or empathy on the part of the criminal"). At the end of the 1800s and the beginning of the 1900s, a more scientific and empirical approach emerged, fuelled by a new area of inquiry, criminology. The first criminologists, such as Cesare Lombroso, took a decidedly biological or medical approach and sought to diagnose what genetic failure, disease, or mental failure led a person to commit a crime.

These *individual-oriented theories* continue to attract considerable theoretical attention and research but they have largely been replaced by *society-oriented theories*.[68] Such theories latch on to different elements in an attempt to explain crime: anomie, capitalism, conflict in society, social disorganisation, differential association, subcultures, self-identification as an offender, and so on. What is common to all the major criminological theories today is that they see crime as the result of a complex interaction between an individual and the surrounding society.

Whereas the individual-oriented theories sought to proceed from a diagnosis of a genetic, medical, or psychological disorder to the identification of a suitable treatment and, in time, "cure" of the individual of their criminal tendencies, the society-oriented theories seek to suggest social (and, at times, political) solutions to crime: better child-raising, better education, early intervention, better community development, better social development, improved identification and correction of situations which may motivate a person to commit a crime, and so on.

Both the individual-oriented and the society-oriented theories have fed into the prevailing approaches around the world to the *treatment of offenders* and were influential throughout the first decades of the UN Crime Programme. Over the years, many different correctional treatment programmes have been developed and considerable thought has been given to how to improve the effectiveness of community-based corrections. Practitioners and researchers have been very active locally, nationally, and internationally in exchanging information and experiences on what works and what (apparently) does not. They have contributed to the public debate on how to develop a rational, effective, and humane criminal justice system. They also largely drove the approach adopted in the UN Crime Programme – an approach adopted until the 1990s, that is.

The basic outline of the democratic process of policy formulation is that the public elects its representatives to govern, policy proposals are developed in consultation with practitioners, academia, and other stakeholders, and the elected representatives engage in a debate on the respective merits of different policy options. This is of particular importance in respect of crime prevention and criminal justice, areas which are imbued with the fundamental values and principles of society, and where the policy choices that are made may involve the use of coercive force by the State against individuals suspected or convicted of blameworthy conduct.

A shift appears to have taken place in this respect nationally and internationally, parallel with the *growing concern with organized crime and terrorism*. A currently fashionable term in social science is "securitization." Broadly speaking, this refers to a process in which a specific phenomenon (such as social disorder, drug use, an increase in uncontrolled migration) is identified as a "security threat" that must be countered by extraordinary measures, which may even require bypassing the usual public debate and democratic procedures.[69] Researchers have identified *signs of securitization* in relation to discussions on such phenomena as climate change and unemployment. One of the topics in which it is especially prevalent is crime control and criminal justice, and the security threat(s) may be due, for example, to increasing (and increasingly uncontrolled) mobility across borders, the potential for increased violence and other crime, and the potential destabilization of the State. This would seem to fit in with what Simon has referred to as "governing through crime" (Simon, 2007; see also Blaustein et al., 2022, pp. 22–27). Broadly speaking, in times of increasing uncertainty, governments are under pressure to demonstrate that they can control the situation, and they do so through a mixture of punitive sentencing and harsh preventive policies, particularly when directed at the disenfranchised and marginalized.

Within the UN Crime Programme, this securitization process is evident in three respects, the topics being discussed, the proposals made, and the language used in the resolutions that are adopted. The process can also be traced directly to the restructuring of the UN Crime Programme at the beginning of the 1990s.

The shift from an expert-driven UN Crime Committee to a government-driven UN Crime Commission resulted in a *growing emphasis on (transnational) organized crime and transnational criminal justice* (international law enforcement and judicial cooperation, measures which, significantly, are the responsibility of the State), with a corresponding decrease in the attention devoted to so-called ordinary crime and the day-to-day working of the criminal justice system: various crime prevention approaches, community-based measures, restorative justice, and improvement of the criminal justice system (which to a large extent can involve the community). This was accompanied by a *shift of focus from "soft law" instruments* (such as standards and norms) *to "hard law" instruments*, in particular UNTOC and UNCAC (Joutsen, 2017).

Perhaps the clearest indication of the shift in priorities has been that, since the restructuring of the Programme in 1991, various aspects of organized crime have featured as separate agenda items at all of the Congresses.[70] Indeed, if only the substantive agenda items of UN Crime Congresses are considered, the Eleventh (2005) and Twelfth (2010) UN Crime Congresses could justifiably be characterized as primarily UN Transnational Organized Crime Congresses: four out of the five agenda items at each Congress dealt with various aspects of transnational issues (see Annex 3).

The same shift can be seen in the work of the UN Crime Commission. Much of the Commission's time is spent on the drafting of resolutions. The substance of these resolutions can be divided very roughly into three groups: (1) transnational and organized crime issues, (2) essentially domestic crime prevention and criminal justice issues (including, for example, violence against women and girls, restorative justice, corrections, and standards and norms), and (3) general procedural and organizational matters. Leaving this third group aside, during the 1990s roughly half of the resolutions dealt with transnational and organized crime, and half with the more traditional domestic issues. Since 2000, when UNTOC was opened for signature, twice as many resolutions have been adopted on transnational and organized crime as on domestic issues.

The language used includes, unsurprisingly, increasing references to "security." One of the first signs of this was in the title of a declaration adopted at the 1995 UN Crime Congress held in Cairo: the "United Nations Declaration on Crime and Public Security (A/RES/51/60, annex). References to security can also be found in the declaration adopted at the Twelfth UN Crime Congress held in 2010, in the form of a recommendation for "stronger coordination between security and social policies, with a view to addressing some of the root causes of urban violence" (para. 45). This same formulation was repeated in preambular paragraph 16 of GA resolution A/RES/68/188 on the rule of law, crime prevention, and criminal justice in the UN development agenda beyond 2015.

In March 2011, soon after the Twelfth UN Crime Congress in Salvador, the Secretary-General established a UN System Task Force on transnational organized crime and drug trafficking "in order to develop an effective and comprehensive approach to the challenge of transnational organized crime and drug trafficking as threats to security and stability." The UN System Task Force is co-chaired by the Department of Political and Peacebuilding Affairs, and UNODC (Blaustein et al., 2022, pp. 185–186).

Recently several ECOSOC resolutions have included references to security. A formulation that can be found in such resolutions is that transnational organized crime "represents a threat to health and safety, security, good governance and the sustainable development of States."[71]

An illustrative example of the extent of the shift is ECOSOC resolution 2014/21, which bears the seemingly "soft" title of "Strengthening social policies as a tool for crime prevention." However, a reading of the text, and in particular of the preambular paragraphs, shows that the resolution is considerably more concerned with security policies than with social policies.

The emphasis on the link between crime and security has not been limited to the UN Crime Commission. On 19 December 2014, the Security Council adopted resolution 2195 on terrorism and cross-border crime, including drug trafficking, as threats to international peace and security.

What can explain this shift in the UN Crime Programme? Has there been such a growth in the threat of transnational organized crime during the last decades of the 1990s and the beginning of the new millennium that discussions of the proper response within the UN Crime Programme could essentially push aside continued discussions on how to prevent "ordinary crime" and how to improve the everyday working of the criminal justice system?

Certainly, there is ample evidence that such essentially transnational crimes as drug trafficking, trafficking in persons, the smuggling of migrants, money laundering, trafficking in wildlife, trafficking in cultural property, terrorism, and corruption were and continue to be serious issues, and by various indicators were becoming more serious and more transnational.[72] Member States were becoming increasingly aware that stronger international cooperation was needed.

The timing of the shift can also be simply explained by the fact that, at the beginning of the 1990s, the expert-oriented UN Crime Committee was replaced by the government-oriented UN Crime Commission and that one of the primary arguments for making the change was the desire for a more effective UN Crime Programme. In searching for "effectiveness" (however defined), the representatives of Member States sitting in Vienna had the recent model of the 1988 UN Drug Convention in front of them, and they began to explore the possibility of adopting hard-law instruments in the UN Crime Programme.

Earlier discussions within the framework of the UN Crime Programme on resolutions had been consensus-oriented and usually they had not excited passions in one direction or another. This could largely be attributed to the fact that the standards and norms were not binding, and therefore whatever was said about them had no direct policy implications for individual states. Once the discussion shifted to transnational organized crime, and especially when the UN started working on the two UN Crime Conventions, the situation changed. This was due both to political sensitivities inherent in some aspects of organized crime and in the response to organized crime and to the fact that the Conventions were hard law instruments that were binding on the States Parties.

One consequence of the shift from an expert-driven to a government-driven UN Crime Programme has been that the themes in the debate and of the output of the debates, increasingly focused on criminalization, police powers, and the operation of the criminal justice system, at the expense of discussions on such issues as prevention, juvenile delinquency, and restorative justice. The latter themes continued to be raised but arguably received less attention.

A change in the Crime Programme that has perhaps been less visible is in those who participate in the discussions in Vienna. In the early years of the UN Crime Programme, through to the 1980s, the participants at meetings tended to be persons "from the capitals" who were knowledgeable about crime prevention and criminal justice. The UN Crime Committee met every other year for eight days, allowing time for interaction both in and outside the meeting rooms. From 1955 to 1990, the UN Crime Congresses lasted for two weeks and were a mix of debate, negotiations, and social events. The tradition arose that consensus was sought on all resolutions and decisions. Calling for a vote on any issue was a measure only used rarely. This came to be called the "Spirit of Vienna."

Since the 1990s, the profile of many of the participants has changed. Largely because of the entry into force of the two UN Crime Conventions, the number of meetings held in Vienna has increased considerably. In addition to the biannual sessions of the two Conferences of the States Parties, these two bodies have set up several subsidiary working groups, which generally meet on an annual basis, for a period ranging from two to five days. The UN Crime Commission, in turn, meets for its regular annual session but also for an annual reconvened session as well as intersessional meetings.[73] In addition, various intergovernmental working groups hold meetings. The result is that the meeting calendar is full, with on the average one or more UN Crime Programme meetings every month. It is logistically and financially difficult for Member States to send experts "from the capitals" to attend short meetings so often, and consequently the participants tend to be diplomats based in Vienna.

3.4   The impact of the adoption of the 2030 Sustainable Development Agenda

The increased influence that governments have on the work carried out in Vienna and the growing importance of hard law UN crime conventions have had several consequences. Two of these have been mentioned in passing: the politicization of various issues and the shift from general crime prevention and criminal justice issues to a focus on organized and transnational crime. This has been accompanied by a tendency to stress *increased efficiency of the criminal justice system* and, to some extent, *punitive measures*. A third consequence has been the increased use of extra-budgetary funding and increasingly severe financial problems.

Politicization of issues. The change in the background of participants in the discussions in Vienna, from experts to diplomats, has inadvertently meant that what were once discussions of policy have become negotiations over the wording of draft resolutions. The earlier discussions within the framework of the UN Crime Programme on standards and norms were consensus-oriented and usually did not excite passions in one direction or another. This could largely be attributed to the fact that the standards and norms were not binding and therefore whatever was said about them had no direct policy implications for individual Member States. Once the discussion shifted to transnational organized crime and to the two hard-law UN Crime Conventions, the situation changed. Certain aspects of organized crime and of the response to organized crime raised political sensitivities. Examples include the repatriation of the proceeds of crime, trafficking in cultural property, and cybercrime.

The politicization has also extended beyond transnational organized crime, most significantly as already noted in the form of a debate over the role of civil society in the local, national, and international response to crime. Other examples include the extended debate on peer review of UNCAC and the debate that often arises over proposed references to structures to which not all Member States belong (such as the Financial Action Task Force).

Financial constraints. During the first half century of the UN Crime Programme (roughly to the 1990s), most of the (extremely limited) activities of the Programme were undertaken on the basis of the regular UN budget. Today, the situation is markedly different: over 95 per cent of the UN Crime Programme budget comes from extrabudgetary sources.[74] Two factors in particular have led to this: the rapid expansion of UN Crime Programme activities (most clearly visible in costs associated with the review of implementation of the UN Convention against Corruption) and a series of worldwide economic crises, which have led the major donor countries to reconsider their commitments.

The impact of the budgetary crunch has been felt for most of the time the UN Crime Commission has been in existence. In 1995, the length of the UN Crime Congresses was shortened from ten to eight days and, in 2005, the annual sessions of the Commission were reduced from eight to five days. Strict limits were instituted on the length of documentation for UN Crime Programme meetings and of the meeting reports; the translation, editing, and processing of documents in the six working languages of the UN is a major expense.

The Secretariat has made commendable efforts to secure extrabudgetary funding, and as a result has succeeded in significantly expanding its technical assistance activities around the world. However, this shift towards a high dependence on extrabudgetary funding has also had negative consequences: the constant necessity to spend considerable time on identifying sources of funding, uncertainty over the sustainability of various projects, competition within the UNODC for resources, and concerns that much of the work that is carried out will remain tied to the interests of the donors. As long as only 5 per cent of its activities are funded through the regular UN budget, the UN Crime Programme will have a tenuous existence.

In 2009, an open-ended intergovernmental working group on finance and government (FINGOV) was established to deal with both the UN Crime Commission and the UN Commission on Narcotic Drugs.

It is unlikely that the financial constraints will be eased anytime soon, particularly since the UNODC is constantly being asked by Member States to take on even more tasks.

In September 2015, the UN Summit adopted the 2030 Agenda for Sustainable Development. This has highlighted the interlinkages between different sectors of policy and also the need for closer cooperation between different UN agencies. It has also marked a recognition within the UN of the relevance of issues dealt with in the UN Crime Programme, including crime prevention, access to justice, victim assistance and protection, and, more broadly, the role of the criminal justice system in society. This has contributed to moving the dial back, from a priority on transnational organized crime, to an approach that recognizes the links between crime prevention and criminal justice and the rule of law (Goal 16), and such other areas as gender equality, the sustainability of cities and communities, and the reduction of poverty.

The 2030 Agenda could contribute to a further transition in the UN Crime Programme, towards a truly global UN Crime Programme that pays increasing attention to how crime prevention and criminal justice can contribute to sustainable development around the world, in both developing and developed countries. Such a UN Crime Programme would continue to deal with pressing questions related to transnational and organized crime but would also deal with the prevention of and response to "ordinary crime." It would continue to identify best practices in international law enforcement and judicial cooperation but would also seek to identify best practices in the strengthening of access to justice, restorative justice, victim support, and community-based sanctions.

The groundwork for this has already been laid by the UN Crime Programme. The extensive body of international standards and norms provides a more general framework for the national and international response to crime, and in so doing can serve to strengthen respect for human rights in the criminal justice system. This provides at least some balance to the punitive direction in which criminal policy has been taken in many countries around the world.

There are several encouraging signs that such a transition is already underway:

- the expansion of UN technical assistance activities covers a broad range of "domestic" issues, and standards and norms as well as human rights concerns have been integrated into these activities; [75]
- similarly, the topics of UN Crime Programme research cover a wide range of issues;[76]

- the agendas of the two most recent UN Crime Congresses (2015 and 2021) and of the next UN Crime Congress to be held in 2026 are more balanced than those from 1995–2010; and
- the themes selected for the annual sessions of the UN Crime Commission cover a wide range and often deal with issues related to "ordinary crime."[77]

There appears also to have been a slight resurgence in the number of "experts from the capitals" attending UN Crime Programme meetings, working alongside the diplomats on such practical issues as prosecutorial and judicial cooperation or the response to cybercrime.

The global Covid-19 pandemic, alongside all the suffering that it has caused, may have indirectly contributed to growing involvement of "experts from the capitals" in the UN Crime Programme. In 2020, governments around the world locked down the population and restricted domestic and international travel. As a result, in-person meetings (such as those that have been held in Vienna) were almost completely replaced in 2021 and 2022 by online and, to some extent, "hybrid" meetings. This opens up the possibility that more national experts could attend UN Crime Programme meetings online.

The government-driven discussions can thus benefit from the input of experts, who can identify what best practices can be adapted to the different circumstances around the world, and meet not only the general needs of Member States but also the ground-level needs of practitioners and local communities, of victims, and of offenders (Joutsen, 2022).

The changes brought about by the adoption of the 2030 Agenda and the Sustainable Development Goals (SDGs) can thus strengthen the UN Crime Programme. The intellectual debate that took place in the early years can be revitalized in order to bring in research and best practices from around the world, channelled, for example, through the UNODC and the Programme Network Institutes so that it is reflected in the discussions at the UN Crime Commission, the UN Crime Congresses, and other UN Crime Programme meetings. The government-driven discussions can also benefit from the input of experts, who can identify what best practices can be adapted to the different circumstances around the world so that these would meet not only the general needs of Member States, but also the ground-level needs of practitioners and local communities, of victims, and of the rehabilitation of offenders.

In his assessment of the work of the UN Crime Commission, Ram has laid out several suggestions for how the work of the Commission (and, indirectly, of the UN Crime Programme itself) can be strengthened (Ram, 2012, pp. 98 ff.). Redo (2012), in turn, in his study of the development of the UN Crime Programme, has emphasized the interrelationship between criminology and the approach that the UN has taken to crime prevention and criminal justice.

The UN Crime Programme has evolved to try and meet very real needs. There is still much to do to meet those needs.

Notes

1 In international law, "soft law" refers to quasi-legal instruments such as resolutions, guidelines, and declarations, which embody political aspirations but are not legally binding. "Hard law" refers, for example, to international conventions which are binding on the States Parties.
2 The Standard Minimum Rules had originally been drafted within the framework of the IPPC, and an early version was endorsed by the League of Nations.
3 Criticism was also directed at the resources made available to the sessions of the ad hoc Group of Experts, and then the UN Crime Committee, and generally to the limited time allotted to these sessions. For example, the UN Crime Committee at its 1978 session called for the Secretariat unit responsible for the UN Crime Programme to be given a position that was "consistent with the political, juridical, humanitarian and developmental nature of the mandates involved." (E/CN.5/558, p. 21).
Following the Sixth UN Crime Congress (1980), the GA requested that the Secretary-General take the necessary steps to provide sufficient resources to ensure that the unit was able to discharge its responsibilities in accordance with its mandate and the recommendation of the Congress (A/RES/35/171, para. 4).
4 The final report of the Secretary-General was submitted to ECOSOC, as requested, in 1987. ECOSOC resolution 1987/53 followed the lines ECOSOC had adopted a year earlier, in calling for the strengthening of the Crime Prevention and Criminal Justice Branch, giving priority attention to the forms of crime identified in the Milan Plan of Action, "including those of international dimensions," strengthening technical assistance, action-oriented research and advisory services, developing practical measures to assist Member States on request in the development of crime prevention and criminal justice, establishing an information system on crime prevention and criminal justice, and developing diversified funding strategies.
In 1987, in A/RES 42/59, the GA approved the recommendations of ECOSOC.
ECOSOC returned to the matter in 1988 (ECOSOC resolution 1988/44; see in particular para. 3) and 1989 (ECOSOC resolution 1989/68).
5 The author served as the secretary for this meeting, as well as host of the 1991 meeting at HEUNI referred to below. The meetings were quite informal, with the participants sitting comfortably around a small table at HEUNI, at times nibbling on take-away pizza and drinking red wine. See Joutsen and Viljanen, 2016.
6 All of the participants at the Helsinki meeting attended the 1988 session of the UN Crime Committee. Dusan Cotic and Bo Svensson served as vice-chairpersons of the session and David Faulkner and Ronald Gainer were members of the Committee.
Between the 1986 and the 1988 sessions of the UN Crime Committee, in 1987, ECOSOC established a Special Commission to conduct a much broader exercise, an "in-depth study of the United Nations intergovernmental structure and functions in the economic and social fields" (ECOSOC decision 1987/112). As Clark notes, 1994, p. 26, this raised concerns that the UN Crime Committee would be merged with other UN bodies, concerns that were dispelled when the chairperson of the Committee, Ms. Simone Rozes, mobilized support on the Special Commission for the maintenance of the UN Crime Committee.
7 The report was entitled "The Need for the Creation of an Effective International Crime and Justice Programme" (E/1990/31/Add.1).
8 The idea of establishing a specialized UN agency to deal with crime prevention and criminal justice can be seen as a throwback to the effort by the IPPC, described in section 2.2, to have the work of the IPPC carried out by such a UN agency. See also Clark, 1994, pp. 50–51 and 311–312.
9 The United States was among the most active in calling for the strengthening of the UN Crime Programme and in criticizing the flow of soft law instruments and other "paper" being produced by the UN Crime Committee. The Eighth UN

Crime Congress was organized in Havana, Cuba. The United States, which had imposed a general economic embargo on Cuba in 1962, did not send an official delegation to the Congress. The official records do not indicate whether individual U.S. citizens attended the Eighth UN Crime Congress, as individual experts or as members of the delegations of non-governmental organizations.

10 Three different elements for such a convention had been proposed at different times by different speakers: (1) a convention that would place the UN standards and norms on a firmer basis, (2) an amalgamation of existing bilateral and multilateral agreements on international cooperation in criminal justice (a rather ambitious undertaking, to say the least), and (3) provisions that would give the UN a pivotal role in the development of (international) criminal policy. See A/ CONF.144/5, paras. 82–86.

  See in particular Clark, 1994, pp. 46–53.

11 On file with the author. Clark, 1994, pp. 30–31, calls this discussion paper "quite influential."

12 Clark, 1994, pp. 32–34, provides more details on the three separate drafts that were before the meeting in Vienna. One, presented by Australia, was a more detailed version of the "Plan for Restructuring," and reflected the extensive consultations in which Australia had engaged with other Member States. A more minimalist draft was presented by the United States, and a more ambitious plan by France.

13 Neither the network of national correspondents nor the Global Crime and Criminal Justice Information Network are active any longer. The latter, which was established in 1986, is described in Clark, 1994, pp. 89–90. It soon fell into disuse and has to a large extent been replaced by the Criminal Justice Knowledge Center, which was created by Mr. Gary Hill. See www.justiceknowledgecenter.org

14 A detailed presentation of the work of the UN Crime Commission is provided in Ram, 2012.

15 Reconvened meetings are formal continuations of the annual meetings. Intersessional meetings are primarily for the preparation of the next session, and for updates on progress achieved.

16 Whether or not such broad issues can be called "priorities" is debatable. On their adoption, a close colleague of the author was overheard grumbling, largely to himself, "The only thing missing is shoplifting by the elderly out in the countryside."

  The "priority themes" established in 1992 were intended to be long term, and should not be confused with the "thematic debate" at the annual session of the UN Crime Commission referred to in section 4.3, which change from one year to the next.

17 At the second session of the UN Crime Commission (1993), disagreement arose over how these priorities should be set. Some Member States proposing draft resolutions wanted the topics dealt with in them designated as priorities and thus, in effect, in an ad hoc manner. Others argued that any decision on prioritization should be made in a comprehensive manner, once all the proposals for priorities were before the Commission. Those arguing for an ad hoc approach won the day. (Personal notes of the author.)

18 The substantive agenda items at all of the UN Crime Congresses from the time of the restructuring of the UN Crime Programme in 1991, to the Fourteenth UN Crime Congress in 2015, dealt predominantly with organized transnational crime and international cooperation. Even so, the more "traditional" issues related to domestic crime prevention and criminal justice, such as youth crime, policing and corrections have been touched upon at some workshops organized at the Crime Congresses. Since the 2015 Crime Congress, these "traditional" issues have been taken up more often as substantive agenda items.

19 The International Opium Conventions of 1912 and 1925 and the Convention for Limiting the Manufacture and Regulating the Distribution of Narcotic Drugs of 1931. The 1925 Convention has subsequently been amended several times with protocols. This series of amendments was extended in 1953 by the Protocol Limiting and Regulating the Cultivation of the Poppy Plant, the Production of, International and Wholesale Trade in, and Use of Opium.

20 Another template that emerged in the course of the 1970s was the work on conventions on terrorism. The first such UN convention was the 1983 Convention on the Prevention and Punishment of Crimes against Internationally Protected Persons, including Diplomatic Agents. However, the emergence of these conventions (and the difficult negotiations involved) was due to a very specific set of circumstances, which include the politicization of terrorism. Since these negotiations take place within the framework of the Security Council and not the UN Crime Programme, they are not considered here.

21 It should be remembered that these proposals were mixed in with the debate that led to the restructuring of the UN Crime Programme in 1991. Some of those participating in the debate saw work on conventions as the way forward in invigorating the UN Crime Programme. Others thought that the restructuring itself could be based on an international convention.

Redo, 2012, p. 177, notes that Barbados, Dominica, India, Jamaica, Sri Lanka, and Trinidad and Tobago proposed to the Preparatory ICC Committee that illicit trafficking in drugs and psychotropic substances be included in the scope of the International Criminal Court. See also Clark, 2022, p. 120.

A detailed description of developments leading up to the drafting of the United Nations Convention against Transnational Organized Crime is to be found in UNTOC, 2006, pp. ix–xxiv. For an overview of the entire process, from the early developments, through to negotiation and ratification, and the belated agreement (in 2018) on a review mechanism, see Tennant, 2020.

22 According to the *Report of the Seventh UN Crime Congress* (para. 87), "Some delegations felt that a convention on international co-operation in crime prevention and criminal justice ... deserved careful consideration, Other delegations, however, stated that while it had its attraction, the negotiation and preparation of such a convention could be a lengthy process, taking up resources of the Secretariat and of Member States which could more profitably be devoted to the tasks."

23 Clark notes that in several respects, the Ignatov draft presaged the UN Convention against Transnational Organized Crime that emerged at the end of the decade. The Costa Rican draft was submitted as a conference room paper, A/CONF.156/ CRP. The text can also be found in Clark, 1994, pp. 304–310.

24 This can be seen as a tactical move. Decisions at the UN Crime Commission in Vienna (and, before that, at the UN Crime Committee) have traditionally required consensus, which presumably would not have been possible at the time. Decisions at the GA, however, could be taken on the basis of a vote. As it happened, no vote was taken on GA resolution 51/120.

25 Personal notes of the author from the session. See also the official report of the session, E/1997/30, para. 65.

26 For example, the U.S. proposal had detailed provisions on the principle of "extradite or prosecute" (art. 3 of the U.S. draft), the rights of a person taken into custody in expectation of extradition (art. 4), mutual legal assistance (art. 6), other forms of cooperation (art. 9), and law enforcement training (art. 10). The Polish draft only dealt with these issues briefly. On the other hand, the Polish draft contained provisions on the monitoring of the implementation of the Convention (arts. 15 and 16 of the Polish draft); the U.S. draft had no proposals on this topic.

27 Several other documents informed the work of the Ad Hoc Intergovernmental Committee. For example, the Organization of American States had adopted international instruments on trafficking in firearms and trafficking in women and children, which were submitted as reference material for work on the two draft protocols related to these issues.

28 At a later stage in the negotiations, this was replaced by a draft submitted by Belgium, Poland, and the United States.

Barberet, 2014, pp. 116 ff. provides context for the international concern over trafficking in persons for purposes of sexual exploitation.

29 At a later stage, Canada and the United States submitted a separate draft, which contained several provisions related to migration policy in general. This was used as a point of reference, with some provisions integrated into the amended Austrian–Italian draft.

30 During the negotiations, Mexico submitted separate drafts for protocols on corruption and on money laundering.

The Ad Hoc Committee decided that these drafts were beyond its mandate so the separate drafts were not considered as such. As separately noted, it was agreed that work would begin at a later stage on what ultimately emerged as the UN Convention against Corruption.

31 The negotiators soon realized that they would have to work long hours if the work was to be accomplished by December 2000, as mandated by the GA. As the French Ambassador warned her colleagues at a late stage of the process, "Forget about your social life" (personal notes of the author).

32 For the first session in January 1999, the Finnish delegation prepared a non-paper analysing the correlation between the 1988 Drug Convention and the draft main convention. This was subsequently updated, most recently for the tenth session in July 2000. (On file with the author.)

33 The chairperson, Ambassador Luigi Lauriola (Italy), was fluent in English, French, and Spanish. Towards the end of the negotiating process, he was inserting some Russian and Arabic phrases into his comments from the chair.

34 During the second session, the Secretariat reported that it was preparing a glossary of terms to ensure that there was agreement on how key words and concepts would be translated into the different UN working languages.

35 The same issue had been debated extensively at the Ninth UN Crime Congress and so it was fresh in the minds of many of the negotiators working on the Convention.

36 The decision on the review of implementation of UNTOC was reached in 2018. See below.

37 Six sessions were held in 1999, on 18–29 January, 8–12 March, 29 April–4 May, 28 June–2 July, 4–15 October, and 6–17 December 1999. A further five sessions were held in 2000, on 10–21 January, 21 February–3 March, 5–16 June, 17–28 July, and 2–27 October.

Although the standard session was two weeks, the amount of time spent on the draft Convention at the sessions varied from four days to the full ten days at each respective session. The rest of the time was allotted to the protocols. In 2000, some informal sessions were held on the Convention, in parallel with the formal discussions on the protocols.

The text of the main Convention was finalized at the tenth session in July 2000. One last four-week session was added to the schedule in order to ensure that the text of the protocols would be finalized in time for the high-level signing event scheduled in Palermo on 12 December 2000. The month of November was needed for processing the texts by the Office of Legal Affairs of the United Nations, for final checks of the translations into the six official UN languages, and for the preparation and adoption, on 15 November 2000, of GA resolution A/RES/55/25 on the Convention.

38 An overview of developments within the UN that led to the drafting and adoption of UNCAC is provided in UNCAC, 2010, pp. xii–xliii.

39 In 1975, the GA adopted resolution 3514(XXX), on Measures against corrupt practices of transnational and other corporations, their intermediaries and others involved, and requested that ECOSOC take up the issue. ECOSOC duly established an ad hoc Intergovernmental Working Group on Corrupt Practices to consider the matter, and then a Committee on an International Agreement on Illicit Payments. In 1979, after two sessions, the Committee had prepared such a draft international agreement (E/1979/104). However, this did not receive sufficient support and despite repeated urging by ECOSOC and the GA, the draft was never finalized. The efforts petered out during the early 1990s. See Jalan, 1993, pp. 44–66.

   The original draft, which was discussed by the Working Group, appeared to be heavily influenced by the Foreign Corrupt Practices Act of the United States. See Young, 1980.

40 At the Sixth UN Crime Congress (1980), corruption was discussed primarily under the agenda item "Crime and the abuse of power: offences and offenders beyond the reach of the law"; at the Seventh UN Crime Congress (1985), under the agenda item "New dimensions of criminality and crime prevention in the context of development: challenges for the future"; and at the Eighth UN Crime Congress (1990), under the agenda item "Crime prevention and criminal justice in the context of development: realities and perspectives of international cooperation" (UNCAC, 2010, pp. xiv–xviii).

41 The United States has been very active in promoting international cooperation against corruption. In the early 1990s, some rather prominent corruption cases in Latin America drew the attention of the United States to the need for regional cooperation, as one way of mobilizing political pressure on individual countries. See, for example, *First Annual Report to Congress on the Inter-American Convention Against Corruption* (available at www.state.gov/p/inl/rls/rpt/3350.htm).

   For a constructivist explanation for the identification and framing of corruption as a "global problem", see Blaustein et al., 2022, pp. 68–69, 126–128, and 144–149. They emphasize the role of moral entrepreneurs such as the World Bank, multinational (and in particular American) corporations, and civil society organizations such as Transparency International in lobbying for a global anti-bribery regime.

42 The main corruption-related provision in UNTOC was article 8, which requires States Parties to criminalize active and passive bribery involving a public official (para. 1), and to consider the criminalization of active and passive bribery involving a foreign public official or international civil servant (para. 2).

   In addition, article 9 of UNTOC requires States Parties to adopt measures to promote integrity and to prevent, detect, and punish the corruption of public officials.

43 The author was a member of the Ad Hoc Committee, and can confirm that this consensus view was reached very quickly.

44 When kleptocrats extract resources to the tune of billions of dollars, much of it does not leave the country but instead is used to maintain and strengthen the kleptocrat's power base, for example, by rewarding supporters and ensuring the allegiance of the military and security apparatus. Nonetheless, many kleptocrats have transferred money abroad as a hedge against a fall from power.

   A clear reflection of the interest of developing countries, particularly, in recovering the proceeds of corruption from abroad is that, after UNCAC entered into force, a number of GA resolutions were adopted urging States Parties to implement UNCAC effectively –especially its provisions on asset recovery. A/RES/67/192 (2012), A/RES/68/195 (2013), A/RES/69/199 (2014), and A/RES/75/194 (2020).

See also ECOSOC resolution 2001/13, which was adopted while UNCAC was still being negotiated.

45 Much of the original rolling text was a consolidation of proposals submitted by Austria and the Netherlands (A/AC.261/IPM/4) and Mexico (A/AC.261/IPM/13). Several other Member States, among them Colombia, France, Peru, and the United States, made extensive proposals that facilitated the negotiations.

46 Three sessions were held in 2002: 21 January–1 February, 17–28 June, and 30 September–11 October. Four sessions were held in 2003: 13–24 January, 10–21 March, 21 July–8 August, and a brief final session, 29 September–1 October.

47 Even this provision has several qualifiers: "consider taking appropriate ... measures," "in accordance with the fundamental principles of its domestic law," and "where applicable."

48 For an assessment of the UN Convention against Corruption, see Argandona, 2007.

49 The following presentation is based on Joutsen, 2023.

50 Other international conventions on cybercrime include the Shanghai Cooperation Council's Agreement on Cooperation in the Field of Ensuring International Information Security (2009), the League of Arab States Convention on Combatting Information Technology Offences (2010), and the African Union Convention on Cyber Security and Personal Data Protection (the Malabo Convention, 2014).

51 See, for example, Joutsen and Graycar, 2012.

52 I am indebted to Mr. Chris Ram for pointing out the relevance of mobile telephones in UN Crime Programme negotiations. (Private communication, 16 February 2023.)

53 An example of a self-executing treaty is the Vienna Convention on Consular Relations.

A separate issue is that States can be divided into two groups, dualist and monistic (with a few hovering in between). Most States are dualist, in that a treaty ratified by the government usually requires additional legislation to incorporate the provisions into domestic law. In monistic states, ratification in itself incorporates the provisions into the domestic legal order (although this may be subject to certain conditions).

54 The functions of depositaries are defined in article 77 of the Vienna Convention on the Law of Treaties (1969).

55 See, for example, https://www.ohchr.org/en/instruments-and-mechanisms Examples of UN Charter-based bodies include the Human Rights Council, special procedures, the universal periodic review, and independent investigations.

On the monitoring of implementation of UN transnational crime treaties, see Redo, 2015, pp. 62–67.

56 Regarding the implementation of the Council of Europe's Criminal Law and Civil Law Convention on Corruption, see www.coe.int/t/dghl/monitoring/greco/default_en.asp. Regarding the implementation of the OECD Convention on Combating Bribery of Foreign Public Officials in International Business Transactions, see www.oecd.org/document/20/0,3343,en_2649_34859_2017813_1_1_1_1,00.html.

57 Rose, 2020, p. 52, notes that although several transnational law conventions have been adopted since the Second World War, many do not contain provisions on a formal monitoring body.

58 Joutsen and Graycar, 2012, describe the evolution of the UNCAC review mechanism. Parts of the following are based on this article.

59 The author prepared a conference room document, which was submitted by Finland to the 2015 session of the UNCAC conference, outlining the debate over the role of non-governmental organizations in the review of implementation of UNCAC; CAC/COSP/2015/CRP.3.

Concerns over participation of non-government organizations in the UN Crime Programme were not new. López-Rey, 1985, pp. 27–28 notes that efforts to restrict individual and non-government organization participation had already been made in the late 1960s and the 1970s, on those instances in respect of UN Crime Congresses. He rather provocatively sees as the probable reason "the fact that since most governments are dictatorial, they are afraid that congresses may be used to criticize their often repressive criminal policies and programmes. Criticism may be well founded in some cases, particularly when it concerns a criminal abuse of power."

Redo, 2015, pp. 65–67, in turn, notes that civil society representatives are involved in the review of implementation of some other UN treaties. For example, they may be invited for an informal dialogue with members of the International Narcotics Control Board, and non-governmental organizations have a clear role in monitoring implementation of the Convention on the Rights of the Child.

60 The author has experience with OECD and Council of Europe peer review and finds it difficult to understand how the use of independent experts, the arrangement of country visits, and the judicious incorporation of relevant information provided, for example, by academia and non-governmental organizations can be construed as intervention in domestic matters.

However, the author can understand how representatives of a State Party under review may question the appropriateness of a general discussion in a monitoring body, on how the country's legislation, policy and practice matches up with its obligations under the convention in question – and, more particularly, how those representatives may object to the monitoring body making recommendations for changes in legislation, policy, and practice and requiring that the State Party reports at a subsequent session on what action it has taken.

61 In addition to the career diplomats, the author was also among those present.

62 Disagreement arose over the definition of a "governmental expert." Those opposed to the peer review concept generally stressed that these experts must be civil servants. The solution found was to have each State Party list who would be available to conduct the review, thus giving the State Party under review the opportunity to challenge anyone they regarded as biased.

63 The terms of reference, guidelines for the conduct of the country review, and the blueprint for the country report and executive summary are available at https://www.unodc.org/unodc/en/corruption/implementation-review-mechanism.html

64 For example, in over 90 per cent of country visits the State Party under review arranged meetings with "other stakeholders" (CAC/COSP/2021/2, paras. 40 and 41).

65 According to CAC/COSP/IRG/2021/5, p. 2, regular budgetary funding was made available for twelve new staff members: one D-1, one P-5, three P-4, three P-3, three P-2, and one General Service.

66 Annually, some three million dollars came from the regular UN budget and some two million from extrabudgetary sources. The amount of extrabudgetary funding that has been made available has decreased considerably since 2019. The status as of early 2023 is provided in CAC/COSP/IRG/2023/4.

67 An overview of the discussion on the UNTOC review mechanism and its operation is provided in Rose.

68 Individual-oriented theories continue to have relevance in helping to explain a predisposition to engage in behaviour that is condoned by society and in suggesting methods of treatment for specific types of offenders.
69 The term is generally associated with what is known as the "Copenhagen School." See, for example, Emmers, 2003, and Stritzel, 2012.
70 In addition, the Sixth UN Crime Congress dealt with abuse of power as a separate agenda item.
71 See, for example, the first preambular paragraph of ECOSOC 2012/19, which is entitled "Strengthening international cooperation in combating transnational organized crime in all its forms and manifestations."
72 See, for example, the many UNODC studies on transnational organized crime noted in Chapter 12.
73 Reconvened meetings are formal continuations of the annual meetings. Intersessional meetings are primarily for the preparation of the next sessions and for updates on progress achieved.
74 Personal communication from John Brandolino, 10 November 2023.
  The regular budget comes from assessed contributions from the Member States and is used to pay for the administrative infrastructure and core normative work. The biennial budget of the UN is decided by the GA.
  Extrabudgetary funds come from voluntary contributions. They can be "general purpose" funds (used to pay infrastructure costs that are not directly related to individual projects) or "special purpose" funds (usually earmarked to pay for projects identified by the donor).
  A key difference between the two is that the regular budget provides more sustainability and predictability in carrying out activities.
  See https://www.unodc.org/documents/commissions/FINGOV/Background_Documentation_2009–2011/Agenda_Item_1/Regular-Budget-and-Extra-Budgetary-Resources.pdf
75 See Chapter 12.
76 See Chapter 12.
77 See section 4.2.

References

Andreas, P. and Nadelmann, E. (2006), *Policing the Globe: Criminalization and Crime Control in International Relations*. Oxford University Press

Argandona, Antonio (2007), *The United Nations Convention Against Corruption and Its Impact on International Companies*, IESE Business School Working Paper No. 656, available at https://papers.ssrn.com/sol3/papers.cfm?abstract_id=960662

Barberet, Rosemary (2014), *Women, Crime and Criminal Justice. A Global Inquiry*, Routledge

Blaustein, Jarrett, Tom Chondor and Nathan W. Pino (2022), *Unravelling the Development – Crime Nexus*, Rowman & Littlefield

Clark, Roger S. (2022), The Concept of International Criminal Law and Its Relationship with Transnational Criminal Law and Conflict of Laws, *Transnational Criminal Law Review*, 1(2), 100–122

Clark, Roger S. (1990), The Eighth United Nations Congress on the Prevention of Crime and the Treatment of Offenders. Havana, Cuba. August 27–September 7, 1990, in *Criminal Law Forum*, 1(3), 513–523

Clark, Roger S. (1994), *The United Nations Crime Prevention and Criminal Justice Program. Formulation of Standards and Efforts at Their Implementation*, University of Pennsylvania Press

Emmers, Ralf (2003), *The Securitization of Transnational Crime in ASEAN*, Institute of Defence and Strategic Studies, Singapore, available at www.tandfonline.com/doi/abs/10.1080/0951274032000085653

Jalan, Abhimanyu (1993), *Control of Accommodation Payments Made by Transnational Corporations*, University of Ottawa, available at https://ruor.uottawa.ca/bitstream/10393/6729/1/MM00571.PDF

Joutsen, Matti (2017), *Four Transitions in the United Nations Crime Programme*, HEUNI, available at https://www.unodc.org/documents/commissions/CCPCJ/CCPCJ_Sessions/CCPCJ_26/E_CN15_2017_CRP4_e_V1703636.pdf

Joutsen, Matti (2023), Negotiating United Nations Crime Conventions: Comparing the Negotiations on the Proposed UN Cybercrime Convention with Earlier Conventions, *PNI Newsletter*, issue 3, Bangkok, pp. 18–22

Joutsen, Matti (2022), Staying Connected: The Impact of the Covid-19 Pandemic on United Nations Crime Programme Meetings, UN Crime Commission Conference Room Paper, E/CN.15/2022a/CRP.5

Joutsen, Matti and Adam Graycar (2012), When Experts and Diplomats Agree: Negotiating Peer Review of the UN Convention Against Corruption, in *Journal of Global Governance: A Review of Multilateralism and International Organizations*, 18(4), 425–439

Joutsen, Matti and Terhi Viljanen (2016), Inkeri Anttila's International Reach, in Raimo Lahti (ed.), *Inkeri Anttila (1916–2013): Rikosoikeuden uudistajan ammatillinen ura ja vaikutus*, University of Helsinki, pp. 207–226

Lombroso, Cesare (2006), *Criminal Man*, translated by Mary Gibson and Nicole Hahn Rafter, Duke University Press

López-Rey de Arroya, Manuel (1985) *A Guide to United Nations Criminal Policy*, Cambridge Studies in Criminology LIV

Ram, Christopher D. (2012), *Meeting the Challenge of Crime in the Global Village: An Assessment of the Role and Future of the United Nations Commission on the Crime Prevention and Criminal Justice*, HEUNI publication no, 73

Redo, Slawomir (2012), *Blue Criminology. The Power of United Nations Ideas to Counter Crime Globally – A Monographic Study*, HEUNI publication no. 72, available at https://www.heuni.fi/en/index/publications/heunireports/reportseriesno.72.bluecriminologythepowerofunitednationsideastocountercrimeglobally-amonographicstudy.html

Redo, Slawomir (2015), The United Nations Criminal Justice System in the Suppression of Transnational Crime, in Neil Boister and Robert J. Currie (eds.), *Routledge Handbook of Transnational Criminal Law*, Routledge, pp. 57–72

Report of the [xx] UN Crime Congress: the reports of, as well as other background documents relating to, the different UN Crime Congresses are available at www.unodc.org/congress/en/previous-congresses.html

Rose, Cecily (2020), The Creation of a Review Mechanism for the UN Convention Against Transnational Organized Crime and Its Protocols, *American Journal of International Law*, 114(1), 51–67

Simon, Jonathan (2007), *Governing Through Crime: How the War on Crime Transformed American Democracy and Created a Culture of Fear*, Oxford University Press

Stritzel, Holer (2012), Securitization, Power, Intertextuality: Discourse Theory and the Translations of Organized Crime, *Security Dialogue*, 43(6), 549–567

Tennant, Ian (2020), *The Promise of Palermo. A Political History of the UN Convention against Transnational Organized Crime*, Global Alliance against Transnational Organized Crime, Geneva

UNCAC (2010), *Travaux Préparatoires* of the Negotiations for the Elaboration of the United Nations Convention against Corruption, United Nations, Sales No. E.10.V.13., available at www.unodc.org/documents/treaties/UNCAC/Publications/Travaux/Travaux_Preparatoires_-_UNCAC_E.pdf

UNTOC (2006), *Travaux Préparatoires* of the Negotiations for the Elaboration of the United Nations Convention against Transnational Organized Crime and the Protocols Thereto, United Nations, Sales No. E.06.V.5., available at www.unodc.org/pdf/ctoccop_2006/04-60074_ebook-e.pdf

United Nations (1948), *Yearbook of the United Nations 1947–48*, United Nation, available at unhcr.org/4e1ee75f0.pdf and https://www.unmultimedia.org/searchers/yearbook/page.jsp?bookpage=613&volume=1947-48

Young, Margaret H. (1980), A Comparison of the Foreign Corrupt Practices Act and the Draft International Agreement on Illicit Payments, *Vanderbilt Journal of Transnational Law*, 13(4777), 795–823

PART II

The parts and the players

4

THE MAIN STRUCTURES IN THE UN CRIME PROGRAMME

4.1   The overall structure

The main UN Crime Programme structures are the *Secretariat*, the *Economic and Social Council (ECOSOC)* (see Acackpo-Satchivi, 1990), and the *General Assembly (GA)* (which formally sets the policy), the *UN Commission on Crime Prevention and Criminal Justice* (which, in practice, develops the policy), and the *UN Congresses on Crime Prevention and Criminal Justice*. In addition, over the past twenty years, two new structures have emerged: the *UNTOC Conference of the States Parties* and the *UNCAC Conference of the States Parties*.

Within the UN system, *ECOSOC* deals with international economic, social cultural, education, health, and related matters, as well as promoting respect for, and observance of, human rights and fundamental freedoms for all.[1] As part of this mandate, it has the primary responsibility within the UN system for issues related to crime prevention and criminal justice.

ECOSOC holds one substantive session each year, in late spring or early summer. These sessions, which last four or five weeks, are held primarily in New York, although some matters may be dealt with in Geneva. Most matters coming before ECOSOC are initially dealt with in one of its three Committees of the Whole, before going to the plenary.[2] Crime prevention and criminal justice issues are dealt with by the Second Committee. Since only three working days are allotted to the Second Committee at each year's substantive session and there are many issues to deal with, the Second Committee's discussion on crime prevention and criminal justice tends to be rather perfunctory (Clark, 1994, pp. 65–70). The subsequent adoption in the ECOSOC plenary tends to take place without debate.

DOI: 10.4324/9781003480907-6

From ECOSOC, major policy statements (including some UN Crime Commission resolutions embodying standards and norms) may proceed to the *GA* for consideration. (Since the establishment of the UN Crime Commission in 1991, the GA has adopted an average of between six and eight resolutions each year related to crime prevention and criminal justice.)[3] Furthermore, some politically sensitive crime issues, such as war crimes, genocide, and terrorism, may be taken up in the GA without prior discussion in subsidiary bodies. The GA sometimes sets up special bodies to deal with specific issues, such as the drafting of new international agreements.

The GA holds one annual meeting, in the autumn, in New York. As with ECOSOC, it operates with a plenary and Committees of the Whole. The GA has six such Committees. Crime prevention and criminal justice issues are dealt with by the Third Committee, which covers social, humanitarian, and cultural matters.[4]

Criminal violations of human rights are the mandate of the *Commission on Human Rights*. It will thus often deal with matters that are also relevant to the UN Crime Programme. Examples of such matters are torture and inhumane treatment in correctional facilities and by the police.

The *UN Commission on Narcotic Drugs* has an extensive mandate which is often directly relevant to crime prevention and criminal justice (and vice versa).

As noted in Chapter 5, in respect of *UN specialized agencies*, for example the Statistical Commission, the Office of the High Commissioner for Refugees, UN Women, the International Labour Office, the World Health Organization, and the International Organization for Migration have a mandate that often involves issues dealt with in the UN Crime Programme.

The *UN regional commissions* (the Economic Commission for Africa, the Economic Commission for Europe, the Economic Commission for Latin America and the Caribbean, the Economic and Social Commission for Asia and the Pacific, and the Economic and Social Commission for Western Asia) are responsible for promoting economic and social development in their respective regions. The programmes developed by the UN regional commissions vary depending on the priorities of the region they serve, but they often contain elements related to the promotion of the rule of law, human rights, and access to justice.

4.2 The UNODC and its field and regional offices[5]

Within the UN Secretariat, issues relating to crime prevention and criminal justice are dealt with by the *UN Office on Drugs and Crime* (UNODC), although related issues are also considered by, for example, the *Office of the United Nations High Commissioner for Human Rights*.

The UNODC acts as the Secretariat to the UN Crime Commission, the UN Commission on Narcotic Drugs, and the Conferences of the States Parties to the two UN Crime Conventions as well as the three drug control conventions.[6]

Eduardo Vetere, who was the Director of the Crime Prevention and Criminal Justice Branch from 1987 to 2005 (as the UN Secretariat unit responsible for the UN Crime Programme was called at the time), provides the following summary of its work (Vetere, 1995, pp. 17–18):

> [the Branch is] charged with the formulation of policy options and the promotion and implementation of United Nations international instruments, resolutions and policies at the international level, as directed by its policy bodies. It works closely with officials of Member States, intergovernmental and non-governmental organizations and through public information activities. It fosters the application of United Nations standards and norms in national legislation, collects and analyses statistics, and conducts studies on various aspects of crime prevention and control and criminal justice administration. It organizes the quinquennial United Nations congresses on the prevention of crime and the treatment of offenders and their regional preparatory meetings, as well as various other expert group meetings on crime prevention and criminal justice matters. Staff members of the Branch coordinate crime prevention and criminal justice activities within the United Nations system, cooperating with other entities such as the Centre for Human Rights, the United Nations International Drug Control Programme and the Office of Legal Affairs.
>
> In addition, the Branch is the central repository of international technical expertise in matters of crime prevention and criminal justice, criminal law reform, and criminological sciences. It bears the primary responsibility within the United Nations system for facilitating technical cooperation between countries in the criminal justice field and providing technical and advisory services. Direct services to requesting Governments are undertaken in the form of the provision of policy advice and the implementation and training of personnel, as well as in highly specific areas such as the introduction of juvenile courts, the creation of open penal institutions, and probation. Another major function is the gathering, analysis and dissemination of data.

Over the years, the UN Secretariat unit dealing with crime prevention and criminal justice has been known by many names (the Social Defence Unit, the Social Defence Section, the Crime Prevention and Criminal Justice Section, the Crime Prevention and Criminal Justice Branch, the Crime Prevention and Criminal Justice Division, and the Centre for International Crime Prevention), and in 1997 it was combined with the Secretariat unit dealing with drug issues to form the UNODC.

For most of its existence, this Secretariat unit remained small. It began with three professional staff members, two of whom had been transferred from the International Penal and Penitentiary Commission. For most of the next 50 years, it had less than a dozen professional staff members, plus some secretarial staff members. The number fluctuated somewhat with temporary secondments from Member States or elsewhere in the Secretariat, in particular in the run-up to the quinquennial UN Crime Congresses. At the time of the restructuring of the Programme in 1992, there were eleven professional officers and six "general service" staff members (Clark, 1994, p. 18, fn 44 and p. 63, fn 32).[7]

Over the past twenty years, largely as a consequence of the adoption of the two UN Crime Conventions (including the need for additional Secretariat staff to assist States Parties in the review of their implementation), the number of professional staff members dealing with substantive crime issues in the UNODC has increased to about 350, serving both at the UNODC headquarters in Vienna and at regional and field offices around the world.[8]

UNODC *regional offices* have been established in Bangkok (Southeast Asia and the Pacific), Cairo (Middle East and North Africa), Dakar (West and Central Africa), New Delhi (South Asia), Nairobi (East Africa), Panama City (Central America and the Caribbean), Pretoria (South Africa), and Tashkent (Central Asia). In addition, the UNODC has 7 national offices and 94 programme offices (https://www.unodc.org/unodc/en/field-offices. html#:~:text=UNODC%20operates%20in%20more%20than,with%20 2%2C400%20UNODC%20personnel%20globally).

The Secretariat of the UN has undergone numerous waves of restructuring, and the unit responsible for crime prevention and criminal justice has followed suit. The unit was originally part of the Division for Social Development and Humanitarian Affairs,[9] which moved from New York to Vienna in 1980.[10] In 1993, when the Division was transferred back across the Atlantic to New York, the small Crime Prevention and Criminal Justice Branch was detached and remained in Vienna, together with the part of the Secretariat dealing with drug issues (Clark, 1994, p. 5). In 1997, as noted above, these two were combined to form the UNODC.

The UNODC is based at the UN Office in Vienna (UNOV), under the Executive Director, who is at the same time the Director-General of the United Nations Office at Vienna itself (which includes several other entities). The current Executive Director is Ms. Ghada Waly.

The UNODC is currently divided into four divisions: operations, treaty affairs, policy analysis and public affairs, and management. Each division is headed by a director.

The division most visible in the UN Crime Programme is arguably the Division for Treaty Affairs (the current director is Mr. John Brandolino). This division is divided, in turn, into three branches: organized crime and illicit trafficking, terrorism prevention, and corruption and economic crime. In the division for policy analysis and public affairs, the research and trend analysis branch is also involved in the Crime Programme.

TABLE 4.1 Evolution of the UN Secretariat unit responsible for crime prevention and criminal justice

Name of Secretariat unit	Director	Comments
Social Defence Unit 1947–1952	Benedict S. Alper 1947 Sir Leon Radzinowicz 1948–1949 Paul Amor 1950–1952	
Social Defence Section 1952–1971	Manuel López-Rey 1952–1961 Edward Galway 1962–1966 Georges Kahale 1966–1968	
Crime Prevention and Criminal Justice Section 1971–1977	William Clifford 1968–1974	
Crime Prevention and Criminal Justice Branch 1977–1996 (moved to Vienna, 1980)	G.O.W. Mueller 1974–1981 Minoru Shikita 1982–1986	Division for Social Development and Humanitarian Affairs moved from New York to Vienna in 1980
Crime Prevention and Criminal Justice Branch detached from Division, remaining in Vienna 1993	Eduardo Vetere 1987–2005	Division transferred back across the Atlantic to New York
Crime Prevention and Criminal Justice Division 1996 Centre for International Crime Prevention 1997 [integrated into the UNODC, 1997]		
	Herman Woltring 2005–2008 John Sandage 2008–2014 John Brandolino 2014– (present)	United Nations Office on Drugs and Crime formed by combining crime and drugs units 1997

4.3 The policy-making body: the UN Crime Commission

As noted in section 3.1, the most notable and ultimately far-reaching change brought about by the restructuring of the UN Crime Programme was that the expert-driven UN Committee on Crime Prevention and Control was replaced by a government-driven UN Commission on Crime Prevention and Criminal Justice (A/RES/46/152).[11] This UN Crime Commission functions as the *governing body* of the UNODC. It coordinates with other UN bodies that have specific mandates in the areas of crime prevention and criminal justice, and is also the preparatory body for the *United Nations Crime Congresses*. The UN

Crime Commission thus acts in practice as the *principal policy-making body* for the UN in the field of crime prevention and criminal justice.

The UN Crime Commission consists of 40 Member States elected by ECOSOC for a term of three years. The sessions of the UN Crime Commission are also attended by a very large number of observer States as well as by other categories of participants: representatives of UN specialized agencies, the UN Crime Programme Network Institutes (PNIs), intergovernmental organizations, and non-governmental organizations.[12]

The delegations from the Member States and observer States tend to be dominated by diplomatic representatives from missions based in Vienna. Since meetings generally last only a few days, most Member States are not prepared to send experts from the capitals to attend them. As is the case with the domestic criminal policy of any Member State, the policy formulated by the UN Crime Commission is not determined solely by the criminological expertise of the participants on such matters as how crime should be defined, how it should be prevented, and how the criminal justice system should operate. As Ram notes (2012b, p. 129):

> political functions, generally brought before it by the Member States' foreign ministries and diplomatic representatives, are also central to the work of the Commission. These include marshalling and contributing financial resources and holding UNODC and other UN bodies accountable for how they are spent, general oversight over the work of the Secretariat, and coordinating the work of the Commission with other bodies, especially in areas such as rule of law, narcotics and human rights, where overlapping or dual-aspect subject matter is often encountered. At its most fundamental level, however, the work of diplomatic representatives in the Commission consists of articulating the political will of various Member States. Diplomatic experts serve as channels of communication, bringing the political views of their governments into the Commission, taking back their assessments of the political views of other States, both individually and collectively, and ultimately conveying the consent of each Member State to join consensus on outcomes. ... Without [diplomatic experts], diplomatic discourse would be sterile and devoid of underlying substance, and with [the substantive experts] there would be substance, but little meaningful discourse or transfer of substantive knowledge from one State to another.

The UN Crime Commission holds annual five-day sessions (usually in May). Since 2009, "reconvened" sessions of two or three days have been held in early December. In addition, "intersessional" meetings have been held as necessary.

When meetings are held, the key persons are the members of the "bureau," in other words the chairperson, the vice-chairpersons (usually three), and the rapporteur. These positions usually rotate among the five regional groups: Africa, Asia-Pacific, Eastern Europe, Latin America and the Caribbean (also known as "GRULAC"), and the "Western European and others" group. The bureau deals with various practical organizational matters (which can at times become somewhat politicized). It may also meet in an "enlarged bureau" composition, which would also include representatives of the five regional groups as well as of the EU and the Group of 77 + China (which essentially consists of developing countries). (These same conference structures are to be found in the Conferences of the States Parties to the two UN Crime Conventions, dealt with below in section 4.4.)

Over the years, the formal agenda of each annual session of the UN Crime Commission has become relatively standard. After the opening of the session, there will be a general debate (usually lasting the first day), followed by what is called a thematic debate related to the special theme selected for that particular session of the UN Crime Commission (usually lasting the second day). On the afternoon of the first day, the UN PNIs and the UNODC organize a workshop related to this theme.

Towards the middle of the annual session, the UN Crime Commission takes up strategic management, budgetary, and administrative questions, followed by "integration and coordination of efforts by the UNODC and by Member States in the field of crime prevention and criminal justice." This includes ratification and implementation of the two UN Crime Conventions and of international instruments related to terrorism, as well as activities of the PNIs, non-governmental organizations, and other bodies.

On Thursday, according to this somewhat standardized agenda, the UN Crime Commission discusses the use and application of UN standards and norms in crime prevention and criminal justice; world crime trends and emerging issues and responses; as well as follow-up to the previous UN Crime Congress and preparations for the next UN Crime Congress.

On the last day of the annual session, Friday, the UN Crime Commission directs its attention to implementation of the Sustainable Developments Goals. The afternoon is reserved for the draft agenda of the next session of the UN Crime Commission, the adoption of resolutions, and the adoption of the report.

The discussion on each of the agenda items follows a relatively standard procedure. Once the Secretariat representative has introduced the agenda item (or the members of a panel or roundtable have given their statements), the chairperson opens the floor for discussion. Regional groups have the option of speaking first, followed by representatives of Member States. If ministers or other dignitaries are in attendance, they will generally be invited to speak first.

TABLE 4.2 Themes selected for the annual sessions of the UN Crime Commission, 2000–2025

Year	Theme
1992	
1993	
1994	
1995	
1996	Measures to regulate firearms (not identified as a theme, but dealt with exceptionally as a separate agenda item)
1997	
1998	
1999	
2000	International cooperation in combating transnational crime; elaboration of an international convention against transnational organized crime, and other possible international instruments
2001	Progress made in global action against corruption
2002	Reform of the criminal justice system: achieving effectiveness and equity; workshop
2003	Trafficking in human beings, especially women and children; workshop
2004	Rule of law and development: the contribution of operational activities in crime prevention and criminal justice; workshop
2005	Consideration of the conclusions and recommendations of the Eleventh United Nations Congress on Crime Prevention and Criminal Justice; workshop on working modalities and substantive results: report on the Eleventh Congress workshops and ancillary meetings
2006	Maximizing the effectiveness of technical assistance provided to Member States in crime prevention and criminal justice; workshop
2007	(a) Crime prevention and criminal justice responses to urban crime, including gang-related activities:
	(i) Preventive measures, including community-based responses;
	(ii) Criminal justice responses, including international cooperation;
	(b) Effective crime prevention and criminal justice responses to combat sexual exploitation of children; sharing of successful practices to combat sexual exploitation of children through:
	(i) Crime prevention responses;
	(ii) Criminal justice responses;
	(iii) International cooperation.
	Successful crime reduction and prevention strategies in the urban context; workshop
2008	Aspects of violence against women that pertain directly to the Commission on Crime Prevention and Criminal Justice; workshop
2009	(a) Economic fraud and identity-related crime;
	(b) Penal reform and the reduction of prison overcrowding, including the provision of legal aid in criminal justice systems.
	Prison overcrowding; workshop

Year	Theme
2012	Violence against migrants, migrant workers, and their families
2013	The challenge posed by emerging forms of crime that have a significant impact on the environment and ways to deal with it effectively; workshop on Emerging forms of crime that have an impact on the environment: lessons learned
2014	International cooperation in criminal matters; workshop
2015	Follow-up to the Thirteenth United Nations Congress on Crime Prevention and Criminal Justice; workshop
2016	Criminal justice responses to prevent and counter terrorism in all its forms and manifestations, including the financing of terrorism, and technical assistance in support of the implementation of relevant international conventions and protocols; workshop on Terrorism in all its forms and manifestations: international and national responses
2017	Comprehensive and integrated crime prevention strategies: public participation, social policies and education in support of the rule of law; workshop on Institutional coordination in crime prevention: international perspectives
2018	Criminal justice responses to prevent and counter cybercrime in all its forms, including through the strengthening of cooperation at the national and international levels; workshop
2019	The responsibility of effective, fair, humane and accountable criminal justice systems in preventing and countering crime motivated by intolerance or discrimination of any kind; workshop
2020	(Abbreviated and highly restricted session, due to Covid-19)
2021	Effective measures to prevent and counter the smuggling of migrants, while protecting the rights of smuggled migrants, particularly women and children, and those of unaccompanied migrant children; workshop on Lessons learned: Impact of the migrant smuggling protocol twenty years later
2022	Strengthening the use of digital evidence in criminal justice and countering cybercrime, including the abuse and exploitation of minors in illegal activities with the use of the Internet; workshop on Improving the criminal justice responses to Internet-related crimes against children
2023	Enhancing the functioning of the criminal justice system to ensure access to justice and to realize a safe and secure society; workshop
2024	Promoting international cooperation and technical assistance to prevent and address organized crime, corruption, terrorism in all its forms and manifestations and other forms of crime, including in the areas of extradition, mutual legal assistance and asset recovery; workshop
2025	Addressing new, emerging and evolving forms of crime, including crimes that affect the environment, smuggling of commercial goods and trafficking in cultural property and other crimes targeting cultural property; workshop

Note: Prior to 2000, no themes were identified. References to "workshop" in the table denote a PNI workshop organized during the session on the same theme; if the PNI workshop theme was a modification, this is indicated.

BOX 4.1 PROCEDURE FOR THE GIVING OF STATEMENTS AT UN CRIME PROGRAMME MEETINGS

The Secretariat keeps the list of speakers, which the chairperson consults in giving speakers the floor. Persons who wish to speak should contact a conference room officer and ask to be placed on the list of speakers, usually on the basis of "first come, first served." The speaker can also ask to be allotted a certain time (such as the first to speak after lunch, or the first to speak after another speaker), as long as this does not endanger the "first come, first served" approach, or speakers whose priority would be affected inform the conference room officer that they agree to this.

The conference room officer will usually ask if the statement is in writing, so that this can be distributed to the interpreters. If so, the written statements should preferably be given to the Secretariat at least an hour in advance, so that the Secretariat has time to deliver them to the interpreters' booths, and the interpreters, in turn, have time to note the availability of the texts, and use them for the interpretation. (The UN interpreters are very competent, and can adjust if the speaker makes changes to the text during delivery.)

Because of the need for interpretation, oral statements should be given at a relatively leisurely pace: not ponderously slow, but definitely not in a rush. Most interpreters prefer simple, straightforward sentences that follow the normal rhythm of conversation. All too often, written statements can include long and convoluted sentence structures which can be difficult to follow, even if the interpreters have a written text in front of them.

The chairperson may limit the length of oral statements. However, even if no limit has been imposed, speakers should avoid trying the patience of the audience, who have to sit through six hours of meetings every day, involving a study stream of oral statements. PowerPoint presentations and even videos may help in getting a point across but, if these are used, the speaker should be mindful that the UN works with six official languages, and consequently possibly the majority of the participants will depend on the interpretation.

Under the rules of procedure, the chairperson has the power to call a speaker to order if their remarks are not relevant to the subject under discussion. This is rarely necessary.

The formal discussion on all of the agenda items at sessions of the UN Crime Commission, with the exception of the PNI workshop, takes place in the plenary. Much of the work of the UN Crime Commission, however, takes place elsewhere, in the informal negotiations (known as "*informals*") and in the *Committee of the Whole*. It is here that most of the negotiation over the draft resolutions takes place.

In addition, various Member States, PNIs, intergovernmental organizations, and non-governmental organizations arrange so-called *side events* (similar to the ancillary meetings organized at UN Crime Congresses) on a large variety of issues.

The participants at UN Crime Commission sessions will have before them extensive documentation produced by the UNODC which are usually made available in advance in all six UN working languages on the unodc.org website. As with the formal agenda, many of these documents follow the same standardized format, and provide background for the discussion of the respective items on the agenda.

The final stage of work at UN meetings involves the *adoption of the report*. The Secretariat generally assists the rapporteur in this process, and the draft text is usually very carefully constructed to provide an impartial summary of the discussions.

BOX 4.2   THE DRAFTING OF UN CRIME PROGRAMME MEETING REPORTS

Drafting UN meeting reports can be called an art in its own right. UN meetings often deal with sensitive points, and the rapporteur (assisted by the Secretariat) seeks to present these in a way that would be acceptable to the different sides on the issues. With some exceptions (such as heads of state or other distinguished speakers) it is not customary for speakers to be identified in the report, even by Member State. The reference will be simply to "one speaker noted" or "several speakers suggested that ...."

Many participants, who may be exhausted by the lengthy negotiations, may assume that the adoption of the report will be a formality. However, on particularly sensitive issues, some representatives may try to expand the presentation of the arguments that their side had made, thus correspondingly diminishing the amount of attention given to opposing points of view. One technique used here is for a representative to argue that their country's position, as given earlier, was not correctly reflected in the report, and then submit a (lengthy) proposal for amending the report to remedy this. The chairperson usually accepts short amendments along these lines. Given that this may, indeed, give a one-sided impression of the discussion, representatives from the other side on the issues may wish to make corresponding amendments based on points made in the discussions by other speakers supporting their views.

4.4   The Conferences of the States Parties of the two UN Crime Conventions

The governing structures of the two UN Crime Conventions steer the respective work of the Member States that are States Parties to the conventions:

- the Conference of the Parties to the UN Convention against Transnational Organized Crime (COP) (https://www.unodc.org/unodc/en/organized-crime/intro/UNTOC.html); and
- the Conference of the States Parties to the UN Convention against Corruption (CoSP) (https://www.unodc.org/unodc/en/treaties/CAC/index.html).

Five working groups have been established under the mandate of the COP of the UN Convention against Transnational Organized Crime (UNTOC) and two working groups as well as one expert group under the mandate of the CoSP of the UN Convention against Corruption (UNCAC), in order to discuss particular topics related to the conventions. Three of the UNTOC working groups deal with each of the three protocols (trafficking in persons, the smuggling of migrants, and trafficking in firearms). A fourth UNTOC working group deals with international cooperation, and a fifth with technical assistance. The UN-CAC working groups deal, respectively, with prevention and asset recovery, and there is an expert group that deals with international cooperation.

The respective Conferences of the States Parties are convened in alternate years. For example, the COP for UNTOC will meet in 2024, followed by the CoSP for UNCAC in 2025. The working groups under the two Conferences, however, generally meet annually.

The work of the Conferences somewhat overlaps with the work of the UN Crime Commission related to, respectively, transnational organized crime and corruption. However, each have somewhat different constituencies (not all UN Member States are parties to UNTOC or its protocols, or to UNCAC), and there are significant differences in the legal obligations involved. The two UN Crime Conventions consist of "hard law," whereas the UN Crime Commission operates on the basis of consensus in its negotiation largely of soft law resolutions and declarations.

4.5   Resolutions, documents, and meeting reports in the UN Crime Programme

Resolutions

With the facilitation of the UNODC, the work of the main structures in the UN Crime Programme (UN Crime Commission and the Conferences of the States Parties to the two UN Crime Conventions), often focuses on the drafting of resolutions. Resolutions are important for a variety of reasons.

On the substantive level, a resolution (when adopted) embodies the sense of the Member States regarding such issues as what are the priority issues in crime prevention and criminal justice, and what should be done by the international community in general. They can, for example, call the attention of the Member States, and the international community as a whole, to the emergence of new challenges, such as the difficulties faced by prisoners with a Covid-19 infection.

On the aspirational level, a resolution may express the collective will of the body adopting the resolution to call upon Member States, or to invite other actors (such as intergovernmental organizations) to take specific action.

On the political level, a resolution may be used to promote a certain political agenda: condemn certain developments, action taken or incidents, welcome other developments, stress the importance of certain principles, and so on.

On the practical level, a resolution often requests that the Secretariat take specific action such as prepare a report, organize a meeting or provide certain assistance to Member States on request.

Finally, on the linguistic level, and as a document reflecting the outcome of UN negotiations, the phrasing and terminology used in resolutions often becomes "agreed language," which may well be referred to in future negotiations.

During the negotiation of draft resolutions, considerable attention is paid to the exact wording. For example, while the UN Crime Commission (and ECOSOC as well as the General Assembly) can "request" that the Secretary-General carry out certain activities, it is (with certain exceptions) not seen to have the mandate to "request" that Member States do or refrain from doing certain activities. To do so would be widely seen as a violation of article 2(7) of the UN Charter, which prohibits the UN from intervening in matters which are essentially within the domestic jurisdiction of a State. Instead, the Commission may, for example, "invite," "encourage" or "urge" Member States to take certain action.

The basic process of the consideration of draft resolutions consists of the following phases:

- a Member State formulates the purpose and content of the envisaged draft resolution, and (preferably) the first draft version for circulation;
- the Member State conducts initial informal consultations with at least some of the key delegations to solicit their views and comments and, ideally, their tentative promise to serve as *sponsors* of the draft in the negotiations, or otherwise to provide support;[13]
- the draft resolution is formally *tabled*, after which it will be translated into all the official UN languages and distributed;
- informal negotiations are conducted with all "interested Member States." These are closed negotiations, which may generally be attended only by

representatives of Member States. Other individuals may be present, if the other participants agree;

- presentation of the results of the informal negotiations in the Committee of the Whole (perhaps with an updated "clean copy" of the text of the draft resolution, as amended); this stage may involve further negotiations; and
- the results of the negotiations are submitted to the plenary for adoption.

The informal negotiations will generally not have the benefit of interpretation into all of the official UN languages. The considerations in the Committee of the Whole and in plenary, in turn, will have interpretation.

The negotiation of draft resolutions can be quite time-consuming, and some sessions of the UN Crime Commission and the Conferences of the States Parties have been marked by very lengthy negotiations on multiple draft resolutions that last far into the night (and even to the early morning). Generally, the negotiations do lead to the adoption of the draft resolution, although often with extensive amendments in "compromise language." If towards the end of a session it appears that consensus on the draft resolution will not be reached (or could be reached only with substantive amendments that do not meet the interests of the sponsors of the draft), the draft resolution may be withdrawn.

BOX 4.3   TERMS USED IN ADOPTING RESOLUTIONS AND IN REFERRING TO OTHER INSTRUMENTS, EVENTS, AND DEVELOPMENTS

One of the peculiarities of "UN English" is that commonly used words may have a specific meaning in the UN. For example, the words *adoption* and *approval* – which most lay observers would regard as synonyms – have specific meanings in the context of the life of a draft resolution.

The UN Crime Commission can (a) *adopt* a resolution (in which case it goes no further up the UN hierarchy), (b) *recommend* to ECOSOC the *adoption* of a resolution (in which case it would become an ECOSOC resolution), or (c) *recommend* to ECOSOC the *approval* of a draft resolution for *adoption* by the GA.

Things can become even more esoteric when a (draft) resolution requests that a body (such as the UN Crime Commission, ECOSOC, or the GA) *endorses* an instrument (such as a standard and norm), event, or development that has been submitted for its consideration or otherwise brought to its attention. Quite often, the body in question will do so. However, if some influential Member States are not fully in support of this instrument, event, or development (but not to the extent that they will block any reference to it in a resolution), other words can and have been used.

At sessions of the UN Crime Commission, this situation arises occasionally in the drafting of a resolution. A Member State may, for example, have organized a meeting on a subject related to the theme of the draft resolution in question, and want the UN Crime Commission to acknowledge the beneficial contribution of this meeting. Other Member States may be less appreciative. If they are not able to have the entire reference deleted, then they may seek a word that conveys something less than full-throated endorsement. Among the alternatives that have been used, in rough order of descending favourability, are "recommends," "welcomes," "takes note with appreciation," "takes note with satisfaction," and the rock-bottom but diplomatic "takes note." (A separate issue is how references are formulated when Member States refer in a negative way to events or developments. Here, again, there are different gradations, such as "noting with concern," "noting with grave concern," "noting with alarm," to "condemning.")

Clark (1994, pp. 137–141) provides several examples of the different language that the GA has used when adopting a resolution incorporating a standard and norm, or in otherwise acknowledging a resolution of another body (generally, the UN Crime Congress) that incorporates a standard and norm.

UNODC documentation and UN Crime Programme meeting reports

One of the major functions of the UNODC is to prepare documentation for the consideration of UN Crime Programme meetings, such as the sessions of the UN Crime Commission, the UN Crime Congresses, and the Conferences of the States Parties to the two UN Crime Conventions. The result is a steady flow of information that has been collected and processed by the Secretariat.

The documentation, which is usually of a very high quality, seeks to provide the conceptual framework for the expected discussion, set out briefly the state of knowledge on the relevant issues, describe what action has been taken, and possibly suggest for consideration what action should be taken. This is a challenging task for several reasons, not least because of the fairly stringent limits on the length of documents that have been imposed in order to keep down the costs of translating and processing the documents into the six official languages.

The final stage of work at UN Crime Programme meetings involves the *adoption of the report*. The Secretariat generally assists the rapporteur in the drafting of the report, and the draft text is usually very carefully constructed to provide what should be an impartial summary of the discussions.

In addition to documentation connected directly with UN Crime Programme meetings, the UNODC has produced, at an increasing pace since the turn of the millennium, many *manuals, handbooks, training materials, reports,* and *compendiums* that are intended to be used in technical assistance projects (https://www.unodc.org/unodc/en/international-cooperation/publications.html). These include:

- model legislation that can be used to give technical assistance in different legal systems in the implementation of the two UN Crime Conventions;
- manuals and handbooks on how to prevent, investigate, and prosecute specific offences (such as trafficking in persons and the smuggling of migrants),
- digests of legal cases showing how different courts have dealt with criminal cases related to the UN Crime Conventions, and
- manuals and handbooks on different aspects of international legal cooperation (such as mutual legal assistance, extradition, the transfer of prisoners, the recovery of assets).[14]

The UNODC continues to produce excellent research publications. Special reference can be made to the annual *Global Report on Trafficking in Persons,* and the *Global Studies on Homicide* and the *World Wildlife Crime Reports.* Reports on different aspects of transnational organized crime, from different regions, have also been published.[15]

Notes

1 The main functions and powers of ECOSOC are defined in article 62 of the UN Charter.
2 The three Committees are the First (Economic) Committee, the Second (Social) Committee, and the Third (Programme and Co-ordination) Committee.
3 The main functions of the GA are defined in articles 10–17 of the UN Charter.
   There is no hard-and-fast rule on what policy pronouncements remain on the level of ECOSOC and which go on to the GA. There are at least two countervailing pressures. On the one hand, the GA does not necessarily want to take on additional matters, since all of this requires time and money to process. On the other hand, the sponsors of various proposals that have been adopted by the UN Crime Commission often regard these as sufficiently important to go not only through ECOSOC, but all the way up to the GA.
   Clark, 1994, pp. 134–135 notes that a resolution of the GA carries more "moral authority" than a resolution of ECOSOC.
4 Clark, 1994, pp. 81–83, provides useful information on the context of discussions at the Third Committee.
5 For further information, see unodc.org
6 The three drug control conventions are: the Single Convention on Narcotic Drugs of 1961, as amended by the 1972 Protocol; the Convention on Psychotropic Substances of 1971; and the UN Convention against Illicit Traffic in Narcotic Drugs and Psychotropic Substances of 1988.
7 In 1958, the Bureau of Social Affairs had eight professional officers and one professional assistant working on social defence questions (E/CN.5/329, 1958, para. 14).
   For example, in 1982 the Crime Prevention and Criminal Justice Branch consisted of the Assistant Director (a D-1 position), the interregional advisor, and nine other professional staff members. Letter from the Crime Prevention and Criminal

Justice Branch to the Finnish Permanent Mission, 20 August 1982 (on file with the author). In 1989, the number of professional staff members had been reduced from eleven to eight. Joutsen, 1989, p. 17.

    Clifford, pp. 5–6, argues that placing this Secretariat unit in the social division of the UN Secretariat contributed to its marginal position. In the early years of the UN, the UN Secretariat was essentially divided into an economic and a social division. In Clifford's words, the economic division gradually "swamped" the social division, which consequently lost influence. Even within the social division, the Social Defence Unit had a low priority.

8 This, however, is only an estimate. The UNODC currently has a total of 2,400 professional and secretarial staff members at the headquarters in Vienna and at field and regional offices around the world. It is difficult to assess precisely how many staff members deal with drug control issues and how many with crime prevention and criminal justice issues, because the UN border management and container control programmes serve both areas.

9 Now known as the Division for Social Policy and Development.

10 The move from New York was opposed by many in the Branch, and by developing countries that did not have a mission in Vienna. There was an extensive debate on this at the UN Crime Committee session held in August 1980. The debate was brought to a close when a senior representative from the Secretariat observed (perhaps with some bemusement) that the Division for Social Development and Humanitarian Affairs had already packed up and moved to Vienna. See the report of the UN Crime Committee, E/1980/112, paras. 39–41.

11 A detailed presentation of the work of the Commission is provided in Ram, 2012a. The author was one of the last to serve on the Committee and was actively involved in drafting the plans for the transition from the Committee to the Commission.

12 Representatives of specialized agencies, PNIs, intergovernmental organizations, and non-governmental organizations may take the floor only if no State wishes to do so. In practice, this means that their contribution to the debate has become indirect and rather marginal.

13 In principal, once a Member State has agreed to co-sponsor a draft resolution, its agreement should be secured before making any amendments to the draft.

14 The UN Crime Programme has also adopted a number of different model agreements. See https://www.unodc.org/unodc/en/international-cooperation/publications.html

15 See Chapter 12.

References

Acackpo-Satchivi, Joseph (1990), The Economic and Social Council, *UNAFEI Resource Materials Series*, vol. 38, UNAFEI, pp. 197–204

Clark, Roger S. (1994), *The United Nations Crime Prevention and Criminal Justice Program. Formulation of Standards and Efforts at Their Implementation*. University of Pennsylvania Press

Clifford, William (1979), *Echoes and Hopes. The United Nations Committee on Crime Prevention and Control*, Australian Institute of Criminology, Canberra, available at https://www.aic.gov.au/sites/default/files/2020-07/echoes-and-hopes.pdf

Joutsen, Matti (1989), Assessment of the United Nations Crime and Criminal Justice Programme, Memorandum for the Subcommittee established by the United Nations Committee on Crime Prevention and Control, 20 March 1989, unpublished paper (on file with the author)

López-Rey de Arroya, Manuel (1985), *A Guide to United Nations Criminal Policy*, Cambridge Studies in Criminology LIV

Ram, Christopher (2012a), *Meeting the Challenge of Crime in the Global Village: An Assessment of the Role and Future of the United Nations Commission on the Crime Prevention and Criminal Justice*, HEUNI publication no. 73

Ram, Christopher (2012b), The Commission on Crime Prevention and Criminal Justice: A Search for Complementarity Between Politics and Criminology, in Slawomir Redo, *Blue Criminology. The Power of United Nations Ideas to Counter Crime Globally – A Monographic Study*, HEUNI publication no. 72, pp. 128–131

Vetere, Eduardo (1995), The Work of the United Nations in Crime Prevention and Criminal Justice, in M. Cherif Bassiouni, *The Contributions of Specialized Institutes and Non-Governmental Organizations to the United Nations Criminal Justice Programme. In Honour of Adolfo Beria di Argentine*, Brill Publishers, pp. 15–63

5

MEMBER STATES, SPECIALIZED AGENCIES, INTERGOVERNMENTAL ORGANIZATIONS, AND EXPERTS

5.1   The main actors: the Member States

The Member States are the most important units in the UN Crime Programme. This is evident in the formulation of GA resolution 46/152, which defines the mandate of the UN Crime Commission as helping *Member States* to prevent crime and to improve the response to crime.

The importance of Member States is increased by the fact that the UN Crime Commission consists of 40 Member States elected by ECOSOC and by the fact that the budget of the UN to conduct this work comes almost entirely from assessments from Member States (the regular UN budget) and from so-called extra-budgetary (voluntary) funds, which are also largely from Member States.

In the UN Crime Programme, the political "weight" of a Member State in discussions at the UN Crime Commission, the UN Crime Congress, or the Conferences of the States Parties to the two UN Crime Conventions is often of less importance than the professional competence and negotiating skill of the individual representative of the Member State in question. Small and large Member States alike have experience, insights, and national concerns to share. The "Spirit of Vienna" that seeks consensus on all issues at UN Crime Programme meetings, without the need to resort to a vote, underlines the importance of getting the cooperation of all Member States.

Given the crowded calendar of the UN Crime Programme, with meetings taking place on average once a month, the fact that most meetings tend to last only two or three days and the fact that only representatives of "least developed countries" have their attendance paid to formal UN meetings by the UN Secretariat mean that fewer and fewer Member States are sending

DOI: 10.4324/9781003480907-7

substantive experts "from the capitals" to attend the meetings. As a result, much of the work of the UN Crime Programme is conducted by diplomatic representatives of the permanent missions based in Vienna.

The representatives of the missions tend to be posted in Vienna for only a few years (depending on the Member State, generally from three to six) before they are rotated to other postings. For this reason, the influence of any one representative will depend on several factors, among the most important of which are their personal and negotiating skills; how interested they are in the UN Crime Programme; how familiar they are with the operation of the UN, with international negotiations, and with crime prevention and criminal justice issues; and how large the mission in question is. (With small missions, individual representatives need to cover several different issues and will often not be able to attend more than selected meetings on the UN Crime Programme agenda.)

As has been noted, now that various UN meetings are held on almost a monthly basis, fewer and fewer Member States – especially those located long distances away – are prepared to send "experts from the capitals" to attend two- or three-day meetings. As a result, the burden is shifting to the diplomatic representatives of the missions, who have negotiating skills and are familiar with the general UN context but on substantive issues on crime and criminal justice often have to rely on written positions sent from the capitals – written positions which may become irrelevant as the negotiations in Vienna proceed.

In the past few years, there appears to have been a resurgence in the attendance of "experts from the capitals" at UN Crime Programme meetings. Among the reasons for this may have been the increase in the number of technical meetings which require substantive expertise, as well as the organization of "side events" sessions at the UN Crime Commission. A second factor may have been a growing awareness among some Member States of the need to combine expertise from the capitals with the negotiating skills of the diplomatic representatives.

In order to promote regional coordination as well as what is known as equitable geographical representation through the UN system, the 193 Member States have been divided into *regional groups* as follows (https://www.un.org/dgacm/en/content/regional-groups):

- the African Group, with 54 Member States;
- the Asia-Pacific Group, with 53 Member States;
- the Eastern European Group, with 23 Member States;
- the Latin American and Caribbean Group (GRULAC), with 33 Member States; and
- the Western European and others Group (WEOG), with 28 Member States, plus one Member State (the United States) as an observer state.[1]

A variety of other regional groupings exist within the UN. Two important ones (in the sense that they engage in regional consultations during sessions of the UN Crime Commission and their respective spokesperson may give statements) are the G-77 + China (an organization of developing countries, with 134 members)[2] and the EU (with 27 members).[3]

As a rule, if any Member State in a regional group objects to the proposed position, there is no consolidated regional position. Should agreement be reached on the regional position, this is presented by the chairperson of the group, after which individual Member States will ask for the floor to offer further arguments. The protocol is that when representatives of individual States speak for the first time after their respective regional group, they begin by emphasizing that they align themselves with the position of the regional group.

5.2 Specialized UN agencies

A number of specialized UN agencies (such as the International Labour Organization, the International Organization for Migration, the World Health Organization, and UN Women) may have an interest in the topics on the agenda of the various UN Crime Programme meetings, in which case they often participate as observers. Strictly speaking, a "specialized UN agency" is an autonomous organization that works with the UN (and other agencies) under the coordination of ECOSOC. However, at times various units of the UN Secretariat itself (such as the UN Development Programme) will send representatives to UN Crime Programme meeting and be listed as a "specialized UN agency."[4]

At UN Crime Congresses and sessions of the UN Crime Commission, the PNIs (see Chapter 7) have generally been classified as belonging to the category of specialized UN agencies. They participate as observers.

5.3 Intergovernmental organizations

According to UN legislation, an intergovernmental organization is one in which the members are national governments. The UN itself is the best-known example. Other intergovernmental organizations that have played an important role in the crime prevention and criminal justice sector are the Council of Europe, the Organization of American States, the African Union, the League of Arab States, the EU, Interpol, and Europol.[5]

Intergovernmental organizations participate in many UN Crime Programme meetings as observers.

5.4 Individual experts

The large majority of persons attending UN Crime Programme meetings represent a Member State or an organization. However, individual experts have played, and continue to play, a role in the UN Crime Programme.

As noted in section 2.3, individual experts, appointed in their personal capacity, advised the Secretary-General during the early years of the UN Crime Programme, first as members of an ad hoc committee of experts, and then as members of the UN Crime Committee.

Experts form a recognized category of participants at UN Crime Congresses. This is a continuation of the tradition of international conferences of experts organized by the International Penal and Penitentiary Commission. At the first five Congresses which took place up to 1975, experts invited by the Secretary-General even presented lectures as part of the formal programme.

Individual practitioners and academics continue to be active in various technical assistance projects and in the drafting of manuals and other documentation being prepared by the UNODC and the PNIs.

Notes

1 The "others" in the "Western European and others" group are Australia, Canada, Israel, New Zealand, and the United States. Strictly speaking, the United States is an observer in the WEOG group. However, for practical purposes, such as in allotting positions in the bureau, it is considered a member.
2 The Group of 77 + China was established in 1964. It has traditionally been active in negotiations in Vienna.
3 Following the entry of the Lisbon Treaty into force in 2009 and the adoption of the EU's Common Foreign and Security Policy, the position of the EU has generally been presented by the European External Action Service.
4 The most recent UN Crime Congress, the Fourteenth, used the following separate sub-categories of specialized UN agencies: the UN; representatives of UN Secretariat units; UN bodies and agencies; the UN Interregional Institute, affiliated regional institutes and centres of the UN Crime Prevention and Criminal Justice Programme Network; and specialized agencies.
5 Although the International Criminal Police Organization is usually listed in this category, strictly speaking it is not intergovernmental, as its membership consists of the criminal police entities of different countries.

6

NON-GOVERNMENTAL
ORGANIZATIONS

6.1   Non-governmental organizations in the UN in general

The role of non-governmental organizations in the UN in general, and in the UN Crime Programme in particular, has evolved considerably over the years, and has at times (including at present) been a source of tension (Willets, 1996; Joutsen, 2018).

When the UN was founded in 1945 as an intergovernmental organization, non-governmental organizations successfully lobbied for a provision in the UN Charter that permits non-governmental organizations to seek consultative status with ECOSOC (Willets, 2000, p. 191 and *passim*). Article 71 of the UN Charter states:

> The Economic and Social Council may make suitable arrangements for consultation with non-governmental organizations which are concerned with matters within its competence. Such arrangements may be made with international organizations and, where appropriate, with national organizations after consultation with the Member of the United Nations concerned.

On the basis of Article 71 of the UN Charter, a distinction continues to be made between non-governmental organizations with consultative status with ECOSOC, and other non-governmental organizations. Those with consultative status have a standing invitation to attend sessions of the UN Crime Commission and the UN Crime Congresses, whereas other non-governmental organizations need to apply to the UN Secretariat for an invitation to attend.

DOI: 10.4324/9781003480907-8

As with specialized agencies and intergovernmental organizations, non-governmental organizations participate in UN Crime Programme meetings as observers. Their involvement can be traced back to the very first years of the UN (Clark, 1994, p. 92 and *passim*).[1] The UN Crime Commission operates, and its forerunner the UN Crime Committee operated, under ECOSOC rules of procedure (www.ohchr.org/Documents/HRBodies/CHR/RoP.pdf), which recognize non-governmental organizations as a specific category of participants.

Non-governmental organizations have been very active in the work of the UN Crime Programme. Some have cooperated with the UNODC and the PNIs in capacity-building and technical assistance. Others have contributed to the formulation of UN standards and norms. Several have participated at UN Crime Programme meetings, providing substantive contributions, including in the organization of ancillary meetings and side events.

Article 71 of the UN Charter makes a distinction between international non-governmental organizations and national non-governmental organizations. An "international non-governmental organization " is an organization that functions in more than one country but is not founded on an international treaty (ECOSOC resolution 288 (X) of 27 February 1950).[2] A "national non-governmental organization" is one that is based in one country. It can be granted consultative status only if it is not a member of an international non-governmental organization or it has "special experience" to offer to ECOSOC. Furthermore, as required by the wording of Article 71, the views of the host Member State of a national non-governmental organization are to be obtained when deciding whether or not to grant a national non-governmental organization consultative status.[3] In the past ECOSOC's preference has been for international non-governmental organization, and up to the 1990s very few national non-governmental organizations were granted consultative status (Willets, 1996, p. 2). Since the mid-1990s, however, national non-governmental organizations have been encouraged to apply for consultative status (Willets, 2000, p. 192).

Under ECOSOC rules, there are three categories of non-governmental organizations with consultative status: "general," "special," and "roster." As described by Redo (J. Redo, 2012, p. 125),

> Those in general consultative status, 'broadly representative' and 'concerned with most of the activities of the Council' must document that their programme outreach and delivery is cross-sectorial. Those in special consultative status, i.e. 'organizations with special competence' in a few ECOSOC fields, should make contributions to the development of the United Nations Crime Prevention and Criminal Justice Programme. Those on the roster 'can make occasional and useful contributions.'

According to the ordinary meaning of the word, when you "consult" with someone on a matter, you discuss this matter with that person or organization in order to obtain their advice or opinion. It would therefore seem to be enough to fulfil the requirements of Article 71 to simply send a letter or an email to an organization that has consultative status with ECOSOC, asking it to submit its opinion in writing, which could then be distributed to the representatives of the Member States attending ECOSOC sessions. However, from the very first days of the work of the UN, the distinction between arrangements for consultation and participation without vote in the deliberations of ECOSOC "has been blurred in practice: NGOs have obtained some participation rights that go beyond consultation, whereas governments have usually prevented NGOS from gaining the same rights as observers" (Willets, 2000, pp. 191–192).

The visible participation of non-governmental organizations in ECOSOC has of course been noted by governments, and has been a source of criticism by some governments. *Which* NGOs participate and *how* they participate have been long-standing subjects for debate. Willets provides a historical account of the political tensions involved in accrediting non-governmental organizations, as well of the evolution of the right of non-governmental organizations to participate. He notes, for example, how the Cold War led the two opposing blocs to put forward their own proxies for consultative status with ECOSOC and to seek to prevent proxy non-governmental organizations put forward by the other side from gaining such status. He also notes how votes were forced on whether or not to grant consultative status to some human rights groups and Jewish and Catholic groups on the grounds that they were "politically motivated," and that the initial practice of allowing non-governmental organizations to submit items for the agenda of sessions of ECOSOC was soon discontinued (Willets, 1996, pp. 5–10).

Willets also notes that although the UN Charter does not grant non-governmental organizations a similar consultative status to other UN bodies, non-governmental organizations "have encroached substantially on the General Assembly; and they are starting to appear on the fringes of the Security Council." The first signs of this were apparent in the early 1960s in the Special Committee on Decolonization, the Special Committee Against Apartheid, and the Committee on Palestinian Rights (Willets, 2000, pp. 196–199). In view of the issues that were debated at these Special Committees, it is understandable that entities other than recognized governments had a political interest in being heard.

On its website (https://www.unodc.org/unodc/en/ngos/DCN0-NGOs-and-civil-society.html) the UNODC provides more examples of non-governmental organization involvement in UN bodies other than ECOSOC:

> The UN General Assembly has on many occasions invited NGOs to participate in the work of its committees and some NGO leaders have been invited

to address plenary sessions. NGOs have been active in the First Committee on disarmament issues, in the Third Committee on human rights matters, and in the GA High Level Dialogue on Financing for Development (FfD) for the follow-up to the Monterrey Conference. NGOs are also very active in a number of commissions, including the Commission on Sustainable Development, the Commission on Social Development, and the Commission on the Status of Women. The constructive and vital NGO role in the creation and support for the International Criminal Court is evident to all.

In addition to the GA, the Security Council, and ECOSOC, much work of the UN is conducted in conferences. Willets has also traced a long-term strengthening of the role of non-governmental organizations. In his view, non-governmental organization participation at conferences and, more importantly, in decision-making at conferences has increased in that

[a]ccess to decision-making has changed from a limited role in the main plenary bodies to significant influence in the committees, to NGO representatives quite often taking part in the small working groups where the more difficult questions are thrashed out. In some fields, such as human rights, population planning, and sustainable development, NGOs have changed from being peripheral advisers of secondary status in the diplomatic system to being high-status participants at the center of policymaking.
(Willets, 2000, pp. 193–194)[4]

Examining the status of non-governmental organizations overall in 2000, Willets (2000, p. 205) came to the conclusion that, as a result of Article 71 of the UN Charter and three major reviews, non-governmental organization participation in ECOSOC has become part of customary international law:

When the UN was formed, it was an established norm that the subjects of international law were states. In diplomatic practice and in academic analysis, it used to be taken for granted that international relations consisted solely of the relations between states. Now such a position cannot be argued. ... the only accurate way to describe what has happened is to recognize that [international] NGOs have become a third category of subjects in international law, alongside of states and intergovernmental organizations.[5]

Willets also stresses that the influence of non-governmental organizations arises from three factors: non-governmental organization access to documents, non-governmental organization access to the buildings in which sessions are held (thus giving them access to the delegates when these are not in closed meetings), and the legitimacy that ECOSOC consultative status gives non-governmental organizations (Willets, 1996, p. 10).

As noted, Willets was writing in the year 2000. This was soon after a review of the consultative status of non-governmental organizations at ECOSOC. ECOSOC resolution 1296 of 1968 was replaced by resolution 1996/31 adopted in 1996, which, among other things, made it easier for national non-governmental organizations to become accredited. The UN Non-Governmental Liaison Service (https://www.un-ngls.org/index.php/11-engage-with-the-un) is of the view that

UN-NGOs relationships changed profoundly in the 1990's, both quantitatively and qualitatively. The involvement of NGOs in the UN-organized world conferences, in particular, marked a turning point. Tony Hill talks about a "second generation" of UN-NGOs relations. This generation "is marked by the much larger scale of the NGO presence across the UN system, the more diverse institutional character of the organizations involved, now including national, regional and international NGOs, networks, coalitions and alliances, and the greater diversity of the issues that NGOs seek to address at the UN. Above all, the second generation of UN-NGOs relations are essentially political and reflect the motivation of NGOs to engage with the UN as part of the institutional architecture of global governance.

The need to strengthen cooperation between the UN and non-governmental organizations has been underlined in various UN documents since the beginning of this century, in particular in the Millennium Declaration of September 2000, but also in the 2005 World Summit Outcome Document (GA resolution 60/1, paras. 172–174).

In 2004, Secretary-General Kofi Annan set up a panel of experts which was asked to formulate recommendations to strengthen the interactions between the UN and civil society. This resulted in the Cardoso Report (A/58/817). Following the Cardoso Report, the Secretary-General issued a set of proposals to bring greater coherence and consistency to UN-non-governmental organization relations. These include simplifying the accreditation process, increasing financial support for the participation of southern non-governmental organizations, improving country-level engagement of UN representatives with non-governmental organizations, and opening up the GA further to non-governmental organizations. Since the Cardoso Report, some concrete developments have taken place; for example, the GA has started to hold informal hearings. A trust fund has also been established to support the work of UN country teams with civil society.

Once the GA had adopted the SDGs in 2015, these came to provide a potential framework for strengthened cooperation between Member States and non-governmental organizations at the local, national, regional, and even global level.

6.2 Evolution of the role of non-governmental organizations in the UN Crime Programme

In the first years of the UN Crime Programme, it was difficult to discern where the line should be drawn between the activity of formal UN structures and non-governmental organization activity. This was due to the fact that both the ad hoc advisory group of experts and the UN Crime Committee (which was replaced by the government-dominated UN Crime Commission in 1992) had a large number of participants who were appointed by the Secretary-General in their personal capacity and were active in various non-governmental organizations. The first advisory group of experts appointed in 1948 consisted of six persons, of whom one (Mr. Stanford Bates, of the United States) was the president and a second (Professor Thorsten Sellin, also of the United States) was the soon-to-be elected Secretary-General, re-spectively, of the International Penal and Penitentiary Commission (IPPC) (Clifford, 1979, p. 8). This dominance of IPPC figures was undoubtedly due largely to the imminent transfer of the responsibility of IPPC functions to the UN, yet another direct connection between formal UN structures and non-governmental organization activity.

A review of the experts appointed as UN Crime Committee members until it was dissolved in 1992 would show that academics and practitioners con-tinued to be well represented, and these academics and practitioners were usually also active members of international non-governmental organiza-tions in the field of crime prevention and criminal justice.[6]

Prior to the restructuring of the UN Crime Programme in 1991–1992, the role of non-governmental organizations had been quite discernible in the drafting of the UN standards and norms on crime prevention and criminal justice, beginning with the first such standard and norm, the Standard Mini-mum Rules on the Treatment of Prisoners (SMRs), which was adopted by the General Assembly in 1955. The SMRs had, indeed, been drafted under the auspices of the IPPC (Röstad, 1985, p. 85). During the time of the UN Crime Committee, other standards and norms were generally drafted by outside experts, who often worked together with various non-governmental organi-zations and academic institutions that were active in respect of the subject matter of the draft. These drafts were then submitted to a UN Crime Con-gress for approval and action.[7]

Currently, however, new standards and norms are generally drafted at UNODC expert meetings and intergovernmental ad hoc expert meetings con-vened in accordance with a mandate given by the UN Crime Commission. The draft will then be submitted to the UN Crime Commission for action.

Four international non-governmental organizations in particular should be mentioned in connection with the early evolution of the UN Crime Programme. The International Penal and Penitentiary Foundation,[8] the

International Association of Penal Law, the International Society of Criminology, and the International Society for Social Defence and Humane Criminal Policy (known collectively within the UN Crime Programme as the "Big Four") are international non-governmental organizations that bring together academics and practitioners with an interest in crime prevention and criminal justice (Joutsen, 1996).[9] Although the four have somewhat different membership and orientation profiles, for many years there was very close networking (and extensive overlap) among the members of the governing boards of these four organizations, the membership of the UN Crime Commission (and earlier, the UN Crime Committee), and the UN Secretariat. For a period stretching from roughly the late 1970s to the early 1990s, there was even an effort to align the main themes of the international conferences of the "Big Four" with the theme and agenda items of the subsequent UN Crime Congresses, and to avoid conflicts in the scheduling of these major events.[10] From 1963 to the mid-1990s, the Big Four held joint conferences that focused on one of the main agenda items of the following UN Crime Congress (Röstad, 1985, pp. 87–88 and Joutsen, 1996).[11]

In addition to the Big Four, many other non-governmental organizations have been, and are, actively involved in crime prevention and criminal justice. The International Scientific and Professional Advisory Council (ISPAC) was established in 1991 to serve as a structure for networking among these non-governmental organizations and academic institutions interested in the work of the UN Crime Programme (Clark, 1994, pp. 92–94).[12] For many years, ISPAC hosted annual coordination meetings of the UN PNIs in Courmayeur, Italy.

More broadly, alliances of non-governmental organizations with ECOSOC consultative and associated status have been established in both New York (1972) and Vienna (1983) (J. Redo, 2012, p. 126).

The role of non-governmental organizations has been particularly strong at the UN Crime Congresses, since the first such Congress held in 1955. As already noted, these Congresses continue a tradition established by the IPPC 150 years ago. Until the Fifth UN Congress in 1975, non-governmental organizations even had the right to vote at UN Crime Congresses "for consultative purposes" (S. Redo, 2012, p. 112).

An expanding part of the UN Crime Congresses has been the so-called ancillary meetings, which are generally organized by non-governmental organizations (Clark, 1994, pp. 78–79). The same is true of many of the side events organized at sessions of the UN Crime Commission.

Consequently, it can be concluded that there has traditionally been less political tension over non-governmental organization within the UN Crime Programme participation than Willets has found in ECOSOC, the GA, and the Security Council.

The stress in the previous paragraph, however, should be on the word *traditionally*. In the course of the past three decades, some national delegations have expressed increasing concern regarding non-governmental organization participation in the work of the UN Crime Programme.

The first signs of tension arose in connection with the restructuring of the UN Crime Programme, in particular with the replacement of the UN Crime Committee (consisting of experts serving in their personal capacity) by the UN Crime Commission (consisting of 40 Member States elected by ECOSOC). As noted in section 3.1, among the arguments put forward in support of a shift to a government-dominated UN Crime Programme was that the expert-driven UN Crime Committee had engaged in excessive drafting of soft law (standards and norms, usually with non-governmental organization support) and the national governments had not had sufficient input.[13]

There was also a debate during the first sessions of the UN Crime Commission as to whether or not to recognize the body of standards and norms that had been produced under the UN Crime Committee or whether these could be treated with "benign neglect," largely on the grounds that they had not been drafted with sufficient input from Member States. As a result of these debates, however, the Commission submitted to ECOSOC a draft resolution on the standards and norms which reaffirmed the important contribution that the use and application of this soft law make to criminal justice systems. ECOSOC adopted this draft without amendment as resolution 1994/18.[14]

After that initial debate on the status of the standards and norms, many years passed without any perceptible tensions regarding non-governmental organization participation in the UN Crime Programme.

This situation changed significantly as a result of a disagreement that arose over the mechanism for the review of the implementation of the UN Convention against Corruption (UNCAC). As noted in section 3.3, the disagreement was originally over the participation of non-governmental organizations as observers in the Implementation Review Group and in other UNCAC subsidiary bodies set up by the Conference of the States Parties to UNCAC. The disagreement arose because for the first time in relation to a UN treaty the UNCAC review mechanism incorporated peer review in which experts from two States Parties assess the implementation of the treaty in the State Party under review. To some government representatives, this appeared to have elements of intervention into matters which are essentially within the domestic jurisdiction of a sovereign State, something which is prohibited by article 2(7) of the UN Charter.

The issue of corruption in itself is sensitive and is often used in internal political campaigns, quite commonly with those not in power claiming that those in power are corrupt and should be voted out of office. In addition, many governments were concerned that reports of corruption in their country may not just have a negative impact on investment but may also cause general reputational damage. Several international (and national) non-governmental organizations are active in anti-corruption. As part of their public advocacy for anti-corruption reforms, they often conduct studies and surveys and report on individual cases of corruption. The annual "corruption perception index" reports put out by Transparency International have been a particular source of criticism (https://www.transparency.org/research/cpi/overview).

The debate was a quite heated one, and continues to this day.[15] As noted in section 3.3, it has so far produced a tenuous compromise on the basis of which non-governmental organizations may not participate in the meetings of the Implementation Review Group (IRG) or of the other working groups set up by the Conference of States Parties. A "briefing" is organized for the non-governmental organizations in connection with the annual meetings of the IRG. The UNCAC Conference of States Parties has called for a continuous dialogue on this issue. At numerous UNCAC meetings, some States Parties supporting a more visible role for non-governmental organizations in the mechanism have returned to this issue and the need for a continuous dialogue (whether or not the issue is featured on the agenda of the meeting), while those opposing a more visible role for non-governmental organizations have responded by referring to the decisions already taken at sessions of the Conference of the States Parties in Doha in 2009 and in Marrakesh in 2011, which in their view decisively shut non-governmental organizations out of the mechanism at the international level.

At the national level, on the other hand, the vast majority of States Parties to UNCAC appear to be seeking to involve non-governmental organizations in the review of implementation of UNCAC and in the strengthening of anti-corruption at the national and local level generally.[16]

This disagreement over non-governmental organizations involvement at the international level has spread from the debate over the review mechanism for UNCAC to other issues and can be seen in different ways. Negotiations on the adoption of a review mechanism for the UN Convention against Transnational Organized Crime (UNTOC) also struggled with the extent to which such a review mechanism would involve non-governmental organizations. The mechanism ultimately adopted in 2018 provided non-governmental organizations with an even lesser role than in the review of implementation of UNCAC.

More generally, some States have raised concerns about the activities of at least some non-governmental organizations at the local or national level in crime prevention and criminal justice, quite apart from the implementation of UNCAC or UNTOC. In recent years, some Member States have questioned the right of specific non-governmental organizations to attend sessions of the Conferences of the States Parties to the two UN Crime Conventions.[17]

Governments critical of non-governmental organizations have, among other points of criticism, questioned the appropriateness or qualifications of non-governmental organizations at the international level, including their perceived "relevance," representativeness, professionalism, and accountability.[18] Some governments have also expressed concerns that non-governmental organizations funded from abroad particularly may be promoting a political agenda that is contrary to the dominant values of the Member State in question or that is openly hostile to the government in power.[19] In this respect, there are marked differences between political systems and between public officials, in attitudes towards the role of non-governmental organizations as advocates and as political actors. For some, such political activity is part and parcel of the freedom of association and the freedom of speech, guaranteed by international human rights standards. Others, however, are of the view that some, if not many, non-governmental organizations act on the basis of insufficient information and use improper channels.

Overall, therefore, diverging views have been expressed within the framework of the UN Crime Programme on the value of non-governmental activity at the local and national level. According to one view, such non-governmental activity should be encouraged as widely as possible. According to a second view, such non-governmental activity should be supervised in order to ensure that the non-governmental organizations in question do not have malevolent intentions or serve as a channel for importing foreign (and undesirable) social and cultural values.

The first view could be described as a bottom-up, community-based approach. Local communities have a wide range of concerns, and crime is one such concern. In both a literal and a figurative sense, the mobilization of the public extends the reach of the criminal justice apparatus in a way that not only enhances the effectiveness of criminal justice but also fosters the trust of the public in the operation of the criminal justice system. One manifestation of this approach is community policing, which is based on the view that the police and the public are jointly responsible for responding to crime and improving the quality of life at the community level. Community policing programmes generally seek to encourage public initiative, recognizing that while the goals of individual civil society groups need not necessarily be in full alignment with police goals the work of these groups supplements the work of the police.[20]

The second view could be described as a top-down approach, which seeks to ensure that civil society activity complies with national law. The concerns expressed, as noted, at times refer to the potential that non-governmental organizations may have as channels for bringing unwanted foreign social and cultural values into a country. As noted in the report on the 2015 UN Crime Congress, in the course of the Congress workshop on Public participation in crime prevention and criminal justice,

A number of speakers noted that the engagement of civil society organizations should take place within the appropriate regulatory framework, in line with national legislation and in coordination with relevant oversight bodies, for example crime prevention councils, while also ensuring that organizations had the skills and knowledge for their functions. One speaker noted that any civil society activities should be framed and moderated by Governments, that non-local non-governmental organizations (NGOs) could propagate ideas or value systems that were foreign to some countries, and that those NGOs should respect the economic, cultural, social and religious values of societies. Some speakers referred to the need to build trust and transparency in that regard.[21]

As one speaker expressed at this UN Crime Congress workshop in 2015, the role of civil society is important if the groups are local and are based in the country and if this role occurs in a certain context. According to this speaker, such groups understand the culture, are subject to regulation, and are moderated by the government. The speaker observed that the groups should be transparent and should respect the social and cultural values of the country in question; in the view of the speaker, this is of particular importance in developing countries.[22]

It should be emphasized that this second view does not question the potential utility of the work of civil society groups. The focus is on ensuring that such groups function in accordance with law – and by extension that they should be under the control of the government.

The key difference between the two views presumably has much to do with the degree of control, intended to ensure the lawfulness of the activity of civil society groups. To what extent, for example, can members of the public exercise their right of association and freedom of speech? To what extent are they required to file for approval of activities such as "Neighbourhood Watch" or restorative justice projects? To what extent can such civil society groups (or members of the public) obtain information on the conduct of the police, on corporate activity, and on public procurement contracts in order to detect possible crime and corruption? And to what extent can they advocate for changes in policy and practice, for example, in respect of how women are treated at different stages of the criminal justice system or how migrants or members of ethnic groups are treated?

6.3 Reflections on the current debate in the UN Crime Programme on the status of non-governmental organizations

The UN Crime Commission and the two Conferences of States Parties operate in accordance with the standard Rules of Procedure according to which there are four categories of participants: Member States (/States Parties), intergovernmental organizations, non-governmental organizations, and UN bodies "and others." (Essentially the same Rules of Procedure apply to the quinquennial UN Crime Congresses.) In respect of bodies under the mandate of the two Conferences of States Parties, however, there has been a long-standing and acrimonious debate over whether or not non-governmental organizations may attend. The present status is that they may not, although the matter is supposed to be kept under review. For UNCAC bodies, a one-day briefing is held for non-governmental organizations during the annual session of the IRG. For UNTOC bodies, a "constructive dialogue" is organized after the meetings of each expert group.

Even where non-governmental organizations may attend meetings and may speak if there are no Member States wanting to take the floor, there is generally little time left for non-governmental organization interventions. This has not stopped many of the non-governmental organizations, including the Non-Governmental Organization Alliance, being very much in evidence outside the meeting rooms, for example, distributing their publications and organizing quite substantive and well-attended side events and ancillary meetings.

Those who work in the criminal justice system, and those who have studied it, tend to understand that the public has a key role in crime prevention and criminal justice. It is the public (the broader community) that is the source of the values, morality, and priorities that form the basis for the criminal law and the criminal justice system. It is members of the public (the victims themselves or witnesses and other third parties) who provide most of the initial reports of suspected offences, and it is the victims and the witnesses who can provide critical information regarding the identity and guilt of the suspect that can be used in criminal procedure. It is from the public that the criminal justice system receives the outreach and manpower necessary to supplement the official criminal justice system through voluntary and, depending on the system, semi-official programmes, such as victim support organizations, mediation projects, community policing projects, and volunteer probation officer projects. And the success of the rehabilitation of offenders will ultimately come down to how well they can be reintegrated into the community. (Need it be added that the criminal justice system should serve the community?)

Criminological research has demonstrated the central importance of informal social control in preventing crime, in restraining individuals from embarking on a criminal career or from committing crime on impulse, and in supporting offenders in desisting from crime and becoming reintegrated into society. There has also been a rich tradition of research on the relationship between the public and the criminal justice system, as shown, for example, by the extensive research that has been carried out on public confidence in the police and the courts and public attitudes towards punishment.

For these reasons, practitioners and researchers alike know that the formal criminal justice system on its own cannot "protect" the public from crime. They know that the operation of the criminal justice system depends on the public and on the relationship between the public and the criminal justice agencies.

In light of this, it may seem peculiar that a debate is underway in the UN that seems to question these self-evident assumptions of the role of the public. The idea of "cooperation with non-governmental organizations" a phrase long used in UN dialogue, has been challenged.[23]

Have the disagreements referred to above in the UN Crime Programme regarding the role of non-governmental organizations, as well as the other developments such as securitization, affected how the UN Crime Programme works?

The easy answer to this is "yes." The concept of non-governmental organizations appears to have almost disappeared from UN Crime Programme texts formulated by consensus and, if it is mentioned, this is usually with some qualifications. There are three main reasons, however, why that would be a misrepresentation of the essence of the UN Crime Programme.

The first is linguistic. Debates in the UN often revolve around the choice of words, and in the meeting rooms where UN decisions are crafted these words may take on meanings that are not immediately apparent to persons who are unfamiliar with how the UN works.

The term "non-governmental organization" has a specific legal meaning in the UN. It is an entity that has a recognized legal structure and purpose and its representatives can act on its behalf (locally, nationally, and internationally). As already noted, non-governmental organizations can apply for consultative status with ECOSOC, and a large number have done so.

Although "non-governmental organizations" is thus a recognized legal concept in the UN and non-governmental organizations continue to have a strong institutionalized role at the UN Crime Commission, at the UN Crime Congresses and in other work of the UN Crime Programme it has become a politically charged term when referring to work being done by other than governmental actors. This is very evident from the rapid change that has taken place, in the space of only a few years, in what terminology is used at UN Congress Declarations.

The term "civil society" is used within the UN with greater inconsistency than the term "non-governmental organization." Most dictionaries define civil society as the aggregate of groups or organizations that work alongside government and the private sector to promote shared interests. Thus, civil society consists not only of non-governmental organizations but also of various other more or less organized structures. However, quite often in UN texts the term "civil society" appears to be used as a synonym for "the community" or "the public."

The term "the community," in turn, seems to be used in UN texts as a general concept to refer to the public at large.

Finally, the term "the public" is used to refer to the mass of people in society in their role as citizens, and thus as a counterpoint, for example, to persons acting in the capacity of civil servants or as representatives of other stakeholders (such as the private sector).

The UNODC has already responded to the concerns raised by some Member States, and appears to have largely replaced the word "non-governmental organization" with a synonym (and arguably a wider concept), "civil society organization." To quote from the UNODC website (https://www.unodc.org/unodc/en/ngos/DCN0-NGOs-and-civil-society.html);

> UNODC recognizes the need to promote strong partnerships with civil society organizations in dealing with the complex issues of drug abuse and crime which undermine the fabric of society. The active involvement of civil society, which includes NGOs, community groups, labour unions, indigenous groups, charitable organizations, faith-based organizations, professional associations and foundations is essential to help UNODC carry out its global mandates.

As the Charter recognizes, civil society organizations are important partners of the UN. Over the past 75 years they have developed a close relationship with the organization, working in a variety of areas such as service delivery, policy development, analysis, and advocacy. Today thousands of accredited non-governmental organizations work with the UN worldwide, serving as important sources of public information about the UN and bringing fresh information and ideas from the field.

The second reason to doubt whether the debate over non-governmental organizations have appreciably affected the UN Crime Programme is that the Programme continues to produce reports, resolutions, and UN Congress Declarations that acknowledge the central importance of public participation in crime prevention and criminal justice. Despite the securitization process referred to in section 3.4, the Programme continues to deal with "soft" issues of public participation.

The third reason is the most important one, the guiding effect of the 2030 Agenda, the SDGs. Although also these SDGs do not contain a single reference to non-governmental organizations, they do refer several times to civil society and, in one connection (para. 41), to civil society organizations.

The 2015 UN Crime Congress in Doha contributed, for its part, to the incorporation of the rule of law, crime prevention, and criminal justice issues into Goal 16 of the SDGs, which now provides the frame of reference for the UN Crime Programme.

In so doing, the SDGs challenge the UN Crime Programme to pay increasing attention to how crime prevention and criminal justice can contribute to sustainable development around the world, in developing and developed countries alike. Such a UN Crime Programme would be framed by the link between Goal 16 and other Goals such as gender equality, the sustainability of communities, and poverty reduction. It would continue to deal with pressing questions related to transnational and organized crime but would also deal with the prevention of and response to "ordinary crime." It would continue to identify best practices in international law enforcement and judicial cooperation, but would also seek to identify best practices in the strengthening of access to justice, restorative justice, victim support, and community-based sanctions.

The intellectual debate in the early years of the UN Crime Programme can be revitalized in order to bring in research and best practices from around the world, channelled, for example, through the UNODC and the PNIs so that it is reflected in the discussions at the UN Crime Commission, the Crime Congresses, and other meetings.

The government-driven discussions in the UN Crime Commission can benefit in this way from the input of experts, who can identify what best practices can be adapted to the different circumstances around the world so that they meet not only the general needs of Member States but also the ground-level needs of practitioners and local communities, victims, and offenders.

Moreover, Goal 17.17 of the SDGs expressly states that the target is to "encourage and promote effective public, public-private and civil society partnerships, building on the experience and resourcing strategies of partnerships."

The soft law and the hard law elements of the UN Crime Programme reinforce one another in strengthening local, national, and international crime prevention and criminal justice and in this way contribute to the ongoing work on the review of the implementation of the 2030 Agenda.

On this point, the common ground will presumably revolve around the right of civil society groups to act in a lawful manner to assist the authorities in crime prevention and criminal justice and around the right of sovereign States to determine what laws and regulations apply to such groups. Given the wide differences between Member States in legal and administrative systems, as well as in economic, political, and social development, there cannot be a "one-size-fits-all" model. Noting the principle of non-intervention in domestic affairs, it should be clear that the UN Crime Commission cannot, for example, determine the specific extent to which States may regulate civil society groups, as long as the right of association and the freedom of speech, as provided in recognized international instruments, are respected.

Civil society will continue to have an important seat at the table of the UN Crime Programme.

Notes

1 Linke (1985) provides an overview of non-governmental organization involvement in the UN Crime Programme after the Secretariat unit responsible for the Programme was transferred from New York to Vienna in 1976.
2 Jolanta Redo estimates that there are some 3,500 international non-governmental organizations working with the UN; J. Redo, 2012, p. 125.
   If an international non-governmental organization is based on an international treaty, then it is referred to as an "intergovernmental organization." Examples are the UN itself, the World Trade Organization, the Association of Southeast Asian Nations, and the World Bank.
3 Recently some Member States have opposed the participation of national non-governmental organizations that do not have consultative status at individual UN Crime Programme meetings, particularly at meetings of the Conference of States Parties to one of the two UN Crime Conventions. When this happens, and informal consultations do not arrive at a solution, the matter is dealt with by the Credentials Committee, which would usually bring the matter to the attention of the plenary body. In most cases the plenary body has voted to allow participation.
4 Willets, 2000, cites as examples the Earth Summit in Rio de Janeiro (1992), the World Social Summit in Copenhagen (1995), and the Beijing Conference on Women (1995). Non-governmental organizations accredited to these conferences could take part in the work of the respective commissions. At Habitat II in Istanbul (1996), non-governmental organizations constituted Committee II, an integral part of the official proceedings.
   Since Willets' 2000 article, the number of special conferences organized by the UN has decreased and been replaced at least in part by special sessions of the GA. Non-governmental organizations have a considerably lower profile at the GA than they do at most UN conferences.
5 Ibid. Willets is more cautious about the status of national non-governmental organizations in the work of ECOSOC because up to the mid-1990s relatively few national non-governmental organizations participated.
6 A list of the members of the UN Crime Committee is to be found in Annex 3 in S. Redo, 2012 (a separate CD).
7 See Chapter 12 on the drafting and adoption of standards and norms in the UN Crime Programme.
8 The International Penal and Penitentiary Foundation has continued the work of the IPPC.
9 Bassiouni, 1995 contains chapters dealing with the activities of each of these four non-governmental organizations and their contribution to the UN Crime Programme.
10 Under this arrangement, each year in a five-year cycle, one of the Big Four would organize its main international conference, leading up to the fifth year, in which the respective UN Crime Congress would be held. At the time, the author was an active member of three of the Big Four and on the governing board of two of them.
11 These joint conferences were facilitated and hosted by the International Science and Professional Advisory Council, under the chairmanship of Dr. Adolfo Beria di Argentine.
   In 1982, an International Committee for Coordination (consisting of the presidents and the secretaries-general of the organizations) was established to formalize the coordination of activities.
12 ISPAC is a member of the UN Programme Network Institutes.
13 See, for example, Clark, 1994, pp. 42–45 and 129–132.
14 Draft UN Crime Commission resolution 1994/18. The author participated in this heated debate as a member of the Finnish delegation.

15 An extensive analysis of this disagreement and a proposal for resolving it are presented in CAC/COSP/2015/CRP.3, 2015, prepared by the author.

16 There has been a marked shift in this respect with the overwhelming majority of States Parties under review arranging for "country visits," during which the representatives of the reviewing States Parties can consult with a broad range of national stakeholders, civil society representatives included.

17 At the eleventh session of the COP-UNTOC (2022), a draft decision was submitted relating to the participation of relevant stakeholders, including non-governmental organizations, representatives of the private sector, and academia, in the constructive dialogues for the Mechanism for the Review of the Implementation of the UNTOC and the Protocols thereto. Due to lack of consensus, the sponsors undertook to postpone action by the Conference to a later date. The Conference will come back to this matter at a time deemed appropriate. The next session of the Conference is scheduled for 14–18 October 2024.

Furthermore at the eleventh session of the Conference, in a departure from the long-standing practice within the UN Crime Programme in Vienna of seeking consensus on all issues and avoiding any votes (the "Spirit of Vienna"), three separate votes were taken. What was at issue was the request of three non-governmental organizations to attend as observers. Some States Parties objected to their participation. A vote was taken thereupon, first, on whether according the status of observer was a matter of substance or of procedure. The majority held it to be one of procedure. This was followed by a vote on whether the status of observer should be accorded to these three organizations jointly or to each individually. The majority held that one voting process should be conducted jointly for all three. In the third vote, these three organizations were granted observer status.

18 These statements are not reflected in the official reports of the respective sessions of the IRG but have been recorded in the notes made by the author, who attended all of the relevant sessions of the IRG, including the briefings.

19 See, for example, para. 15 of the Report on Workshop 4 of the Thirteenth United Nations Congress on Crime Prevention and Criminal Justice, Doha, 12–19 April 2015, A/CONF.222/L.4/Add.1.

20 López-Rey (1985), pp. 27–28, has an extensive critique of what he sees as the UN Crime Congresses coming under "excessive governmental control," using arguments that could also be extended to support extensive non-governmental organization involvement in other aspects of the UN Crime Programme.

21 Report on Workshop 4 of the Thirteenth United Nations Congress on Crime Prevention and Criminal Justice, Doha, 12–19 April 2015, A/CONF.222/L.4/Add.1, para. 15.

22 Personal notes of the author, who served as one of the chairpersons at the Thirteenth UN Crime Congress and chaired the session at which this discussion took place.

23 See the analysis and the examples cited in Joutsen, 2018.

References

Bassiouni, M. Cherif (1995), *The Contributions of Specialized Institutes and Non-Governmental Organizations to the United Nations Criminal Justice Programme. In Honour of Adolfo Beria di Argentine*, Brill Publishers

Clark, Roger S. (1994), *The United Nations Crime Prevention and Criminal Justice Program. Formulation of Standards and Efforts at Their Implementation*, University of Pennsylvania Press

Clifford, William (1979), *Echoes and Hopes. The United Nations Committee on Crime Prevention and Control*, Australian Institute of Criminology, Canberra, available at https://www.aic.gov.au/sites/default/files/2020-07/echoes-and-hopes.pdf

Finnane, Mark (2007), *JV Barry: A Life*, University of New South Wales Press

Joutsen, Matti (1996), "Le Quatre Grand" and the United Nations Crime Prevention and Criminal Justice Programme, unpublished paper, HEUNI

Joutsen, Matti (2018), What is the Role of the Public in Crime Prevention and Criminal Justice? The Debate in the United Nations, *UNAFEI Resource Material Series 105*, UNAFEI, pp. 49–69, available at https://www.unafei.or.jp/publications/pdf/RS_No105/No105_9_VE_Joutsen_2.pdf

Linke, Robert (1985), The Cooperation Between Non-Governmental Organizations and the United Nations in the Field of Crime Policy, in *Course on United Nations Criminal Policy. Report of the European Course Held in Helsinki, Finland, 25–29 March 1985*, HEUNI publication no. 6, pp. 90–95

López-Rey de Arroya, Manuel (1985) *A Guide to United Nations Criminal Policy*, Cambridge Studies in Criminology LIV

Redo, Jolanta (2012), Non-Governmental Organizations in the United Nations Crime Prevention and Criminal Justice Programme, in S. Redo, *Blue Criminology. The Power of United Nations Ideas to Counter Crime Globally – A Monographic Study*, HEUNI publication no. 72, pp. 125–126

Redo, Slawomir (2012), *Blue Criminology. The Power of United Nations Ideas to Counter Crime Globally – A Monographic Study*, HEUNI publication no. 72, available at https://www.heuni.fi/en/index/publications/heunireports/reportseriesno.72.bluecriminologythepowerofunitednationsideastocountercrimeglobally-amonographicstudy.html

Röstad, Helge (1985), The History of International Collaboration in Crime Prevention and Treatment of Offenders – with Special Emphasis on the Activities of the International Penal and Penitentiary Foundation, in *Course on United Nations Criminal Policy. Report of the European Course Held in Helsinki, Finland, 25–29 March 1985*, HEUNI publication no. 6, pp. 79–89

Willets, Peter (1996), Consultative Status for NGOs at the UN, City University London, available at www.staff.city.ac.uk/p.willets/NGOS/CONSSTAT.HTM

Willets, Peter (2000), From "Consultative Arrangements" to "Partnership": The Changing Status of NGOs in Diplomacy at the UN, *Global Governance*, 6(2), 191–212

7
THE UN CRIME PROGRAMME NETWORK INSTITUTES

The UN Crime Prevention and Criminal Justice Programme Network Institutes (PNIs) has grown over the years to consist of seventeen institutes, the International Scientific and Professional Advisory Council (ISPAC), and (strictly speaking) the United Nations Office on Drugs and Crime (UNODC).[1] These institutes have different mandates. Nonetheless, they all share a commitment to working together within the framework of the UN Crime Programme.

Over the years, the PNIs individually and collectively have produced an extensive body of work. The institutes and entities have been and continue to be very active in producing research reports, technical manuals, policy guides, and other publications that can be used, for example, in policy development and the training of practitioners.[2]

Several of the institutes are also very active in technical assistance, usually in the form of training programmes. For example, the regional institute for Asia and the Far East, the Asia and Far East Institute for the Prevention of Crime and the Treatment of Offenders (UNAFEI), has organized close to 200 international seminars and courses, involving more than 6,200 criminal justice practitioners mostly from around Asia and the Pacific, but also from the Middle East, Africa, and Latin America. In addition, several institutes work closely on request with Member States in technical assistance projects.

7.1 Evolution of the UN PNIs

At the time the UN Crime Programme was established, there were plans to establish regional institutes in order to meet the specific needs of different parts of the world: "UN leadership in criminal policy was never understood as aiming for uniformity" (López-Rey, 1985, pp. 28–29). However,

DOI: 10.4324/9781003480907-9

the path towards their establishment was not at all swift and straightforward but long and winding, with a few false starts and changes in (potential) host governments.

The first calls for the establishment of regional institutes were made in the early 1950s, and were repeated several times in subsequent years. For example, during the preparations for the First UN Crime Congress in 1955, Mr. Philippe de Seynes, Under-Secretary for Economic and Social Affairs, advocated for a Latin American and an Asia and Far East regional institute, and a separate recommendation was made for an institute for the Arab countries.[3]

TABLE 7.1 The UN PNIs listed by mandate

	Established	Location	Comments
UN Interregional Crime and Justice Research Institute (UNICRI; originally UN Social Defence Research Institute) https://unicri.it	1968	Turin, Italy	

Institutes with a primarily regional mandate

	Established	Location	Comments
UN Asia and Far East Institute for the Prevention of Crime and the Treatment of Offenders (UNAFEI) https://www.unafei.or.jp	1962	Tokyo, Japan	Oldest institute; training and technical assistance
Latin American Institute for the Prevention of Crime and the Treatment of Offenders (ILANUD) https://www.ilanud.or.cr	1975	San José, Costa Rica	Research and technical assistance
European Institute for Crime Prevention and Control, affiliated with the UN (HEUNI) https://heuni.fi	1981	Helsinki, Finland	Research and policy guidance
African Regional Institute for the Prevention of Crime and the Treatment of Offenders (UNAFRI) https://www.unafri.or.ug	1987	Kampala, Uganda	Research and technical assistance
Naif Arab University for Security Sciences (NAUSS; originally Arab Security Studies Training Centre) https://nauss.edu.sa/ar-sa/Pages/default.aspx	1972	Riyadh, Saudi Arabia	Not officially a regional institute but active among Arab countries in forensics, research, and higher educatio

TABLE 7.1 (Continued)

	Established	Location	Comments
Specialized institutes and entities			
International Center for Criminal Law Reform and Criminal Justice Policy (ICCLR & CJP) https://icclr.org	1991	Vancouver, Canada	Technical assistance
International Scientific and Professional Advisory Council of the UN Crime Prevention and Criminal Justice Programme (ISPAC) https://ispac.cnpds.org	1991	Milan, Italy	Liaison and research
Siracusa International Institute for Criminal Justice and Human Rights (SII) https://www.siracusainstitute.org/	1972	Siracusa, Italy	Technical assistance
Raoul Wallenberg Institute of Human Rights and Humanitarian Law (RWI) https://rwi.lu.se	1984	Lund, Sweden	Technical assistance
International Centre for the Prevention of Crime (ICPC) https://cipc-icpc.org/en/home	1994	Montreal, Canada	Technical assistance
Institute for Security Studies (ISS) https://issafrica.org	1991	Pretoria, South Africa	Several offices located around Africa
Basel Institute on Governance / International Centre for Asset Recovery https://baselgovernance.org	2003	Basel, Switzerland	Technical assistance and policy guidance
National institutes			
Australian Institute of Criminology (AIC) https://www.aic.gov.au	1973	Canberra, Australia	Research
Korean Institute of Criminology and Justice (KICJ) https://www.kicj.re.kr/international/	1989	Seoul, Republic of Korea	Research
National Institute of Justice (NIJ) https://nij.ojp.gov	1968	Washington, D.C., U.S.	Research and the funding of research
College for Criminal Law Science (CCLS)	2005	Beijing, China	Research
Thailand Institute of Justice (TIJ) https://www.tijthailand.org	2011	Bangkok, Thailand	Research and technical assistance

At the 1958 session of the ad hoc committee of experts, Mr. de Seynes returned to the possibility of decentralizing UN social defence activities *inter alia* with the help of regional institutes. These institutes, which were to be established under the UN Technical Assistance Programme, would be responsible for training, research, the organization of regional meetings, liaison with regional correspondents, and furnishing regional information to the Bureau of Social Affairs, the other institutes, and the European Consultative Group. The work programmes of the regional institutes would be established within the general framework of the activities of the UN in the field of social defence, "taking into account the recommendations of the Committee of Experts and of the congresses" (E/CN.5/329, para. 11).

The 1958 Secretariat report "Progress of Work in the Field of Social Defence" (E/CN.5/AC.9/R.4, 1958, para. 11) states:

> Special references should be made to the organization of two Regional Institutes on the Prevention of Crime and the Treatment of Offenders, sponsored by the United Nations, one for Asia and the Far East and the second for Latin American countries. With respect of the first, which will be located in Lahore, Pakistan, the international agreement governing the functioning of the Institute had already been submitted to the Government of Pakistan, and it is expected that the Institute will start its activities in 1958. With respect to the Latin American Institute, negotiations are already well advanced between the Government of Brazil and the United Nations.[4]

In the negotiations with the early potential host Member States, the Secretariat offered the host government partial funding, at least during the initial years, by undertaking to cover the salary and other expenses of the director and possibly some other staff members. The Secretariat usually also discussed with other Member States in the region whether they would be willing to provide financial and other support. The host government, in turn, was expected to provide the facilities, the rest of the staff, and the operational budget. An implied assumption was that the government was committed to supporting the proposed institute in the long term.[5]

Those first plans for regional institutes located in Pakistan and Brazil did not materialize. The UN PNIs finally began to emerge in 1962, with the establishment of UNAFEI in Tokyo. This was followed by four waves of PNI expansion.

In the first wave, UNAFEI was joined by the interregional research institute (the UN Interregional Crime and Justice Research Institute (UNICRI)) and three regional institutes, the Latin American Institute for the Prevention of Crime and the Treatment of Offenders (ILANUD) for Latin America and the Caribbean (San José, Costa Rica; 1975), the Naif Arab University for Security Sciences (NAUSS) for the Arab region (Riyadh, Saudi Arabia, 1979), and the European Institute for Crime Prevention and Control, affiliated with the United Nations HEUNI for Europe (Helsinki, Finland, 1981).[6] One additional regional institute, however, was short-lived. In 1972, negotiations between the UN Secretariat and Egypt resulted in the establishment of a UN-affiliated Institute of Social Defence in Cairo, operating within the pre-existing National Centre for Social and Criminological Research. Its primary purpose was to provide training facilities for Africa and the Middle East. However, the agreement between the UN and Egypt lapsed ten years later, in 1982 (López-Rey, 1985, p. 30).[7]

In the second wave of PNI expansion (roughly the 1980s and 1990s), the interregional UN institute and the regional institutes were joined by one more regional institute, the African Regional Institute for the Prevention of Crime and the Treatment of Offenders (UNAFRI) as well as by four pre-existing institutes: the Australian Institute of Criminology (AIC) (Canberra; originally established 1973), the Siracusa International Institute for Criminal Justice and Human Rights (SII) (Siracusa, Italy; originally established 1972), the International Centre for the Prevention of Crime (ICPC) (Montreal, Canada; 1994), and the International Centre for Criminal Law Reform and Criminal Justice Policy (ICCLR & CJP) (Vancouver, Canada; 1991). In addition, the International Scientific and Professional Advisory Council (ISPAC) (Milan, Italy; 1991) joined the Programme Network.

These second-wave institutes (as well as the institutes brought in during the third and fourth wave) were *pre-existing* institutes, with a mandate that was not necessarily tailored to the UN Programme. Nonetheless, each institute undertook to cooperate with the UNODC.

During the third wave, the PNIs were joined by the National Institute of Justice (NIJ) (Washington, D.C.; originally established in 1968), the Korean Institute of Criminology and Justice (KICJ) (Seoul, Republic of Korea; 1989), the Institute of Security Studies (ISS) (Pretoria, South Africa; 1991), and the Raoul Wallenberg Institute of Human Rights and Humanitarian Law (RWI) (Lund, Sweden; originally established 1984).

A fourth wave of PNI expansion started in 2007 with the inclusion of the Basel Institute on Governance/International Centre for Asset Recovery (Basel, Switzerland), to be followed in 2011 by the College for Criminal Law Science (CCLS) at the Beijing Normal University (Beijing, China), and in 2016 by the Thailand Institute of Justice (TIJ) (Bangkok, Thailand; established 2011). The contributions of the Basel Institute enhance international assistance for the recovery of stolen assets (in line with chapter V of the UN Convention against Corruption). The College contributes to the internationalization of domestic criminal justice reform through increasingly practical exchanges and engagements, according to UN criminal policy recommendations. The TIJ, the newest member of the PNIs, is very active in research, capacity-building, and policy guidance in crime prevention, criminal justice, and the rule of law.

7.2 The status and mandate of the institutes

UNICRI, UNAFEI, ILANUD, HEUNI, UNAFRI, and ISPAC were established specifically within the framework of the UN Crime Programme. NAUSS, the six specialized institutes, and the five national level institutes each have their own original mandate, but have agreed to cooperate with the UNODC and the UN Crime Programme.[8]

The administrative status of the institutes varies considerably. The UN-ODC is, of course, part of the UN Secretariat. UNICRI is a UN entity and subject to the administrative and financial regulations of the UN; however it is not funded through the regular UN budget but through voluntary contributions.[9] UNAFEI, ILANUD, HEUNI, and UNAFRI were established on the basis of agreements signed between the UN and the host government. NIJ, AIC, KICJ, and TIJ are part of their respective government structures, each in somewhat different ways. These national institutes, as well as the other "pre-existing" institutes and entities, are part of the PNIs on the basis of, for example, a letter or memorandum of understanding with the UNODC.

The report of the Secretary-General to the first session of the UN Crime Commission (1992) laid out the functions of the PNIs (E/CN.15/1992/3, para. 5):

(1) service as a link between the UN and the Member States in the different regions;
(2) promotion of interregional, regional and subregional cooperation;
(3) fostering UN criminal policy;
(4) keeping Member States abreast of the work and perspectives of the UN;
(5) advising the Secretariat of the special needs, concerns and priorities of the region; and
(6) assistance in the implementation of the UN Crime Programme.

The PNIs have different governing structures, different levels of staffing, and different resource bases. They also vary to a considerable extent in the way in which they support the work of the UNODC in Vienna and the UN Crime Programme. The work of the individual PNIs, both institutes and entities, can be divided into four categories:

- activities that are carried out in accordance with mandates formulated by the UN Crime Commission. Examples include organization of workshops at the UN Congresses and the workshop connected with the thematic debate at annual sessions of the UN Crime Commission;

- activities that directly support the work of the UNODC. Examples include assisting the UNODC in the preparation of documentation for the UN Crime Congresses and the sessions of the UN Crime Commission, assistance in organizing regional preparatory meetings for the UN Crime Congresses, and organization together with the UNODC of various expert meetings preparing new standards and norms or other documentation intended for the consideration of the UN Crime Commission;
- activities that contribute to implementing UN mandates in crime prevention and criminal justice. Examples include various training programmes, technical assistance, and research projects; and
- activities that are conducted primarily in accordance with mandates coming from sources other than the UN. This is particularly the case with the national institutes, which are primarily accountable to their respective national government.

The two clearest examples of the contribution of the PNIs to the UN Crime Programme are assistance with the organization of the UN Crime Congresses and assistance with the organization of the annual sessions of the UN Crime Commission.

The PNIs have had two specific roles to play in the organization of the UN Crime Congresses. First, in the preparations for the next UN Crime Congress, some institutes (such as ILANUD, but also, for example, HEUNI, UNAFRI, and NAUSS) have been instrumental in organizing regional preparatory meetings and in mobilizing regional interest in participation. Second, beginning with the joint organization by HEUNI and UNICRI of a workshop at the 1985 UN Crime Congress in Milan on juvenile justice, the PNIs have assumed a considerable share of the responsibility for the UN Crime Congress workshops. This role of the institutes was formally recognized by the UN GA in 2001 (A/RES/56/119, para. 2 (f)).

The discussions at these workshops are considered by many participants to have been very substantive. Indeed, Ram argues that

> the workshops and other specialised meetings are often the only occasions in which truly global expert discussions of some issues take place [at the Congresses], and in which experts can make connections among related or overlapping substantive issues. This aspect of the Congresses has, if anything, increased in its importance as the same sort of expert function has declined in the Commission itself.
>
> *(Ram, 2012, p. 113)*

Since 2001, the PNIs have organized side events at the sessions of the UN Crime Commission and ancillary meetings at the UN Crime Congresses. The PNIs have also been responsible, together with the UNODC, for the organization of the workshop associated with the respective theme of each session.[10]

7.3 Coordination among the PNIs

The GA, ECOSOC, the UN Crime Committee (later the UN Crime Commission), and the PNIs themselves have repeatedly called for the reinforcement and coordination of the activities of the PNIs. The need for adequate support has been underlined, and closer collaboration has been requested between the PNIs and the UNODC. Measures to do so include the sharing of information, technical backstopping of activities, secondment of personnel,[11] exchange of expertise and joint programming, the organization of seminars and training courses on priority issues of concern to Member States of the respective regions, and (since 2022) the publication of the PNI Newsletter.

The structure for PNI coordination consists primarily of annual coordination meetings, a tradition that began in 1984 when NAUSS (called at the time the Arab Security Studies and Training Centre), in cooperation with UNICRI, hosted representatives of the UNODC and the directors and other representatives of the various PNIs at the first such meeting in Riyadh. In addition, the Italian Government, largely thanks to the efforts of Professor Beria di Argentine, provided generous financial support for PNI coordination, including for the organization of several annual coordination meetings.

This PNI coordination had become well entrenched by the time the UN Crime Committee was dissolved and the UN Crime Commission was established in 1992. Consequently, when the architecture of the new UN Crime Programme was designed, special mention was made about the role of the interregional and regional institutes and about coordination (A/RES/46/152, annex):

1. United Nations institutes for the prevention of crime and the treatment of offenders
    35. The activities of the United Nations institutes for the prevention of crime and the treatment of offenders should be supported by Member States and the United Nations, with particular attention being given to the needs of such institutes located in developing countries. Given the important role of such institutes, their contributions to policy development and implementation, and their resource requirements, especially those of the United Nations African Institute for the Prevention of Crime and the Treatment of Offenders, should be fully integrated into the overall programme.

2. Coordination among the United Nations institutes for the prevention of crime and the treatment of offenders

36. The institutes should keep one another and the commission on crime prevention and criminal justice informed on a regular basis about their programme of work and its implementation.

37. The commission may request the institutes, subject to the availability of resources, to implement select elements of the programme. The commission may also suggest areas for inter-institute activities.

38. The commission shall seek to mobilize extrabudgetary support for the activities of the institutes.

The Secretary-General submitted the first progress report on the PNIs at the first session of the Commission in 1992 (E/CN.15/1992/3). Such reports were submitted also at the fourth and fifth sessions of the Committee. Beginning with the ninth session of the UN Crime Commission (2000), the activities of the PNIs have become a standard part of the agenda. Indeed, one of the five specific functions of the Commission (together with providing policy guidance to the UN on crime prevention and criminal justice, implementing the Programme, mobilizing the support of Member States for the Programme, and preparing the UN Congresses) is to facilitate and help coordinate the activities of the interregional and regional institutes (A/RES/46/152, annex, para. 26(c)). The Commission may request the PNIs, subject to the availability of resources, to implement selected elements of the Programme. The Commission may also suggest areas for inter-institute activities.

The UN Crime Commission thus has specifically been assigned the function of facilitating and helping to coordinate the activities of the PNIs. It should be noted, however, that other than a few references in resolutions adopted in 1992, the Commission has not engaged in practice in very much discussion on the PNIs or on coordination (ECOSOC Res 1992/22 and A/RES/46/152, Annex, para. 28; see also E/CN.15/1992/3, paras. 103 and 109). The major exception to this has been in relation to the involvement of PNIs in organizing UN Congress workshops and contributing to the thematic debate at annual sessions of the Commission.

7.4   The role of the UNODC in coordination of the PNIs

The Secretariat is charged with the practical implementation of the UN Crime Prevention and Criminal Justice Programme and, according to GA/RES/46/152, the PNIs provides Programme support. The opening paragraph of ECOSOC resolution 1992/22 (I para. 1) sets out the framework for the relationship between the UNODC and the PNIs:

Under the guidance of the Commission, the secretariat of the programme should be responsible for facilitating the planning, coordination and implementation of practical activities in the field of crime prevention and criminal justice, in close collaboration with governments and interregional and regional institutes.

In his report to the first session of the Commission, the Secretary-General had this to say:

> To make the network viable, support is needed for strengthening and consolidated action on the part of the Secretariat. The Secretariat's support requires continuous advisory, monitoring and follow-up action. Effective coordination of the institutes' work programmes and activities is necessary to programme performance and impact.
>
> *(E/CN.15/1992/3, para. 104)*

From the outset the UNODC was considered an integral part of the PNIs. Furthermore, since the regular staff of the UNODC are able to develop day-to-day working routines, it is in a better position than the UN Crime Commission to understand the different elements of the work of the PNIs and to strengthen coordination. This is most evident in the fact that the UNODC representative has traditionally chaired the PNI coordination meetings. It is also evident in the formal role of the UNODC in reporting to the annual sessions of the Commission on the work of the PNIs.

Furthermore, a UNODC representative is either formally or informally a part of the advisory board, management board, or equivalent of many of the PNIs. This allows it to follow, and potentially influence, the actual work of the PNIs.

Individual entities or staff members of the PNIs have either co-organized or participated in UNODC activities implementing the Programme. This includes the hosting by some regional institutes of regional preparatory meetings for the Congresses, the organization of expert meetings, and a wide variety of technical assistance activities.

Since the Secretariat has the principal responsibility for implementing the UN Crime Programme under the direction of the UN Crime Commission, it would follow – in a rational world – that the role of the PNIs would be to work closely with the Secretariat to implement the priorities determined by the UN Crime Commission.

However, this ideal scheme of cooperation between the Secretariat and the PNIs has been significantly hampered by a number of factors, in particular the differences in the mandates, priorities, orientation, capacities, and funding bases of the institutes. Only the interregional and the regional institutes have been specifically designed to work with the Secretariat and more broadly to contribute to the UN Crime Programme. The other institutes must remain mindful of their original mandate, which in the case of the national institutes in Australia, South Korea, and the United States is understandably focused on national priorities in crime and justice.

There are also inherent limitations in relation to the orientation, capacities, and funding of the different PNIs. Some of the institutes focus on research, others on training. Some of the institutes (such as the national institutes, as well as the regional institute for Asia and the Pacific, which is funded primarily by the host government) have a relatively stable funding base, allowing them some flexibility when deciding whether or not to assist the Secretariat. Others rely on voluntary contributions, and in many cases these voluntary contributions are fairly meagre. Such factors may explain why the discussions at the UN Crime Commission on coordinating the work of the institutes have usually been quite limited. The Commission often finds that the institutes are unable to respond to requests and, therefore, will understandably not bother to ask.

As for the scope of direct PNI involvement in carrying out Commission-approved mandates under the guidance of, and in cooperation with the Secretariat, it would appear that, after a relative lull towards the end of the 1990s and the beginning of the 2000s, individual PNIs are once again becoming more active in this respect.

7.5 Assessment of changes in the contribution of the PNIs to the UN Crime Programme

Three phases can be detected in the evolution of the work of the PNIs.

The first phase, lasting from the 1960s to the 1980s, marked the creation of the PNIs. Only a few of the individual PNIs had difficulty getting their programme established and work underway during this stage.[12]

Beginning during the 1990s, the profile of the PNIs in the UN Crime Programme declined for a period of approximately twenty years. The main factor was the transition from the UN Crime Committee to the UN Crime Commission. The Member States forming the UN Crime Commission were represented to an increasing extent by diplomatic representatives based in Vienna, and these diplomats (who were often rotated in and out of Vienna for very short periods, in some cases three or four years) had considerably less understanding, and appreciation, of the work of the PNIs than had previously been the case with the members of the UN Crime Committee.[13]

A second factor was the increasing sense of financial austerity around the world, which led individual governments to cut back on their financial support for some of the institutes, seriously curtailing their ability to undertake projects. Several PNIs became largely dependent on extrabudgetary funding, generally in the form of outside grants for research or technical assistance activities.

A third factor was domestic. The policy of some host governments became less supportive of international cooperation, and the management of the institutes in question had to respond to newly instituted programme restraints by reducing international work, to focus on more pressing (and politically more prioritized) domestic concerns.

Even during the second phase (roughly the 1990s and the first decade of the new millennium), however, many individual PNIs continued to do important and significant work within their mandates, and the PNIs collectively provided substantive and practical assistance to the UNODC in the organization of the formal workshops at the UN Crime Congresses. Several institutes engaged in important ad hoc cooperation among themselves and continued their extensive research and technical assistance work.

Over the past decade, there has been a third phase, which has seen an appreciable improvement in PNI cooperation, as shown for example in their participation in the annual coordination meetings and the organization of joint activities. The PNIs as a collective and as individual entities still have considerable potential to contribute to the UN Crime Programme.

Notes

1 A somewhat dated overview of the work of different PNIs is provided in *The United Nations and Crime Prevention*, 1995, pp. 17–21. The list at that time did not include the Basel Institute, CCLS, ISS, KICJ, NIJ, RWI, or TIJ.

   Although the first institutes were established during the 1960s and the 1970s, the earliest use of the term "Programme Network" in this context was in 1996 in a UNODC document to the UN Crime Commission; United Nations African Institute for the Prevention of Crime and the Treatment of Offenders. Report of the Secretary-General, A/51/450, paras. 25 and 51.

   The terminology has evolved over the years. At the time when the PNIs comprised just UNICRI and the regional institutes, the reference was simply to "UNICRI and the regional institutes." See, for example, the wording used in the Secretariat report to the first (1992) session of the UN Crime Commission, outlining the activities of the institutes (E/CN.15/1992/3).

   After specialized institutes and national institutes had joined the network, the corresponding reports to the Commission in the years 1993, 1994, and 1995 referred to ""UNICRI and other institutes." As of 1996, the term became "institutes comprising the UN crime prevention and criminal justice programme network" (see, for example, E/CN.15/1996/21).

   However, different terminology was used initially in the list of participants at these same sessions of the UN Crime Commission. In 1992 and 1993, the institutes represented at the sessions of the UN Crime Commission were listed under "UN bodies and affiliated institutes." From 1994 to 2000, UNICRI was listed separately under the heading, "United Nations," whereas the other institutes were listed under the heading "Affiliated regional institutes and associated institutes." From 2001 onwards, all of the institutes were once again listed under the heading, "UN bodies and affiliated institutes."

2 Information on PNI publications can be obtained from the websites of the respective PNIs, listed in Table 7.1.

3 Report of the Advisory Committee, 1974, E/CN.5/516, para. 183.

In 1954, the First United Nations Asia and Far East Conference for the Prevention of Crime and the Treatment of Offenders, held in Rangoon, Burma (now Yangon, Myanmar) adopted a resolution calling for the establishment of a UN regional training institute in Asia (UNAFEI, 2020).

4 Footnote 1 to the paragraph states that "The Government of the State of Sao Paulo has offered to act as host to the Institute."

Apparently the first negotiations were not successful, as a note from the Secretariat ten years later, in 1969, stated that the plans for a Latin American institute needed to be "reactivated" (E/CN.5/C.2/R.2, 1966, para. 72). The report on the fourth session (1970) of the Advisory Committee of Experts (E/CN.5/457, 1970, paras. 21–22) notes that the Advisory Committee stressed the "urgent" need to establish regional institutes, particularly in the Latin America region and in Africa south of the Sahara, and recognized a need to establish "possibly in Eastern Europe ..., a regional institute to bridge the gaps of communication, research and training within the larger European Area." In para. 40 reference was made to the willingness of Venezuela to host a second social defence institute in the Latin American region (in addition to the one being discussed at that time with Brazil).

5 As the Social Defence Section was, in the view of the Committee of Experts, understaffed and underfunded, the Committee welcomed proposals for the establishment of regional institutes, but argued that this should not lead to a reduction of the Secretariat staff dealing with crime prevention and criminal justice. See, for example, E/CN.5/329, 1958, para. 18.

When the European regional institute was established in 1981, the UN no longer offered to cover the salary of the director for the initial years (personal notes of the author).

6 The original name of UNICRI was the UN Social Defence Research Institute (UNSDRI). The establishment of UNAFEI and UNSDRI is described in Alper and Boren, 1972, pp. 104–112. The establishment of the first wave of institutes is dealt with more generally in Finnane, 2007, pp. 235–245 and 249–250.

Although it was not formally established as a regional UN institute, NAUSS (originally called the Arab Security Studies and Training Centre) has a clear regional mandate and is a member of the PNIs.

7 During its ten years of existence, the effectiveness of the institute in Cairo appears to have been somewhat limited due to insufficient technical assistance from the UN. However, it held training courses on human rights in the administration of justice, social defence for Arab States, narcotics control, crime detection, and criminal statistics. It also prepared background papers for the Arab region preparatory meeting for the Fifth UN Crime Congress. See *Report of the UN Crime Committee*, 1974, E/AC/21/Rev1, paras. 177–182, and Progress Report on United Nations Activities in Crime Prevention and Control, Report of the Secretary-General, 7 August 1980, para. 74.

At the 1995 session of the UN Crime Commission, held a month after the organization of the Ninth UN Crime Congress in Cairo, an open-ended intergovernmental working group was established to consider the proposal of the Egyptian Government to establish a regional centre, which was to be based in Cairo, for training and research in crime prevention and criminal justice for the Mediterranean States. *Report on the Fourth Session of the UN Crime Commission*, E/CN.15/1995/13, p. 5 and ECOSOC resolution 1995/27, at I(B) para. 8. However, the regional centre envisaged was never established.

8 In 1994, soon after the restructuring of the UN Crime Programme, ECOSOC adopted a resolution (Resolution 1994/23) on affiliation of institutes or centres with the PNIs.

9 Statute of the UN Interregional Crime and Justice Research Institute, ECOSOC resolution 1989/56, arts. III and VII. The Italian Government is the primary source of UNICRI's financial support.
10 At the 2008 session of the Commission, the Commission "agreed that the workshop should, if possible, be continued and that it should continue to take place in the context of the first meeting of the Committee of the Whole, at a meeting to be organized on the morning of the first day of the session, prior to the informal consultations of the Committee of the Whole on draft resolutions." Report of the UN Crime Commission at its 2007 session (E/2007/30/Rev.1, para. 170).
11 There has been extensive cooperation among the PNIs in, for example, the organization of joint training sessions and research. On the other hand, secondment of personnel among the PNIs has remained very rare in practice.
12 Perhaps the most notable exception was UNAFRI, which at the time of establishment had received promises from many African countries that they would provide it with sustained financial and other support. In the majority of cases these promises were not kept. A second exception was the short-lived (1972–1982) Institute of Social Defence, in Cairo.
13 In practice, one clear sign of this lack of understanding was the opposition of some diplomatic representatives at sessions of the UN Crime Commission to the insertion into draft resolutions of earlier "agreed language," according to which the UNODC would be requested to carry out activities "in cooperation with the Programme Network Institutes." Some of these representatives simply had not heard of the PNIs before and had difficulty in understanding their relevance and usefulness within the framework of the UN Crime Programme. Others may have equated the PNIs with non-governmental organizations, and were reluctant to include references in draft resolutions to entities that were not directly under the control of Member States.

References

Alper, Benedict S. and Jerry F. Boren (1972), *Crime: International Agenda, Concern and Action in the Prevention of Crime and Treatment of Offenders, 1846–1972*, Lexington Books

Finnane, Mark (2007), *JV Barry: A Life*, University of New South Wales Press

López-Rey de Arroya, Manuel (1985), *A Guide to United Nations Criminal Policy*, Cambridge Studies in Criminology LIV

Ram, Christopher (2012), *Meeting the Challenge of Crime in the Global Village: An Assessment of the Role and Future of the United Nations Commission on the Crime Prevention and Criminal Justice*, HEUNI publication no. 73

The United Nations and Crime Prevention (1995), UN Department of Public Information, New York, available at https://www.unodc.org/documents/congress// Previous_Congresses/9th_Congress_1995/029_The_United_Nations_and_Crime_ Prevention.pdf

UN Asia and Far East Institute for the Prevention of Crime and the Treatment of Offenders (UNAFEI) (2020), *United Nations Asia and Far East Institute for the Prevention of Crime and the Treatment of Offenders* (brochure). Tokyo, p. 6, available at https://www.moj.go.jp/content/001323828.pdf

PART III

The product

8

THE EVOLUTION OF TOPICS IN THE UN CRIME PROGRAMME

8.1   Does the UN have its own criminal policy?

The concept of criminal policy is generally understood to refer to the approach that Member States take in preventing and responding to crime. This criminal policy provides the framework for guiding the work of the police, prosecutors, judges, correctional staff, social workers, and other actors.

The UN as a body does not have the power to define authoritatively what conduct is or should be criminal in Member States, nor does it have the power to interpret provisions of criminal law. It also does not have its own police force, prosecutors, or judges (except, for example, in connection with UN peacekeeping and peacebuilding operations). Nonetheless, it does seek to prevent and respond to crime by promoting the exchange of experience, providing technical assistance to Member States on request, and developing standards and norms. The UN advocates for a fair, effective, and humane criminal policy, in line with international human rights and the growing body of UN standards and norms. It can thus be said to have its own evolving criminal policy. Furthermore, the UN is an intergovernmental organization and can receive criminal policy mandates from its Member States.[1]

Perhaps the most fundamental way in which the UN promotes a criminal policy is by bringing Member States and other entities together to formulate strategies for preventing and responding to crime. What Roger Clark refers to as a "subtle process of symbiosis" is at play (Clark, 1994, p. 23, fn 61). The issues dealt with at sessions of the UN Crime Commission, the UN Crime Congresses, the Conferences of the States Parties to the two UN Conventions, the UN Programme Network Institutes, and other meetings organized within the framework of the UN Crime Programme can have an effect on

DOI: 10.4324/9781003480907-11

how policy-makers and practitioners around the world approach their work. At the same time, the views, concerns, concepts, and proposals that are raised by the participants at these meetings often find their way into the outcome, into what here is called UN criminal policy. The criminal policy of the UN has changed and continues to change. At the same time it can influence the criminal policy of Member States.

These changes can be due to a number of factors. Society itself has changed considerably since the end of the Second World War, when the UN and the UN Crime Programme were established. These changes have been the result of (unequal) economic development and industrialization, the process of urbanization, the increase in internal and international migration, changes in social structure, and changes in the socio-political system that functions in any given Member State. Developments in transportation, communications, and financial instruments bring with them new types of crime and facilitate the movement of offenders and the transfer of the profits from crime. Also, technological change (such as the advent of computers and the Internet) create new criminal opportunities, but also new ways to respond to crime.

Sections 8.2–8.4 look at how three of the main topics in UN criminal policy have changed over the past 75 years: corrections, youth crime, and development, social defence, and crime. (The evolution of two other topics, transnational organized crime and corruption, is described in section 3.2.) Section 8.5. looks at how gender has been reflected in the UN Crime Programme. The final section provides a brief description of how certain topics were introduced into and dealt with in the UN Crime Programme; access to justice, victims, and cybercrime.

The introduction of a topic and its evolution have sometimes been slow (as with youth crime and correctional treatment), and at other times very fast (as with cybercrime). There is sometimes considerable resistance among Member States to consideration of a topic (such as "the new International Criminal Justice Order"), or a topic may receive so much attention that it seems to preclude others, at least in the short term (as with transnational organized crime at the turn of the millennium).

8.2   Corrections

In the first decades of UN work on crime prevention and criminal justice, the focus was almost solely on corrections and youth crime ("juvenile delinquency," as it was referred to at the time). For example, the agenda items at the first two UN Crime Congresses, in 1955 and 1960, dealt solely with these two traditional topics.[2] However, *how* correctional treatment and youth crime have been conceived and analysed and what criminal policy recommendations have been made have evolved considerably.

In respect of correctional treatment, the focus in the UN Crime Programme was initially almost solely on *institutional treatment*. This was in line with the positivist approach of criminology at the time, which emphasized the need for rehabilitation and treatment. The dominant school of thought was that the "cause" of crime could be identified. Doing so was believed to require a careful examination of the offender, and a diagnosis of where his (the assumption was generally that the offender was male) development had gone wrong. Once the diagnosis had been given, it would be possible to apply the proper treatment.

This "proper treatment" was widely presumed to require an extended period in a closed institution. According to the progression system, incoming prisoners would be interviewed and classified, to make it possible to select the proper course of treatment for each individual. Gradually over the course of the incarceration, a prisoner who responded well to the treatment (i.e., "progresses") would be granted more privileges. This was intended to motivate the prisoner to better himself.[3] The final stage would be parole, during which period the released offender would be subjected to supervision to ensure that "he had learned his lesson" and could be safely reintegrated into society.

In the 1960s and 1970s, initially in northern Europe and North America, increasing criticism was directed against the focus on rehabilitation through extended institutional treatment. It had proved to be difficult to find a form of institutional treatment that was effective for broad categories of offenders.[4] Predicting who would reoffend and, conversely, who could be safely released back into the community had also proved to be difficult. Some criminologists and criminal policy experts pointed out that there was often a lack of proportionality between the seriousness of the offence and the term of institutional treatment that was considered necessary for rehabilitation. Human rights advocates noted that the prisoner was in effect being coerced into accepting treatment, and argued that such coercive treatment was generally ineffective. Several observers pointed out that the social, economic, and human costs of incarceration were increasing. In many countries, the prisons were getting bigger and becoming increasingly difficult to manage. A number of institutions suffered from gang violence and other breakdowns in order. Illegal drugs and communicable diseases were also causing problems. When there was a breakdown in prison management, it was doubtful whether prisons could provide effective rehabilitation and treatment. Their function was increasingly simply to "warehouse" the prisoners until their sentence had been served. During their stay in the institution, they would often fail to become rehabilitated and, instead, learn new means of committing offences, form new criminal alliances, and become more ingrained in a "criminal mindset." On release, ex-prisoners often found that there were few if any reintegration services available to them. Unable to find housing or gainful employment and rejected by the community, they would return to crime.

Among the first signs of a change in UN correctional policy were discussions of *short-term imprisonment* and *non-custodial sanctions*.[5] At the Second UN Crime Congress (1960), the recommendation was made that short imprisonment sentences should be avoided (Neudek, 1993, p. 71).[6] The *prevention of recidivism*, the *training of staff*, and the use of probation were discussed at the Third UN Crime Congress (1965) (Neudek, 1993, pp. 71–72). At both the Fourth and the Fifth UN Crime Congresses (1970 and 1975), there were separate agenda items on implementation of the Standard Minimum Rules for the Treatment of Prisoners.

At the Sixth UN Crime Congress (1980), *prison overcrowding* was a specific topic on the agenda, a topic to be taken up again at several subsequent UN Crime Congresses. The inclusion of the phrase "deinstitutionalization of corrections" in this agenda item was in line with discussions at earlier UN Crime Congresses on community-based measures (as designated agenda items at the First, Third, and Fifth UN Crime Congresses, respectively in 1955, 1965, and 1975). However, it was also in part a reflection of concern about the increase in the prison population in many countries, with the accompanying difficulties in prison management and in the rehabilitation of offenders in severely overcrowded prisons. Whereas earlier, the debate had largely been on proper identification of which offenders "merited" a sentence of imprisonment due to the severity of the offence and/or the risk that they posed to society, more and more practitioners and academics were suggesting a need for fundamental changes in criminal policy in order to reduce the use of imprisonment.[7]

The Eighth UN Crime Congress (1990) included an agenda item on "Criminal justice policies in relation to problems of imprisonment, other penal sanctions and alternative measures," the last time in a 30-year period that a corrections-related theme was included as a separate topic at a UN Crime Congress. However, the PNIs helped to keep corrections on the Congress agenda. The Eighth UN Crime Congress was the first to have a workshop organized by the PNIs, and the topic was "Alternatives to imprisonment." Corrections-related workshops were organized also at the Eleventh (2005), Twelfth (2010), and Fourteenth (2021) UN Crime Congresses.

Among the resolutions adopted by the Eighth UN Crime Congress was one on draft standard minimum rules for non-custodial measures. The Sixth UN Crime Congress (1980) adopted a resolution entitled "Alternatives to imprisonment," encouraging Member States to expand the use of such measures. This led in 1984 to the first UN Crime Programme resolution on this theme being adopted (ECOSOC resolution 1984/46). It also led to UN Asia and Far East Institute for the Prevention of Crime and the Treatment of Offenders taking the initiative and hosting a meeting of experts in 1988, to prepare draft standards that were then submitted to the Eighth UN Crime Congress, from where they went to the UN Crime Committee and ECOSOC, to ultimately be adopted by the GA in 1990 (A/RES/45/110).[8] Due to their provenance, this set of standards and norms is known as the "Tokyo Rules."

The way in which the UN Crime Programme has considered the specific issue of the treatment of *women in corrections* is covered in section 8.5.

The discussion on non-custodial sanctions gradually led to an interest in mediation and restorative justice. The issue was raised by non-governmental organizations at the Ninth (1995) and Tenth (2000) UN Crime Congresses, and found its way into the Congress resolutions in 2000 and 2005. In 2002, ECOSOC adopted the "Basic principles on the use of restorative justice programmes in criminal matters" (ECOSOC resolution 2002/12). To assist Member States with implementation of these new standards and norms, the UNODC produced a *Handbook on Restorative Justice Programmes* in 2006. Following the collection of new experience from around the world in restorative justice, as well as the adoption of the SDGs in 2015, an updated version of the *Handbook* was published in 2020 (https://www.unodc.org/documents/justice-and-prison-reform/20-01146_Handbook_on_Restorative_Justice_Programmes.pdf).[9]

Together with the interest in non-custodial measures, restorative justice, and the treatment of women in corrections, institutional corrections has remained a mainstay in the UN Crime Programme, just as it has remained the central element of the response of all UN Member States to crime. The first UN standards and norms ever adopted, the 1955 Standard Minimum Rules for the Treatment of Prisoners (the SMRs), has clearly been the most important and most influential UN standard. Considerable UN technical assistance has been provided to Member States on request in order to help them in its implementation.

The adoption of the SMRs also contributed to an ECOSOC resolution setting out the importance of "alternatives to imprisonment" within the context of comprehensive crime prevention and criminal justice policy (E/RES/2017/19).

However, ideas about what is proper correctional treatment evolve over time. Furthermore, relevant "hard law" international instruments were adopted after the SMRs entered into force, among them the International Covenant on Civil and Political Rights, the International Covenant on Economic, Social and Cultural Rights, and the Convention against Torture and Other Cruel, Inhuman or Degrading Treatment or Punishment. Although several new standards and norms have been adopted over the years on implementation of the original SMRs, for example, extending it to persons arrested or imprisonment without charge (ECOSOC resolution 2076 (LXII) (1977) and ECOSOC resolution 1984/47, respectively), various proposals were made to update them. This caused some concern, in particular concerns that rewriting the SMRs could lead to attempts to weaken some of the human rights protection that had been incorporated in them. This weakening did not take place, and 60 years after the adoption of the SMRs, with due consideration given to the ongoing work at that time on the SDGs, the up-dated Standard Minimum Rules on the Treatment of Offenders were adopted by the GA in 2015 (A/RES/70/175).[10] The South African Government had provided extensive support to the review process, so in honour of Nelson Mandela, who had passed away in 2013, the new standard is known as "The Nelson Mandela Rules."

The Covid-19 pandemic had an impact on correctional institutions around the world.[11] This was a factor in UNODC making the decision to cooperate with the UN Office of the High Commissioner for Human Rights and the UN Department of Peacekeeping in the preparation of a UN System Common Position on Incarceration (https://www.unodc.org/res/justice-and-prison-reform/nelsonmandelarules/UN_System_Common_Position_on_Incarceration_09-06-2021.pdf).[12] The Position Paper, however, was in preparation before the outbreak of the pandemic; it seeks to shift the criminal policy of Member States away from incarceration and towards crime prevention and the use of non-custodial sanctions. It also seeks to improve prison management and prison conditions, thus promoting the rehabilitation and social integration of offenders. As noted in the Common Position,

> It addresses prison and associated challenges at the global, regional and national levels and constitutes the common framework for United Nations support to Member States in relation to incarceration. The paper reflects a 'One UN' approach aimed at supporting efforts to rethink the current overreliance on and implementation of incarceration, including through better coordination and integrated efforts.

The Position Paper is a welcome and integrative development. Its importance lies in the fact that it will be used in UN Crime Programme technical assistance work as a framework in assisting Member States on request to improve their approach to corrections.

At the time of writing, work is underway on a new UN standard and norm that should help Member States in this process: guidelines on reducing reoffending through rehabilitation and reintegration.[13] The work has been promoted in particular by the Japanese Government and UNAFEI.

8.3   Youth crime (juvenile delinquency)

Juvenile delinquency (currently referred to the UN Crime Programme as "youth crime") is the second theme that the UN Crime Programme has considered from the very beginning.

A hundred and fifty years ago, long before the UN Crime Programme was established, the First International Congress on Crime Prevention and the Repression of Crime, including Penal and Reformatory Treatment (London, 1872) brought together practitioners from many countries interested in learning from one another about how to deal with offenders. Among the issues considered at that first international congress were juvenile reformatories and, more broadly, how society should deal with delinquent children.[14]

Juvenile justice was first addressed in its own right on the international level in 1882, when the first International Congress on Child Welfare was held in Paris. This was followed by the International Congress for the Welfare and Protection of Children in 1896 in Florence. The Third International Congress for the Welfare and Protection of Children (London, 1902) considered the problem of neglected children and the probability (not "possibility") that such children would become delinquents if due care was not taken.

When the League of Nations was established a few years later, juvenile justice became one of its main areas of activity. In 1919 the League of Nations established the Child Welfare Committee in order to examine the rights of children, primarily to identify the measures that states should take in respect of street children, slavery, child labour, child trafficking, and the prostitution of minors.[15]

The first criminal policy programme drafted under the aegis of the UN was produced by the Temporary Social Commission in 1948. This programme shows a heavy orientation towards "social defence" in criminal policy. Such an orientation is understandable in the light of the contemporary discussion about criminal policy in Europe and North America, the mainstay of UN membership at that time.[16]

Of the nine items in this first programme, three dealt specifically with youth:

- the promotion by medical and educational measures of the readjustment of children with antisocial tendencies;
- the organization of vocational training for children leaving school and the employment and protection of such children; and
- the treatment of juvenile offenders according to medical and educational methods by which punishment should be replaced by special measures.

(López-Rey, 1985, p. 2)

When compared to discussions conducted at international conferences in the 1800s and, to some extent, the 1900s, general agreement seemed to have been reached by the time the UN Crime Programme began its work on some issues related to juvenile delinquency:[17]

- young suspects and offenders should be kept separated from adult suspects and offenders;
- young offenders should be dealt with by youth courts and in facilities where the staff have been trained to take into consideration the special needs and circumstances of young persons;

- social inquiries should be prepared for young suspects coming before the court;
- individual cells for incarcerated young offenders should be avoided. They should be kept "congregate" (in group facilities), with a clear preference for small, almost home-like facilities; and
- young offenders should be provided with a mix of education and physical and vocational training.

There was no general consensus on a number of other issues and from the earliest days of the UN Crime Programme, the discussions reflected the divided opinions familiar to practitioners and policy-makers today. Some examples are:

- Should attention be focused on those who have committed a criminal act or should measures also encompass children at risk of becoming delinquent?
- What is the proper scope of treatment and punishment?
- What are the criteria for success or failure of treatment?
- Where should the age limits be set?

One of the earliest results of UN work on youth crime was a publication series entitled "Comparative Studies on Juvenile Delinquency," which primarily contained reviews of the laws in different countries. Issue nos. 7–8 of the *International Review of Criminal Policy*, published in 1955, focused exclusively on "The Prevention of Juvenile Delinquency." It sought to provide a global overview of the following topics:

- concepts in the field of juvenile delinquency (age limits, delinquency and maladjustment, pre-delinquency, and potential delinquency);
- the extent of juvenile delinquency;
- the question of the determining factors of juvenile delinquency;
- the scope and meaning of prevention;
- approaches to prevention (the role of the state, community, family, school, police, social services, and others), research, and the relation between prevention and treatment;
- the role of courts and administrative bodies with jurisdiction over juveniles and treatment measures in the prevention of juvenile delinquency; and
- review of the existing situation.

Work also began on preparations for the First UN Crime Congress (1955), at which one of the five topics was "The Prevention of Juvenile Delinquency." At the Second UN Crime Congress, one of the topics was "New Forms of Juvenile Delinquency: Their Origin, Prevention and Treatment," while a second topic dealt with "Special Police Services for the Prevention of Juvenile Delinquency." While the First UN Crime Congress lumped together delinquent, abandoned, orphaned, and maladjusted youth as "juvenile delinquents," the Second UN Crime Congress five years later made a distinction between juvenile delinquency caused by maladjustment and juvenile delinquency caused by other factors.[18]

In 1965, the overall theme at the Third UN Crime Congress was "Prevention of Criminality," and one of the topics was "Special Preventive and Treatment Measures for Young Adults." Youth crime was not discussed at the 1970 and 1975 Crime Congresses. In 1980, the Congress had as one of its topics "Juvenile justice before and after the onset of delinquency," and the 1985 UN Crime Congress, which adopted the Standard Minimum Rules for the Administration of Juvenile Justice, had as one of its topics "Youth, crime, and justice." The Congress in 1985 also saw a special research workshop on youth, crime, and justice, to which extensive documentation on current research was submitted.[19] The Eighth UN Crime Congress (1990) discussed "Prevention of delinquency, juvenile justice, and the protection of the young: policy approaches and directions." The Discussion Guide for the Congress indicated that the focus had increasingly shifted to children at social risk (1/ CONF.144/PM.1, para. 58).

The Beijing Rules

In 1985, the GA adopted the Standard Minimum Rules on the Administration of Juvenile Justice (the Beijing Rules) (A/RES/40/33). The idea for drafting the Beijing Rules arose during the Sixth United Nations Congress discussions on "Juvenile delinquency: before and after the onset of delinquency" (A/ CONF.87/14/Rev.1). The report of the Congress called for the development of "model rules on juvenile justice administration." The UN Secretariat requested that Professor Horst Schüler-Springorum prepare a draft for such model rules, which he then presented to a UN ad hoc Meeting of Experts on Youth, Crime, and Justice held on 2–8 November 1983 in Newark, New Jersey. Following extensive rounds of consultations, including within the framework of a five-week international seminar held at UNAFEI in 1983, meetings organized by both ILANUD and HEUNI, as well as the Sixth Joint Colloquium organized by the Big Four non-governmental organizations[20] the draft "Standard Minimum Rules on the Administration of Juvenile Justice" were discussed at the Interregional Preparatory Meeting held in Beijing in 1984 (A/CONF.121/IPM/1, paras. 55 and 56), and then at the Seventh UN Congress in Milan. On the recommendation of the Seventh Congress, the Beijing Rules were adopted by the GA (A/RES/40/33).

Together with the UN Declaration on the Rights of the Child (GA resolution 1386 (XIV)) and the 1990 Convention on the Rights of the Child

(A/RES/44/25), the Beijing Rules set an international standard for dealing with juveniles. As noted by the Director-General of the UN Office in Vienna at the preparatory meeting for the Eighth UN Congress (A/CONF.144/IPM.4, p. 27),

> The aim and spirit of those instruments, as well as scientific evidence and practical experience, provided a basic international premise: that young person's rights, well-being, status and interest had to be protected and upheld. Specific measures therefore had to be provided for the large number of the young who are not in conflict with the law but who were abandoned, neglected, abused and, in general, were endangered or at social risk.

Among the topics covered by the Beijing Rules are the improved professionalization of juvenile justice personnel, specialization within the police to handle juvenile cases, enactment of specific statutes such as Child Welfare Acts and Codes of Procedure, information sharing (clearinghouses, study tours, courses, advisory services), and research and pilot projects.

In the drafting of the document, a number of problematic issues had to be considered. One of the most debated issues was the determination of the age range in question. Several Latin American countries proposed an upper age limit of 24 years, while Nordic countries favoured a limit more in line with their legislation, 18 years.[21] The Beijing Rules skirted this issue by leaving it to national legislation and policy: Rule 2-2 defines a juvenile as "a child or young person who, under the respective legal system, may be dealt with for an offence in a manner which is different from an adult."[22]

Another difficulty had to do with the scope of the Beijing Rules. For example, certain jurisdictions, such as the United States, made use of the concept of status offences, which involve behaviour which, in the case of an adult, would not be criminal (for example, drinking alcohol, violation of curfews, and non-attendance of school). It was decided that the Rules would also be applied, *mutandis mutanda*, to these forms of conduct.

Another problem lay in the definition of the type of custody in question. According to Rule 11(b), deprivation of liberty

> means any form of detention or imprisonment or the placement of a person in another public or private custodial setting from which this person is not permitted to leave at will by order of any judicial, administrative or other public authority.

In the implementation of the Beijing Rules, special attention should be focused on its key tenets, which include:

- less severe and punitive sanctions for youth;
- the increased use of diversion;

- the restriction of imprisonment;
- the limitation of the scope of the definition of delinquency; and
- the guarantee of procedural and substantive rights.

The Riyadh Guidelines

Although some of the drafters of the Beijing Rules argued that prevention is an essential part of juvenile justice, others regarded this as too broad an issue to be included in the Beijing Rules and wanted to focus on the structure and operation of the juvenile justice system (Schüler-Springorum, 1983, p. 4). For this reason, the Beijing Rules do not include provisions on prevention. Nonetheless, the drafters recognized the importance of the issue. On the same day as the GA adopted resolution 40/33 approving the Beijing Rules, the GA adopted resolution 40/35, which drew attention to the need for standards and norms on the prevention of juvenile delinquency. "Specific measures therefore had to be provided for the large number of the young who were not in conflict with the law but who were abandoned, neglected, abused and, in general, were endangered or at social risk" (A/CONF.144/IPM.3, para. 4).

The first draft for what became the Riyadh Guidelines was prepared by Professor Allison Morris. The draft was circulated among experts in juvenile justice and then discussed at an International Meeting of Experts on the development of UN Draft Standards for the Prevention of Juvenile Delinquency held at the Arab Security Studies and Training Centre[23] in Riyadh 28 February–1 March 1988. From there, the draft went to the regional preparatory meetings and the respective interregional preparatory meeting for the Ninth Congress, and then on to the GA for adoption (A/RES/45/112 of 14 December 1990. See A/CONF.144/16, para. 26).

Formulating an international standard on the prevention of juvenile delinquency is an ambitious undertaking. The approach adopted by the UN was to focus on "primary prevention" (policies and proposals designed to prevent the conditions that may give rise to delinquency), with some references to "secondary prevention" (efforts to identify high-risk juveniles and reduce the likelihood of offending). Some of the assumptions underlying the guidelines were as follows (Morrison, 1988):

- some involvement in juvenile delinquency is a normal part of socialization;
- persistent offending is rare. Some early signs of possible future involvement in persistent offending are troublesome, anti-social, and aggressive behaviour at an early stage of development; and
- factors that are somewhat correlated with persistent offending include poor parental child-rearing practices, poor parental supervision, social deprivation, and low intelligence and attainment.

The Havana Rules

In November 1990, the GA adopted rules for the protection of juveniles deprived of their liberty. The International Covenant on Civil and Political Rights, the Standard Minimum Rules for the Treatment of Prisoners, and the Beijing Rules are designed in part to reduce the incarceration of children and youth. However, when these instruments were adopted, it was already clear that incarceration of children and youth would remain a widespread practice. Instead of calling for more and better prisons for juveniles, the Havana Rules were designed to encourage the use of alternatives to imprisonment and to ensure that juveniles in custody have their basic rights protected (A/CONF.144/IPM.3, para. 10). These Rules were developed by an open-ended[24] working group of non-governmental organizations established by Defence for Children International in cooperation with the UNODC. The text was circulated for comment, following which the draft was developed by the Max-Planck Institute for Foreign and International Criminal Law (Germany) (A/CONF.144/IPM.3, paras. 3 and 65–67). As with the Riyadh Guidelines, the draft went to the regional preparatory meetings and the respective interregional preparatory meeting for the Ninth Congress for discussion, and then on to the GA for adoption (A/RES/45/113 of 14 December 1990. See A/CONF.144/16, para. 26).

The Havana Rules clearly follow the model and the language of the 1955 Standard Minimum Rules for the Treatment of Prisoners. Among the issues covered are juveniles under arrest, awaiting trial, or sentenced. The bulk of the document deals with management issues, such as the keeping of records, classification and placement, accommodation, education and work, medical care, contacts with the wider community, and disciplinary procedures.

Children as victims

As has been noted earlier, during the 1990s and the first decade of the 2000s, the UN Crime Programme was heavily focused on (transnational) organized crime. However, the topic of young offenders was not completely eclipsed. Nonetheless, there were inversions and shifts in the focus. Whereas the focus had previously been on children and young persons as offenders and as "in need of care" in order to prevent them from becoming offenders, in the 1990s and the early 2000s, the focus when speaking of children and young people shifted to them as victims of crime and, in part, as witnesses in the criminal justice system.

The first sign of this was the adoption by the GA of resolution A/RES/45/115 (1990) on the "Instrumental use of children in criminal activities." Largely as part of the overall realignment of the UN Crime Programme to focus on (transnational) organized crime and in view of the increasing online availability of child sexual abuse material, considerable attention was paid to the sexual abuse or exploitation of children. The following resolutions were adopted over the course of twenty years:

- ECOSOC resolution 2002/14, Promoting effective measures to deal with the issues of missing children and sexual abuse or exploitation of children;
- UN Crime Commission resolution 16/2, Effective crime prevention and criminal justice responses to combat sexual exploitation of children (2007);
- ECOSOC resolution 2011/33, Prevention, protection and international cooperation against the use of new information technologies to abuse and/ or exploit children;
- GA resolution A/RES/69/194, UN Model strategies and practical measures on the elimination of violence against children in the field of crime prevention and criminal justice (2014);
- GA resolution A/RES/74/174, Countering child sexual exploitation and sexual abuse online (2019); and
- ECOSOC resolution 2022/14, Strengthening national and international efforts, including with the private sector, to protect children from sexual exploitation and abuse (2022).

Regarding children in criminal procedure, ECOSOC resolution 1997/30 adopted the Guidelines for Action on Children in the Criminal Justice System. The entry into force of the Convention on the Rights of the Child in 1990 imposed obligations on States Parties. It also provided a basis for cooperation among not only the States Parties but also different UN agencies (such as the UNODC, the Centre for Human Rights, the UN Children's Fund, and the Committee on the Rights of the Child), as well as a broad range of non-governmental organizations, professional groups, the media, academic institutions, and other stakeholders. In order to provide guidelines for this cooperation, ECOSOC resolution 1996/13 called for a plan of action. This was drafted at an expert group meeting held in Vienna 23–25 February 1997. The draft was submitted to the UN Crime Commission two months later, and during the autumn of that same year the Vienna Guidelines were adopted by ECOSOC (resolution 1997/30).

This was followed a few years later by ECOSOC resolution 2005/20 on Guidelines on justice in matters involving child victims and witnesses of crime.

One agenda item at the Twelfth UN Crime Congress (2010) was "Children, youth and crime; and making the United Nations guidelines on crime prevention work", and the Fourteenth UN Crime Congress (2021) had a workshop on "Education and youth engagement as key to making societies resilient to crime."

More general child justice reform issues are dealt with in ECOSOC resolution 2007/23, Supporting national efforts for child justice reform, in particular through technical assistance and improved United Nations system-wide coordination and, two years later, ECOSOC resolution 2009/26, Supporting national and international efforts for child justice reform, in particular through improved coordination in technical assistance.

8.4   Development, social defence, and crime

An enduring theme in the work of the UN, and also of the UN Crime Programme, has been "development." How this concept has been understood, however, has changed in the course of time.

As noted in section 2.2, at the time the UN Crime Programme was established, criminologists understood crime to be due largely to a pathology on the part of the individual offender. Although many pure biological theories of the cause of crime (such as the anthropological theory that "born criminals" could be identified by congenital stigmata) had long since been discredited, many criminologists during the immediate post-Second World War period continued to assume that the "cause" of crime in an individual offender could be diagnosed, and that they could be rehabilitated through the application of suitable therapy (rehabilitation). Several of the key persons involved in early UN criminal policy were strongly influenced by the ideology of "*social defence*" which had initially focused on the "dangerous" personality of offenders, "safety measures," and resocialization. Reference can be made in particular to Professor Marc Ancel (France), and to Dr. Manuel López-Rey (Bolivia), who served as the head of the UN Secretariat unit on crime prevention and criminal justice (aptly named the Social Defence Section) from 1952 to 1961, and who served in this capacity at the time of the First and Second UN Crime Congresses.[25]

Adler and Mueller describe the social defence approach taken during the early years of the UN Crime Programme as follows:

> guided only by humanitarianism, society had the right to defend itself against internal aggression (crime), as much as it could defend itself against foreign aggression (war). Ideologically neutral, social defence took no position on such philosophical concepts as free will or determinism, classicism or positivism, retribution or rehabilitation" (Adler and Mueller, 1995, p. 5).[26]

Although the term "social defence" can thus be seen to be part of the UN Crime Programme lexicon up to the time of the Fourth UN Crime Congress (1970), the social defence ideology was abandoning its earlier focus on crime as pathology and had come to see crime as an interaction between society and the individual. This is not to detract from the continuing relevance of so-called bio-social theories of crime, which seek to identify and treat pathologies that increase the risk that an individual will engage in criminal conduct. Dr. Marc Ancel in particular sought to encourage this evolution in the understanding of social defence, with the publication of his *La défense sociale nouvelle*. The first edition appeared in 1954, with revised editions in 1966 and 1981.

However, by the end of the 1980s, the term "social defence" appears to have been retired from use in the UN Crime Programme.[27]

Beginning in the 1940s, emerging theories in criminology stressed factors such as increasing disorganization in society, a weakening in informal and formal social control, and the development of subcultures. Such theories fitted in nicely with the corollaries of the *modernization thesis*. In the wider context of the work of the UN, development was at first thought to be synonymous with economic development and economic growth. The underlying idea was that the increase in economic resources (as measured by the gross national product) would have a trickle-down effect throughout society, enhancing the general standard of living (Vetere, 1995, p. 38). According to the modernization thesis, societies in the process of industrializing and developing were seen to go through different stages. These stages tend to involve considerable economic and social changes, such as rural-urban migration, a shift in the industrial structure, and changes in the pattern of time use. Many of these changes were seen to be criminogenic: rising unemployment, increased leisure time, the breakdown of families, greater availability of coveted goods, and the increased ease with which crime can be committed.

An implicit (and often explicit) assumption of the modernization these is that the values of Western countries have made industrialization and modernization possible, and that these values should be emulated elsewhere. At the same time, developing countries should be assisted in managing the anticipated criminological consequences of rapid modernization (presumably under the guidance of Western economists and criminologists).

Towards the end of the 1960s, social, political, and cultural factors were also being considered alongside economic factors within the framework of development. One of the first signs of a shift in the UN Crime Programme was the 1960 Secretariat report, Prevention of types of criminality resulting from social changes and accompanying economic development in less developed countries, which was submitted to the Second UN Crime Congress (1960) (A/CONF.17/4).[28]

The title of the report was intended to echo the last substantive agenda item at the Second UN Crime Congress (1960), "Criminality resulting from social change and economic development in less developed countries." The report and ensuing discussion at the Congress marked two significant shifts in the approach to crime prevention and criminal justice. One was that the perspective was being expanded beyond the industrialized Western countries to examine crime and the response to crime in other regions and in developing countries.[29] The second was the shift in criminological thinking noted above, away from individualistic theories that saw crime as a pathology which could be diagnosed and treated, towards theories that were seeking to understand the impact that cultural, technical, economic, and social changes have on the level and structure of crime in society. As noted by Manuel López-Rey, in his capacity as representative of the Secretary-General, the improvement of material living conditions and welfare policies could not alone stop the increase in crime, since new forms of crime would inevitably appear as the result of development (Report of the Second UN Crime Congress, para. 46).

In 1969, the GA adopted a "Declaration of Social Progress and Development" which mentions as one of its many goals "the provision of social defence measures and the elimination of conditions leading to crime and delinquency."[30]

In the late 1960s and throughout the 1970s, there was a growing conviction that the emphasis on domestic growth, which stimulated industrialization but also led to internal and external migration, was contributing to increased poverty and to the inability of a growing sector of the population to have access to basic health care, education, social services, and gainful employment. Especially in urban areas, formal social control weakened. Poverty, social injustice, poor living conditions, and lower-class status were increasingly found to be correlated with crime (López-Rey, 1985, p. 83).[31] There was also a growing conviction that crime was no longer solely a national (much less local) problem. Crime was becoming transnational, and the factors that appeared to be promoting crime were to a significant extent beyond the scope of national economic, social, and criminal policy.

At the time of the Sixth UN Crime Congress (1980), the political debate in Latin American countries particularly featured references to the "New Economic International Order," which was an effort by developing countries to replace the so-called Bretton Woods Agreement with a structure that would provide them, in their view, with more favourable terms of trade as well as greater control over multinationals operating within their country.[32]

At the Sixth UN Crime Congress (1980), Egypt submitted a brief draft resolution entitled "Towards a new international order for the prevention of crime and the treatment of offenders." It expressed the need for a "new international order governing relations between States in the field of crime prevention and the treatment of offenders complementary to and integrated with the new international economic order" and invited ECOSOC to undertake a study that would lead to the elaboration of the principles of such an order, as well as the preparation "as appropriate, of draft international instruments in the fields of international criminal law and international co-operation in combating criminality," with a view to submitting such a study to a "special international Congress to be convened promptly for the purpose of laying the foundations for the new international order" (Report of the Sixth UN Crime Congress, paras. 130 and 132; the draft is to be found on pp. 61–62).[33] Several delegations objected in particular to the proposal for such a study that could lead to the preparation of draft international instruments. Because of these objections, Egypt withdrew the draft on the understanding that the matter would be submitted to the Seventh UN Crime Congress in 1985 (Report of the Sixth UN Crime Congress, para. 112).

Language related to the proposal, however, found its way into the Sixth UN Crime Congress Declaration, the "Caracas Declaration," which was adopted after lengthy debate. The Declaration recognized that "crime prevention and criminal justice should be considered in the context of economic development, political systems, social and cultural values and social change, as well as in the context of the new international economic order" (Report of the Sixth UN Crime Congress, p. 3, at operative para. 2). In a way, this presaged the SDGs (adopted by the GA 35 years later, in 2015) by declaring that "all crime prevention policies should be co-ordinated with strategies for social, economic, political and cultural development."

As promised, the supporters of a "New International Criminal Justice Order" returned to the matter five years later, at the Seventh UN Crime Congress (1985). This time the draft resolution was more detailed and included an annex setting out 47 draft "guiding principles." The draft was negotiated at length in a working group, which resulted in the deletion of all references to a New International Criminal Justice Order and deletion of the proposal for work on draft international instruments. The heavily negotiated text was at last adopted by the Congress, from where it went to ECOSOC and the GA. However, even with these modifications, the GA exceptionally set the draft aside.

The efforts continued five years later, at the Eighth UN Crime Congress (1990). Once again, there were lengthy negotiations and the result, a resolution entitled "International co-operation for crime prevention and criminal justice in the context of development" was adopted not only by the Congress but also by the GA, as resolution 45/107. The document, however, was quite different from the one negotiated five years earlier. The annex was briefer (29 paragraphs as opposed to the earlier 47) and consisted not of "guidelines" but of the softer term "recommendations." With the exception of a passing reference in the second preambular paragraph, all references to the New International Economic Order had been deleted, to be replaced with "in the context of development." Language such as calls for "restructuring of the international economic system," the need for crime prevention and criminal justice policies to "take into account the structural causes, including socio-economic causes, of injustice, of which criminality is often but a symptom," and the obligation of Member States to refrain from committing "acts aimed at harming the development of other countries" disappeared from the draft.

At the time of the Eighth UN Crime Congress, work was already underway on the restructuring of the UN Crime Programme. This offered an opportunity to specifically formulate the underlying assumptions on which the UN Crime Programme rests and to define its goals. The GA resolution that established the new Programme, resolution 46/152, contained very few references to development.

In the Milan Plan of Action and the Guiding Principles, the broader New International Economic Order merited a passing reference in the ninth preambular paragraph, in which the GA referenced

> the principles contained in the Milan Plan of Action and the Guiding Principles for Crime Prevention and Criminal Justice in the Context of the New International Economic Order as well as other pertinent instruments formulated by United Nations congresses on the prevention of crime and the treatment of offenders and approved by the General Assembly.

Operative paragraph 9 of the resolution encouraged "all developed countries to review their aid programmes in order to ensure that there is a full and proper contribution in the field of criminal justice within the overall context of development priorities."

In the annex to the resolution establishing the restructured UN Crime Programme (A/RES/46/152), which contained the statement of principles and programme of action, the preambular paragraph cited above is repeated in full.[34] Otherwise, there are only a few rather general paragraphs that refer to the link between crime and development:

- according to paragraph 3, "the lowering of the world crime rate is related to, among other factors, the improvement of the social conditions of the population. The developed countries and the developing countries have experienced difficult situations in this respect. Nevertheless, the specific problems encountered by the developing countries justify priority being given to dealing with the situation confronting these countries."
- paragraph 4 states that "We believe that rising crime is impairing the process of development and the general well-being of humanity and is causing general disquiet within our societies. If this situation continues, progress and development will be the ultimate victims of crime."
- paragraph 5, in dealing with the growing internationalization of crime, states that organized crime is exploiting the relaxation of border controls designed to foster legitimate trade "and, hence, development."

The restructured UN Crime Programme, as presented in GA resolution 46/152, could not therefore be said to have provided a cohesive vision of the role of crime and criminal justice in development. As has been noted in the foregoing, the government-dominated UN Crime Commission turned much of its attention to questions related to the prevention and, more importantly, control of transnational organized crime, which was regarded as a security threat to an increasing extent.

Ten years after the restructuring, a second opportunity arose for the UN Crime Programme to set out its understanding of the link between development and crime, with the discussion on the formulation of the Millennium Development Goals (MDGs). However, there was relatively little discussion in the UN Crime Commission regarding the negotiations on the MDGs, and in particular on whether and how the Commission should become involved in this process. The opportunity – if there was one – was not seized. Other, perhaps more politically attuned elements of the UN system participated in framing the eight overall objectives: the eradication of extreme poverty and hunger, the achievement of universal primary education, the promotion of gender equality and the empowerment of women, the reduction of child mortality, the improvement of maternal health, the combating of HIV/AIDS, malaria, and other diseases, ensuring environmental sustainability, and the development of a global partnership for development (A/RES/55/2; Blaustein et al., 2022, pp. 159–166).

The timeline set for the MDGs ran until 2015. Although their effectiveness has been questioned, they did generate considerable political attention. Within the UN Crime Programme, thoughts turned to whether the international profile of crime prevention and criminal justice issues (and, on the part of the UN Drug Programme, drug issues) could be raised by integrating them in future UN-wide objectives. When work began on the SDGs, a new opportunity arose. As with the MDGs, there was no lack of stakeholders for different issues, and issues relating to drugs and crime were only regarded as part of the mix. This time, however, questions of security and access to justice were incorporated in Goal 16.[35]

The idea of sustainable development was not a new one in the UN Crime Programme, nor did the SDGs represent the first time a connection had been made between sustainable development and crime prevention and criminal justice. This had been done twenty years earlier with a GA resolution on human rights in the administration of justice (A/RES/50/181; Redo, 2012, p. 83).

The SDGs also provide an opportunity to incorporate the concept of *alternative development* into the UN Crime Programme more clearly than has been the case previously.

Within the UN system, early efforts to get farmers to grow licit crops led to what is known as the alternative development approach in drug policy. Attempts to assist farmers in growing licit crops broadened to efforts to improve the standard of living in general in areas producing illicit drugs. The UNODC defines alternative development as follows:

> a process to prevent and eliminate the illicit cultivation of plants containing narcotics and psychotropic substances through specifically designed rural development measures in the context of sustained national growth and sustainable development efforts in countries taking action against drugs, recognizing the particular socio-economic characteristics of the target communities and groups, within the framework of a comprehensive and permanent solution to the problem of illicit drugs.[36]

This process seeks not only to address rural poverty and economic factors which lead farmers to grow illicit drugs but also to provide members of local communities with health care, education, and social services, a way of securing rights to land and access to credit, and technical assistance in selecting, growing, packaging, and marketing their products.

The process also seeks to strengthen basic human rights, including the rights of indigenous people to citizenship, gender mainstreaming, and participation in local decision-making. Alternative development further seeks to provide irrigation, potable water, electricity, roads, and infrastructure, used not only to provide access to the market far beyond local communities but also to allow access to other services available in more developed areas of the country.

One of the earliest and arguably most successful practical illustrations of alternative development has been in Thailand. A notable aspect of the Thai experience is that the alternative development approach, although commonly associated with drug policy, has almost from the outset been applied to many other forms of crime (Joutsen, 2021).

The ethnic minorities in the mountainous regions of northern Thailand cultivated the opium poppy because they believed that they did not have any other viable options to earn a living. Some individuals were also beginning to become engaged in other criminal activities. Rural communities that become impoverished and vulnerable may not restrict the criminal activities they turn to to drug trafficking. In many places throughout the world, corresponding situations have led to an increase in, for example, trafficking in persons, illicit logging, trafficking in endangered species, trafficking in firearms, smuggling, and even terrorism. The alternative development approach should not be seen only in the context of preventing and controlling drug trafficking; the lessons can and should also be applied to other forms of crime.

The lessons learned in mountainous and rural areas can also be adapted to the slums, favelas, barrios, and overcrowded tenements in urban areas.[37] Ethnic minorities, the impoverished, and other vulnerable groups, especially in our larger cities, often face the challenges of lack of access to viable livelihoods and many turn to crime out of despair. Their physical proximity to modern and bustling shopping malls, gated communities, and conspicuous signs of inequalities in the distribution of wealth may increase their sense that they have been dealt with unfairly and that they and their families have been abandoned in the national pursuit of development. For them, drug trafficking, petty thefts, burglaries, street robberies, and confidence games may seem the only option, and joining criminal gangs may become a rite of passage. They need to be provided with legitimate paths to provide for themselves and their families.

8.5   Gender issues in the UN Crime Programme

In the early years of the UN Crime Programme, little attention was given to gender.[38] The predominant focus in criminology and criminal justice was on the offender, the assumption was that offenders were usually male and the context was generally the "ordinary crime" that came to the attention of the authorities.[39] Furthermore, the reality was that both the practitioners in the criminal justice system and the policy-makers were themselves overwhelmingly male.

A telling example of the prevailing paternalistic attitudes in these early years is embedded in the report of the First UN Crime Congress (1955). In connection with a discussion on the role of the family in the prevention of juvenile delinquency, reference was made to the role of the mother in the home. According to the report,

> Several speakers emphasized the need for the mother to remain at home, contending that for the child she represented the essential element in family life. Women should be able to have a career if they so desired, but if the mother had to leave the home and go out to work for economic reasons, the necessary steps should be taken to ensure that the child does not suffer.
> *(Report of the First UN Crime Congress, para. 344)*

This opinion was reflected in the conclusions of the Congress, according to which "In particular it is desirable ... to avoid the necessity for mothers to work outside the home for economic reasons alone and to protect children where the family is broken or where the mother must work" (Report of the First UN Crime Congress, p. 79, para. 7).

The Second UN Crime Congress (1960) drew passing attention to the perceived need for women police services to help in the prevention of juvenile delinquency and this point was picked up occasionally in subsequent UN Crime Programme discussions (e.g. Report of the Second UN Crime Congress, paras. 144(1) and 180).[40] Beyond these odd mentions, the reports reflect almost no discussion relating to gender prior to the 1970s.

In the 1970s, several strands of criminological research started to increase the amount of attention given to women as victims and to the lack of equality in society between men and women generally (Barberet, 2014, pp. 79–134 and *passim*). One such strand resulted in a growing awareness of the extent of the "dark figure," i.e., hidden crime, offences that did not come to the attention of the authorities. Particular attention was paid to domestic violence and sexual assault. A second and related strand drew attention to the difficulties that women face in seeking justice when they have been victimized. In addition to research on women as victims, interest was also being taken in women as offenders.

It was not long before these issues filtered through to the UN Crime Programme. At the Fifth UN Crime Congress (1975), reference was made to rapidly increasing female criminality as a social phenomenon (Report of the Fifth UN Crime Congress, paras. 107–110). The Sixth UN Crime Congress (1980) adopted a brief resolution on Specific needs of women prisoners. Three of the four operative paragraphs deal with women as offenders. The last paragraph called for future UN Crime Congresses and the UN Crime Committee to set aside time for the "study of women as offenders and as victims." This same paragraph "urges Governments to include appropriate representation of women in their delegation" (Report of the Sixth UN Crime Congress, pp. 12–13).[41] The silence on gender issues in the UN Crime Programme had been broken and clear lines of discussion emerged.

The most active line of discussion had to do with women as victims. The Seventh UN Crime Congress (1985) formulated a draft resolution on domestic violence which was then adopted by the GA (A/RES/40/36).[42] The draft resolution was notable in signifying the recognition of entrenched sexism not only in society in general but also in the criminal justice system. Paternalistic and sexist attitudes on the part of many criminal justice practitioners had made them reluctant to intervene in what happens in the home, making domestic violence very much a hidden crime. The topicality of the issue was enhanced by the fact that the 1980s had been recognized by the UN as the "Decade for Women."

The subsequent stepping stones along this line of discussion on women as victims of crime were as follows:[43]

- GA resolution A/RES/48/104, containing the Declaration on the Elimination of Violence against Women (1993);
- UN Crime Commission Resolution 3/1 on Violence against women and children (1994);
- activities of UN bodies and institutions with regard to the issue of violence against women and children, Report of the Secretary-General (E/CN.15/1995/5);
- the Ninth UN Crime Congress (1995) resolution on Violence against women;

- ECOSOC resolution 1996/12, on Elimination of violence against women;[44]
- GA resolution A/RES/52/86, Crime prevention and criminal justice measures to eliminate violence against women (1997), by which it adopted a new standard and norm, *the Model Strategies and Practical Measures on the Elimination of Violence against Women in the Field of Crime Prevention and Criminal Justice*;
- ECOSOC resolution 2006/29, Crime prevention and criminal justice responses to violence against women and girls;
- UN Crime Commission Decision 17/1, Strengthening crime prevention and criminal justice responses to violence against women and girls (2008);
- GA resolution A/RES/65/228, Strengthening crime prevention and criminal justice responses to violence against women (2010), by which it updated the Model Strategies and Practical Measures on the Elimination of Violence against Women in the Field of Crime Prevention and Criminal Justice; and
- GA resolutions A/RES/68/191 (2013) and A/RES/70/176, both entitled Taking action against gender-related killing of women and girls (2015).

The question of women as victims of trafficking returned to the UN agenda in connection with the negotiation of the UNTOC and its protocols. One of the issues considered in negotiating the protocol on trafficking in persons was specifically whether the protocol should be generic or whether it should cover only women and children, in line with what had been the focus in the work of the League of Nations.[45] As noted in section 3.2, a compromise was reached, which was reflected in the title of the protocol: "Protocol to Prevent, Suppress and Punish Trafficking in Persons, Especially Women and Children."

A second important strand in the discussion in the UN Crime Programme had to do with the treatment of women in the criminal justice system. The correctional treatment of women had been discussed at the Sixth UN Crime Congress (1980), albeit briefly.[46] A growing number of practitioners and policy-makers realized that not only was a growing proportion of the prison population female but that correctional facilities had been designed with male offenders in mind. It was not enough, for example, to allow pregnant female offenders a postponement of sentencing until they had given birth, or to set up creches in a few prisons so that prisoners with infants could continue to serve their sentence.

Almost three decades after women in corrections had been discussed at the Sixth UN Crime Congress (1980), the question of women prisoners was raised again by Thailand. Under the guidance of Her Royal Highness Princess Bajrakitiyabha, Thailand's Ministry of Justice initiated a project in 2008 called "Enhancing Lives of Female Inmates." The project evolved to have a strong international element, with an open-ended intergovernmental expert group meeting organized in Bangkok to develop draft standards and norms to provide a clear gender supplement to the Standard Minimum Rules for the Treatment of Prisoners, as well as to the Tokyo Rules on non-custodial measures. The resulting draft was presented to and supported by the Twelfth UN Crime Congress (2010).[47]

Immediately after the Twelfth Congress, Thailand presented a draft resolution at the UN Crime Commission, which ultimately led to the adoption by the GA of the UN Rules for the Treatment of Women Prisoners and Non-Custodial Measures for Women Offenders (the Bangkok Rules). These rules are applicable to all categories of women deprived of their liberty, including both untried and convicted women and women subjected to non-custodial measures.

A broader perspective had been taken by ECOSOC in its resolution 1984/49, Fair treatment of women by the criminal justice system. Since the turn of the century, there has clearly been an interest in integrating a gendered perspective more widely into the treatment of victims, witnesses, survivors, suspects, and offenders in the criminal justice system. This was reflected at the beginning of the millennium at the Tenth UN Crime Congress (2000), which included a workshop on women in the criminal justice system.[48]

The UN Crime Programme has paid less attention to women than men as criminal justice professionals, despite the early attention referred to above to the need for more women police officers at the First and Second UN Crime Congresses.[49]

The wider gender perspective was also reflected, soon after the adoption of the SDGs, in UN Crime Commission resolution 26/3, Mainstreaming a gender perspective into crime prevention and criminal justice policies and programmes and into efforts to prevent and combat transnational organized crime (2017).

One gender issue with clear crime policy dimensions that has seldom been raised in the UN Crime Programme is the question of sexual identity, including the criminalization of homosexuality.[50] The apparent assumption is that this is more a human rights issue and should therefore be dealt with by the UN Human Rights Council in Geneva.

The mainstreaming of a gender perspective, called for in the 1995 Beijing Platform for Action, has become clearly evident in the day-to-day work of the UNODC, and in the research and technical assistance provided by the PNIs.

On the policy level, the UN has adopted system-wide Enabling Environment Guidelines (2019) in response to the Secretary-General's Gender Parity Strategy. The UN Office in Vienna and the UNODC have adopted strategies for gender equality and the empowerment of women. The UNOV/UNODC Second Strategy for Gender Equality and the Empowerment of Women, which covers the period 2022–2026 (https://www.unodc.org/unodc/es/gender/unov-unodc-gender-strategy-2022-2026.html), calls for:

- improved assistance to Member States;
- provision of a comprehensive set of norms, policies, and standards;

- enhancement of gender-sensitive research;
- strengthening of gender-sensitive data and knowledge;
- enhancement of women's participation;
- enhancement of access to justice; and
- strengthening of male engagement.

According to the UNODC website (https://www.unodc.org/unodc/en/gender/the-gender-strategy.html):

> UNODC programmes need to take into account how men and women, girls and boys, including variations in gender, sexual orientation, or bodily characteristics, are impacted differently by drugs, crime and terrorism as they will have different experiences going through for instance the criminal justice system. These different aspects must be reflected in any support that UNODC provides to Member States.

The UNOV/UNODC Gender Team has developed guidance on how to mainstream gender in practice through Programme documents, in the area of corruption, health and livelihoods, justice, organized crime and illicit trafficking, and terrorism (https://www.unodc.org/unodc/en/gender/gender-and-thematic-areas/gender-thematic-areas-1.html). The Gender Team has also published a triannual news bulletin since 2020 (https://www.unodc.org/unodc/en/gender/newsletter_-gender-bulletin.html).

For the past two decades, the UNODC and various PNIs have prepared and made available a large variety of policy guides, research, and other documentation directly related to gender issues in crime prevention and criminal justice. Among recent publications is a study prepared by the UNODC, UN Women, and Interpol on *Women in Law Enforcement in the ASEAN Region* (2020). A corresponding study on the position of women as lawyers, prosecutors, and judges in ASEAN was published by TIJ: *Women as Justice Makers: Perspectives from Southeast Asia* (Lapouge, 2017).

Recent publications related to women as victims include:

- the UNODC study *Abused and Neglected: A Gender Perspective on Aggravated Migrant Smuggling Offences and Response* (2021);
- the European regional institute HEUNI published Inka Lilja, Anni Lietonen, and Julia Korkman, *Step Forward – A Tool for Developing an Organisational Strategy to Provide Victim-Centred Support for Migrant Women Victims of Gender-Based Violence* (2022), Anni Lietonen and Inka Lilja, *A Toolkit for Enhancing Counselling for Victims of Gender-Based Violence* (2021), and Anni Lietonen and Inka Lilja, *Handbook on Counselling Asylum Seeking and Refugee Women Victims of Gender-Based Violence* (2019); and

- the Australian Institute of Criminology has published Bridget Harris and Delanie Woodlock, *Spaceless Violence: Women's Experiences of Technology-Facilitated Domestic Violence in Regional, Rural and Remote Areas* (2022) and Hayley Boxall, Anthony Morgan, and Rick Brown, *The Prevalence of Domestic Violence among Women during the COVID-19 Pandemic* (2020).

The TIJ was established soon after the adoption of the Bangkok Rules at the initiative of HRH Princess Bajrakitiyabha and has become in effect the custodian of the Bangkok Rules. Its research, publications, and technical assistance activities provide extensive guidance on the implementation of the Bangkok Rules. Among the more recent TIJ publications relating to gender issues are the following:

- *Guidance Document on the Bangkok Rules: Implementing the United Nations Rules on the Treatment of Women Prisoners and Non-custodial Measures for Women Offenders* (2022);
- *Women's Pathways Into, Through and Out of Prison. Understanding the Needs, Challenges and Successes of Women Imprisoned for Drug Offending and Returning to Communities in Thailand* (2021);
- *Toolkit on Gender-Responsive Non-Custodial Measures* (published in collaboration with the UNODC) (2020); and
- *Towards Gender-Responsive Criminal Justice: Good Practices from Southeast Asia* (2019).

The topic of "Gender in the UN Crime Programme" can also be examined through the lens of who guides the Programme. It was noted above that at the time the UN Crime Programme was established both the practitioners in the criminal justice system and the policy-makers were overwhelmingly male. The same was true of those involved in the UN Crime Programme. Although the first and longest serving professional staff member in the Secretariat unit was a woman, Ms. Irene Melup, women long remained almost totally absent from senior and executive positions.[51] With the exception of Ms. Sarah Margery Fry (United Kingdom), who chaired the second meeting of the International Group of Experts in 1950, for over twenty years all the experts advising the Secretary-General on the Programme were male.[52] Photographs taken at the earlier UN Crime Congresses tend to show predominantly male participation. The Second UN Crime Congress, in London in 1960, even had a separate "programme of interest to the wives of participants," including among things a fashion show, a visit to a cosmetics company, and a visit to a department store.[53]

Change in this respect was slow to come. Women did in fact attend the First and Second UN Crime Congresses, but their input was not to be seen in the documentation. Among the 140 experts who advised the UN on the Crime Programme, there were only 3 women: Ms. Sarah Margery Fry, as mentioned above, Dr. Inkeri Anttila (Finland), and Ms. Simone Rozes, President of the Cour de Cassation of France, who served on the Committee from 1978 to 1992.

A glass ceiling was broken in 1975 at the Fifth UN Crime Congress. The year had been declared "International Women's Year," and the first world conference on the status of women was convened in Mexico that year. When a decision was taken just a few months before the Fifth UN Crime Congress to move the venue from Toronto to the UN headquarters in Geneva, the practice of appointing the head of the host delegation as Congress president could not be followed because the venue was the UN headquarters. A diplomatic solution was found. The Congress agreed that the highest-ranking female head of a national delegation attending the Congress would be elected, and Dr. Inkeri Anttila, who was serving at the time as Minister of Justice of Finland, served as president.

The opportunity to see women holding senior positions on the podium of a UN Crime Congress would not be repeated until almost half a century later, when Ms. Yoko Kamikawa, Minister of Justice of Japan and head of the delegation of the host country, was elected President of the Fourteenth UN Crime Congress (2021). Sitting alongside her on the podium for the official opening was Ms. Ghada Waly, the recently appointed Executive Director of the UNODC, and Secretary-General of the Congress. Ms. Jo Dedeyne-Amann, as Executive-Secretary of the Congress, was also to be found on the podium throughout the Congress.

The change in gender roles in the UN Crime Programme between 1955 and 2021 could not have been more marked.

8.6   Examples of the evolution of other topics in the UN Crime Programme

Access to justice

Goal 16 of the SDGs, adopted by the GA in 2015, calls for the promotion of peaceful and inclusive societies for sustainable development, the *provision of access to justice for all*, and the building of effective, accountable, and inclusive institutions at all levels. Among the targets set for Goal 16 is ensuring responsive, inclusive, participatory, and representative decision-making at all levels.

The concept of access to justice has evolved over time. The concept is not defined in any UN document but is universally accepted as an element of "good governance" (in itself, a contentious concept) (Redo, 2012, p. 83).[54] In the criminal justice context, access to justice has widely been understood as the ease with which *victims* of crime can turn to the law enforcement authorities and the court or other conflict resolution mechanisms in order to protect themselves against the offender and bring them to justice, and the ease with which *suspects* can receive legal assistance when accused of an offence. The emphasis has been on the *access* element of "access to justice." The self-evident remedy suggested was to seek to make it easier for a victim to report an offence to the law enforcement authorities and for the suspect to be advised of their rights as a suspect, including the right to obtain legal counsel.

Merely arranging for a consultation with a lawyer or legal aide, however, is insufficient if the criminal justice system itself is ineffective, slow, and cumbersome. In the 1960s, there was increased concern in many Member States that the views and concerns of the victim were not being given sufficient consideration within the criminal justice system. In 1985, this concern led the GA to adopt the Declaration of Basic Principles of Justice for Victims of Crime and Abuse of Power, Articles 4–7 of which deal with access to justice and fair treatment. Extensive work has been carried out since then to make the criminal justice system more "victim-centred."

At the same time, there was widespread concern that the internationally recognized rights of suspects and convicted offenders were not being effectively protected. These concerns, in turn, led to the adoption of a series of UN standards and norms, among them the Code of Conduct for Law Enforcement Officials (1979), the Basic Principles on the Independence of the Judiciary (1985), the Body of Principles for the Protection of All Persons under Any Form of Detention or Imprisonment (1989), the Basic Principles on the Role of Lawyers (1990), the Guidelines on the Role of Prosecutors (1990), and the Guidelines on Justice in Matters involving Child Victims and Witnesses of Crime (2005).

Most directly relevant to the topic of access to justice, the GA adopted the Principles and Guidelines on Access to Legal Aid in Criminal Justice Systems (2012). These establish minimum standards on the right to legal aid in criminal justice systems and provide practical guidance on how to ensure access to effective criminal legal aid services. The UN Crime Commission adopted resolution 25/2 (2016), on promoting legal aid, including through a network of legal aid providers.

In the 1970s and 1980s, the focus expanded to include an examination of how to make the criminal justice system more fair, more efficient, and more responsive to the concerns of members of the community. This included managerial reforms (such as improved case management), judicial specialization, and an emphasis on straightforward language. In the 1980s there was an increasing interest in criminal justice in exploring the possibility of "alternative" dispute resolution mechanisms, such as mediation and restorative justice, and in enhancing customary justice and indigenous practices. In 2002, ECOSOC adopted the Basic Principles on the Use of Restorative

Justice in Criminal Matters, which was followed up by UN Crime Commission resolution 27/6 (2018) on restorative justice.

An even more recent approach to access to justice has focused on the *justice* element of the concept. This involves, for example, a consideration of the benefits of greater and more effective popular participation in the drafting of laws and the formulation of legal policy, including criminal policy. Such an approach is in line with Goal 16 of the SDGs, and it also helps to widen the discussion of access to justice from the perspective of the individual victim or suspect needing legal assistance to structural inequities that may prevent groups and entire communities not just from securing rights in the criminal justice system, but from having those rights recognized in the first place.

Access to justice concerns not only the victim and the offender but also the community, since this access is an essential component of the feeling of security in the community, as well as a contributing factor to confidence in and satisfaction with the agents of criminal justice and the establishment of a culture of lawfulness. The structural inequalities in question may include discriminatory laws and practices, cultural and language barriers, lack of accessibility, financial constraints, lack of access to information and digital technology, and gaps in education and literacy levels, which may, in turn, result in a lack of knowledge regarding existing rights and where to go for advice or assistance in exercising these rights.

The UN Crime Commission has focused on the need to strengthen the position of several groups that often meet with structural barriers.

For women victims, the barriers to reporting a crime often begin with the definition of crimes. Although most manifestations of violence against women are generally recognized in criminal law as offences, the legal institutions are often poor at enforcing the law. Women's rights are often not sufficiently recognized in patriarchal systems, and women may face considerable difficulties in securing access to justice. These legal difficulties may be related to social and economic barriers, which may vary considerably among cultures. Women victims may lack legal awareness of their rights and be uninformed of the legal process. They may lack faith in the legal system and not believe that they can be helped. Many female victims are poor and illiterate or come from socially vulnerable communities (such as minority groups and migrants) and are therefore often unable to seek legal aid. The representatives of the criminal justice system with whom they come into contact are generally male, and may be dismissive or uninterested in the concerns of female victims.

Children may come into contact with the criminal justice system as victims, witnesses, or suspects. Even for adults, dealing with the police, prosecutors, and courts can be a daunting experience. For children, it is even more so. They are usually not aware of their rights, or how to access justice. Even if they are, they are often not prepared to assert these rights in order to secure access, especially if their parents or other figures of authority tell them (often wrongly) that this cannot or should not be done. They may reasonably fear that they will be subjected to violence or intimidation, or abandoned, if they seek their rights.

Migrants, especially smuggled migrants, are often subjected to exploitation and other criminal acts. Smuggled migrants may be exposed to life-threatening risks, which require an immediate response to assist and protect them. However, if they are in the host country illegally or clandestinely, they may well be reluctant or even unable to seek help from the authorities. They may also be unable to speak the local language or be familiar with the domestic legal system. They may come from a cultural context in which they had little trust in the authorities. For them, access to justice may be particularly difficult, and yet it may be a question of life or death.

In 2018, the GA adopted resolution A/RES/73/185, on enhancing the role of the UN Crime Commission in contributing to the implementation of the 2030 Agenda for Sustainable Development. In preambular paragraph 12 of this resolution, the GA:

> [emphasized] its commitment and strong political will in support of effective, fair, humane and accountable criminal justice systems and the institutions comprising them, encouraging the effective participation and inclusion of all sectors of society, thus creating the conditions needed to advance the wider United Nations agenda, and recognizing the responsibility of Member States to uphold human dignity, all human rights and fundamental freedoms for all, in particular those affected by crime and those who may be in contact with the criminal justice system, including vulnerable members of society, regardless of their status, who may be subject to multiple and aggravated forms of discrimination, and to prevent and counter crime motivated by intolerance or discrimination of any kind.

Among the first steps in demonstrating the commitment and strong political will of the GA to do so would be ensuring that all sectors of society have effective means of access to justice.

Victims

The international development of victim policy has been very rapid. This can be seen in research, in practical action, and even in the models for administrative and legislative reform. It is also apparent in the adoption of various international standards.

Both research results and the goals of the victim movement spread quickly from country to country. Interest in victimology has been percolating in criminology for some time.[55] Support increased in many Member States in the 1960s particularly for "victim policy," measures designed to take into account the interests and concerns of the victim in the criminal justice system. The channels used included scientific and professional meetings as well as journals, other publications, and informal contacts. The first specialized international victimological forum, the International Symposium on Victimology, was held in Jerusalem in 1973, followed by similar symposia at three-year intervals. The first victimological journal (*Victimology: An International Journal*) was established in 1976, and the World Society of Victimology was established in 1979. The trickle of victimological literature through these and other channels has turned into a flood. An international breakthrough took place in 1990, when a victim survey was carried out in a number of countries using the same methodology.[56]

Researchers, practitioners, and victim advocates acting on the international level have produced recommendations on various aspects of victim policy. For example, in 1976 the International Association of Penal Law discussed the presentation of civil claims in the criminal process. The International Association of Judges produced a report on the same subject in 1983. Also in 1983, the International Association of Chiefs of Police adopted a "Crime Victim Bill of Rights," in which the Association urged police forces to establish procedures and train personnel to implement the "incontrovertible rights of all crime victims" (Waller, 1990, pp. 139–140).

The early work on victim policy led also to hard law instruments. In 1983, the Council of Europe produced a convention on State compensation for victims of crime. Soon afterwards, it also adopted two recommendations of direct relevance to victims: a 1985 recommendation on the position of the victim within the framework of criminal law and procedure and a 1987 recommendation on assistance to victims and the prevention of victimization.

It was in this context that "Victims of crime" was proposed as a topic for the Seventh UN Crime Congress (1985). In preparation, an interregional expert meeting was organized in Ottawa in 1984. The meeting not only discussed the issue, it also prepared a draft for a declaration on victims' rights.[57] The drafting was facilitated by the participation of several international experts with experience in both research and practice but was made more complex because of the desire to integrate the perspective of both victims of crime and victims of abuse of power into the same Declaration.[58]

The Seventh UN Crime Congress thus contributed to the globalization of this discussion on victim policy, in particular by adopting what became named the Declaration of Basic Principles of Justice for Victims of Crime and Abuse of Power. The UN Victim Declaration went on to the GA for approval (A/RES/40/34; López-Rey, 1985, pp. 121–123).

Work on implementation of the UN Victim Declaration took the form of two new standards, Implementation of the Declaration of Basic Principles of Justice for Victims of Crime and Abuse of Power (ECOSOC resolution

1989/57) and Action for the implementation of the Declaration of Basic Principles of Justice for Victims of Crime and Abuse of Power (ECOSOC resolution 1998/21, annex).[59]

Although broader victim issues did not appear as a separate agenda item at subsequent UN Crime Congresses, a victim perspective can be seen on the agenda of several of the Congresses since 1995. One agenda item at the Ninth UN Crime Congress (1995) dealt with "Crime prevention strategies, in particular as related to crimes in urban areas and juvenile and violent criminality, including the question of victims: assessment and new perspectives." One agenda item at the Tenth UN Crime Congress (2000) dealt with "Offenders and victims: accountability and fairness in the justice process," and one workshop dealt with "Women in the criminal justice system."

At the Eleventh UN Crime Congress (2005), victim issues were dealt with peripherally in connection with a workshop on criminal justice reform, including restorative justice. At the two subsequent Congresses, victim issues were dealt with in connection with specific forms of transnational organized crime: an agenda item at the 2010 Congress dealt with violence against migrants, and a workshop at the 2015 Congress dealt with trafficking in persons.

The Fifteenth UN Crime Congress, to be held in 2026, may well deal with victim issues under the agenda item dealing with people-centred, inclusive, and responsive criminal justice systems, and in a workshop dealing with access to justice.

As for the UN Crime Commission, ECOSOC, and the GA, victim issues have generally been dealt with in the context of specific forms of crime, such as kidnapping (ECOSOC resolutions 2002/16, 2003/28, and 2009/24 as well as GA resolution A/RES/59/154), trafficking in persons (GA resolutions A/RES/58/137 of 2003, ECOSOC resolution 2006/27 and GA resolution A/RES/61/179 of 2006), and child victims and witnesses of crime (ECOSOC resolution 2004/27 and 2005/20).

Ten years before the UN Victim Declaration was adopted, domestic violence was dealt with in a draft resolution at the Seventh UN Crime Congress (1975). This went on to be adopted by the GA (A/RES/40/36). Domestic violence against children and domestic violence against women were the two main strands that had contributed to the broader emerging interest in victim issues. The issue had been identified almost in passing by the previous Sixth UN Crime Congress.[60] The topicality of the issue was enhanced by the fact that the 1980s had been recognized by the UN as the "Decade for Women."

The specific issue of violence against women was taken up in the Declaration on the Elimination of Violence against Women (GA resolution 48/104, of 20 December 1993), and almost twenty years later in the adoption of the Updated Model Strategies and Practical Measures on the Elimination of Violence against Women in the Field of Crime Prevention and Criminal Justice (GA resolution 65/228, annex, of 21 December 2010).

Similar work on standards and norms related to children resulted in the adoption of the Guidelines on Justice in Matters involving Child Victims and Witnesses of Crime (ECOSOC resolution 2005/20, annex, of 22 July 2005), and the UN Model Strategies and Practical Measures on the Elimination of Violence against Children in the Field of Crime Prevention and Criminal Justice (GA resolution A/RES/69/194, annex, of 18 December 2014).

At the Eleventh UN Crime Congress (2005), a workshop dealt with "Enhancing criminal justice reform, including restorative justice." One agenda item at the Twelfth UN Crime Congress (2010) dealt with "Criminal justice responses to the smuggling of migrants and trafficking in persons, and links to transnational organized crime; and Crime prevention and criminal justice responses to violence against migrants, migrant workers and their families." One workshop at the Thirteenth UN Crime Congress (2015) dealt with "Trafficking in persons and smuggling of migrants: successes and challenges in criminalization, in mutual legal assistance and in effective protection of witnesses and trafficking victims."

Computer systems and cybercrime

The interest in the UN Crime Programme in computers was at first directed at, the ability of computers to facilitate the work of the criminal justice system. In 1987, issue 14/15 of the UN Crime Prevention and Criminal Justice Newsletter focused on the computerization of criminal justice information, and during the same year HEUNI organized a European Seminar on the same topic in Popowo, Poland.[61] In 1990, the Secretariat issued a report on "Computerization of Criminal Justice Administration," to be followed up by reports in 1992 and 1994.[62]

In 1990, the GA adopted a resolution on computerization of criminal justice (A/RES/45/109), and workshops on the computerization of the administration of criminal justice and the development, analysis, and policy use of data were organized by PNIs at both the Eighth (1990) and Ninth (1995) UN Crime Congresses.

It was during this period that the World Wide Web was launched (1989) and the Internet began to connect computer users. International concern began to grow about cybercrime and found expression within the UN Crime Programme. In 1994, the Secretariat issued its first manual on the prevention and control of computer-related crime, and in 1998 UNAFEI, in cooperation with the UNODC, organized an expert meeting on the topic.[63]

At the end of the 1990s, the Russian Federation introduced a draft resolution on cybercrime in the GA, which resulted in the adoption of GA resolution 53/70 (1999). The Secretary-General prepared a report on "Effective Measures to Prevent and Control High-Technology and Computer-Related Crime" (E/CN.15/2001/4), followed up by a progress report on the same issue (E/CN.15/2002/8).

Workshops at the next two UN Crime Congresses, in 2000 and 2005, focused specifically on computer-related crimes, and at the Twelfth UN Crime Congress (2010), the topic was discussed in connection with one of the substantive agenda items.

The Twelfth UN Crime Congress (2010) was a pivotal moment in the discussion of cybercrime in the UN Crime Programme. Previously, the discussion had focused largely on aiding Member States in computerization of their criminal justice systems and in preventing and controlling cybercrime. A number of Member States, however, were of the view that the UN should begin negotiation of an international agreement on cybercrime. As noted in section 3.2, some other Member States were of the view that existing agreements (particularly the agreement drafted within the framework of the Council of Europe) provided a sufficient basis for international cooperation, and that the available resources should be devoted to implementation of those agreements and to technical assistance to Member States on request.

The discussions at the Twelfth UN Crime Congress grew heated, and (exceptionally for UN Crime Congresses up to that time) continued late into the night and through to the early morning of the last day. There was wide agreement on the need to assist Member States in preventing and responding to cybercrime; what was at issue was exactly how to find a formulation that would find consensus on an international agreement. The language of paragraph 42 of the Salvador Declaration was a masterclass in constructive ambiguity on this point:

> We invite the Commission on Crime Prevention and Criminal Justice to consider convening an open-ended intergovernmental expert group to conduct a comprehensive study of the problem of cybercrime and responses to it by Member States, the international community and the private sector, including the exchange of information on national legislation, best practices, technical assistance and international cooperation, with a view to examining options to strengthen existing and to propose new national and international legal or other responses to cybercrime.

On the basis of the Salvador Declaration, which had been adopted by the Twelfth UN Crime Congress, the GA, in resolution 65/230, requested that the UN Crime Commission establish an open-ended intergovernmental expert group to study cybercrime and how Member States, the international community, and the private sector respond to it, "with a view to examining options to strengthen existing and to propose new national and international legal or other responses to cybercrime." The initial meetings of the expert group could be described as difficult, in particular the second meeting, which considered a draft report submitted by the Secretariat. However, at the third meeting the expert group agreed on an agenda for future meetings, with the focus on technical issues, and not (in particular) on whether or not to proceed with negotiations on a new UN Convention on the topic (https://www.unodc.org/unodc/en/cybercrime/egm-on-cybercrime.html).

As noted in section 3.2, on 27 December 2019, following a close vote, the GA established an ad hoc intergovernmental committee of experts to elaborate a comprehensive international convention on countering the use of information and communications technologies for criminal purposes (UN cybercrime convention; GA resolution 74/247). The goal of the negotiations is to finalize such a convention during the summer of 2024.

In the meantime, discussions continued elsewhere on the prevention and response to cybercrime. In each of the subsequent UN Crime Congresses (2015, 2021, and the proposed Congress in 2026), one of the substantive agenda items deals with "new and emerging" forms of crime, a formulation which is understood to include cybercrime. Cybercrime was specifically addressed at workshops at both the 2015 and 2021 Congresses, and the use of information technology in responding to crime will be dealt with in one of the workshops at the Fifteenth UN Crime Congress in 2026, under the topic "Turning the digital age into an opportunity: promoting the responsible use of technologies in crime prevention and criminal justice."

Notes

1 Both López-Rey, 1985, and Redo, 2012, speak of UN criminal policy, and López Rey, 1985, pp. 11–12 and 40, seeks to define it.
2 This focus on corrections and youth crime continued almost unabated throughout the 1950s. For example, the 1958 meeting of the Advisory Group formulated six projects, all of which were on these two topics. E/CN.5/329, para. 28. See also the Report of the Second (1960) Crime Congress, para. 33.
   These were not the only topics in the early UN Crime Programme, despite their dominance. The list of 21 UN Crime Programme research and study topics that Clark, 1994, pp. 14–15, notes were on the agenda as of 1951 also includes criminal statistics (item no. 3), "police programs and activities directed at the prevention of crime" (no. 15), and a general item (no. 21) on collecting information that can be used in crime prevention and criminal justice.
3 "He" is used deliberately here. As appears in section 8.5 below, it took many years before the language of criminal policy, and of the UN Crime Programme, confronted the reality that both men and women were held in prison.
4 The seminal contribution to this debate is widely deemed to be an article by Robert Martinson published in 1974, entitled simply "What Works? Questions and Answers about Prison Reform," *The Public Interest*, Spring 1974, pp. 22–54. The article examines 231 studies of different prison rehabilitative programmes, and concludes that the treatment of offenders was largely ineffective in stopping them from continuing their criminal activity. Subsequent research, including by Martinson, was somewhat more optimistic in arguing that some programmes do have an impact, at least on some groups of offenders.
5 Both terms, non-custodial sanctions (or a wider term, non-custodial measures) and community-based measures, are used. The term "alternatives to imprisonment" – as used, for example, at the 1980 UN Crime Congress – is currently generally

avoided, as it implies that imprisonment is the presumptive sanction and all other sanctions are somehow exceptions.

6 Short-term sentences were regarded as providing insufficient time for "treatment," and as carrying the added danger that the offender would be subjected to the negative influence of other offenders in prison. (Although different Member States have very different sentencing policies, here, broadly speaking, "short-term sentences" refers to sentences of up to six months.)

7 Among the key figures in this debate were Professor Andrew von Hirsch, whose influential book *Doing Justice* appeared in 1976 (Hill and Wang), and Professor Nils Christie, whose equally influential article "Conflicts as Property" appeared a year later, in 1977 (*British Journal of Criminology*, 17(1), pp. 1–15).

8 The report is available in UNAFEI, 1988, and E/AC.57/1988/CRP.2.

9 Criminal Justice Handbook Series, United Nations publication, Sales No. E.06.V.15.
   See Yvon Dandurand, in Redo, 2012, pp. 88–90.

10 Two years later, the GA adopted a further resolution, A/RES/72/193, Promoting the practical application of the United Nations Standard Minimum Rules for the Treatment of Prisoners (The Nelson Mandela Rules) (2017).

11 See, for example, the UN Position Paper on COVID-19 preparedness and responses in prisons (2020), available at https://www.unodc.org/documents/justice-and-prison-reform/COVID-19/20-02110_Position_paper_EN.pdf

12 This is only the second UN System Common Position Paper that has been prepared. In 2018, the first such paper was issued on drug control policy; available at https://unsceb.org/united-nations-system-common-position-supporting-implementation-international-drug-control-policy

13 See ECOSOC resolution 2022/13. A draft is available in E/CN.15/2023/13.

14 Questions 45–50 on the programme dealt with such questions as what to do about "children hovering on the verge of criminality" and "what is the best organization of reformatory institutions for juveniles, that which rests on the congregate or the family principle." See https://books.google.co.th/books?id=nYsIAAAAQAAJ&printsec=frontcover&dq=First+International+Congress+on+Crime+Prevention+and+the+Repression+of+Crime&hl=th&sa=X&ved=0ahUKEwi12ayRyLHRAhXBs48KHW6RDhMQ6AEIKjAB#v=onepage&q=First%20International%20Congress%20on%20Crime%20Prevention%20and%20the%20Repression%20of%20Crime&f=false, p. 22.

15 See, for example, Alper and Boren, 1972, pp. 55–60.

16 López-Rey, 1974, p. 490, notes that of the 24 Member States in 1950, only six were non-European: Argentine, Egypt, Japan, New Zealand, the Union of South Africa, and the United States.

17 See, for example, Alper and Boren, 1972, pp. 41–43 and 59–60.
   However, concerns were also increasingly raised about the operation of the juvenile court. The Child Welfare Committee of the League of Nations had considered a different model, the Nordic child welfare boards. Alper and Boren, 1972, p. 57.

18 López-Rey, 1985, pp. 100–107, provides a detailed description of the changes that took place in this regard between 1946 and 1985. See also López-Rey, 1985, pp. 21–22.

19 See in particular Zvekic, 1986.

20 The Big Four term has been used to refer to the International Association of Penal Law, the International Penal and Penitentiary Foundation, the International Society of Criminology, and the International Society of Social Defence and Humane Criminal Policy. The term is no longer in wide use, largely because the four have

discontinued their joint activities. Several other non-governmental organizations have now become very active within the framework of the UN Crime Programme.

21 The Beijing Rules do not set an age below which a child is deemed not to have criminal liability.

22 At the time of the Seventh UN Crime Congress (1985) work was underway on the Convention on the Rights of the Child, which was to define a child as a person under the age of 18 years. The Convention entered into force in 1990. Consequently, when the UN Rules for the Protection of Juveniles Deprived of their Liberty were adopted in 1990, these defined a juvenile as "every person under the age of 18" (rule 11(a)).

23 Now known as the Naif Arab University for Security Sciences.

24 In this context, "open-ended" means that the meeting in question is, in principle, open to any non-governmental organization interested in attending the meeting.

25 Dr. Marc Ancel has written extensively on social defence and was very active in the UN Crime Programme. Other influential advocates of social defence included Dr. Gerhard Mueller (United States), who served as the head of the Section from 1974 to 1981, and Dr. Adolfo Beria di Argentine (Italy). On social defence, see Redo, 2012, pp. 64–66.

   For an insightful analysis of social defence and its influence on the UN Crime Programme during the 1950s and 1960s, see Blaustein et al., 2022, pp. 100–114.

26 Redo, 2012, pp. 64–65, traces social defence back "at least" to 1831. He notes that its major programmatic objective was the resocialization of the offender, thus strengthening the security of society. He also emphasizes that it has evolved over the decades: "Up to the present, social defence has continued to change its content and direction."

27 Blaustein et al., 2022, p. 116, associate what they see as the "perceived failure" of social defence with, among other factors, the rise of neoliberalism during the 1970s, "widespread disillusionment among criminological experts and practitioners with social crime prevention," and "the growing popularity of efficient and cost-effective neoclassical criminological approaches and theories." The authors do, however, caution that various criminologists have questioned the generalizability of this largely Anglo-American narrative.

   Having been closely involved in UN Crime Programme debates since the 1970s, I would question these generalizations. Perhaps most relevant is the fact that correctional systems and many judges in most of the world continued to evidence strong support for approaches based on treatment and rehabilitation. I would also note that during this period, there was a steady decrease in the proportion of participants in the debates who were familiar with criminological theories or the characteristics of neoclassicism.

28 A Secretariat document with the same title was issued in 1953 (E/CN.5/AC.7/L.5), which proposes research on the topic. However, the background for the study noted in paras. 8–12 of the document aligns well with the modernization thesis and presages the 1960 document.

29 Despite criminological theory widening its focus to include other regions, comparative and international criminology initially remained hampered by assumptions that Western criminological concepts and hypotheses could readily be transferred from one region to another.

30 GA resolution 2542 (XXIV), article 11(c). Vetere, 1995, pp. 39–40, notes that while the importance of social progress as a component of development was recognized in principle, the emphasis in UN policy very definitely remained on economic development. López-Rey, 1985, p. 7, was somewhat more optimistic, and emphasized the importance of the Second UN Crime Congress in moving away from a

policy focused on treatment to one that looked at the correlation between development and crime and to the instrumental use of planning in crime prevention. He also stressed the "growing awareness that certain changes in the socioeconomic structure and cultural patterns resulting from economic growth and social change might affect deviance and criminality" See López-Rey, 1985, pp. 7–8 and 83–93.

31 Blaustein et al., 2022, p. 35 and Chapter 5, argue that at this stage crime was seen as a consequence of modernization and, increasingly during the 1970s, an obstacle to economic development.

32 In 1974, the GA adopted the Declaration for the Establishment of a New International Economic Order (GA resolution 3201 (S-VII)).

33 See also López-Rey, 1985, pp. 93–95 and Redo, 2012, pp. 68–70 and 80.

34 This is repeated as the fourth preambular paragraph in the annex to the resolution.

35 Blaustein et al., 2022, pp. 167–203, provide a detailed description of the involvement of elements of the UN Crime Programme in these negotiations.

36 Action Plan on International Cooperation on the Eradication of Illicit Drug Crops and on Alternative Development, 20th special session of the UN General Assembly, 1998. GA resolution S-20/4 E, available at https://www.unodc.org/documents/alternative-development/UNGASSAc tionPlanAD.pdf

A recent extensive presentation of alternative development is provided in *World Drug Report 2015*, UNODC, Vienna, pp. 77–119, available at https://www.unodc.org/documents/wdr2015/World_Drug_Report_2015.pdf

37 See Sagredo, 2016, for an examination of experience in Latin America in preventing crime, in the context of the SDGs.

38 In 1949 the UN adopted the Convention for the Suppression of the Traffic in Persons and of the Exploitation of the Prostitution of Others. However, this work was based on a League of Nations draft from 1937 and was considered directly by the Social Commission, without any involvement by the fledgling UN Crime Programme. See Report of the Social Commission at its Fourth Session, C/CN.5/152, pp. 4–10.

In the context of the UN Crime Programme, trafficking in women and children was not discussed until almost 50 years later, in the lead-up to the negotiations on the UNTOC protocol on trafficking in persons.

39 For a comprehensive and comparative review of research on women and offending, see Barberet, 2014, pp. 137–158.

40 At subsequent Congresses, a few speakers referred to the role of women police officers in their Member State.

41 The UN Convention on the Elimination of All Forms of Discrimination against Women was adopted in 1979.

42 Paragraph 6 of the resolution invited the Eighth UN Crime Congress (1990) "to consider the problem of domestic violence under a separate agenda item dealing with domestic violence." This invitation was not taken up.

The background reports to the 1985 Congress included "The Situation of Women as Victims of Crime," A/CONF.121/16, and "The Fair Treatment of Women by the Criminal Justice System," A/CONF.121/17.

43 Much of this work has been done in close cooperation with UN Women and the Commission on the Status of Women. See Clark, 1994, p. 112 and fn 79, as well as https://www.un.org/womenwatch/daw/vaw/v-esc-csw.htm An overview of UN work in this field (up to 1989) is provided in *Violence Against Women in the Family* (1989), UN Office in Vienna, pp. 3–4.

44 When the draft resolution was being negotiated in the UN Crime Commission, one ambassador very strongly objected, saying that the major problem with regard to violence was violence against men. He was persuaded to withdraw his objection. (Personal notes of the author. The ambassador was presumably referring to the

observation that men are more often the victims of lethal stranger-to-stranger violence than women.)

45 The issue had already been raised in connection with the negotiation of ECOSOC resolution 1998/20, Action to combat international trafficking in women and children.

46 A brief four-paragraph resolution (resolution 9) was adopted on this theme at the Sixth UN Crime Congress, entitled "Specific needs of women prisoners." Report of the Sixth UN Crime Congress, pp. 12–13.

See also Neudek, 1993, p. 75. On p. 81, Neudek calls for the development of standards and norms that specifically address the situation of women detainees.

47 An excellent overview of women in prison around the world is provided in Barberet, 2014, pp. 159–188. For an early assessment of the Bangkok Rules, see ibid., pp. 173–176.

48 This workshop was organized by HEUNI. The proceedings, edited by Natalia Ollus and Sami Nevala, were published by HEUNI in 2001.

Gender issues were also raised at the Thirteenth UN Crime Congress (2015), which featured a workshop on standards and norms, including on "meeting the unique needs of women and children."

49 A notable exception is Lapouge, 2017, who provides an overview of the challenges faced by women lawyers in Southeast Asia.

50 An exception is a publication by the International Center for the Prevention of Crime, one of the PNIs: *Report on Hate Crimes Based on Sexual Orientation and Gender Identity: An Overview of Global Trends and Prevention Modalities,* Montreal, 2019.

51 This did not change until the millennium. Among the women currently in senior positions are Ms. Angela Me, Head of the Research and Trend Analysis Branch, and Ms. Jo Dedeyne-Amann, Chief of the Secretariat to the Governing Bodies at the UNODC.

52 In other respects Sara Margery Fry fits the profile of the first experts. She was British and very active in prison reform.

It was not until 1972 that a second woman reached this status, when Dr. Inkeri Anttila (Finland) was elected to the UN Crime Committee. She eventually became by far the longest serving member (along with Mr. Jorge Arturo Montero Castro, Costa Rica), serving on the Committee from 1972 to 1991.

53 Apparently it was not expected that the accompanying spouses would be male. Although it is perfectly possible men enjoyed fashion, cosmetics, and shopping, some might have preferred a visit to a local pub.

54 Vincent del Buono provides background on what he refers to as "sustainable access to justice"; Redo, 2012a, pp. 85–87.

55 Among the generally acknowledged pioneers in victimology were Professor Hans von Hentig (*The Criminal and His Victim: Studies in the Sociobiology of Crime,* 1948, Yale University Press), Prof. Stephen Schafer (*The Victim and His Criminal: A Study in Functional Responsibility,* 1968, Random House), and Prof. Marvin Wolfgang (*Patterns of Criminal Homicide,* 1958, University of Philadelphia Press).

56 See, for example, van Dijk, 1999.

57 The drafting group was chaired by Professor Cherif Bassiouni. (The author was among the participants.) The draft for the Victim Declaration benefited from written and other contributions by many persons. One key person was Ms. Irene Melup, a long-time UN staff member. Key persons providing written contributions included Professor LeRoy Lamborn, Professor Irvin Waller, and, on the topic of victims of abuse of power, Dr. Walter Schwarz.

58 Clark, 1994, pp. 180–197, provides a detailed description of the genesis of the Victim Declaration, as well as the difficulties in integrating the perspectives of

victims of crime with those of victims of abuse of power, and an analysis of the
provisions of the Victim Declaration.

See also Joutsen, 1987, pp. 63–69 and 298–324.
59 ECOSOC dealt subsequently with implementation of the UN Victim Declaration
in its resolutions 1990/22, 1996/14, 1997/31 and 2000/15.

Various non-governmental organizations, in particular the World Society of
Victimology, had advocated for a UN convention on the rights of victim, which
would have turned the soft law Victims Declaration into hard law. See Redo,
2012, p. 63. However, no formal initiative was made by a Member State at the
UN Crime Commission.
60 The Sixth UN Crime Congress had adopted a brief resolution entitled "Specific
needs of women prisoners."
61 HEUNI publication 12, *Computerization of Criminal Justice Information Systems: Realities, Methods, Prospects and Effects: Report of the European Seminar
Held in Popowo, Poland, 18–22 May 1987* (1987).
62 The signum of the report is A/CONF.144/14. The 1992 report is ST/ESA/STAT/
SER.F.58, Guide to Computerization of Information Systems in Criminal Justice,
and the 1994 report is E/CN.15/1994/3, Progress made in the improvement of
computerization in criminal justice management, with emphasis on strengthening
national capacities for the collection, collation, analysis and utilization of data.
63 ST/ESA/SER.M/43–44 *United Nations Manual on the Prevention and Control of
Computer-Related Crime* (1994) (E.94.IV.5).

E/CN.15/1999/CRP.10 Report of the Experts Meeting on Crime Related to the
Computer Network, held at Fuchu, Japan, 5–9 October 1998.

References

Adler, Freda and Gerhard Mueller (1995), A Very Personal and Family History of the
United Nations Crime Prevention and Criminal Justice Branch, in Bassiouni, M.
Cherif (ed.), *The Contributions of Specialized Institutes and Non-Governmental
Organizations to the United Nations Criminal Justice Programme. In Honour of
Adolfo Beria di Argentine*, Brill Publishers, pp. 3–13
Alper, Benedict S. and Jerry F. Boren (1972), *Crime: International Agenda, Concern
and Action in the Prevention of Crime and Treatment of Offenders, 1846–1972*,
Lexington Books
Ancel, Marc (1954), *La Défense sociale nouvelle. Un mouvement de politique
criminelle humaniste*, Cujas
Barberet, Rosemary (2014), *Women, Crime and Criminal Justice. A Global Inquiry*,
Routledge
Blaustein, Jarrett, Tom Chondor and Nathan W. Pino (2022), *Unravelling the
Development – Crime Nexus*, Rowman & Littlefield
Christie, Nils (1977), Conflicts as Property, *British Journal of Criminology*, 17(1),
1–15
Clark, Roger S. (1994), *The United Nations Crime Prevention and Criminal Justice
Program. Formulation of Standards and Efforts at Their Implementation.* Univer-
sity of Pennsylvania Press
Handbook on Restorative Justice Programmes (2006), UNODC
Handbook on Restorative Justice Programmes (2020), UNODC and the Thailand
Institute of Justice

International Center for the Prevention of Crime (2019), *Report on Hate Crimes Based on Sexual Orientation and Gender Identity: An Overview of Global Trends and Prevention Modalities*

International Review of Criminal Policy, United Nations, issue 7, January 1955

International Review of Criminal Policy, United Nations, issue 8, July 1955

Joutsen, Matti (2021), *Crime Prevention and Criminal Justice within the Context of the Sustainable Development Goals*, Thailand Institute of Justice

Joutsen, Matti (1987), *The Role of the Victim of Crime in European Criminal Justice Systems*, HEUNI publication no. 11

Lapouge, Magali (2017), *Women as Justice Makers: Perspectives from Southeast Asia*, Thailand Institute of Justice

López-Rey de Arroya, Manuel (1985) *A Guide to United Nations Criminal Policy*, Cambridge Studies in Criminology LIV

Martinson, Robert (1974), What Works? Questions and Answers about Prison Reform, *The Public Interest*, Spring, pp. 22–54

Morrison, Allison (1988), The Prevention of Juvenile Delinquency: Background Paper on the Development of United Nations Guidelines on the Prevention of Juvenile Delinquency, Interregional Preparatory Meeting on Topic IV of the Eighth United Nations Congress, 18–22 April 1988, conference room paper

Neudek, Kurt (1993), United Nations Crime Prevention and Criminal Justice Programme, *European Journal of Crime, Criminal Law and Criminal Justice*, 1(2), 185–201

Ollus, Natalia and Sami Nevala (eds.) (2001), *Women in the Criminal Justice System: International Examples & National Responses*. Proceedings of the Workshop held at the Tenth United Nations Congress on the Prevention of Crime and the Treatment of Offenders. Vienna, Austria, 10–17 April 2000, HEUNI

Redo, Slawomir (2012), *Blue Criminology. The Power of United Nations Ideas to Counter Crime Globally – A Monographic Study*, HEUNI publication no. 72, available at https://www.heuni.fi/en/index/publications/heunireports/reportseriesno.72.bluecriminologythepowerofunitednationsideastocountercrimeglobally-amonographicstudy.html

Report of the [xx] UN Crime Congress: the reports of the different UN Crime Congresses are available at http://www.unodc.org/congress/en/previous-congresses.html

Sagredo, Javier (2016), Towards the Definition of Sustainable Development-Led Approaches in Crime Prevention and Treatment of Offenders: Key Conceptual References (draft), Thailand Institute of Justice, available at https://www.tijthailand.org/public/files/highlight/055/5-Development-Led%20Paper.pdf

Schafer, Stephen (1968), *The Victim and His Criminal: A Study in Functional Responsibility*, Random House

Schüler-Springorum, Horst (1983), Report on the Standard Minimum Rules for the Administration of Juvenile Justice and the Handling of Juvenile Offenders, submitted to the United Nations ad hoc Meeting of Experts on Youth, Crime and Justice, 2–8 November, Newark, New Jersey (on file with the author)

UNAFEI (1988), Report on the Meeting of Experts on the United Nations Draft Standard Minimum Rules for Non-Custodial Measures ("The Tokyo Rules"), *UNAFEI Resource Material Series*, no. 84, UNAFEI, pp. 209–225

UN Office in Vienna (1989). *Violence Against Women in the Family* van Dijk, Jan (1999), The Experience of Crime and Justice, in Graeme Newman (ed.), *Global Report on Crime and Justice*, UNODC, pp, 25–41

Vetere, Eduardo (1995), The Work of the United Nations in Crime Prevention and Criminal Justice, in M. Cherif Bassiouni, *The Contributions of Specialized Institutes and Non-Governmental Organizations to the United Nations Criminal Justice Programme. In Honour of Adolfo Beria di Argentine*, Brill Publishers, pp. 15–63

von Hentig, Hans (1948), *The Criminal and His Victim: Studies in the Sociobiology of Crime*, Yale University Press

von Hirsch, Andrew (1976), *Doing Justice*, Hill and Wang

Waller, Irvin (1990), The Police: First in Aid?, in A. Lurigio, W. Skogan and R. Davis, *Victims of Crime. Problems, Policies and Programs*, Sage Publications, pp. 139–156

Wolfgang, Marvin (1958), *Patterns in Criminal Homicide*, University of Philadelphia Press

Zvekic, Ugljesa (ed.) (1986), *Action-Oriented Research on Youth Crime. An International Perspective*. Publication no. 27 of the UN Interregional Crime and Justice Research Institute, Rome

9

SOFT LAW

UN standards and norms

9.1   Standards and norms in the UN Crime Programme

The structure and operation of the criminal justice system, as well as the definition of how, for example, law enforcement officials, judges, and correctional officials should conduct themselves, are closely linked to national (and local) values and traditions. Until relatively recently, societies have seen little reason to look beyond their borders for models or guidance in the development of criminal law or the criminal justice system.

That changed with the first international conferences on crime and delinquency (discussed in section 2.1.), when practitioners and academics gathered to share their experiences and theories regarding "what works" in crime prevention and criminal justice, in other words "good practice."

At the same time that the UN was established, increased attention was being paid to human rights. At the domestic level, various minimum legal safeguards and mechanisms were adopted in criminal justice systems, where they had previously been absent or inconsistently recognized. It has been argued that respect for human rights promotes effective crime prevention and control (E/CN.15/1997/14, para. 41). In particular the 1948 Universal Declaration of Human Rights and the 1966 Covenant on Civil and Political Rights have direct implications for the operation of the criminal justice system.

The concept of good practice has been used to promote human rights in different ways, at different times, and in respect of different issues, such as the prevention of delinquency, child protection, the investigation of offences, legal representation of suspects in court, correctional treatment, and greater use of mediation and restorative justice.

DOI: 10.4324/9781003480907-12

One key way in which good practice and human rights have been brought together is in the form of international standards and norms, a concept that has found a welcoming home in the UN Crime Programme.

A "standard and norm" is an instrument that contains normative elements. It defines how members of the target audience – individuals, members of a certain profession, public officials, and so on – should conduct themselves, and may even define the minimum level acceptable. An "international standard and norm" on justice, accordingly, is an instrument that is intended to apply to target audiences in different countries, which may be at different stages of development and have very different legal and administrative systems.

A standard and norm can be set out in an international agreement, national law, or other binding instrument. In the context of the UN Crime Programme, the term refers to a set of instruments adopted by the GA and ECOSOC (and in a few exceptional cases, by other bodies) that have been designed as benchmarks for the development of crime prevention and the criminal justice system. As noted on the UNODC website (https://www.unodc.org/unodc/en/commissions/CCPCJ/ccpcj-standards-and-norms.html), "These standards and norms provide flexible guidance for reform that accounts for differences in legal traditions, systems and structures whilst providing a collective vision of how criminal justice systems should be structured."

Over the years, a considerable number of UN standards and norms have been adopted (https://www.unodc.org/unodc/en/justice-and-prison-reform/compendium.html; see Clark, 1994, and Redo and Platzer, 2014, pp. 284–290). The first to be adopted were the Standard Minimum Rules on the Treatment of Prisoners, known as the SMRs. Originally adopted in 1955, these were updated in 2015. The revised version is known as the Nelson Mandela Rules.

Other key standards and norms deal with:

- *corrections,* such as the UN Standard Minimum Rules for Non-Custodial Measures (the Tokyo Rules), the UN Rules for the Treatment of Women Prisoners and Non-Custodial Measures for Women Offenders (the Bangkok Rules), and the Basic Principles on the Use of Restorative Justice Programmes in Criminal Matters;
- *torture and capital punishment,* such as the Declaration on the Protection of All Persons from Being Subjected to Torture and Other Cruel, Inhuman or Degrading Treatment or Punishment, and the Safeguards Guaranteeing Protection of the Rights of those Facing the Death Penalty;
- *justice for children,* such as the UN Standard Minimum Rules for the Administration of Juvenile Justice (the Beijing Rules), the UN Guidelines for the Prevention of Juvenile Delinquency (the Riyadh Guidelines), the UN Rules for the Protection of Juveniles Deprived of Their Liberty, and the UN Model Strategies and Practical Measures on the Elimination of Violence against Children in the Field of Crime Prevention and Criminal Justice;

- *crime prevention*, such as the Guidelines for Cooperation and Technical Assistance in the Field of Urban Crime Prevention, and the Guidelines for the Prevention of Crime;
- *violence against women*, such as the Declaration on the Elimination of Violence against Women, and the Updated Model Strategies and Practical Measures on the Elimination of Violence against Women in the Field of Crime Prevention and Criminal Justice;
- *victims of crime*, such as the Declaration of Basic Principles of Justice for Victims of Crime and Abuse of Power; and
- the *operation of the criminal justice system*, such as the Code of Conduct for Law Enforcement Officials, the Basic Principles on the Use of Force and Firearms by Law Enforcement Officials, the Basic Principles on the Independence of the Judiciary, the Guidelines on the Role of Prosecutors, the Basic Principles on the Role of Lawyers, and the UN Principles and Guidelines on Access to Legal Aid in Criminal Justice Systems.

A special category of UN standards and norms is formed by *model treaties on international judicial cooperation*. These include the following:

- the Model Agreement on the Transfer of Foreign Prisoners;
- the Model Treaty on Extradition;
- the Model Treaty on the Transfer of Proceedings in Criminal Matters;
- the Model Treaty on the Transfer of Supervision of Offenders Conditional Sentenced or Conditionally Released; and
- the Model Treaty for the Prevention of Crimes that Infringe on the Cultural Heritage of Peoples in the Form of Movable Property.

These model treaties form a special category in that they are intended for use as templates when two or more Member States seek to enter into international agreements on these topics. The other standards and norms are designed primarily to guide Member States in the development of their domestic law, policy, and practice in crime prevention and criminal justice.[1]

9.2   How UN standards and norms are drafted and adopted

Historically, the drafting of a UN standard and norm on crime prevention and criminal justice has generally gone through the following stages (Mueller, 1990, p. 37):

- an initiative comes from individual experts or non-governmental organizations;
- a draft is prepared (generally by an academic expert in the field);
- the draft is discussed at one or more international expert meetings;

- the draft is discussed at the UN Crime Commission (previously, the UN Crime Committee);
- the draft is discussed at a UN Crime Congress; and
- the draft is submitted to ECOSOC and/or the GA for adoption.[2]

In the first four decades of the UN Crime Programme, various non-governmental organizations were active in the drafting of UN standards and norms, to the extent that in some cases they brought advanced drafts to sessions of the UN Crime Committee and to a UN Crime Congress, where there was generally little time to discuss the drafts, let alone negotiate them.[3] When the UN Crime Programme was being restructured, some Member States questioned the general validity of these earlier standards and norms, specifically on the grounds that they had not been drafted by Member States.[4]

Consequently, following the restructuring of the UN Crime Programme in 1991, Member States began to take a greater interest in, and control of, the drafting of new standards and norms. Since that time, the initiative has been brought by a Member State to a session of the UN Crime Commission in the form of a draft resolution. If the mandate to proceed is approved, the first draft is generally prepared by an expert consultant assisting the UNODC and then considered at a meeting with "equitable geographical representation." There have also been calls for such meetings to be open-ended intergovernmental meetings, which would mean that any Member State could send an expert if they so wished. This, however, has financial implications for the host government – especially if there is an increased demand for the availability of interpretation into all six UN working languages.

However, no firm guidelines have been established by the UN Crime Commission, let alone ECOSOC, for how this drafting of future standards and norms is to be done. Currently, the sponsoring government will generally cooperate with the UNODC in the organization of one or more drafting meetings, with the UNODC working to ensure there is a proper balance in the participation. The results are then submitted to the UN Crime Commission.

These strictures imposed by the UN Crime Commission have not resulted in a decrease in the number of of new standards and norms. On the contrary the Commission has continued to mandate work on new standards and norms. Indeed, it could be argued that (ignoring the 1985 and the 1990 UN Crime Congresses, each of which produced several new instruments) the pace has increased. Since the UN Crime Commission took up its work in 1992, 22 new standards and norms have been formulated.[5] Even a selective chronological list shows the scope of the work over the past 30 years:

- Declaration on the Elimination of Violence against Women (1993);
- Guidelines for Cooperation and Technical Assistance in the Field of Urban Crime Prevention (1995),

- International Code of Conduct for Public Officials (1996);
- Safeguards Guaranteeing Protection of the Rights of Those Facing the Death Penalty (1996);
- Guidelines for Action on Children in the Criminal Justice System (1997);
- Firearm Regulation for Purposes of Crime Prevention and Public Health and Safety (1997);
- Status of Foreign Citizens in Criminal Proceedings (1998);
- Principles on the Effective Investigation and Documentation of Torture and Other Cruel, Inhuman or Degrading Treatment or Punishment (2000);
- Basic Principles on the Use of Restorative Justice Programmes in Criminal Matters (2002);
- Guidelines for the Prevention of Crime (2002);
- Guidelines on Justice in Matters involving Child Victims and Witnesses of Crime (2005);
- Bangalore Principles of Judicial Conduct (2006);
- the Bangkok Rules (2010);
- Updated Model Strategies and Practical Measures on the Elimination of Violence against Women in the Field of Crime Prevention and Criminal Justice (2010);
- UN Principles and Guidelines on Access to Legal Aid in Criminal Justice Systems (2012);
- UN Model Strategies and Practical Measures on the Elimination of Violence against Children in the Field of Crime Prevention and Criminal Justice (2014);
- International Guidelines for Crime Prevention and Criminal Justice Responses with Respect to Trafficking in Cultural Property and Other Related Offences (2014); and
- the Nelson Mandela Rules (2015), which are an update of the original 1955 Standard Minimum Rules on the Treatment of Prisoners.

At the time of writing, work is underway on a new standard and norm, Reducing Reoffending Through Rehabilitation and Integration (A/RES/76/182, 2021, and ECOSOC resolution 2022/13). The initiative was taken by the Japanese Government, which has proceeded cautiously, to test the interest of Member States at the Fourteenth UN Crime Congress (2021) and then to sponsor resolutions at subsequent sessions of the UN Crime Commission, which has resulted in a mandate to work on such a standard and norm being given by the GA. Significant work has been done by the UNODC and the Japanese Government to obtain wide support from Member States for this initiative.

9.3   Implementation of UN standards and norms

UN standards and norms are commonly referred to as *soft law* instruments, in the sense that they provide guidance but are not legally binding.[6] They embody an earnest request to their addressees (Member States, members of a criminal justice profession, other stakeholders) to apply the contents but not an absolute obligation to undertake a certain course of action (Castaneda, pp. 7–8 and 193–195).[7]

This does not mean that standards and norms, as soft law, are meaningless and have no practical effect. The significance of soft law, including standards and norms, does not lie in any assumed legally binding effect. The significance lies elsewhere, at both the national and the international level.

At the national level, international standards and norms may have an instrumental value in guiding the development of national law, policy, and practice.[8] They may be used as persuasive arguments by decision-makers in individual jurisdictions when these decision-makers seek to justify certain courses of action that they would have preferred even if the standard or norm in question did not exist. When selecting from various alternative approaches to achieve a certain end, decision-makers may defend their choice by referring to specific provisions in, for example, the Nelson Mandela Rules, the Bangkok Rules, or the Tokyo Rules.

Similarly, international standards and norms can also be used by practitioners, professional, and other non-governmental organizations, academics, and other stakeholders when trying to influence their government to change laws and policy in a certain direction.

Work by the UNODC and other stakeholders to promote implementation has generally taken one of three different forms: dissemination of information on the standards and norms, a reporting procedure, and provision of technical assistance to Member States on request.[9]

The *dissemination of information* involves, for example, encouraging Member States to translate the standards and norms into the local language(s) (if needed) and circulate them among the professional groups and other stakeholders concerned.

The UNODC and PNIs also disseminate information, such as the text of the standards and norms themselves, guidance on implementation, and reports on implementation. The UNODC has prepared a *Compendium* of the UN standards and norms which is particularly helpful (https://www.unodc.org/unodc/en/justice-and-prison-reform/compendium.html).[10] In the compendium, which has been published in all the UN official languages, the material is divided by theme:

1. Persons in custody, non-custodial sanctions and restorative justice;
2. Justice for children;
3. Crime prevention, violence against women and victim issues;
4. Good governance, the independence of the judiciary, the integrity of criminal justice personnel and access to legal aid; and
5. Legal, institutional and practical arrangements for international cooperation.

The UNODC and PNIs have also conducted extensive research and issued policy guidance publications related to various standards and norms.

The *reporting procedure* within the UN Crime Programme is voluntary and has generally involved the UNODC sending out requests to all Member States to report on the implementation of (specific) standards and norms, including whether they have been translated into the local languages, have been made available to practitioners and other stakeholders, have been used as the basis for the development of laws and policy, and whether any particular difficulties have been encountered in implementation.

A reporting procedure was instituted for the first UN standard and norm adopted, the Standard Minimum Rules on the Treatment of Prisoners, with questionnaires sent out in 1957, 1967, 1974, 1979, 1985, and 1989 (Clark, 1994, pp. 234–242).[11] A second reporting procedure was introduced by ECOSOC in 1973 in respect of capital punishment, requesting reports at five-year intervals (Clark, 1994, pp. 242–243).

The 1985 UN Crime Congress produced a large number of new standards and norms. In considering the results of the Congress, the GA requested that the UN Crime Committee make recommendations on their implementation, which could be done by mandating the UNODC to send out further requests to Member States to report on what action they had taken (A/RES/40/53; see Clark, 1994, pp. 243–248).

The UN Crime Committee did as requested. At the same time, however, there was a growing realization that with the proliferation of standards and norms the process was becoming rather complicated. At the end of the 1980s, it may be recalled, several Member States were becoming concerned with what they regarded as the excessive preoccupation with soft law standards and norms. They pointed out that the increasing number of questionnaires on the implementation of the standards and norms was becoming burdensome to practitioners and policy-makers. They also noted that several of the questionnaires had met with a relatively low response rate, rendering the validity of the data questionable.

The UN Crime Committee responded in 1989 by setting up a working group to consider ways in which the process of reporting could be simplified and consolidated. The report of the working group recommended what became known as a "cluster approach," with the main standards and norms grouped into four "clusters" (Clark, 1994, pp. 248–254). The intention was that one questionnaire would be sent out that dealt with implementation of all the standards and norms contained in each respective cluster, instead of separate questionnaires on each standard and norm. Furthermore, the UNODC sought to streamline the questionnaires, minimizing (as far as possible) the amount of information that would be collected, and formulating questions so that they could be answered as quickly and simply as possible.

The 1990 UN Crime Congress produced seven new standards and norms, a record: the Basic Principles for the Treatment of Prisoners, the UN Standard Minimum Rules for Non-Custodial Measures (the Tokyo Rules), the UN Guidelines for the Prevention of Juvenile Delinquency (the Riyadh Guidelines), the UN Rules for the Protection of Juveniles Deprived of Their Liberty, the Basic Principles on the Use of Force and Firearms by Law Enforcement Officials, the Guidelines on the Role of Prosecutors, and the Basic Principles on the Role of Lawyers. The 1990 Congress also adopted five model treaties, on, respectively, extradition, mutual assistance in criminal matters, the transfer of proceedings in criminal matters, the transfer of supervision of offenders conditionally sentenced or conditionally released, and the prevention of crimes that infringe on the cultural heritage of peoples in the form of movable property.

When the new UN Crime Commission took up its role, two years after the 1990 UN Crime Congress and following the restructuring of the UN Crime Programme, one of the questions that it had to consider was how to deal with the added burden on reporting. The 1994 ECOSOC resolution that was cited above as endorsing the existing body of standards and norms also endorsed the questionnaires that the UNODC had prepared, in line with the cluster approach (ECOSOC resolution 1994/16, arts. 5 and 6).

Over the course of the next decade, the UNODC continued to send out questionnaires, and reported to the UN Crime Commission on the results. However, in 2006 and 2007, a few members of the Commission returned to the issue, and repeated their complaints about the overburdening of practitioners. They noted that some of the questionnaires covered issues that involved several different national agencies or (in federal states) even state agencies, making coordination of the national response complicated (E/CN.15/2006/20, para. 137 and E/CN.15/2007, paras. 116 and 117).[12] Since that time, the UN Crime Commission has appeared to be quite reluctant to mandate the UNODC to send out questionnaires on implementation of standards and norms.

However, this should not be understood as implying that the UN Crime Commission wanted to abandon the possibility of reporting completely. When the Commission was established, it stressed the importance of the UN standards and norms in a rather instrumental way: it decided that the implementation of standards and norms would become a standing agenda item at the annual sessions of the Commission (ECOSOC resolution 1992/22, part VII, para. 3; see Clark, 1994, pp. 258–259). Many Member States have taken the opportunity to provide information in their national statements on what measures they have taken to implement specific standards and norms.

Furthermore, several of the themes that the UN Crime Commission has selected for its annual sessions, as well as several of the substantive topics and workshop topics selected for the different UN Crime Commissions have provided a suitable framework for discussing implementation of the standards and norms. For example, the 2005 Congress considered the topic of "Making standards work," the 2010 Congress examined guidelines on crime prevention, and the 2015 Congress featured a workshop devoted to standards and norms.

The third method of encouraging implementation is through the provision of *technical assistance* to Member States on request. As noted in Chapter 12, the UNODC and a number of PNIs have increasingly incorporated standards and norms into their training, research, and technical assistance projects.

9.4 From soft law to hard law: the example of standards and norms on juvenile justice

It is difficult to analyse the actual impact of UN standards and norms for a number of reasons: the absence of an obligation to report, the variation in the criminal justice systems of different Member States, the possibility of different interpretations of the same text, and the difficulty in determining if a specific change in national law, policy, or practice was due to the influence of a UN standard and norm or to other factors.

Nonetheless, many reports from Member States to the UNODC cite examples of the impact of the standards and norms, and the literature shows several further examples of their impact. In many states, the standards and norms are becoming part of the national discourse on crime prevention and criminal justice.[13]

Furthermore, on the international level, soft law may be seen as an intermediate stage in the formulation of ideas and concepts that emerge as *hard law*. When ideas are embodied in standards and norms, the recognition and declaration of certain principles and even detailed rules may be intended to have a direct influence on the practice of Member States. If this happens, they contribute to the creation of *customary international law*, which is widely recognized as binding on states. Even if they are not in themselves binding, standards and norms may thus become a source of international law, particularly if they are drafted in the form of an obligation (for example, "states *shall*" do something, as opposed to "states *may consider*" doing something, or "states *are invited*" to do something).

Examples of this process are provided by soft law UN standards and norms on juvenile justice which in the space of just a few years have found their way into the hard law Convention on the Rights of the Child (CRC), and into the practice of the Committee on the Rights of the Child. The CRC was adopted in 1989 by GA resolution A/RES/44/25 (https://www.ohchr.org/en/instruments-mechanisms/instruments/convention-rights-child).

There are several provisions of the CRC that are relevant to juvenile justice (General Comment No. 10, para. 4), including those related to non-discrimination (article 2), the best interests of the child (article 3), the right to life, survival, and development (article 6), the right to be heard (article 12), the deprivation of liberty (article 37), and the treatment of a child in conflict with the law (article 40).

The Committee on the Rights of the Child provides guidelines – "General Comments" – for implementation in specific areas. The General Comments are recommendations and are not binding. However, they have proved to be influential. Special reference should be made to General Comment no. 10 (2007), which deals with the rights of children in respect of juvenile justice.

General Comment No. 10 deals with several issues, among them the age of criminal responsibility. There is considerable disparity around the world in this respect. Many countries have set an absolute minimum age of criminal responsibility, often 14 or 16 years. Others use two age limits, with a higher age limit at which all persons will be presumed to have full criminal responsibility, and a lower age limit above which a person can be treated either as a juvenile or an adult, depending on the circumstances. There are also countries where quite young children, aged 6 or 7, can be held to be criminally liable (General Comment No. 10, para. 30).

Rule 4 of the Standard Minimum Rules on the Administration of Juvenile Justice (the Beijing Rules; A/RES/40/33) calls upon States to ensure that the age of criminal responsibility is not fixed at too low an age level. CRC article 40(3), in turn, requires that States Parties establish "a minimum age below which children shall be presumed not to have the capacity to infringe the penal law." Neither of these provisions can be seen to provide clear guidance as to what, exactly, the age of criminal responsibility should be.

However, in its General Comment no. 10, the Committee on the Rights of the Child does seek to provide guidance on the legislative technique to be used in establishing age limits for criminal responsibility. It even specifies what it considers to be the internationally accepted minimum age of criminal responsibility (General Comment no. 10, para. 32):

> Rule 4 of the Beijing Rules recommends that the beginning of MACR [minimum age of criminal responsibility] shall not be fixed at too low an age level, bearing in mind the facts of emotional, mental and intellectual maturity. In line with this rule the Committee has recommended States Parties not to set a MACR at a too low level and to increase the existing low MACR to an internationally acceptable level. From these recommendations, it can be concluded that a minimum age of criminal responsibility below the age of 12 years is considered by the Committee not to be internationally acceptable. States Parties are encouraged to increase their lower MACR to the age of 12 years as the absolute minimum age and to continue to increase it to a higher age level.

The right to be heard is particularly important given the diversity of procedures and structures for dealing with children in conflict with the law: child welfare boards, administrative hearings, juvenile courts, and so on. This is also dealt with in General Comment No. 10.

Beijing rule 14.2 guarantees the juvenile the right to be heard: "The proceedings shall be conducive to the best interests of the juvenile and shall be conducted in an atmosphere of understanding, which shall allow the juvenile to participate therein and to express herself or himself freely."

Article 12 of the CRC has transformed this right to be heard into hard law:

1. States Parties shall assure to the child who is capable of forming his or her own views the right to express those views freely in all matters affecting the child, the views of the child being given due weight in accordance with the age and maturity of the child.
2. For this purpose, the child shall in particular be provided the opportunity to be heard in any judicial and administrative proceedings affecting the child, either directly, or through a representative or an appropriate body, in a manner consistent with the procedural rules of national law.

In its conclusions on the reports of States Parties, the Committee on the Rights of the Child has repeatedly returned to these issues, and recommended that laws be changed, policy be developed, more resources be given, and closer attention be given to the right to be heard. Furthermore, in its General Comment no. 10 (para. 45), the Committee has clarified its position on the child's right to be heard in any proceedings regarding them:

The child should be given the opportunity to express his/her views concerning the (alternative) measures that may be imposed, and the specific wishes or preferences he/she may have in this regard should be given due weight. Alleging that the child is criminally responsible implies that he/she should be competent and able to effectively participate in the decisions regarding the most appropriate response to allegations of his/her infringement of the penal law .... It goes without saying that the judges involved are responsible for taking the decisions. But to treat the child as a passive object does not recognize his/her rights nor does it contribute to an effective response to his/her behaviour. This also applies to the implementation of the measure(s) imposed. Research shows that an active engagement of the child in this implementation will, in most cases, contribute to a positive result.

A hundred years ago, when the League of Nations was founded, the concern was with "children hovering at the verge of criminality." The basic approach was quite paternalistic: the child was regarded as a "passive object" who should be guided on the way to their full role as a well-adjusted citizen. It was also assumed that each Member State was free to develop its own juvenile justice system, although there was a growing interest in seeing how other States were dealing with child and juvenile offenders.

The UN standards and norms have contributed to changes in approach to crime prevention and criminal justice. As with UN standards and norms in other areas, they are a distillation of "what works" in different legal and administrative systems and at different stages of development.

They have also contributed to hard law, as shown by the example of the CRC and the work of the Committee on the Rights of the Child. The Committee has taken a particularly active but carefully considered role in building on the UN standards and norms as well as the text of the Convention in order to provide guidance to States Parties.

It continues to be individual Member States that are responsible for the development of crime prevention and criminal justice in their own domestic system. However, we have learned a great deal from one another's successes (and failures) over the course of 150 years. One result is that this international experience is guiding individual Member States in finding the right response – through the exchange of experience, through soft law, and ultimately through hard law. The UN standards and norms have contributed to this process.

Notes

1 All six model treaties were prepared in the 1980s. The first five were adopted as annexes to GA resolutions. A presentation of the context in which these were drafted and an analysis of their content can be found in Clark, 1994, pp. 198–228.
2 However, there have been a number of changes in the process. Clark, 1994, pp. 126–141, provides a detailed and critical description of different modes used particularly in the standards and norms that went through the Seventh (1985) and Eighth (1990) UN Crime Congresses.
3 For example, the Declaration on the Protection of All Persons from Being Subjected to Torture and Other Cruel, Inhuman or Degrading Treatment or Punishment was exceptionally drafted during the two-week Fifth UN Crime Congress in September 1975, and adopted by the GA only four months later.
    Clark, 1994, pp. 100–103, describes the tactical reasons given by Amnesty International (the primary proponent of the draft) for this approach.
4 The matter was resolved, after extensive debate, by ECOSOC resolution 1994/16, which essentially reaffirmed the importance of the entire body of UN standards and norms (para. 1).
5 If one counts the Congress Declarations adopted in 2000, 2005, 2010, 2015, and 2012, as well as two model bilateral agreements, all of which are included in the *Compendium*, then the average comes out to one each year since 1992.
6 A fuller discussion of whether or not standards and norms are legally binding is provided in Joutsen, 2016.

7 Some writers on international law deny the existence of soft law. See in particular Klabbers, 1996. Essentially, he argues that either something is law or it is not; there is no intervening category of soft law, nor is there any need for such a concept.

8 The most widely known example of a standard and norm guiding national development is the Nelson Mandela Rules and its predecessor, the SMRs. It is evident that they have guided national practice in corrections and, in several cases, helped bring about legal reform.

Nonetheless, in assessing the impact of the SMRs almost 40 years after their adoption, Clark, 1994, pp. 177–179, offers a much more nuanced assessment. According to him, the SMRs have had a substantial impact in some countries but only a marginal one in others.

9 Clark, 1994, pp. 240–242 and 280–283, who is perhaps the world's leading authority on UN standards and norms on crime prevention and criminal justice, argues forcefully that the UN Crime Commission has the authority to institute different forms of procedures for implementation, such as a complaints procedure, the establishment of thematic working groups, and the appointment of special rapporteurs.

He also makes the point (ibid., p. 240) that all remedies "available under international law or set forth by other UN bodies and agencies for the redress of violations of human rights" remain in force.

10 The first edition of the *Compendium* was issued in 1992, and was mandated by ECOSOC resolution1989/63. The most recent edition was published in 2016.

As Clark, 1994, p. 98, fn 3, notes, the first publication of the Compendium surprised many with the extent of the material that had been produced by the UN Crime Programme. He also notes that the UNODC had to make some choices as to what material should be included and what omitted.

11 These questionnaires were usually sent out in advance of UN Crime Congresses and the results were reported to the subsequent Congress.

12 Even the intergovernmental expert meeting dealt with in E/CN.15/2004/9/Add. 1 was criticized by one speaker for not being "sufficiently representative" and for being conducted in English only; E/CN.15/2004/16, para. 119.

13 See Redo and Platzer, 2014, pp. 284–290 on the impact of standards and norms.

References

Castaneda, Jorge (1969), *Legal Effects of United Nations Resolutions*, Cambridge University Press

Clark, Roger S. (1990), The Eighth United Nations Congress on the Prevention of Crime and the Treatment of Offenders. Havana, Cuba, August 27 – September 7, 1990, *Criminal Law Forum*, 1(3), 513–523

Compendium of United Nations Standards and Norms in Crime Prevention and Criminal Justice (2016), UNODC, available at https://www.unodc.org/unodc/en/justice-and-prison-reform/compendium.html

General Comment no. 10 (2007), Committee on the Rights of the Child, Children's Rights in Juvenile Justice, 25 April 2007 (CRC/C/GC/10)

Joutsen, Matti (2016), International Standards and Norms as Guidance in the Criminal Justice System, *UNAFEI Resource Material Series* no. 98, UN Asia and Far East Institute for the Prevention of Crime and the Treatment of Offenders, Fuchu, pp. 54–67

Klabbers, Jan (1996), The Redundancy of Soft Law, *Nordic Journal of International Law* 65(2), 167–182

Mueller, Gerhard (1990), United Nations Norms and Guidelines on Crime Prevention and Criminal Justice, *UNAFEI Resource Materials Series*, vol. 38, UNAFEI, pp. 34–45

Redo, Slawomir and Michael Platzer (2014), The United Nations' Role in Crime Prevention and Control, in Philip Reichel and Jay Albanese (eds.), *Handbook of Transnational Crime and Justice*, second edition, Sage, pp. 283–301

10

THE UN CRIME CONGRESSES[1]

10.1   The mandate of the UN Crime Congresses

Paragraph (d) of GA resolution 415 (V) provides the original mandate of the UN Crime Congresses:

> The United Nations shall convene every five years an international congress similar to those previously organized by the IPPC (International Penal and Penitentiary Commission). Resolutions adopted at such international Congresses shall be communicated to the Secretary-General and, if necessary, to the policy-making bodies.

The very first item on the agenda of the first meeting of the ad hoc Advisory Committee (1953) was the "organization of the World Quinquennial Congress in the field of the prevention of crime and the treatment of offenders" (Clifford, 1979, p. 9). Given the focus of the mandate of the new UN Crime Programme on corrections, it was not surprising that four out of the five agenda items of this first UN Crime Congress dealt with corrections: the (draft) Standard Minimum Rules for the Treatment of Prisoners, the selection and training of correctional personnel, open correctional institutions, and prison labour. A fifth agenda item dealt with the prevention of juvenile delinquency.

In planning the First UN Crime Congress, the ad hoc Advisory Committee emphasized that the Congresses were designed to be *expert bodies*, and *not policy-making bodies* of the UN.[2] They would, in effect, be a sounding board for experts on developments in crime and criminal justice, a body for an exchange of views and experiences on what works and what does not

DOI: 10.4324/9781003480907-13

work in crime prevention and criminal justice. To ensure this, the ad hoc Advisory Committee called for the participants to be a mixture of national delegations, specialized UN agencies, intergovernmental organizations, non-governmental organizations, and individual participants. This mixture of different participants still remains the case.

The expertise of the Congresses has been strengthened from the outset by the fact that many national delegations have included a mix of senior criminal policy-makers, practitioners from different fields, and academics. Indeed, the letter of invitation to the First UN Crime Congress sent out to governments specified that members of national delegations were to express their personal opinion on the different issues on the agenda, and not their national position.[3]

Speaking at the First UN Crime Congress in 1955, Dr. Manuel López-Rey, as the representative of the UN Secretary-General at the Congress, identified three ways in which the new UN Crime Congresses differed from the earlier conferences organized by the IPPC. He noted that the items on the agenda "were part of the extensive United Nations work programme on social questions" and should not be seen in isolation from that work programme. Second, the Congress was part of the broader UN Crime Programme envisaged by GA resolution 415 (V). And third, the Congress recommendations would be forwarded to the Secretary-General for the appropriate follow-up action by the respective UN bodies, in particular by the Social Commission of ECOSOC (Report of the First UN Crime Congress, para. 37).

The mandate of the UN Crime Congresses remained essentially the same for the first 30 years of their existence, until the end of the 1980s. The Advisory Committee (and later the UN Crime Committee) selected the agenda items, the Committee members usually attended the Congresses, and when these Committee members convened again in a session of the Committee, they sought to ensure the appropriate follow-up for the outcome of the Congresses.

The UN Crime Committee never engaged in a fundamental debate on a possible need to review the overall mandate and structure of the UN Crime Congresses. The concept of these quinquennial events was apparently regarded as working quite well. At the end of the 1980s, however, questions began to be raised as to whether UN Crime Congresses needed to be continued. The restructuring of the UN Crime Programme provided a suitable opportunity to consider which elements were necessary and which were not. One national delegation argued that the Congresses were not effective or particularly useful and that other professional international fora existed. Given that it had been agreed that the restructuring would involve the replacement of the expert-driven UN Crime Committee with a government-driven UN Crime Commission, which would meet every year, it was the view of this delegation that the Congresses could be discontinued.

However, this remained a minority view, and the Congresses continued to have a place in the new UN Crime Programme.[4] Their functions were specified for the first time. According to paragraph 29 of the annex to GA resolution A/RES/46/152:

The United Nations congresses on the prevention of crime and the treatment of offenders, as a consultative body of the programme, shall provide a forum for:

(a) The exchange of views between States, intergovernmental organizations, non-governmental organizations and individual experts representing various professions and disciplines;
(b) The exchange of experiences in research, law and policy development;
(c) The identification of emerging trends and issues in crime prevention and criminal justice;
(d) The provision of advice and comments to the commission on crime prevention and criminal justice on selected matters submitted to it by the commission;
(e) The submission of suggestions, for the consideration of the commission, regarding possible subjects for the programme of work.

Before the restructuring, the Congresses reported directly to the GA.[5] With the restructuring, they were to report to the newly established UN Crime Commission. In addition, phrases referring to the function of Congresses in "provision of advice and comments" and "submission of suggestions" underline that the *UN Crime Congresses do not set UN policy* on crime and justice. This mandate is reserved for the UN Crime Commission.

Paragraph 30 of the same annex specifies that the UN Crime Congress would continue to be held every five years, for a period of between five and ten working days, and that the UN Crime Commission is to "select precisely defined topics for the congresses in order to ensure a focused and productive discussion."

Finally, para. 30 (c) provides for regional preparatory meetings:

Quinquennial regional meetings should be held under the guidance of the commission on issues related to the agenda of the commission or of the congresses, or on any other matters, except when a region does not consider it necessary to hold such a meeting.[6] The United Nations institutes for the prevention of crime and the treatment of offenders should be fully involved, as appropriate, in the organization of those meetings. The commission shall give due consideration to the need to finance such meetings, in particular in developing regions, through the regular budget of the United Nations.

When the UN Crime Commission met at its first session in 1992, it recommended for the consideration of ECOSOC a resolution on the preparations for the next UN Crime Congress in 1995, the ninth in order (ECOSOC resolution 1992/24). The wording of the resolution reflected a heightened interest in efficiency and timeliness. For example, the draft noted that the Congress "should deal with a limited number of precisely defined substantive topics, which reflect the urgent needs of the world community" and that "there should be action-oriented research and demonstration workshops related to the topics." These workshops were to be organized in cooperation with the UN PNIs. To staunch the possibility of resolutions being submitted to the Congress at the last minute (as had frequently happened at the Eighth UN Crime Congress in 1990), the draft resolution specified that draft resolutions on the selected topics were to be submitted "well in advance of the Ninth Congress" (ibid, paras. 2 and 4).

Ten years later, in January 2002 (following the organization of two UN Crime Congresses in 1995 and 2000), the UN Crime Commission returned to the question of how the UN Crime Congresses could be organized in an effective matter. This resulted in GA resolution A/RES/56/119, on the "Role, function, periodicity and duration of the United Nations congresses on the prevention of crime and the treatment of offenders." The formal nature of the UN Crime Congresses as "a consultative body of the United Nations Crime Prevention and Criminal Justice Programme" was reaffirmed. The GA recognized that they

> have been a forum for promoting the exchange of experiences in research, law and policy development and the identification of emerging trends and issues in crime prevention and criminal justice among States, intergovernmental organizations and individual experts representing various professions and disciplines

and that they played a role "in preparing suggestions, for consideration by the Commission, on possible subjects for its programme of work."

In this new GA resolution, the basic elements of the UN Crime Congresses remained the same: regional preparatory meetings, a number of substantive agenda items, workshops (involving panels of experts that maintain "an open dialogue with the participants" and avoid the "reading of statements"),[7] and ancillary meetings. To streamline the Congress preparations and cut costs, the resolution stated that the Commission should "request the Secretary-General to prepare only those background documents which are absolutely necessary for implementing the programme of work of the congress."

The 2002 GA resolution incorporated two innovations that had been introduced at the Tenth UN Crime Congress (2000): a high-level segment (at which statements would be given by participants of ministerial rank or above) and consolidation of the formal outcome of the Congress into a single Declaration. In addition, the UN Crime Congresses were renamed the United Nations Congresses on Crime Prevention and Criminal Justice.

The resolution once again underlined that it was the UN Crime Commission, and not the UN Crime Congress, that set UN policy on crime and justice. The resolution did this by noting that "any action suggested to the Commission regarding its programme of work, contained in the declaration of the congress, shall be undertaken through individual resolutions of the Commission." In practice, this meant that the outcome of the UN Crime Congresses goes to the UN Crime Commission, which decides whether or not to take any initiatives forward.

10.2   *The participants at the UN Crime Congresses*

The participants at the earlier, IPPC conferences had been a mix of members of national delegations, representatives of various organizations interested in crime and justice issues, and individual experts. This same broad mix continued when the UN took over the responsibility for the organization of Congresses. With the advent of intergovernmental organizations (such as the African Union, the Association of Southeast Asian Nations, the Council of Europe, and the Organization of American States), a new category was added, as was a category consisting primarily of specialized UN agencies.

National delegations

Among the different categories, national delegations have been and continue to be privileged. From the outset, it was their votes on resolutions that counted, although up to the 1970 Congress, non-governmental organizations and individuals could also vote for "consultative purposes" (Report of the Fifth UN Crime Congress (1975), para. 464).[8]

At the First and Second UN Crime Congresses, the rules of procedure gave members of national delegations priority in taking the floor.[9] Beginning with the Third UN Crime Congress, the chairperson had the power to give the floor to speakers regardless of whom they represented.[10] However, in practice when the list of speakers is drawn up, national delegations continue to have priority.

The chairpersons and other elected officials are selected solely from the members of national delegations.[11]

Perhaps the most important respect in which members of national delegations are privileged in respect of other participants is that, since the restructuring of the UN Crime Programme, they are the only ones who can sit in on negotiations on the most visible and politically most important outcome of the Congresses, the resolutions and, as from 2000, the Congress Declarations. Other categories of participants do not have the right to be present at these negotiations even as observers.

National liberation movements (such as the Palestine Liberation Organization) have generally been listed separately at the end of the national delegation category.

Specialized UN agencies

A number of specialized UN agencies (such as the International Labour Organization, the International Organization for Migration, and the World Health Organization) sometimes have an interest in the topics on the agenda of the various UN Crime Congresses and they often participate as observers.

With the establishment in 1962 of the UN Asia and Far East Institute for the Prevention of Crime and the Treatment of Offenders (UNAFEI), a new subcategory was created, which is generally grouped under "specialized UN agencies," although at times it has been listed separately as the "members of the UN Crime Programme Network Institutes." These institutes have a formal role at UN Crime Congresses in that they have the primary responsibility for the organization of the research and demonstration workshops that have been a feature of the Congresses since 1985.

Intergovernmental and non-governmental organizations

Intergovernmental organizations, such as the African Union, the Association of Southeast Asian Nations, the Council of Europe, the EU, and the Organization of American States, have the right to participate in UN Crime Congresses as observers. They have done so quite actively, and several of them have submitted reports to the various Congresses.

Non-governmental organizations have been active at all the UN Crime Congresses, since the first such Congress held in 1955. Up to the Fifth UN Crime Congress in 1970, non-governmental organizations (and experts attending in a personal capacity) had the (theoretical) right to vote at UN Crime Congresses for "consultative purposes."[12]

In addition, non-governmental organizations have organized so-called ancillary meetings at the UN Crime Congress, which have drawn a broad mix of participants.[13] These have often been of a very high quality, and the number of such meetings has increased with each successive Congress.

Individual experts

In keeping with the tradition of the IPPC, the UN Crime Congresses have been attended by individual experts from the outset. These participants can even submit papers to the Congress. The official report of the First UN Crime Congress lists 65 such papers that were submitted and assigned a Congress document signum. The available documentation for most subsequent UN Crime Congresses does not include such a list. However, the website of the most recent Congress, the Fourteenth UN Crime Congress (2021), provides links to the fifteen individual expert papers submitted.[14]

At the First UN Crime Congress, a process was devised by which individuals could seek to attend the Congress. The report of the First UN Crime Congress specifies that the Congress was open to persons in the following categories (Report of the First UN Crime Congress, para. 9):

(a) "Officials of competent ministries and departments, police officials, officials of institutions for adult and juvenile delinquents;
(b) Members of judicial bodies;
(c) Members of the Bar;
(d) Members of the teaching staff of universities;
(e) Persons who have done distinguished scientific work in the field of prevention of crime and treatment of offenders;
(f) Representatives of governmental or private social agencies which are concerned with offenders or with the prevention of crime; and
(g) Persons, or representatives of organizations, invited by the Secretary-General."

Somewhat similar criteria were used at the Second and Third UN Crime Congresses (1960 and 1965). For the Fourth UN Crime Congress in Kyoto in 1970, the criteria was simplified to "individual participants having a direct interest in the field of social defence, including representatives of criminological institutes and of national non-governmental organizations concerned with social defence matters."[15] The reference to "social defence" was abandoned for the Fifth UN Crime Congress in 1975, to be replaced by "individual members having a direct interest in the field of crime prevention and criminal justice, including representatives of criminological institutes and of national organizations concerned with crime prevention and criminal justice." [16]

The rules of procedure for the Seventh UN Crime Congress (1985) no longer sought to define the background of who could request the right to attend in their personal capacity, other than by referring to them as "individual experts in the field of crime prevention and the treatment of offenders."[17] This terminology has been used at subsequent UN Crime Congresses.[18]

TABLE 10.1 Participants at the UN Crime Congresses, 1955–2021

UN Crime Congress	National delegations	Specialized UN agencies	Intergovernmental organizations	Non-governmental organizations	Individual experts	Total participants
First (Geneva, 1955)	51	3	2	43	257	512
Second (London, 1960)	68	4	4	50	632	1,046
Third (Stockholm, 1965)	74	3	2	39	658	1,083
Fourth (Kyoto, 1970)	79	3	2	31	556	998
Fifth (Geneva, 1975)	101	3	4	33	240	909
Sixth (Caracas, 1980)	102	2	6	38	170[i]	920
Seventh (Milan, 1985)	125	16	9	58	ca. 400	1,395
Eighth (Havana, 1990)	127	21	6	49	ca. 250	1,127
Ninth (Cairo, 1995)	138	22	17	73	ca.420[ii]	1,899
Tenth (Vienna, 2000)	137	15	20	58	ca. 400	1,902
Eleventh (Bangkok, 2005)	129	32	25	35	ca. 1,110	ca.3,000
Twelfth (Salvador, 2005)	102	29	17	45	181[iii]	ca.3,000
Thirteenth (Doha, 2015)	142	31	23	47	475[iii]	ca. 4,000
Fourteenth (Kyoto, 2021)	156	40	26	109	1,126	ca. 5,560

[i] Para. 15 of the Report of the Sixth UN Crime Congress states that the number of individual experts about 250.

[ii] Para. 14 of the Report of the Ninth UN Crime Congress states that the number of individual experts was

[iii]At both the Twelfth and Thirteenth UN Crime Congresses, the national delegation of the host Member was exceptionally large: 1,551 persons at the Twelfth UN Crime Congress and 555 at the Thirteenth UN Crime Congress.

At all of the other UN Crime Congresses, a large proportion of the individual experts came from the Member State.

otes

The basic source for the number of Congress participants from 1955 to 2005 in different categories is UN-DC (2010). Individual Congress reports and other sources provide somewhat different figures. One source of ror is double-counting; the same participant might appear on the list of participants in two or more categories, r example, as a member of a national delegation and as a representative of a non-governmental organization.

The official list of participants at the Seventh UN Crime Congress did not include individual experts. Their mber was calculated on the basis of the total number of participants reported by the UN (1,395), minus mbers of national delegations (706) and members of other delegations (283). Some members of "other del-ations" were listed also as members of national delegations, and so these counts must be taken as estimates. The national delegation of the host Member State of the Seventh UN Crime Congress, Italy, consisted of 5 members.
The official list of participants at the Eighth UN Crime Congress did not include individual experts. Their mber was calculated on the basis of the total number of participants reported by the UN (1,127), minus mem-'s of national delegations (694) and members of other delegations (187).

Due to the Covid-19 pandemic and stringent restrictions on entry into the country imposed by Japan, the jority of participants at the Fourteenth UN Crime Congress participated online.

10.3   The preparation and structure of the UN Crime Congresses

Preparation of the UN Crime Congresses

The UN Crime Congresses are held in five-year cycles, in relatively standard-ized steps:

- the UN Crime Commission[19] invites governments to make suggestions for the theme, agenda items, and workshop topics of the Congress (usually, the first year of the cycle);
- the UN Crime Commission decides on the theme, agenda items, and work-shop topics of the Congress (usually, the second year of the cycle);
- the UN Crime Commission accepts the invitation of the future host Mem-ber State to organize the UN Crime Congress (usually, the second or third year of the cycle);
- the Secretariat and the host country negotiate the "host country agree-ment" that is required to hold a UN Crime Congress (finalization of this agreement may continue until almost the time of the Congress);
- the Secretariat drafts the Discussion Guide that sets out the main issues and possible questions for discussion in respect of each agenda item and workshop topic; input on the Discussion Guide is received from the Pro-gramme Network Institutes responsible for organizing the respective workshops (usually, the third year of the cycle);[20]
- the Discussion Guide is approved by the UN Crime Commission (usually, the third year of the cycle);

- regional preparatory meetings are organized (usually, during the first four months of the fourth year of the cycle);[21] and
- informal negotiations begin on the text of the Congress Declaration (once the regional preparatory meetings have been held, building to a large extent on the conclusions and recommendations of these meetings).[22]

At the session of the UN Crime Commission immediately following the Congress, the Congress report will be considered, and the Commission decides on possible follow-up action. At subsequent sessions, the Secretariat and national delegations report on what action they have taken for implementation.

Throughout the cycle, the Secretariat makes the necessary and often quite extensive technical, logistical, and other preparations for the organization of a smooth Congress. This includes the organization of the regional preparatory meetings and the negotiation of the host country agreement. In cooperation with the host country, the many practical preparations include identification of a suitable range of accommodation alternatives for the participants, local transport arrangements, protocol arrangements, and ensuring that there are a suitable number of meeting rooms for both the official sessions and smaller informal meetings. Separately, the Secretariat compiles the necessary (and often quite voluminous) documentation, which includes background reports on the different agenda items, reports of the regional preparatory meetings, and other UN Secretariat reports requested by the UN Crime Commission or otherwise regarded as necessary in view of the items to be discussed.[23] The identification of the official documentation is currently done in consultation with the extended Bureau of the UN Crime Commission.[24]

Governments are encouraged to make their own national preparations for the upcoming UN Crime Congress. This includes not only identification of the members of the national delegation but also preparation of material for the Congress. Governments are encouraged to "be represented at the highest possible level ... for example by Heads of State or Government, Government ministers or attorneys general," and to send "legal and policy experts, including practitioners with special training and practical experience in crime prevention and criminal justice."[25] In addition, governments are encouraged "where appropriate" to establish national preparatory committees.

Ancillary meetings have been organized in connection with the Congresses from the outset.[26] These have generally been organized by non-governmental organizations, professional organizations, and geographical interest groups. The Secretariat is requested "to take appropriate action to encourage the participation of the academic and research community" in these meetings. Governments are encouraged to participate in these meetings "as they provide an opportunity to develop and maintain strong partnerships with the private sector and civil society organizations."[27] For several of the most recent UN Crime Congresses, the coordination of these ancillary meetings has been done by the International Scientific and Professional Advisory Council, in practice by one individual working in close coordination with the Secretariat and the host government, Mr. Gary Hill. Under his guidance, arrangements for the ancillary meetings have been made so that, as far as possible, these do not overlap with formal sessions or other ancillary meetings covering similar issues.[28]

Structure of the UN Crime Congresses

The basic (formal) programme of the UN Crime Congresses consists of work in a plenary body and in two or more committees (referred to as "sections" at the first Congresses). Generally speaking, the different agenda items (including possible recommendations, conclusions, and resolutions) are debated in the committees, and the results are reported at the end of the Congress to the plenary body for adoption.[29]

At the Fifth (1975) and Seventh (1985) UN Crime Congress, a new formal element was introduced, research and demonstration workshops (Report of the Fifth UN Crime Congress, para. 471). These are intended to be more practical and technical than the more policy-oriented discussions on the different agenda items, of particular interest to practitioners.

The Tenth (2000) UN Crime Congress added a further new element, the high-level segment, at which heads of national delegations of ministerial rank or higher (and selected other participants) discuss the Congress topics. Furthermore, the respective Congress Declaration is adopted during the high-level segment, thus giving it more political visibility.[30] As noted at an intergovernmental meeting held in 2006 to review the work of the UN Crime Congresses,

> As a result of the introduction of the high-level segment as an integral part of the congresses in 2000, commitments were being made at the highest possible level of national representation and the importance of ensuring that such commitments would be honoured was stressed.
>
> (E/CN.15/2007/6, p. 16)

The officials of the Congress (referred to collectively at the first Congresses as the steering committee, and at subsequent Congresses as the general committee) consist of the president (by tradition, the head of the delegation of the host government),[31] and vice-presidents (vice chairpersons) to preside over each of the sections (or to substitute as necessary for the president), as well as a general rapporteur. At the more recent UN Crime Congresses, a distinction has been made between the general category of vice-presidents (of whom there were 27 at the Thirteenth and Fourteenth UN Crime Congresses (2015 and 2021), selected on the basis of equitable geographical representation, with an additional person designated as first vice-president) and the two persons who serve as chairpersons of the two Committees.

Each section has, in addition, a vice chairperson and a rapporteur. At the First and Second UN Crime Congresses, the function of the section rapporteur was not limited to reporting on the proceedings (in accordance with the title). Instead, these first two Congresses adhered to the practice at professional and academic meetings whereby the rapporteur initiated the debate by providing background and context. At the Third UN Crime Congress (1965), the discussions were initiated and guided by small panels selected for equitable geographical representation (Report of the Third UN Crime Congress, para. 29). At the Fourth (1970) and subsequent UN Crime Congresses, the use of such geographically balanced panels to launch the discussion was at the discretion of the chairperson, and in practice these panels were very rarely used.[32] Instead, a representative of the Secretariat would generally present a summary of the official background documentation.

The Secretary-General is represented by a senior UN official referred to as the Secretary-General of the Congress, who is assisted by the Executive Secretary. The extensive responsibilities of the Executive Secretary include overseeing all the Secretariat preparations referred to earlier, including the preparation of all of the official documentation, organization of the preparatory meetings, ensuring all support services, including the technical facilities and the translation and interpretation services in the official languages,[33] servicing the meetings, and assisting the rapporteurs in the drafting of the reports. (To a large extent many of the support services, including the preparation of the extensive meeting facilities and arrangement of security, are carried out in cooperation with the host government.)

As noted above, a number of ancillary meetings are organized at the UN Crime Congresses. The level of discussion at such meetings has often been quite high. At the Thirteenth and Fourteenth UN Crime Congresses (2015 and 2021), some ancillary meetings were designated as "special events" and were given more publicity by the Secretariat.

Various professional visits have been arranged in connection with the Congresses, at first primarily to correctional institutions. In addition, exhibitions have been part of the Congress programme from the outset; at the First and Second UN Crime Congresses, these dealt with prisons. The scope of these exhibitions has expanded over the years, and, as with the ancillary meetings, the arrangements have been coordinated by the International Scientific and Professional Advisory Council in cooperation with the UNODC and the host government.

The programme of the first UN Crime Congresses also contained lectures given by eminent criminal justice professionals and scholars, with equitable geographical distribution. Usually one expert was selected from each region to give a lecture on an issue related to the respective agenda items. This format is no longer followed.

At all the UN Crime Congresses except one, participants have been free to move from one session to another. At the Fourth UN Crime Congress (1970), participants were required to register for sections in order to be recognized as being "qualified to speak in that section." Participants could register for a maximum of two sections and no participant could be registered for meetings that were to be held simultaneously on the same day (Rule 8 of the Rules of Procedure, Report of the Fourth UN Crime Congress, p. 63). This stringent rule was no longer applied at subsequent Congresses, presumably due to the practical difficulty that members of smaller delegations had as they often had to take part in discussions going on simultaneously in two or more places.

From 1955 to 1990, the UN Crime Congresses lasted a leisurely two weeks, with the intervening weekend set aside for recreational and social activities. Since the restructuring of the UN Crime Programme in 1991, UN Crime Congresses have been shortened to an uninterrupted span of eight days, plus one day reserved in advance of the UN Crime Congress for "pre-Congress negotiations."

The two most recent Congresses, the Thirteenth (2015) and Fourteenth (2021), were preceded by a "Youth Forum" at which young participants discussed selected items on the Congress agenda. The report of the Youth Forum was submitted to the Congress.

10.4   Overview of the individual UN Crime Congresses[34]

The *First UN Crime Congress* (Geneva, 22 August–3 September 1955) focused almost exclusively on the traditional criminological and criminal justice concerns about the proper treatment of young offenders and prisoners. This selection of focus was due to the fact that the number of young offenders and prisoners had risen dramatically in post-war Europe, the geographical area with which most of the participants were familiar. Among the agenda items considered by this Congress were the possibilities of "open" penal and correctional institutions (a new concept for many participants), the selection and training of prison personnel, and the proper use of prison labour. The work was dealt with in three sections, which reported back to the plenary. The seven resolutions of the Congress were communicated to the Secretary-General.[35]

One of the agenda items at the First UN Crime Congress was the draft Standard Minimum Rules for the Treatment of Prisoners, which had been drafted by the IPPC and had been endorsed by the League of Nations. The Standard Minimum Rules were subsequently formally approved by ECOSOC (ECOSOC res. 663 C (XXIV) of 31 July 1957). These Standard Minimum Rules became the prototype for a rapidly expanding set of UN standards and norms on crime prevention and criminal justice.

In opening the *Second UN Crime Congress* (London, 8–19 August 1960), the Right Honourable Viscount Kilmuir, Lord Chancellor of England, expressed concern that "the problems of crime were growing in gravity" and that there was a "disproportionate increase of crime among young people at a time of unparalleled economic prosperity, when unemployment was negligible and educational and social welfare services were highly developed" (Report of the Second UN Crime Congress, para. 39). He saw as the proper response an increase in the resources allotted to crime prevention and criminal justice, continued research, a "fundamental re-examination of the whole philosophy of the nature of crime and legal punishment," and an attempt "to reach a coherent criminal policy embracing alike the criminal law, the agencies for enforcing the law, the judicature, and the methods of treatment" (Report of the Second UN Crime Congress, para. 42).[36]

The choice of agenda items at the Second UN Crime Congress seemed appropriate in order to expand on the issues raised by the Rt. Hon. Viscount: the origin, prevention, and treatment of new forms of juvenile delinquency, as well as special police services for the prevention of juvenile delinquency; short-term imprisonment; prison labour; pre-trial treatment and after-care and assistance to dependents or prisoners; and criminality resulting from social change and economic development in less developed countries.

Conclusions and recommendations were adopted on each of the themes of the Congress. In addition, two resolutions were adopted by the Congress, one on UN social defence activities and one an expression of gratitude to the host of the Congress.

The *Third UN Crime Congress* (Stockholm, 9–18 August 1965) was the first to have a Congress theme: "Prevention of criminality." At the time the Nordic countries were undergoing a shift from rehabilitation-oriented criminal justice (as epitomized in the UN Crime Programme by the social defence ideology) to a broader societal focus on crime as an interaction between society and the individual. There was also an increasing interest in empirical criminological research. Accordingly, the Congress featured a special plenary session designed to identify research problems connected with the development of policy and programmes (Report of the Third UN Crime Congress, para. 17).

In opening the Congress, Mr. Herman Kling, the Minister of Justice of the host country, Sweden, stressed the importance of humane approaches to criminal justice and warned against the dangers that could result from overly punitive measures, with their stress on efficiency in criminal justice (Report of the Third UN Crime Congress, para. 38). In turn, Mr. Philippe de Seynes, the representative of the UN Secretary-General, referred to the recent adoption by ECOSOC of a resolution that endorsed the principle that the prevention of youth crime and adult crime should form part of comprehensive economic and social development plans (Report of the Third UN Crime Congress, para. 46).

Mr. Kling's opening comments were in line with the overall prevention orientation of the Congress. All six agenda items represented a clear shift from the focus at the First and Second UN Crime Congresses on the formal criminal justice system and formal control to examining how formal and informal social control could strengthen one another.

The themes also marked a move away from the original focus of criminology, which assumed that the causes of crime could be found through a study of the personality of the offender, to an approach which looked at the interplay between social factors and the potential offender. At the time, Swedish (and more widely Nordic) criminal policy was making a distinction between "delinquency" and "crime." As society changes, societal attitudes also change. What was earlier regarded as unacceptable and even "criminal" behaviour (such as homosexuality) can become acceptable, and what was earlier regarded as acceptable (such as domestic violence) may be redefined as criminal.[37]

One of the issues that was featured for the first time at the Third UN Crime Congress was technical assistance. The Congress recommended the employment of UN regional advisors. The issue of technical assistance would remain a mainstay of UN Crime Programme discussions, with repeated calls for the UNODC and other stakeholders, as well as Member States, to expand their technical assistance to developing countries on request. (Five years previously, at the Second UN Crime Congress, the theme had been addressed in passing, under the agenda item "Prevention of types of criminality resulting from social changes and accompanying economic development in less developed countries.")

Only one brief resolution was adopted by the Third UN Crime Congress, consisting of five paragraphs. The resolution welcomed the Secretary-General's proposals for strengthening the activities of the UN "in the field of social defence," expressed the wish for the continuation of technical assistance in this field, noted with satisfaction the decision of the Secretary-General to establish a social defence trust fund (ECOSOC resolution 1086 B (XXXIX) of 30 July 1965), and expressed gratitude to the host of the Third UN Crime Congress.

The *Fourth UN Crime Congress* (Kyoto, 17–26 August 1970) was the first to be held outside Europe. It had as its theme "Crime and development." As with the Third UN Crime Congress, the agenda items reflected a continuing shift from viewing crime solely as an issue of individual conduct to viewing crime as an issue of economic and social development.[38] The Congress discussed social defence policies in relation to development planning, public participation in crime prevention and control, the Standard Minimum Rules on the Treatment of Prisoners in the light of recent developments, and the organization of research for policy development in social defence.

The Fourth UN Crime Congress was the first to have regional preparatory meetings, held in Africa, the Arab countries, Asia, and Latin America and the Caribbean (Report of the Fourth UN Crime Congress, para. 20).[39]

In the planning of the Fourth UN Crime Congress, the Advisory Committee of Experts "was firmly opposed to the oral delivery of national statements, since valuable time was used which might be required for more important exchanges of view. It strongly recommended, therefore, that national statements should be provided in writing only" (Report of the Advisory Committee, E/CN.5/443, para. 19.)

Ten ancillary meetings were held during the Fourth UN Crime Congress (Report of the Fourth UN Crime Congress, para. 32). In view of the large number of UNAFEI alumni in attendance at the Congress in Kyoto, a meeting of the ad hoc Advisory Committee of the Institute was held (Report of the Fourth UN Crime Congress, para. 33).[40]

The Fourth UN Crime Congress adopted a three-paragraph document called, for the first time, a "Congress Declaration."[41] The Declaration called upon governments to take effective measures to coordinate and intensify their crime prevention efforts within the context of their economic and social development; urged the UN and other international organizations to give high priority to crime prevention, particularly technical aid; and recommended that special attention be given to the administrative, professional, and technical structure necessary for more effective action in crime prevention.[42]

The *Fifth UN Crime Congress* (Geneva, 1–12 September 1975) was originally scheduled to be held in Toronto, Canada. In the early summer of 1975 the Palestine Liberation Organization gave notice that it would send a delegation to the Congress. One month before the scheduled beginning of the Congress, the Canadian Government requested a postponement of one year for further negotiations. The Committee of Conferences of the GA decided not to accede to the request and transferred the venue to the UN headquarters in Geneva and held the Congress on the same dates as originally planned (Report of the Fifth UN Crime Congress, para. 433; Adler and Mueller, 1995, pp. 9–10).

Two of the five substantive agenda items, one dealing with law enforcement and the other with corrections, reflected the continued interest in the UN Crime Programme in the development of new standards and norms and in implementing existing ones. The other three agenda items brought in new perspectives.

The agenda item on the prevention of crime dealt with "traditional" issues in the operation of the formal criminal justice system but it also included "other forms of social control." This marked a strengthening of the attention that was given by the Third UN Crime Congress (1965) to informal social control.

The agenda item on research and planning marked a continuation of an issue dealt with extensively ten years earlier at the Third UN Crime Congress.

The Fifth Congress broadened the focus beyond the social consequences of crime to include the economic consequences. The Congress recommended that a cost-benefit approach be encouraged (Report of the Fifth UN Crime Congress, para. 24 (a) and (l)). The report summarizing the discussion on the costs of crime – such as several paragraphs dealing with "redistributing the costs of crime" – reads almost like a comprehensive manual for integrating data on the costs of crime into national policy-making (Report of the Fifth UN Crime Congress, paras. 302–371).[43]

A new element that was introduced at the Fifth UN Crime Congress was a workshop, which was organized by the UN Interregional Crime and Justice Research Institute (UNICRI). The topic was evaluative research (Report of the Fifth UN Crime Congress, para. 471).

The Fifth UN Crime Congress was the first UN Crime Congress to discuss organized crime and the transnational aspects of crime. It also expanded the discussion beyond crime prevention and criminal justice to consider human rights standards. It approved the Declaration on the Protection of All Persons from Being Subjected to Torture and Other Cruel, Inhuman or Degrading Treatment or Punishment.[44] The Fifth UN Crime Congress adopted recommendations on the abuse of economic power, drug trafficking, terrorism, theft and destruction of cultural property, interpersonal violence, and changing expectations of police performance. The last point laid the basis for the Code of Conduct for Law Enforcement Officials, which was adopted by the GA in resolution A/RES/34/169 of 17 December 1979 (A/CONF.203/15).

The *Sixth UN Crime Congress* (Caracas, 25 August–5 September 1980) was the first to be held in a developing country. The overall theme of the Sixth UN Crime Congress was "Crime prevention and the quality of life."[45]

In addition to the regional preparatory meetings that had been held for earlier UN Crime Congresses, advance interregional expert meetings were organized for the first time on each agenda item. In addition, "pre-Congress consultations" were held on-site among national delegations for the first time to deal primarily with procedural and organizational matters, such as the identification of candidates for the various positions on the General Committee (Report of the Sixth UN Crime Congress, para. 7).

In connection with a substantive agenda item on crime trends, the Congress was presented with the results of the first UN survey of crime trends and operations of criminal justice systems, based on information received from 65 Member States (A/CONF.87/4).[46]

Several difficult and somewhat politicized issues were raised at the Sixth Congress: the concept of a "New International Criminal Justice Order," the death penalty, torture and inhuman treatment, and the prevention of the abuse of power.

In addition to the Caracas Declaration, the Congress adopted 19 resolutions and 1 decision. Most of these were adopted by consensus, which was reached relatively easily, as in the case of recommendations for standard minimum rules on juvenile justice, public participation in crime prevention, and improved statistics. Two draft resolutions, on "Effective measures to prevent crime" and "Extra-legal executions," were adopted, as orally amended, with no votes against but several abstentions (Report of the Sixth UN Crime Congress, paras. 133, 203–212, and 214–216).

In respect of the draft resolution on the death penalty, several Member States objected to provisions in the draft that implied eventual and universal abolition of the death penalty. The draft resolution was not adopted by the Sixth UN Crime Congress on the understanding that it would be submitted to the next UN Crime Congress (Report of the Sixth UN Crime Congress, paras. 130 and 132, and pp. 58–61).[47]

In addition, draft resolutions on "Torture and inhuman treatment" and "Prevention of the abuse of power" were adopted as orally amended, but – exceptionally – only by majority vote.

The theme of the *Seventh UN Crime Congress* (Milan, 26 August–6 September 1985) was "Crime prevention for freedom, justice, peace and development."

Of the five substantive agenda items, four can be seen as a continuation of the debate on similar issues at earlier UN Crime Congresses: crime prevention and criminal justice in the context of development, criminal justice processes, youth crime, and the UN standards and norms. The fifth agenda item, with the very short and simple title of "Victims of crime," reflected a broad new approach to crime prevention and criminal justice, one that looked at the victim's perspective. As noted in section 8.6, interest in victimology had been percolating in criminology for some time; in the 1960s especially support increased for "victim policy," with measures designed to take into better account the interests and concerns of the victim in the criminal justice system. The Seventh UN Crime Congress contributed to the globalization of this discussion, particularly through its adoption of the Declaration of Basic Principles of Justice for Victims of Crime and Abuse of Power, which went on to the GA for approval (A/RES/40/34).

At the Seventh UN Crime Congress, UNICRI and HEUNI organized a research workshop on "Perspectives in action-oriented research: youth, crime and juvenile justice."

The Seventh UN Crime Congress adopted a record 32 different instruments. Among these were the three-page "Milan Plan of Action," the UN Standard Minimum Rules for the Administration of Juvenile Justice, and the Basic Principles on the Independence of the Judiciary. The Congress also adopted the first UN model bilateral treaty on crime issues, the Model Agreement on the Transfer of Foreign Prisoners.

The Milan Plan of Action contains eighteen points and can be seen as the forerunner of the considerably more detailed action plans adopted in the aftermath of the Tenth UN Crime Congress (2000), and also of the Congress

Declarations adopted at all UN Crime Congresses since the Tenth UN Crime Congress. The Milan Plan of Action outlined a worldwide programme for crime prevention and criminal justice. Although much of its language is generic (in referring to crime in general), it identified as key priority areas illicit drug trafficking, transnational organized crime, and terrorism. The Milan Plan of Action also stressed the need for action-oriented research and providing technical assistance to developing countries.

Among the other instruments adopted was a twelve-page document entitled "Guiding Principles for Crime Prevention and Criminal Justice in the Context of Development and a New International Economic Order." This was forwarded with the other instruments to the GA for action but was not adopted by the GA.[48]

The theme of the *Eighth UN Crime Congress* (Havana, 27 August–7 September 1990) was "International co-operation in crime prevention and criminal justice for the 21st century." Each of the five agenda items had lengthy names:

- Crime prevention and criminal justice in the context of development: realities and perspectives of international co-operation;
- Criminal justice policies in relation to problems of imprisonment, other penal sanctions and alternative measures;
- Effective national and international action against: a) organized crime; b) terrorist criminal activities;
- Prevention of delinquency, juvenile justice and the protection of the young: policy approaches and directives; and
- United Nations norms and guidelines in crime prevention and criminal justice; implementation and priorities for further standard-setting.

UNICRI and HEUNI again cooperated in the organization of a research workshop, this time on "Alternatives to imprisonment." In addition, HEUNI organized a demonstration workshop on "Computerization of criminal justice administration."

The record set by the previous UN Crime Congress in the number of instruments adopted was easily surpassed in Havana. The Eighth UN Crime Congress approved model treaties on extradition, mutual assistance in criminal matters, transfer of proceedings in criminal matters, and transfer of supervision of offenders conditionally sentenced or conditionally released; the UN Standard Minimum Rules for Non-Custodial Measures; the Basic Principles for the Treatment of Prisoners;[49] the UN Guidelines for the Prevention of Juvenile Delinquency; the UN Rules for the Protection of Juveniles Deprived of Their Liberty; the Basic Principles on the Use of Force and Firearms by Law Enforcement Officials; the Guidelines on the Role of Prosecutors; and the Basic Principles on the Role of Lawyers.

All in all, the Eighth UN Crime Congress recommended 13 draft instruments and resolutions for adoption by the GA, and adopted 3 other instruments, 30 other resolutions, and 1 decision, for a grand total of 47 separate documents. The subject matter of these ranged from computerization of criminal justice to domestic violence, from instrumental use of children in criminal activities to the role of criminal law in the protection of the environment, and from corruption in government to terrorist criminal activities. With one exception, the drafts were all adopted by consensus. The exception was a draft resolution on the death penalty, which after a difficult passage through committee, was ultimately voted down in the plenary, having fallen four votes short of the two-thirds majority vote required under the rules of procedure.[50]

The *Ninth UN Crime Congress* (Cairo, 28 April–5 May 1995) was the first UN Crime Congress to be held after the restructuring of the UN Crime Programme. It can therefore be seen as a congress in a state of transition towards the vision of more "efficient" congresses that would better serve the interests of the governments of Member States in responding to what they saw as growing, and increasingly transnational, crime problems.

One indicator of this search for efficiency was that the preparations had been somewhat streamlined. The interregional expert meetings that had been held during the three previous UN Crime Congress cycles on each of the agenda items were abandoned.

A further indicator of increasing governmental pressure for the Ninth UN Crime Congress to "get results" and to increase the efficiency and effectiveness of international cooperation in responding to crime was the discussions on developing model UN instruments on international cooperation. These led to the adoption of a resolution on the topic.[51]

Another issue dealt with at the Ninth UN Crime Congress for the first time in a coordinated manner (as one of the workshop topics) was the role of the mass media in crime prevention. The workshop raised issues that would increase in importance in the years to come, such as the role of a free press, and the role of the Internet in shaping the information highway (Report of the Ninth UN Crime Congress, paras. 288 and 292–293). The workshop also addressed the question of "media as educator," which presaged the attention that the UN Crime Programme would give to the role of education in crime prevention, an issue returned to separately at the Twelfth UN Crime Congress in 2010 and at the Fourteenth UN Crime Congress in 2021, in connection with the concept of "a culture of lawfulness."[52]

The Ninth UN Crime Congress was more successful than those immediately preceding it in reducing the flow of draft instruments and resolutions. This was largely due to the innovation of combining recommendations relating to the four substantive topics at the Congress in an "omnibus resolution" with 68 operative paragraphs, making this broadly comparable to the consolidated declarations adopted at subsequent UN Crime Congresses.[53]

In addition to this omnibus resolution, the resolution on the development of UN model instruments, the resolution on a possible convention against transnational organized crime, six other resolutions, and an expression of thanks to the host country were adopted at the Ninth UN Crime Congress. The six other resolutions dealt with a range of issues, from the links between terrorist crimes and transnational organized crime, to violence against women, to children as victims and perpetrators of crime.

The *Tenth UN Crime Congress* (Vienna, 10–17 April 2000) was held at the turn of the millennium and had as its self-evident theme "Crime and justice: Meeting the challenges of the twenty-first century."

The Congress was held at the time of the finalization of the UN Convention against Transnational Organized Crime and its three protocols, and largely for this reason limited itself to one general agenda item related to transnational organized crime: "International cooperation in combating transnational crime: new challenges in the twenty-first century."

The Tenth UN Crime Congress introduced a high-level segment at which speakers of ministerial rank and above could take the floor. Statements were made by a total of 76 high-level participants.

The Congress, as directed by the GA, formulated a single Declaration, the "Vienna Declaration on Crime and Justice: Meeting the Challenges of the Twenty-first Century."[54] The Declaration was about three pages (29 paragraphs) in length. The text of the draft Declaration had been negotiated extensively in advance of the Congress, and the negotiations continued throughout the Congress, sometimes late into the night, until its adoption at the high-level segment at the end of the Congress. In summarizing this document, the UNODC stated:

In the Vienna Declaration, Member States set out an international agenda in crime prevention and criminal justice at the beginning of the new millennium. The Vienna Declaration captures the essence of the work carried out over many years and sets out specific key commitments that should reflect a vision for the future work of the United Nations Crime Prevention and Criminal Justice Programme and of Governments. More specifically, Member States pledged to take resolute and speedy measures to combat: terrorism; trafficking in human beings; illicit trade in firearms; smuggling of migrants; and money-laundering. The Vienna Declaration stressed the need for an effective international legal instrument against corruption, independent of the United Nations Convention against Transnational Organized Crime (GA resolution 55/25, annex I).

(A/CONF.203/15, paras. 40 and 41)

Since the Tenth UN Crime Congress, more attention has been focused on following up the Congress recommendations. Although the Congresses do not have the mandate to set policy, they do produce suggestions as to what measures governments, the Secretariat, and other stakeholders might consider taking. Previously the GA had usually invited governments to be guided by the resolutions and recommendations of the various Congresses and had requested the Secretary-General to take the appropriate operational follow-up action.[55]

The procedure after the Tenth UN Crime Congress was different. First, instead of a broad resolution dealing with the Tenth UN Crime Congress as such (as was done with the previous Congresses), one GA resolution adopted the consolidated Vienna Declaration (A/RES/55/59) and a separate GA resolution considered follow-up to the Congress (A/RES/55/60).[56]

Second, the rather brief (three paragraph) GA resolution on follow-up used stronger language than earlier resolutions. The first operative paragraph begins "Urges Governments, in their efforts to prevent and combat crime, especially transnational crime ...." Here, the more exhortative "urges" has replaced "invites" as used in earlier, corresponding GA resolutions. The addition of the words "especially transnational crime" is once again a sign of the growing concern of the drafters about transnational (organized) crime.

Third, the second paragraph of the GA resolution requests that the UN Crime Commission continue its consideration of the findings and recommendations contained in the Vienna Declaration at its next session. No similar request for renewed consideration had been made after earlier Congresses.

Finally, the third paragraph "requests the Secretary-General to prepare, in consultation with Member States, draft plans of action to include specific measures for the implementation of and follow-up to the commitments undertaken in the Declaration for consideration and action by the Commission" at its next session. This third paragraph of the GA resolution lays the basis for what has become a recurring item on the agenda of the UN Crime Commission: each year, at the same time as the Commission discusses preparations for the next UN Crime Congress according to the five-year cycle, it reviews what has been done to follow up on the Declaration from the previous Congress.[57]

The focus at the *Eleventh UN Crime Congress* (Bangkok, 18–25 April 2005) on transnational organized crime was very clear, with four of the five agenda items and three of the six workshops dealing with this topic in one way or another.

This focus on transnational organized crime should be seen in the light of the fact that by the time of the Congress the UN Convention on Transnational Organized Crime (with two of its three protocols related to trafficking in persons and on the smuggling of migrants) had entered into force. The UN

Convention against Corruption also entered into force a few months after the Congress was held.

As with the previous Congress, the Eleventh UN Crime Congress ended with a high-level segment, during which statements were made by 88 heads of national delegations and the Bangkok Declaration was adopted.

In the discussions at the UN Crime Commission, held soon after the Eleventh UN Crime Congress, extensive appreciation was expressed to the host government, Thailand, for hosting the Congress, and to the Secretariat for servicing the Congress. At the same time, a number of Member States were critical of the way in which the UN Crime Commission was planning the Congresses. In their view, the Commission should "adopt a more disciplined approach" to Congress preparations, by, for example, defining the agenda items better and allocating more time to each agenda item (E/CN.15/2005/20 (2005), para. 40).

As a direct result of this discussion, a follow-up event was held in Bangkok at the invitation of the Thai Government: a meeting of an intergovernmental group of experts to review the organization, structure, and methods of work of the UN Crime Congresses (E/CN.15/2007/6). The meeting produced a number of specific recommendations, dealing with such matters as the need to have carefully selected and sharply focused agenda items and topics, to have technical workshops that emphasize an interactive exchange of views and experience (as opposed to the delivery of prepared statements), to have a Congress Declaration that is focused and streamlined, to publish and ensure wide dissemination of the proceedings and outcome of each Congress, and to ensure adequate follow-up at the international and national levels (E/CN.15/2007/6, paras. 35–40 and *passim*).

The intergovernmental meeting also recommended more coherent follow-up to the Congresses. One result of this has been that the Secretariat reports, and governments are invited to report, at subsequent sessions of the UN Crime Commission on their efforts to implement the commitments taken at the preceding Congress. At the next session of the UN Crime Commission, Thailand submitted a template for a checklist that governments could use when reporting on implementation of the Bangkok Declaration (E/CN.15/2007/CRP.1).

The *Twelfth UN Crime Congress* (Bahia de Salvador, 12–19 April 2010) marked the third time a Congress has been held in the Latin American and Caribbean region. As had been the case at the preceding Congress, (transnational) organized crime issues dominated the agenda items; however, the workshops dealt with more "traditional" crime and justice issues.

A sub-text of much of the discussion at the Twelfth UN Crime Congress was the role of the criminal justice system in national development and in strengthening the rule of law. In 2000, the UN GA had adopted the MDGs (A/RES/55/2).

As was the case with the Bangkok Declaration before it, the Salvador Declaration had been extensively negotiated in advance of the Congress and was the focus of very lengthy negotiations at the Congress itself, at times until the early hours of the morning. It consisted of 9 pages, 55 paragraphs.

Three days after the Twelfth UN Crime Congress began, eruptions of the Eyjafjallajökull Volcano in Iceland led to the closing of much of the north Atlantic airspace, which remained closed until after the Congress was over. This caused many of the participants to leave the Congress earlier than intended, in order to use alternative, and often rather difficult, travel arrangements.

The last days (and nights) of the Eleventh UN Crime Congress were filled with their own drama, with intensive and protracted debate over the issue of whether or not a UN convention should be negotiated on cybercrime and how the views of the opposing sides should be reflected in the report.[58]

The *Thirteenth UN Crime Congress* (Doha, 12–19 April 2015) was convened at the time when the GA was finalizing its work on the post-2015 development agenda, the SDGs. One of the key issues being debated by the GA in New York was whether or not crime and justice issues (such as security and the rule of law) would be included in the SDGs. The theme of the Congress quite clearly reflected an interest in influencing this process: "Integrating crime prevention and criminal justice into the wider United Nations agenda to address social and economic challenges and to promote the rule of law at the national and international levels, and public participation."

On this occasion, a more methodical approach was taken to the structuring of the agenda. The four agenda items were selected to cover different broad areas of policy on crime prevention and criminal justice: fundamental policy issues, international cooperation, forms of crime, and crime prevention. The four workshops were formulated so that each one was closely tied ("interlocked") with one of the four agenda items, and they were designed to be more focused and more technical. Furthermore, each workshop was held in advance of the corresponding agenda item, so that the discussion on the agenda item could benefit from input from the workshop.

A second, major adjustment was that the high-level segment was moved from the end of the Congress (where it had been positioned at the three preceding Congresses) to the beginning of the Congress. This allowed adoption of the Congress Declaration, which had been negotiated in advance of the Congress, on the first day of the Congress. This, in turn, meant that many key participants no longer needed to engage in hours of negotiation on the Declaration at the Congress itself (negotiations which, at preceding Congresses, had at times extended far into the night), but were able to take an active part in the discussions on the agenda items, in the workshops, and in the ancillary meetings.

For the first time at any UN Crime Congress, the high-level segment included statements by the Secretary-General of the UN, the President of the

GA, and the President of ECOSOC. A total of 96 high-level speakers gave statements.

At twelve pages, the Doha Declaration was considerably longer than any of the preceding three consolidated Congress Declarations (www.unodc. org/documents/congress//Documentation/ACONF222_L6_e_V1502120. pdf). In view of the ongoing work at the GA on Agenda 2030, the Declaration forcefully argued for the interconnected nature of crime prevention and criminal justice and sustainable development. Paragraph 2, for example, reaffirms "the cross-cutting nature of crime prevention and criminal justice issues and the consequent need to integrate those issues into the wider agenda of the United Nations in order to enhance system-wide coordination," and paragraph 3 recognizes "the importance of effective, fair, humane and accountable crime prevention and criminal justice systems and the institutions comprising them as a central component of the rule of law."

Paragraph 4 states:

We acknowledge that sustainable development and the rule of law are strongly interrelated and mutually reinforcing. We therefore welcome the inclusive and transparent intergovernmental process for the post-2015 development agenda, which is aimed at developing global sustainable development goals to be agreed by the General Assembly, and acknowledge the proposals of the Open Working Group of the General Assembly on Sustainable Development Goals as the main basis for integrating sustainable development goals into the post-2015 development agenda, while recognizing that other inputs will also be considered. In this context, we reiterate the importance of promoting peaceful, corruption-free and inclusive societies for sustainable development, with a focus on a people-centred approach that provides access to justice for all and builds effective, accountable and inclusive institutions at all levels.

The politicization of some discussion in the UN Crime Programme became apparent at the Thirteenth UN Crime Congress. Although previous Congresses had included conclusions and recommendations as part of the outcome of the discussion in the workshops, there was an extended debate at the Thirteenth UN Crime Congress on the status of these conclusions and recommendations. (With only one and a half days allotted to each workshop, there was in practice very little time for negotiation of each set of conclusions and recommendations.) Instead of referring to the outcome of this debate as "conclusions and recommendations," the report on the Thirteenth UN Crime contained the formulation "The Chair, in summarizing the discussion, invited the participants to consider the following ...." The impact of this wording is unclear, since the workshops are designed to be a forum for an exchange of views and experiences, and not for a discussion of policy.

The Thirteenth UN Crime Congress was preceded by a "Youth Forum" at which young participants discussed selected items on the Congress agenda. The report of the Youth Forum was submitted to the Congress during the high-level segment.

The *Fourteenth UN Crime Congress* (Kyoto, 7–12 March 2021) had the distinction of being the first major UN conference in any field to be organized after the outbreak of the Covid-19 pandemic. (The pandemic forced a postponement of the Congress by a year, from 2020 to 2021.) It was organized as what is now termed a *hybrid conference*, with only a very few, some 260, participants on-site, and the vast majority, some 5,300, participating remotely from their office or home.

As this was the first UN Crime Congress to be held after the adoption in 2015 of the 2030 Agenda, with its SDGs, the theme of the Congress was appropriately formulated as "Advancing crime prevention, criminal justice and the rule of law: towards the achievement of the 2030 Agenda."

The Congress Declaration (the Kyoto Declaration) was adopted by consensus at the opening ceremony, which was attended by many dignitaries, including Her Imperial Highness, Princess Takamado, Prime Minister Yoshihide Suga, Mr. Antonio Guterres, the Secretary-General of the UN (in a live telecast from New York), and the Presidents of the GA and ECOSOC (in video statements).

The hybrid model tested in Kyoto had both drawbacks and benefits. Trying to connect over 5,000 participants around the world, when almost all of them were using their own equipment, meant that individual connections were occasionally broken. As this was a global conference, the hybrid model also meant that many attendees were tuning in from different time zones and had to stay alert at unusual times. They tended to try to link in only for very specific events, discussions, or panels, perhaps to give a statement, and then close the link after that was over without doing "virtual roaming" to see what other discussions were underway in other fora at the Congress.

Perhaps the main drawback to the hybrid model is that it does not provide the same vibrant mix of different participants gathered in one place, allowing for networking and one-on-one exchanges of experience and views between members of national delegations (representing many different agencies and fields), representatives from UN special agencies, PNIs, intergovernmental organizations, non-governmental organizations, and individual experts on an equal basis.

There are also benefits, such as the savings in the travel budget. As people could participate online no matter where they were around the world, the number of participants could readily be expanded (although those participating from other time zones may have had to stay up in the middle of the night in order to do so). This was also reflected in the large number of ministers or other very senior officials with substantive responsibility for crime prevention and criminal justice in their own government, who were able to provide a video statement during the high-level segment.

10.5   Output of the UN Crime Congresses: From resolutions to declarations

Each UN Crime Congress since 2000 has produced a single document called a Congress Declaration "containing recommendations derived from the deliberations of the high-level segment, the round tables and the workshops, to be submitted to the Commission for its consideration." The draft is negotiated in advance of the Congress, using as its basis the recommendations and conclusions from the regional preparatory meetings.

The Congress Declaration is not the only outcome of each Congress. In addition to the official report of the Congress, each Congress produces a considerable amount of documentation, such as the official background documents prepared by the Secretariat (which have been of very high quality), the reports of the regional preparatory meetings, a number of conference room documents, a large number of documents submitted by various participants in the different categories, and the unofficial report of the ancillary meetings.

At the more recent UN Crime Congresses, the respective UN PNIs that had the lead role in organizing each workshop has usually produced a report containing the various panel presentations and related material. In respect of the Thirteenth and the Fourteenth UN Crime Congresses, thanks to cooperation between the UNODC and the respective host government, much of this material has been made available through the Congress website (www.unodc. org/congress/en/previous/previous-13.html), thus providing information for those practitioners, policy-makers, and researchers around the world who had not participated, and in this way increasing the impact of the Congresses.

Over the past two decades, both the UN Secretariat and the UN Crime Commission have devoted greater attention to ensuring that the UN Crime Congresses are not "one-off" events, which are forgotten as soon as preparations begin on the next five-year cycle. A standing item on the agenda of the UN Crime Commission is the UN Crime Congresses, during which implementation of action points raised by the previous Congress is reviewed and discussed, at the same time as the preparations for the next Congress are advanced. This ensures continuity in the process.

The introduction in 2000 of Congress Declarations as the main output of UN Crime Congresses resulted in a perceptible change in the nature of these global events. The first UN Crime Congresses had been large gatherings where the participants "talked shop" with other criminal justice experts or stakeholders involved in crime prevention and criminal justice. These

Congresses brought together representatives of governments, intergovernmental organizations, and non-governmental organizations, as well as a large number of persons attending in their personal capacity (usually, criminal justice practitioners and representatives of research and academia). Resolutions were adopted, but they either marked the culmination of a longer process (adoption of a standard or norm) or they related to a specific issue, which was generally (but not always) being dealt with at that particular Congress.

Once the concept of Congress Declarations was introduced, these focused the attention of the governmental representatives on the written outcome of the Congress. Less attention was paid by them to what was said at the Congress itself and more to what was said in the Congress Declaration. Although the UN Crime Congress has no formal policy-making role, many participants began to take the view that a global Congress representing almost every country, with a broad spectrum of stakeholders and a few scattered heads of state and several governmental ministers in attendance, should take precedence over annual sessions of the UN Crime Commission. Accordingly, they came to view the Congress Declarations as establishing the framework for the UN work programme in crime prevention and criminal justice for the next five years.[59]

10.6   Changes in the UN Crime Congresses over 75 years

If participants at the first UN Crime Congress, held in Geneva in 1955, had been able to jump in a time capsule to attend the most recent UN Crime Congress, held in Kyoto in 2021, they would have found much that was familiar (having overcome their astonishment at the fact that, due to the pandemic, most of the participants at the Kyoto Congress attended online). The participants represent Member States, specialized agencies, intergovernmental organizations, and non-governmental organizations. In addition (and this is unusual among major UN conferences and is a legacy from the IPPC conferences), a number of individual experts attend. The participants discuss specific agenda items, and a report is prepared on the proceedings. Much has thus stayed more or less the same.

However, the format and substance of the UN Crime Congresses have evolved considerably. Among the more important changes are the following:

- the participants come from a larger number of Member States, and the number of participants has increased;
- the topics discussed have changed considerably, from the early focus almost solely on corrections and juvenile delinquency to the focus on transnational crime, especially at the turn of the millennium;

- Congress workshops have been added to the formal proceedings, and during the 2015 and 2021 UN Crime Congresses the workshop topics were "interlocked" with the respective substantive discussion item;
- the number of ancillary meetings has expanded;
- a "high level segment" has been added to the UN Crime Congresses (since 2000);
- instead of adopting separate resolutions on different topics, the more recent UN Crime Congresses (since 2000) have adopted a single consolidated Congress Declaration; and
- since the 1990s more attention has been paid to follow-up to the Congress discussions.

As major international events in the calendar of the global crime prevention and criminal justice community, the UN Crime Congresses provide a touchstone for examining how our understanding of crime and criminal justice has changed over the years.

In the early years of the UN Crime Congresses (the first three Congresses in 1955, 1960, and 1965), the largely Western participants appeared optimistic that, with sufficient research and debate, the "cause of crime" (be it at the level of the individual or society) could be identified and remedied. The UN Crime Congresses held in 1970 and 1975, which benefited from more global participation, were not as sanguine, but the participants were nonetheless able to reach consensus on how to respond to a growing range of issues, including organized crime and terrorism. The Congresses in 1980, 1985, and 1990 reflected a (partial) rejection of a solely Western perspective on crime and criminal justice, and there were political overtones to discussions on society and development, in particular economic development, and their impact on crime.

Following the restructuring of the UN Crime Programme in 1991, the formal sessions at the UN Crime Congresses from 1995 to 2010 tended to increasingly address crime as a threat to security, and less to address crime as an interplay between society and the individual. There has been considerably more focus on serious forms of (transnational) organized crime and terrorism and repeated calls for improved efficiency in international law enforcement and judicial cooperation. Coinciding with the adoption by the GA of the Social Development Goals in 2015, there has been a more balanced consideration at the 2015 and 2021 Congresses of transnational crime on the one hand, and "ordinary crime" and the day-to-day operation of the criminal justice system at the domestic and local level, on the other.

Over a 70-year span, therefore, the UN Crime Congresses have reflected shifts in the way crime has been viewed by national governments, and changes in their understanding of what the response of the international community should be.

TABLE 10.2 Timeline of the evolution of the UN Crime Congresses, 1955–2021

UN Crime Congress	Changes in the approach to crime, as reflected in the Congresses	Changes in the Congresses	Notable UN developments
First Geneva, 1955	Social defence theory; gradual shift from individual-oriented to society-oriented theories of crime	50 national delegations, 500 participants; First UN standard and norm adopted	
Second London, 1960	Expansion of criminological concepts beyond a purely Western perspective	Number of participants reaches 1,000; Russian added as official language	1962: UNAFEI (first PNI) established
Third Stockholm, 1965	*New:* attention to prevention and informal social control; *New:* attention to the impact of social change on crime	Growing participation by developing countries; First Congress workshop; Technical assistance becomes recurring agenda item	
Fourth Kyoto, 1970	First references to terrorism; First references to organized crime	First Congress held outside Europe; Regional preparatory meetings organized for the first time	1972: ad hoc UN Crime Committee becomes permanent
Fifth Geneva, 1975	Concept of transnational (organized) crime introduced; *New:* attention to economic costs of crime	Number of national delegations exceeds 100; Outcome routed to different addressees (e.g., GA, ECOSOC)	
Sixth Caracas, 1980	*New:* human rights issues raised; *New:* crime and development considered; *New:* abuse of power considered; *New:* prison overcrowding considered	First Congress to be held in a developing country; Arabic and Chinese added as official languages; Interregional expert preparatory meetings organized; First pre-Congress consultations; First UN crime survey given to Congress; Votes on several resolutions	

Congress	New topics / attention	Organizational and participation developments	External developments
Seventh Milan, 1985	*New*: victim issues considered	32 different documents adopted	
Eighth Havana, 1990	*New*: domestic violence considered	45 separate resolutions adopted	1991: UN Crime Committee replaced by UN Crime Commission
Ninth Cairo, 1995	Growing attention to transnational (organized) crime; *New*: environmental crime considered	Interregional expert preparatory meetings no longer organized; Congress shortened to 8 days; Number of participants nears 2,000; "Omnibus" resolution	
Tenth Vienna, 2000	*New*: rule of law considered	First high-level segment (held at the end of the Congress); First consolidated Congress Declaration; No separate resolutions; Institutionalized Congress follow-up; Number of participants reaches 3,000	2000: MDGs adopted; 2002: GA res 56/119 on the Congresses; 2003: UNTOC enters into force
Eleventh Bangkok, 2005	Crime increasingly seen as threat to national security		2005: UNCAC enters into force; 2006: expert group meeting on Congresses
Twelfth Salvador, 2010	*New*: cybercrime considered; *New*: education for justice considered		
Thirteenth Doha, 2015		Congress workshops "interlocked" with topics; High-level segment shifted to beginning of Congress; Number of national delegations exceeds 140; Number of participants nears 4,000	2015: SDGs adopted
Fourteenth Kyoto, 2021		First major UN conference to be held in a hybrid format (260 on-site participants and 5,300 online participants)	

At the same time as the Congresses have provided snapshots of the approach that has been taken at different times to crime prevention and criminal justice, they have changed our understanding of what the key issues are. By providing a forum for the exchange of ideas and experiences in how local, national, and international responses to crime can be improved, they have promoted the global spread of the latest academic thinking in criminology, victimology, and criminal justice studies. The first four UN Crime Congresses gradually drew in an expanding global audience. The selection of Kyoto, Japan, as the venue for the Fourth UN Crime Congress (1970) contributed to disseminating the latest thinking among practitioners and policy-makers in the Asian and Pacific region. The Sixth and Eighth UN Crime Congresses (1980 and 1990), held in Caracas and Havana respectively, fulfilled the same function for the Latin American and Caribbean region.

The Third UN Crime Congress (1965) served to direct attention to crime prevention strategies, the role of informal social control, and the impact of social change on crime. The Fourth UN Crime Congress (1970) raised awareness of the national and international dimensions of organized crime and terrorism, a process continued at the Fifth UN Crime Congress (1975), which introduced the concept of "transnational crime" to the world.

The Fifth UN Crime Congress was also significant in bringing the issue of human rights into the criminal justice framework, as well as in providing criminologists and criminal justice policy-makers with better conceptual tools to understand and analyse the economic impact of crime.

The Sixth UN Crime Congress (1980), the first to be held in a developing country, changed the tone of the discussion by examining issues of crime and development in depth. It also introduced many to the concept of "abuse of power," with its implications for criminological research and the identification of "offences and offenders beyond the reach of the law." The Sixth UN Crime Congress drew attention to the problems associated with prison overcrowding. The Seventh UN Crime Congress was significant in spreading awareness of and interest in the new approach to victims (victimology and victim policy), and in highlighting the "hidden crime" of domestic violence.

The Eighth UN Crime Congress (1990) was a watershed event in producing a wealth of soft-law instruments that have had an impact on practice and policy in a wide range of issues, from the application of non-custodial measures to the prevention of juvenile delinquency, and from the use of force and firearms by law enforcement officials to the work of both prosecutors and lawyers. At the same time, dissatisfaction with the plethora of draft resolutions that had to be dealt with strengthened support for the restructuring of the UN Crime Programme, with the attendant emphasis on effectiveness and efficiency.

The Ninth UN Crime Congress (1995) was marked by a focus on transnational organized crime. It also brought to global attention the potential harm caused by environmental crime. The Tenth UN Crime Congress (2000) gave increased attention to the rule of law, and the Eleventh and Twelfth Crime Congresses (2005 and 2010) revisited the role of standards and norms. The Thirteenth UN Crime Congress (2015) contributed in part to the incorporation, in the 2030 Agenda, of references to rule of law, security, and crime prevention and criminal justice, as part of Goal 16. The Fourteenth UN Crime Congress in 2021 continued this work.

There has been considerable evolution in examining the UN Crime Congresses from a structural and organizational point of view. The first Congresses were not very different from many other typical professional and academic conferences at the time, with lectures and learned debates (and a ladies' programme for accompanying spouses), resulting in soft-law instruments adopted by consensus. With the addition of workshops, the expansion of the number of ancillary meetings, and the shortening of the Congresses from two weeks to eight days, their schedule has become fuller and tighter. However, many of the innovations adopted at the Thirteenth UN Crime Congress in 2015 in particular (such as interlocking each workshop with a related agenda item) served to clarify the structure and maximize the potential for the technically oriented workshops to inform the discussions on the respective agenda item. Placing the high-level segment at the beginning of the Congress and having the Congress Declaration adopted in the course of it have also been of organizational benefit.

Continuous refinements are needed, and the Congresses will undoubtedly continue to evolve. The UN Crime Congresses have reached a stage where we can pause to reflect on their past achievements, and seek to ensure that they still have the vigour needed to try to identify and come to grips with what needs to be done.

Even at the age of 70, the UN Crime Congresses are not ready for retirement. They are workhorses that can still be harnessed for the benefit of the UN Crime Programme.

Notes

1 This chapter is largely based on Joutsen, 2021.
2 The ad hoc Advisory Committee stated that "although the Congress was to express the opinion of the experts, it was nevertheless essential to bear in mind the fact that its recommendations would be submitted to the policy-making organs of the United Nations, which are made up of Government representatives." Report of the First UN Crime Congress, para. 12, citing E/CN.5/298, para. 11.

   The same point was noted in para. 5 of the Report on the First UN Crime Congress: "The Congress ... was designed to give experts from the entire world an opportunity to express and compare their opinions ...."
3 The footnote to Rule 18 of the Rules of Procedure for the First UN Crime Congress (www.unodc.org/congress/en/previous/previous-01.html) notes that "[a]s stated in the note of invitation to governments, it is understood that in view of the nature of the Congress, the participants will express their own personal opinions."

4 At the time the author was a member of the UN Crime Committee and was actively engaged in this debate.
5 The Eighth UN Crime Congress (1990) reported to the GA through ECOSOC.
6 This subclause was inserted largely to refer to the European region. A few Member States were of the view that the annual sessions of the UN Crime Commission
provided the European Member States sufficient opportunity for consultations.
7 It has often proved difficult to wean participants – and the expert panellists – away
from the reading of prepared statements and draw them into an "open dialogue."
This difficulty is all too familiar at conferences around the world, no matter
what the subject. The difficulty is all the greater when the UN Crime Congress
workshops bring in hundreds of participants, representing different cultures and
backgrounds, with different debating styles. As a final touch, the participants are
working with six different official languages.
8 The amended rules of procedure were adopted by GA resolution 32/60.
9 At the first two UN Crime Congresses, furthermore, a time limit was placed on
statements: ten minutes for the first statement, and (in 1960) five minutes on subsequent statements by the same speaker (Rule 13 of the Rules of Procedure for the
First UN Crime Congress (1955), and Rule 12 of the Rules of Procedure for the
Second UN Crime Congress (1960)). The Rules of Procedure for later Congresses
gave the chairperson discretion to limit the length of interventions. See, for example, the Rules of Procedure for the Third UN Crime Congress.
  In the author's experience, most speakers do not exceed the patience of the
audience, and consequently it has rarely been necessary for the chairperson to call
a speaker to order for speaking too long. At the Thirteenth UN Crime Congress
(2015), one chairperson adopted a useful innovation: after he had announced the
maximum time to be allowed for each speaker, a timer was shown on the back-
drop, clicking down to zero. This method was adopted also at subsequent sessions
of the UN Crime Commission.
10 Rule 20 of the Rules of Procedure at the Third UN Crime Congress (1965) stated
that in giving the floor to speakers, the chairperson should give due regard to geographical representation and the points which each speaker proposes to discuss.
11 Present practice is that the Congress officials are elected on the basis of equitable
geographical representation.
12 See, for example, Rule 21 of the Rules of Procedure of the First UN Crime Congress, available at www.unodc.org/congress/en/previous/previous-01.html In
advance of the Fifth UN Crime Congress (1975), the Rules of Procedure were
amended to limit the right to vote to governmental delegations to bring the Rules
"into conformity with current practice in other United Nations bodies." Report
of the Fifth UN Crime Congress, para. 464.
13 Such ancillary meetings had been organized since the First UN Crime Congress.
14 At the Fourteenth UN Crime Congress, which was held during the COVID-19
pandemic, almost all participants attended online. This may help to explain why
so few individual expert papers were submitted. The list is available at https://
www.unodc.org/unodc/en/crimecongress/statements.html
  Papers submitted by individual experts (or, indeed, by other participants, including national delegations) are not "official" Congress documents, which would
need to be translated into the six official languages of the UN. Moreover, the
Secretariat will not assist in the distribution of unofficial documents other than by
setting aside tables on which delegations and individual experts can leave documents they believe would be of interest to the participants. With some exceptions,
only official documents may be placed in the "pigeonholes" set aside for each
individual delegation or distributed inside the meeting rooms to the seats of the
individual delegations.

15 Report of the Fourth UN Crime Congress, para. 10 and Rule 1 (c) of the Rules of Procedure, provided at p. 62 ff of the Report of the Fourth UN Crime Congress.
16 Rule 1 (b) of the Rules of Procedure, provided at p. 79 ff of the Report of the Fifth UN Crime Congress.
17 Rule 58 (1) of the Rules of Procedure for the Seventh UN Crime Congress, available at www.unodc.org/congress/en/previous/previous-07.html
18 Formally speaking, the Secretariat "invites" qualified individuals to attend the Congresses. In practice, interested individuals apply for permission to attend.
    Most individual experts come from the host Member State or from within the region in question. The hosts of the different UN Crime Congresses have taken quite different approaches to this issue. When the Congress was organized in Milan in 1985, the delegation of the host country consisted of 185 members. This was considerably surpassed in 2010, when the Congress was organized in Bahia de Salvador. The national delegation of the host country, Brazil, consisted of 1,551 members.
19 Formally speaking, the UN Crime Commission submits the decision through ECOSOC to the GA for approval.
    References to the UN Crime Commission should be understood as referring, up to and including preparations for the Eighth UN Crime Congress (1990), to the UN Crime Committee. Whereas the UN Crime Commission is convened every year, its predecessor, the UN Crime Committee, held sessions every second year.
20 Governments are invited to be "actively involved" in the drafting of the Discussion Guides.
21 The regional preparatory meetings are aligned with membership in the five UN Economic Commissions: Africa, Asia and the Pacific, Europe, Latin America and the Caribbean, and Western Asia. Following the Ninth UN Crime Congress (1995), the organization of European regional meetings was discontinued because some Member States argued that, with the UN Crime Commission holding annual sessions in Vienna, the European countries had sufficient opportunity for European preparation. However, European regional preparatory meetings were revived in preparation for the Fourteenth UN Crime Congress (2021).
    During the cycles for the preparation of the Sixth, Seventh, and Eighth UN Crime Congresses (1980–1990), interregional expert meetings were organized on each of the agenda items. This practice was discontinued after the 1990 Congress, following the restructuring of the UN Crime Programme.
22 Although a (brief) Congress Declaration was adopted at the Fourth UN Crime Congress (1970), this had been negotiated during the Congress itself. Since the Tenth UN Crime Congress in 2000, each Congress has adopted as its main output a Congress Declaration, which has been extensively negotiated in advance of the Congress.
23 Since the Sixth UN Crime Congress in 1980, a report on the "State of crime and justice worldwide" has been part of the official documentation.
24 The extended Bureau of the UN Crime Commission currently consists of the chairperson, the three vice-chairpersons and rapporteur of the Commission, the chairpersons of the five regional groups, an EU representative, and a representative of the "Group of 77 and China" group of developing countries.
25 See, for example, A/RES/72/192, paras. 14 and 15.
26 See, for example, para. 32 of the report of the First (1955), para. 35 of the report of the Second (1960), and para. 35 of the report of the Third UN Crime Congress (1965). The reports of several of the Congresses do not indicate how many ancillary meetings were held. Ten such meetings were held at both the Fourth and the Fifth UN Crime Congress (para. 32 of the report of the Fourth UN Crime Congress

and para. 465 of the report of the Fifth UN Crime Congress). Thirty-five such meetings were held at the Tenth UN Crime Congress (2000), 42 at the Eleventh (2005), 82 at the Twelfth (2010), and 195 at the Thirteenth UN Crime Congress (2015) (Gary Hill, private communication, 1 March 2019). At the Fourteenth UN Crime Congress, held in special circumstances due to the COVID-19 pandemic, 151 online ancillary meetings were held, estimated at being half the number that would have been held under normal circumstances.

27 See, for example, A/RES/72/192, para. 17.

28 Through the efforts of Mr. Hill and his team of volunteer "interns," ancillary meetings at the more recent UN Crime Congresses have also been provided with interpretation as needed, and summaries of the different ancillary meetings have been made available.

29 The plenary body is used for the formal opening, closing, and (since the Tenth UN Crime Congress in 2000) high-level segment. It may also deal with an agenda item (as was done at the Fourteenth UN Crime Congress), as a result of which the formal proceedings of the Congress may be conducted simultaneously in three different conference halls.

Before the Tenth UN Crime Congress in 1990, when the Congress was to consider separate resolutions, these resolutions were discussed in a Committee and then forwarded to the plenary for formal adoption.

30 The high-level segment does increase political visibility but in some respects it is problematic. Because of the large number of participants of ministerial rank or higher attending the Congresses and wishing to speak, the time allotted to each can be quite short, generally about 5–7 minutes (with more time given to a head of state). Each speaker will of course speak to their national priorities, as a result of which it becomes difficult to form an overview of possibly a hundred different statements given over the course of two or three days.

Various permutations have been suggested, such as identifying in advance which high-level speakers intend to address certain issues, and bringing them together in themed mini-segments, perhaps even in a roundtable format. However, these have so far remained suggestions.

31 In 1975, when a decision was taken only a few months in advance of the Fifth UN Crime Congress to move the venue from Toronto to UN headquarters in Geneva, Switzerland, this practice was not followed. A diplomatic solution was found: as the UN Secretary-General had declared 1975 to be the "Year of the Woman," the Congress agreed that the highest-ranking female head of a national delegation attending the Congress, Minister of Justice Inkeri Anttila of Finland, would serve as president.

A quarter of a century later (2000), when the Congress was held at the UN headquarters in Vienna, Mr. Penuell Mpapa Maduna, Minister of Justice of South Africa, was elected president.

32 See, for example, Rule 9 of the Rules of Procedure of the Fourth UN Crime Congress.

33 The six official working languages of the UN are Arabic, Chinese, English, French, Russian, and Spanish. At the First UN Crime Congress (1955), there were three official working languages, English, French, and Spanish. Russian was added at the Second UN Crime Congress (1960), and Arabic and Chinese were added at the Sixth UN Crime Congress (1970).

34 More information on the different UN Crime Congresses is provided in Joutsen, 2020.

35 One resolution was adopted on each of the five agenda items. A sixth, one-paragraph resolution dealt with technical assistance, and the seventh resolution was essentially an expression of thanks to the Secretary-General, the IPPC, and

the Swiss authorities for the success of the First UN Crime Congress. Report of the First UN Crime Congress, p. 82.

36 Such dire comments in an opening statement about an increase in crime would presumably have been regarded by most participants as totally appropriate at any of the UN Crime Congresses.

37 In a Secretariat document published a year after the Third UN Crime Congress, it was noted that "Since criminality is a product of interacting individual and social factors, it cannot be assumed that it can be eradicated from society; there will always be deviations from the legal norms of society." International Action in the Field of Social Defence (1966–1970). Note by the Secretariat, E/CN.5/C.2/R.2, 1966, para. 14.

38 An additional factor behind the selection of the theme was that the UN was entering its Second Development Decade.

39 However, the First UN Crime Congress had been preceded by "regional consultative group" meetings that had examined some of the items on the agenda. Report of the First UN Crime Congress, para. 13.

40 UNAFEI, the oldest of the UN PNIs, was established in 1962.

41 A Congress Declaration was also adopted by the Sixth UN Crime Congress in 1970. Since the Tenth UN Crime Congress in 2000, the outcome of each Congress has been consolidated into a single Declaration.

42 The Advisory Committee of Experts, meeting in 1969, considered the proposal of the Secretariat that a "broad declaration of statements summing up the sentiments of a Congress could well be prepared …" (E/CN.5/443, paras 21–22), given the view of the Secretariat that working out resolutions at meetings with more than 1,000 participants was difficult.

43 Redistributing the costs of crime is dealt with in paras. 365–368 of the report of the Congress. The rapporteur responsible for this section of the report was Mr. Warren Woodham, Permanent Secretary of the Ministry of National Security and Justice of Jamaica.

It is the author's understanding that the rapporteurs at the first UN Crime Congresses, who tended to be academics or otherwise persons with extensive experience in summarizing and presenting views, by and large wrote the reports by themselves, with the assistance of the Secretariat. In some cases, the rapporteur finalized the report after the meeting, based on their notes. With some rapporteurs, as with Mr. Woodham on the costs of crime, the report takes the form of a well-structured, comprehensive, and authoritative statement of what (in the light of the discussion) is known about the topic.

A shift has occurred in this respect, in that the Secretariat almost invariably prepares first drafts of the reports in order to assist the rapporteur (and the rapporteur general) in their work. Although the reports continue to be of high quality, they are more of a summary of the debate than of the "state of the art," and abound with qualifiers along the lines of "the participants agreed that …," "several speakers noted that …," and "one delegation cautioned that …."

Since this shift, the draft report presented at the end of each Congress (in all six official languages) has been more or less final. Subsequent changes to the report are primarily limited to linguistic editing of the different language versions.

44 This was subsequently adopted as GA resolution 3452(XXX), which was the genesis of the Convention on the same topic adopted by the Commission on Human Rights (1987).

45 Yet again, there was a last-minute change of venue. The Sixth UN Crime Congress was originally to be held in Sydney, Australia. A year before the Congress, Australia withdrew its offer. Venezuela almost immediately offered to host the Congress. Adler and Mueller, 1995, pp. 10–11.

46 The corresponding results of the second, third, and fourth UN surveys were presented to the next three UN Crime Congresses. Since the Tenth UN Crime Congress (2000), the title of the report has been "The state of crime and criminal justice worldwide –Report of the Secretary-General." See, for example, A/CONF.187/5.

47 The somewhat ungainly formulation of the agenda item under which the death penalty was discussed ("United Nations norms and guidelines in criminal justice: from standard-setting to implementation, and capital punishment") was due to disagreement in the UN Crime Committee between some (largely abolitionist) delegations who wanted to discuss this as a separate agenda item and some (retentionist) delegations who regarded further discussion of the subject as not necessary. Discussing capital punishment under a separate agenda item would have given the issue a higher profile, required the Secretariat to prepare a separate background report, and increased the time allotted to the discussion. The merger of two proposed agenda items was a compromise.

48 Redo, 2012, p. 70, concludes that this marked the failure of the concept of the New International Criminal Justice Order at the Seventh UN Crime Congress, and ultimately within the context of the UN Crime Programme. However, the linking in the UN of the issues of crime, criminal justice, and development continued under the banner of sustainable development.
   On the background to this discussion and the draft resolution, see section 8.4.

49 This should not be confused with the Standard Minimum Rules on the Treatment of Prisoners, adopted at the First UN Crime Congress. The "Basic Principles" consist of eleven brief, human rights related points.

50 The dry text of the Report of the Ninth UN Crime Congress does not convey the passion of the debate; paras. 335–352 and 356–359. Clark, 1990, pp. 518–519 provides some background to and a fuller description of the debate.
   This vote at the Ninth UN Crime Congress was the last time that a vote has been necessary on any issue at the UN Crime Congresses to date.

51 Several UN model agreements had already been developed. A model agreement on the transfer of foreign prisoners was adopted at the Seventh UN Crime Congress (1985). Five years later, at the Eighth UN Crime Congress (1990), model treaties on extradition, mutual assistance in criminal matters, transfer of proceedings in criminal matters, and transfer of the supervision of offenders were adopted (respectively, GA resolutions A/RES/45/116, A/RES/45/117, A/RES/45/118 and A/RES/45/119, annexes).

52 The concept of "a culture of lawfulness" is discussed in A/CONF.234/RPM.1/CRP.1.

53 There was a strong push at the 1995 Congress to consolidate as many resolutions as possible into what the participants began to refer to as an "omnibus resolution." The push was not totally successful as in addition to this one "omnibus resolution" there were also eight separate resolutions.

54 The GA subsequently adopted this as an annex to its resolution 55/59.

55 See, for example, GA resolution A/RES/45/120, adopted after the Eighth UN Crime Congress (1990), and A/RES/50/145, adopted after the Ninth UN Crime Congress (1995).

56 Both GA resolutions had been drafted at the session of the UN Crime Commission that immediately followed the conclusion of the Tenth UN Crime Congress.

57 The plans of action called for in this third paragraph were adopted through GA resolution A/RES/56/261. A follow-up GA resolution on this was adopted a year later (A/RES/57/170).
   In the aftermath of subsequent UN Crime Congresses in 2005, 2010, 2015, and 2021, the process of preparing action plans was no longer followed. However,

since the 2021 Congress, the UN Crime Commission has organized intersessional meetings dealing with the different "pillars" of the Kyoto Declaration. See https://www.unodc.org/unodc/en/commissions/CCPCJ/Mandate_Functions/thematic-discussions-kyoto.html

58 See, for example, para. 45 of the report on the Twelfth UN Crime Congress. The result of this long debate was an invitation to the UN Crime Commission to set up an expert group to consider the proper response to cybercrime.

59 Not that there was less 'talking shop' at the Congresses; the growing number of ancillary meetings, on a broad range of topics (although not on the formal Congress agenda), attracted a growing number of practitioners, non-governmental representatives, and researchers to the Congresses, thus indirectly fulfilling the main purpose: the exchange of information and experiences.

References

A/CONF.87/4 (1980), Crime Trends and Crime Prevention Strategies. Working paper prepared by the Secretariat, available at www.unodc.org/documents/congress//Previous_Congresses/6th_Congress_1980/005_ACONF.87.4_Crime_Trends_and_Crime_Prevention_Strategies.pdf

A/CONF.187/5 (2000), The State of Crime and Criminal Justice Worldwide. Report of the Secretary-General, available at /www.unodc.org/documents/congress//Previous_Congresses/10th_Congress_2000/012_ACONF.187.5_The_State_of_Crime_and_Criminal_Justice_Worldwide.pdf

A/CONF.203/15 (2005), Fifty Years of United Nations Congresses on Crime Prevention and Criminal Justice: Past Accomplishments and Future Prospects. Report of the Secretary-General of the Congress, available at https://undocs.org/A/CONF.203/15

A/CONF.234/RPM.1/CRP.1 (2019), Promoting the Rule of Law by Fostering a Culture of Lawfulness. Conference room paper submitted by the Institutes belonging to the UN Crime Prevention and Criminal Justice Programme Network, available at www.unodc.org/documents/congress//Documentation_14th_Congress/RPM1Asia/A_CONF234_RPM1_CRP1.pdf

Adler, Freda and Gerhard Mueller (1995), A Very Personal and Family History of the United Nations Crime Prevention and Criminal Justice Branch, in M. Cherif Bassiouni, (ed.) (1995), *The Contributions of Specialized Institutes and Non-Governmental Organizations to the United Nations Criminal Justice Programme. In honour of Adolfo Beria di Argentine*, Brill Publishers, pp. 3–13

Clark, Roger S. (1990), The Eighth United Nations Congress on the Prevention of Crime and the Treatment of Offenders. Havana, Cuba. August 27–September 7, 1990, in *Criminal Law Forum*, 1(3), 513–523

Clifford, William (1979), *Echoes and Hopes. The United Nations Committee on Crime Prevention and Control*, Australian Institute of Criminology, Canberra, available at https://www.aic.gov.au/sites/default/files/2020-07/echoes-and-hopes.pdf

E/CN.5/C.2/R.2 (1966), International Action in the Field of Social Defence (1966–1970). Note by the Secretariat, New York

E/CN.5/443 (1969), Report of the Advisory Committee of Experts on the Prevention of Crime and the Treatment of Offenders (Third Session, Rome, 24–30 June)

E/CN.15/2005/20 (2005), Commission on Crime Prevention and Criminal Justice. Report on the Fourteenth Session (23–27 May)

E/CN.15/2007/6 (2007), Report of the Meeting of the Intergovernmental Group of Experts on Lessons Learned from United Nations Congresses on Crime Prevention and Criminal Justice, held in Bangkok 15–18 August 2006, available at https://undocs.org/E/CN.15/2007/6

E/CN.15/2007/CRP.1 (2007), Implementation of the Bangkok Declaration on Synergies and Responses: Strategic Alliances in Crime Prevention and Criminal Justice. Reporting checklist developed by the Government of Thailand, available at www.unodc.org/documents/commissions/CCPCJ/CCPCJ_Sessions/CCPCJ_16/E-CN15-2007-CRP1/E-CN15-2007-CRP1_E.pdf

Hill, Gary (2019), Private communication, 1 March

Joutsen, Matti (2021), *The Evolution of the United Nations Congress on Crime Prevention and Criminal Justice*, Thailand Institute of Justice

Redo, Slawomir (2012a), *Blue Criminology. The Power of United Nations Ideas to Counter Crime Globally – A Monographic Study*, HEUNI publication no. 72, available at https://www.heuni.fi/en/index/publications/heunireports/reportseriesno.72.bluecriminologythepowerofunitednationsideastocountercrimeglobally-amonographicstudy.html

Report of the [xx] UN Crime Congress: the reports of, as well as other background documents relating to, the different UN Crime Congresses are available at www.unodc.org/congress/en/previous-congresses.html

Rules of Procedure for the First UN Crime Congress (1955), available at www.unodc.org/congress/en/previous/previous-01.html

Rules of Procedure for the Second UN Crime Congress (1960), Report of the Second UN Crime Congress, pp. 93–94

Rules of Procedure of the Fourth UN Crime Congress (1970), Report of the Fourth UN Crime Congress, pp. 62–65

Rules of Procedure for the Seventh UN Crime Congress (1985), available at www.unodc.org/congress/en/previous/previous-07.html

11

THE IMPACT OF THE UN CRIME CONVENTIONS

The two UN Crime Conventions (together with the 1988 UN Drug Convention) have influenced international cooperation in at least three respects.[1] As global conventions, they have considerably expanded the geographical scope of cooperation on the types of crime in question. They provide common definitions of certain key offences, and require (or, in some cases, at least encourage) States Parties to criminalize these acts; and they have standardized and contributed to the development of procedural forms of cooperation.

Global scope. The UN Conventions are specifically global instruments, open to countries around the world. Most earlier agreements were bilateral or, at most, regional. The UN Conventions provide a relatively clear basis for cooperation between countries at opposite ends of the earth, regardless of their legal system or the underlying principles of the operation of their criminal justice system. As of October 2023, both the UN Convention against Transnational Organized Crime (UNTOC) and the 1988 UN Drug Convention have a grand total of 192 parties (the three protocols to UNTOC have somewhat fewer), and the UN Convention against Corruption (UNCAC) has two fewer, 190 parties. All three thus have considerable geographical scope.

Criminalization requirements. The major significance of the 1988 Drug Convention was the integration of procedural provisions on international cooperation with substantive provisions on a specific form of crime, drug offences. The 1988 Drug Convention calls for criminalization of a range of conduct, including the organization, management, or financing of drug offences (art. 3). According to article 6, the offences criminalized by the 1988 Drug Convention are by definition extraditable offences, and the Convention itself can be regarded as providing the necessary legal basis for extradition and mutual assistance. Article 5 contains provisions on confiscation, article

DOI: 10.4324/9781003480907-14

7 on mutual assistance, article 8 on the transfer of proceedings, and article 11 on controlled delivery. One notable aspect of the 1988 Drug Convention is that a State Party may not refuse to render mutual legal assistance on the grounds of bank secrecy. Traditionally, this had been a commonly used reason for refusing assistance.

The 1988 Drug Convention also introduced, for the first time for most of the States which became parties to it, the requirement to criminalize money laundering. One of the main motivations for the commission of crime is illegal profit. Domestic criminal law has traditionally sought to ensure that offenders could not benefit from the proceeds of crime. In international cooperation, on the other hand, the focus has been on apprehending fugitives and bringing them to justice. Less attention had been paid, at least until recent years, to requests that other States take measures and provide assistance in relation to confiscation of the proceeds of crime.

UNTOC requires that States Parties criminalize four types of conduct: participation in an organized criminal group (art. 5), money laundering (art. 6), corruption (art. 8), and obstruction of justice (art. 23). In particular the first two of these articles marked a considerable shift in thinking in many countries. During the negotiations, the definition of participation in an organized criminal group proved difficult, since, at the time, few States had anything in their laws that would cover the concept. The definition ultimately represented a marriage of the common law concept of conspiracy with elements of the Italian and U.S. concept of a racketeering influenced criminal organization. Article 8, in turn, was essentially a widening of the definition of money laundering used in the 1988 Drug Convention: while the 1988 Drug Convention limited its scope to the laundering of the proceeds of drug crime, UNTOC referred more broadly to the "proceeds of crime."

Each of the three protocols to UNTOC, the Protocol to Prevent, Suppress and Punish Trafficking in Persons, especially Women and Children, the Protocol against the Smuggling of Migrants by Land, Sea and Air, and the Protocol against the Illicit Manufacturing of and Trafficking in Firearms, Their Parts and Components and Ammunition, all provide for the first time a globally binding definition of the key offences in question, and require that States Parties criminalize them.

UNCAC contains a number of criminalizations. The provisions on money laundering and obstruction of justice (arts. 23 and 25) are broadly similar to those to be found in UNTOC. Understandably, UNCAC goes into greater detail than UNTOC in requiring the criminalization of corruption offences, such as bribery, and misappropriation or other diversion of property by a public official (arts. 15, 16(1), and 17). In addition, UNCAC contains definitions of some conduct that States Parties are encouraged to criminalize, although there is no requirement to do so. This non-mandatory approach is the result of the fact that, during the negotiations, many States were dissatisfied with what they saw as the vagueness of the definitions in UNCAC of such offences as trading in influence (art. 18), abuse of functions (art. 19), and illicit enrichment (art. 20). In addition, some States Parties opposed making bribery in the private sector (art. 21) a mandatory offence.

To illustrate the impact of the three Conventions on procedural cooperation, Table 11.1. summarizes what cooperation was typically like before the Conventions entered into force (referred to here as "traditional cooperation") and compares this with the "new, improved" cooperation to which the three conventions contributed.

Introduction of new investigative means. Because of the diversity of legal systems, investigative techniques that have proven useful in one State may not be allowed in another. This applies, for example, to such techniques as electronic surveillance, controlled delivery, undercover operations, the promising of immunity from prosecution or a reduced sentence in return for cooperation in investigations, and the use of anonymous witnesses. If an investigative technique is legal in one State (A) but not legal in another (B), this may result in at least two types of problems. The first is that A will be frustrated by the inability of the law enforcement authorities of B to use what A regards as an effective tool. The second is that the judicial authorities of B may not allow the use of any evidence that has been gathered through the use of what, for B,

TABLE 11.1 Two regimes of cooperation

The traditional cooperation regime	*The "new, improved" cooperation regime*
Each State uses its own "traditional" investigative means	Introduction of various modern investigative means
Each State carries out its own criminal investigation	Possibility of joint investigations
Limited scope of offences; lists of offences	Broad scope of offences; no offence lists
Limited scope of mutual assistance available	Many possible forms of mutual assistance available
No provisions on confiscation of the proceeds of crime	Such provisions are included, as are provisions on mutual assistance related to confiscation
Use of diplomatic channels in requesting and giving assistance	Use of a central authority, and the possibility of direct contacts between lower-level authorities
Bureaucratic	"Good practice" standards followed; e.g. the possibility of consultation before possible refusal
Requested State applies solely its own laws in granting assistance	Procedures requested by the requesting State can be applied if these are not contrary to the laws of the requested State
Extradition of nationals not possible	Nationals can be extradited, although conditions may be imposed

are illegal techniques, even if the evidence has been obtained in a jurisdiction where the evidence was acquired legally.

In response to this problem, the UN Conventions encourage States Parties to allow the use of certain special investigative techniques. The 1988 Drug Convention introduced controlled delivery (art. 11). Article 20 of UNTOC and article 50 of UNCAC refer not only to controlled delivery, but also to electronic and other forms of surveillance and undercover operations. These techniques are especially useful in dealing with sophisticated organized criminal groups because of the dangers and difficulties inherent in gaining access to their operations and gathering information and evidence for use in domestic prosecutions or in other States Parties in the context of mutual legal assistance schemes.[2]

Possibility of joint investigations. A number of provisions in the UN Conventions focus on overcoming problems that result when each State Party carries out their own criminal investigations. Among the innovations are the possibility of the establishment of joint investigation teams,[3] cooperation in the protection of witnesses,[4] the establishment of formal channels for the exchange of operational and general information between police agencies,[5] and the possibility of appointing liaison officers.

Broad scope of offences. The earliest treaties were based on lists of offences. If an offence was not included in the list, a State Party would not provide mutual legal assistance or grant. The reason for this was that States traditionally wanted to specify in respect of what offences they would consider providing assistance. This led to several difficulties, including the technical ones that arise due to differences in definitions of even the most basic offences, such as assault or robbery. The 1988 Drug Convention stipulated that cooperation should be provided in respect of all the offences defined in it. UNTOC went further, and essentially provided a generic definition of "transnational organized crime," in respect of which cooperation could and should be provided.

Broader range of forms of assistance. The earliest agreements on mutual legal assistance treaties concerned merely the service of summons. Over time, the range of measures has gradually widened. For example, the 1988 Drug Convention (art. 8), UNTOC (art. 21), and UNCAC (art. 47) include specific provisions on the transfer of criminal proceedings, whereby if a person is suspected of having committed an offence under the law of one State Party, that State Party may request another State Party to take action on its behalf in accordance with the Convention, and the latter would prosecute the alleged offender under its own laws.

It has been only relatively recently that international agreements began to contain provisions on assistance in identifying, tracing, and freezing or seizing proceeds of crime for the purpose of eventual confiscation (which can be regarded as a special form of mutual legal assistance). The need to come to grips with the profit motive behind the rapid growth of drug crime led the drafters of the 1988 Drug Convention to require that States Parties criminalize money laundering. The 1988 Drug Convention also requires States Parties to create domestic mechanisms for the tracing, restraint, and confiscation of the proceeds of drug-related crime. International cooperation was recognized in that States Parties are also required to be able to respond to requests presented by other States for the tracing, restraint, and confiscation of the proceeds of drug offences. The 1988 Drug Convention was the primary point of reference in the formulation of the respective provisions in UNTOC (arts. 12 and 13) and UNCAC (Chapter V).[6]

UNTOC and UNCAC allow several forms of assistance that were not envisaged under earlier international instruments. Examples include video conferences (art. 18(18) UNTOC and art. 32(2) UNCAC), and what is known as the "spontaneous transmission of information," which means that the authorities are allowed, even without a prior request, to pass on information to the competent authorities of another state that they believe might be of use (art. 18(4) and (5) UNTOC and art. 46(4) UNCAC).

Use of a central authority. Traditional mutual legal assistance treaties required that requests be sent through diplomatic channels. What this entails is that, for example, a request for evidence, usually originating from the prosecutor, is authenticated by the competent national court in the requesting State, and then passed on by that State's Foreign Ministry to the embassy of the requested State. The embassy sends it on to the competent judicial authorities of the requested State, generally through the Foreign Ministry in the capital. Once the request has been fulfilled, the chain is reversed.[7]

The 1988 Drug Convention introduced a significant innovation, the concept of a central authority (art. 7(8)), a concept that was then incorporated into UNTOC (art. 18(13)) and UNCAC (art. 46(13)).[8] Although each State Party may continue to require diplomatic channels, the 1988 Drug Convention requires that they identify an authority – in practice, often the Ministry of Justice, although also for example Supreme Courts have been designated as such – to specialize in the transmission of international requests, and to provide guidance for practitioners. This has tended to shorten the chain of authorities involved, and accordingly speed up the process of obtaining assistance.[9]

Adoption of "good practice" standards. One of the major problems in mutual legal assistance worldwide is that the requested State is often slow in replying, and suspects must be freed due to absence of evidence. There are many understandable reasons for the slowness: a shortage of trained staff, linguistic difficulties, differences in procedure that complicate responding, and so on. Nonetheless, it can be frustrating to find that a case must be abandoned because even a simple request is not fulfilled in time. The 1988 Drug Convention does not make any explicit reference to an obligation on the part of the requested State to be prompt in its reply. UNTOC, however, stresses the importance of promptness in two separate provisions. Article 18(13) of the TOC Convention provides that, if the central authority itself responds to the request, it should ensure speedy and prompt execution. If the central authority transmits the request to, for example, the competent court, the central authority is required to encourage the speedy and proper execution of the request. Article 18(24) provides that the request is to be executed "as soon as possible" and that the requested State is to take "as full account as possible of any deadlines suggested by the requesting State Party and for which reasons are given."[10]

Difficulties may also arise due to different legal standards. An example of this is the concept of "prima facie evidence of guilt" which some States require as a condition for extradition.[11] Since different States apply different rules of evidence, it may be difficult for a practitioner in one State to know what evidence should be provided. Both UNTOC (art. 16(8)) and UNCAC (art. 44(9)) call upon States Parties to simplify their evidentiary requirements in this respect.

Possibility of applying the law and procedures of the requesting State. Since the procedural laws of States Parties differ considerably, the requesting State may require special procedures (such as notarized affidavits) that are not recognized under the law of the requested State. Traditionally, the almost immutable principle has been that the requested State follows its own procedural law. This principle has led to difficulties, in particular when the requesting and the requested State represent different legal traditions. For example, the evidence transmitted from the requested State may be in the form prescribed by the laws of this State, but such evidence may be unacceptable under the procedural law of the requesting State.

The modern trend is to allow more flexibility in respect of procedures. According to article 7(12) of the 1988 Drug Convention, a request shall be executed in accordance with the domestic law of the requested State. However, the article goes on to say that, to the extent not contrary to the domestic law of the requested State and where possible, the request shall be executed in accordance with the procedures specified in the request. Thus, although the 1988 Drug Convention does not go so far as to require that the requested State comply with the procedural form required by the requesting State, it does clearly exhort the requested State to do so. This same provision was taken verbatim into article 18(17) of UNTOC and article 46(17) of UNCAC.

Extradition of nationals. One of the most cherished principles in extradition law has been that States will not extradite their own nationals and will, at most, undertake to bring them to trial in their own courts. Today, more and more States allow extradition of their own nationals, although some conditions may be placed, such as that the national, if convicted, should be returned to their own State to serve the sentence. UNTOC (art. 16(11)) and UNCAC (art. 44(12)) incorporate provisions that reflect this development, by allowing for the possibility of "temporary surrender" of the fugitive on the condition that this person will be returned to the requested State Party for the purpose of serving any sentence imposed. In cases where the requested State refuses to extradite a fugitive on the grounds that the fugitive is its own national, that State is often seen to have an obligation to bring the person to trial. Where extradition is requested for the purpose of enforcing a sentence, the requested State may also enforce the sentence that has been imposed in accordance with the requirements of its domestic law. (See art. 24 of UNTOC and arts. 32 and 33 of UNCAC.)

Notes

1 For more on the UN crime conventions, see UNTOC, 2006, and UNCAC, 2010. This section is largely based on Joutsen, 2011. The discussion in Chapter 3, which also deals with the UN Crime Conventions, focuses on the negotiation of the Conventions, and on review of their implementation. The present chapter looks separately at their impact on international police and judicial cooperation.
2 See *Legislative Guides for the Implementation of the United Nations Convention against Transnational Organized Crime and the Protocols thereto,* United Nations Office on Drugs and Crime, New York 2004, p. 183, para. 384.
3 See article 9, para. 1 (c) of the 1988 Drug Convention, article 19 of UNTOC, and article 49 of UNCAC. Joint investigation teams can be set up when a criminal investigation requires close cooperation among two or more States. They consist of representatives of law enforcement agencies or other competent authorities of the States in question. The members of the team carry out their operations in accordance with the law of the host State.
4 See article 24 of UNTOC and articles 32 and 33 of UNCAC.
5 For example, article 27 of UNTOC Convention encourages States Parties to cooperate closely with one another by enhancing and, where necessary, establishing channels of communication between their competent authorities, agencies, and services in order to facilitate the secure and rapid exchange of information concerning all aspects of the offences covered by the Convention, strengthen the cooperation in conducting inquiries, provide items for analytical and investigative purposes, exchange information on the modus operandi of offenders or exchange personnel, including the posting of liaison officers. See also article 9 of the 1988 Drug Convention and article 48 of UNCAC.
6 Another strand in this development was the UN Convention for the Suppression of the Financing of Terrorism, which was negotiated in the aftermath of the terrorist attacks in the United States in September 2001. This Convention requires that States Parties take measures for the identification, detection, freezing, and confiscation of funds used or allocated for the purpose of committing the terrorist acts that States are required to criminalize under the Convention (art. 8).
7 Many commentators have pointed out that one of the main disadvantages of letters rogatory is the inefficient, costly, and time-consuming way in which they are transmitted.
8 This concept was originally developed in civil law, and introduced in the 1965 Hague Convention on the Service Abroad of Judicial and Extrajudicial Documents in Civil or Commercial Matters.
9 Article 7(8) of the 1988 Drug Convention, article 18(13) of UNTOC, and article 46(13) of UNCAC also allow for the possibility that, in urgent cases and when

the countries in question agree, the request can be made through the International Criminal Police Organization, if possible.

10 Other elements of "good practice" in mutual legal assistance have also worked their way into UNTOC and UNCAC, making the life of the practitioner easier than under, for example, the 1988 Drug Convention. According to article 18(24) of UNTOC and article 46(24) of UNCAC, the requested State should respond to reasonable requests by the requesting State for information on progress of its handling of the request, and the requesting State should promptly inform the requested State when the assistance sought is no longer required.

11 Essentially, this means that the evidence at first sight appears to indicate the guilt of the suspect. This should not be confused with the principle of the presumption of innocence, according to which a person is to be considered innocent unless and until proven guilty in a criminal trial.

References

Joutsen, Matti (2011), The Impact of United Nations Crime Conventions on International Cooperation, in Cindy Smith, Sheldon X. Shang and Rosemary Barberet (eds.), *Routledge Handbook of International Criminology*, Routledge, pp. 112–124

Legislative Guides *for the Implementation of the United Nations Convention against Transnational Organized Crime and the Protocols thereto*, United Nations Office on Drugs and Crime (2004), UNODC

UNCAC (2010), *Travaux Préparatoires* of the negotiations for the elaboration of the United Nations Convention against Corruption, United Nations, Sales No. E.10.V.13., available at http://www.unodc.org/documents/treaties/UNCAC/Publications/Travaux/Travaux_Preparatoires_-_UNCAC_E.pdf

UNTOC (2006), *Travaux Préparatoires* of the negotiations for the elaboration of the United Nations Convention against Transnational Organized Crime and the Protocols thereto, United Nations, Sales No. E.06.V.5., available at www.unodc.org/pdf/ctoccop_2006/04-60074_ebook-e.pdf

12

UN CRIME PROGRAMME TECHNICAL ASSISTANCE, RESEARCH, AND PEACEBUILDING

12.1   UN Crime Programme technical assistance

The UN Crime Programme and PNIs provide technical assistance to Member States on request. This technical assistance can take the form of the provision of expertise and advice, training, equipment, or other forms of support, to help Member States design, implement, monitor, and evaluate their crime prevention and criminal justice policies and programmes. These services may include conducting assessments, analyses, reviews, or evaluations; providing recommendations, suggestions, or feedback; facilitating dialogue, coordination, or cooperation; or supporting advocacy, awareness-raising, or dissemination activities.

The provision of technical assistance is specifically on the request of a Member State, and is preferably coordinated through a single national office (usually, the ministry responsible for national planning). The Member State in question is expected to define the nature and scope of the problem involved. Although the projects are usually done in direct cooperation with the Member State in question, the UNODC and PNIs also emphasize the importance of consensus-building, and the involvement of all the relevant stakeholders, including civil society organizations and bilateral and multilateral donors.

The UN Crime Programme has provided technical assistance since its formation, and this role was part of the original mandate of the PNIs. The format in which it has been provided, however, has changed over time. At first, it was in the form of UNODC fellowships and the appointment of ad hoc consultants. In the year following the decision of ECOSOC to establish the UN Crime Programme,

consultants were provided to the Philippines and Bolivia to advise on measures for the prevention and treatment of juvenile delinquency and the

DOI: 10.4324/9781003480907-15

establishment of juvenile courts. Thirty-seven fellowships for study and observation of other countries' programmes for the treatment of juvenile delinquency, probation and after-care of prisoners were arranged for officials of twenty different countries.

(Sokalski, 1989, p. 62)

Between 1947 and 1953, 130 UNODC fellowship grants and 18 scholarships were granted, two-thirds of which were in the area of juvenile delinquency. Over the next decade, each year an average of a dozen or so fellowships were granted and the services of about a dozen experts were provided to Member States on request (Alper and Boren, 1972, pp. 86–88).

The granting of UN fellowships in crime prevention to individuals in developing countries continued during the 1960s, as did the appointment of individual consultants. However, this ad hoc format proved to be expensive, and resources were limited. According to a 1968 UN Secretariat document, "the Committee, at its 1965 meeting, recommended the expansion of advisory services to developing countries, particularly through the appointment of inter-regional advisors and the establishment of regional social defence institutes" (E/CN.5/398, paras. 22–34, quoted in E/CN.5/C.2/R.2, para. 70). This recommendation may have been due to the belief that it was more cost-effective to work through one (or more) interregional advisors, augmented by the contribution of the interregional and regional institutes (the first PNIs). As a result, throughout the 1980s, the total number of UN-funded persons engaged in technical assistance in crime prevention and criminal justice amounted to one interregional advisor, whose services were paid for out of the regular UN budget (Joutsen, 1989, p. 15).[1] One of the responsibilities of the interregional advisor became to seek to identify sources of extrabudgetary funding with which to cover the expenses of any training or other external activity that they recommended to the Member State in question.

The first interregional advisors were Edward Galway and Torsten Eriksson, who served from 1970 to 1974 (Redo, 2012, p. 149). Pedro David was the longest-serving interregional advisor (from 1982 to 1993; David, 1985, *passim*),[2] and he was followed by Matti Joutsen, Vincent del Buono, Fausto Zucarelli, Mark Shaw, Samuel Gonzalez-Ruiz, Dagmar Thomas, and Sandra Valle.

These respective interregional advisors were kept busy. As an example, over 100 requests for the services of the interregional advisor were received between 1982 and 1989, and in 1991 and 1992 alone, over 50 requests were received, and 32 missions were undertaken (Vetere, p. 18).[3]

At the same time, as called for by the UN Crime Committee in 1965, the network of "social defence institutes" (the PNIs) was created and expanded, to include a total of eighteen entities currently in operation around the world (see Chapter 7). The institutes do not all work in the same way, but collectively, they provide expertise, advice, training, and other forms of technical assistance. They also provide a gradually expanding source of manuals, policy guides, and research which can be used in technical assistance.[4]

In 1997, the UN Crime Programme and UN Drug Programme secretariat staff were merged to form the UNODC. In subsequent years, the network of regional and national UNODC offices was expanded, and the potential for providing technical assistance was increased. A further expansion in capacity came when the launch of the UNCAC review mechanism led to an increase in UNODC staff members.

Particularly within the framework of the "One UN" initiative,[5] the UNODC has strengthened its cooperation with other agencies in delivering technical assistance. The agencies involved include the following:

- the United Nations Development Programme (UNDP), which seeks to provide technical assistance in eradicating poverty, reducing inequalities, and building resilience. The UNDP works through its headquarters in New York, its regional hubs, and its country offices. The UNDP has worked closely with the UNODC to provide integrated and comprehensive support to Member States on various aspects of crime prevention and criminal justice reform;
- the United Nations Children's Fund (UNICEF), which is the lead UN agency for children's rights, has the mandate of protecting and promoting the rights of every child. UNICEF provides technical assistance through its headquarters in New York, its regional offices, and its country offices, and supports Member States in implementing the Convention on the Rights of the Child and Its Optional Protocols. UNICEF also focuses on ensuring that children in contact with the law are treated in accordance with their best interests, dignity, and special needs and that their rights are respected and protected;
- the United Nations Entity for Gender Equality and the Empowerment of Women (UN Women). UN Women is the lead UN agency for gender equality and women's empowerment, and has the mandate of advancing the rights of women and girls. UN Women provides technical assistance through its headquarters in New York, its regional offices, and its country offices, and supports Member States in implementing the Convention on the Elimination of All Forms of Discrimination against Women and Its Optional Protocol. UN Women also focuses on addressing the specific needs and challenges of women and girls as victims, offenders, or actors in the criminal justice system, and promoting gender equality and non-discrimination;
- the Office of the United Nations High Commissioner for Human Rights (OHCHR). OHCHR is the lead UN agency for human rights and has the mandate of promoting and protecting all human rights for all people.

OHCHR provides technical assistance through its headquarters in Geneva, its regional offices, its field presences, and its special procedures mechanisms. OHCHR also supports Member States in implementing their human rights obligations under various international treaties and instruments, and monitors and reports on human rights violations and abuses in different contexts.

Over the years, UN Crime Programme technical capacity has come to involve a wide range of topics, such as:

- *crime prevention*: developing and implementing evidence-based policies and programmes to prevent crime and violence, especially among vulnerable groups and communities;
- *police reform*: strengthening the capacity, professionalism, accountability, and integrity of law enforcement agencies, and enhancing their cooperation with other actors;
- *judiciary and prosecution*: improving the efficiency, independence, impartiality, and accessibility of the judicial system, and ensuring respect for due process and fair trial rights;
- *access to legal aid*: ensuring that all persons have access to quality and affordable legal assistance and representation in criminal proceedings, especially those who are poor, marginalized, or subjected to discrimination;
- *restorative justice*: promoting alternative dispute resolution mechanisms that involve the participation of victims, offenders, and communities in repairing the harm caused by crime;
- *victims*: protecting the rights and interests of victims of crime, providing them with adequate assistance and support, and facilitating their participation in criminal justice processes;
- *gender-sensitive justice*: addressing the specific needs and challenges of women and girls as victims, offenders, or actors in the criminal justice system, and promoting gender equality and non-discrimination;
- *child-friendly justice*: ensuring that children in contact with the law are treated in accordance with their best interests, dignity, and special needs, and that their rights are respected and protected;
- *non-custodial measures*: developing and applying non-custodial measures and sanctions that are proportionate, appropriate, and effective for different categories of offenders; and
- *prison reform*: improving the management, conditions, and services of prisons and other places of detention, and ensuring the safety, health, rehabilitation, and reintegration of prisoners.

Substantive priority areas include organized crime and illicit trafficking (including trafficking in persons, the smuggling of migrants, cybercrime, and money laundering), corruption and economic crime, and the prevention of terrorism. Technical assistance is provided, for example, on preventive and security measures, the identification and monitoring of the extent, dynamics, and actors involved in crime, the criminal justice response, and international cooperation and information exchange. The UNODC has developed an extensive Criminal Justice Assessment Toolkit to be used in this work (https://www.unodc.org/unodc/en/justice-and-prison-reform/Criminal-Justice-Toolkit.html).

The technical assistance covers, for example, legislative advice (including support in the drafting of legislation), assistance in the development of national policy and strategies, and capacity building. The two UN Crime Conventions as well as the UN standards and norms provide the basic framework, which needs to be tailored to the national and local situation, including not only the assessed needs and priorities but also the legal and administrative system, the human and technical resources, and the cultural and political context.[6]

The tools used by the UN Crime Programme in the provision of technical assistance include a growing library of manuals, handbooks, guidelines, checklists, and other resources produced by the UNODC and the PNIs to assist Member States in implementing the UN standards and norms and improving their crime prevention and criminal justice systems. These tools provide practical guidance, best practices, and case studies on various topics. Some examples, available through the unodc.com website, are the *Criminal Justice Assessment Toolkit* (2006), the *Handbook on Crime Prevention Guidelines* (2010), the *Handbook on Effective Police Responses to Violence against Women* (2010), the *Handbook on Women and Imprisonment* (2014), and the *Handbook on Ensuring Quality of Legal Aid Services in Criminal Justice Processes* (2019).

The UN Crime Programme also provides training and capacity-building to enhance the knowledge, skills, and competencies of various actors involved in crime prevention and criminal justice, such as policy-makers, legislators, judges, prosecutors, lawyers, police officers, prison staff, social workers, civil society organizations, and community leaders. These activities may include organizing workshops, seminars, courses, or study visits; developing curricula, modules, or materials; or supporting peer learning, mentoring, or coaching.

In the planning of UN Crime Programme technical assistance projects, attention has increasingly been given to the importance of adopting an *integrated approach*, as opposed to carrying out short-term, piecemeal, specialized initiatives that do not take into account the broader need in the target Member State for institutional reform, institution building, and capacity building. This entails taking into consideration such cross-cutting issues as gender mainstreaming, the promotion of human rights, and support for the participation of civil society. Such an emphasis has been strengthened by the adoption by the GA in 2015 of the SDGs.

Furthermore, in 2012, the UN established the Global Focal Point for the Rule of Law as a coordination mechanism for the numerous UN agencies involved in work on the rule of law.[7] The Global Focal Point has a broad mandate in providing support to Member States on request in the areas of police, security, justice, and correctional service reform. It also seeks to promote gender mainstreaming and human rights-based approaches. Much of its work has been in connection with peacekeeping, peacebuilding, and transitory justice (see below, section 12.3). The Global Focal Point is co-chaired by the UN Development Programme and the UN Department of Peace Operations. It also includes the UNODC, the Executive Office of the Secretary-General, the Office of the High Commissioner for Human Rights, the UN High Commission for Refugees, the UN Office for Project Services, and UN Women.

The UNODC and the PNIs seek to promote evidence-based projects and emphasize the importance of evaluating the effectiveness and impact of the assistance provided.

Technological development, particularly the use of *video technology*, is rapidly changing the way in which the UNODC and the PNIs are developing and conducting technical assistance projects. In project development, a wide range of stakeholders in the country in question can be consulted online, and they can provide important details on the national or local context. Similarly in the preparation of technical assistance materials, online meetings can be used to prepare and finalize the drafts. The training can be and is being provided online to practitioners and other stakeholders. And finally, in evaluating the results of the programme, a wide range of stakeholders can be interviewed individually or together online. This facilitates a more comprehensive assessment than what would be possible with cost-intensive in-person meetings.

12.2   UN Crime Programme research

From the outset, the purpose of UN Crime Programme research has not been to engage in primary research on the "cause" of crime. The first ad hoc expert meetings in 1949 and 1950, advising the Secretary-General on the UN Crime Programme, stated that UN "social defence" activities should not engage in the study of general social, economic, and cultural measures directed at the improvement of living conditions nor in fundamental research on what causes crime and delinquency (López-Rey, 1985, pp. 14–15). Instead, the UN Crime Programme should seek to support the capacity of Member States to collect and analyse their own data to develop evidence-based policies.

This does not mean that the UN Crime Programme has refrained from collecting and analysing data. In 1950, a Statistical Report on the State of Crime

1937–1946 was presented to the Temporary Social Commission (Alvazzi del Frate, 2012, p. 164). However, during the first decades of the UN Crime Programme, the Secretariat had very few resources to engage in its own research projects. Despite this lack of resources, some of the reports of the Secretariat for sessions of the UN Crime Committee, and background reports for the respective UN Crime Congresses, can be regarded as independent efforts to assess the "state of the knowledge" regarding the various topics to be dealt with, and were received with gratitude by the Committee and the Congresses.

Gradually, the UNODC began to undertake research of its own on a more consistent basis. One of the first signs of this was the launching of the Surveys of Crime Trends and Operations of Criminal Justice Systems, the first sweep of which was made in 1972, covering data for the year 1970 (E/AC.57/17, 1974, paras. 11–13, E/AC.57/21/Rev.1, 1974, paras.162–165, and E/AC.57/27, 1976, para. 6). Since then, the sweeps have been conducted on a fairly regular basis. The purpose has been to gather base-line data on the number of offences reported to the police, and on the operation of the police, the prosecutors, the courts, and the correctional system. The sweeps were also designed to encourage Member States to collect such data.

HEUNI was the first to provide a regional assessment of the data produced by these UN Surveys, covering Europe and North America, and continued to do so at irregular intervals. The most recent publication in this series, which appeared in 2014, provides an extensive analysis of the difficulties in compiling international statistics, and numerous cautions regarding the interpretation of the data.[8] In 1982, UNAFEI provided an assessment of the situation in the Asia and the Pacific (UNAFEI, 1982).

The crime and criminal justice data reports submitted to the Sixth, Seventh, and Eighth UN Crime Congresses (1980, 1985, and 1990) included tables showing comparative rates among countries, an issue which caused some methodological and political concern. The methodological concern was due to the fact that the definition of offences, reporting practice, and the way in which statistics are compiled varies immensely from country to country, and consequently considerable caution should be exercised in comparing rates. The political concern arose in part because comparisons based on tables showing, for example, the number of robberies or murders reported in different countries could perhaps too readily be used to make assumptions about the quality of life in different countries, or about the intrinsic superiority of one country over another. Reasons such as these led to a change, beginning with the Ninth UN Crime Congress in 1995. Since that time, reports of the Secretary-General have usually only provided data for sets of countries, such as the countries in different regions, and not for individual countries (Redo, 2012, p. 169).

One of the major difficulties, other than the differences in definition of offences in, and the statistical systems of, the various Member States, was that many Member States did not have the capacity to collect and process statistical data. For this reason, the UNODC has engaged in long-term work on standardization of offence definitions and statistical processes (Alvazzi del Frate, 2012, pp. 163–167). One early result, building on the experience with the UN Surveys, was ECOSOC Resolution 1997/27, which *inter alia* urged Member States to strengthen their coordination of data collection and to co-operate with the UNODC in collecting and analysing data on crime and the operation of criminal justice systems.

As noted, a fundamental difficulty was that the Member States have very different definitions even of the most common types of crime, as well as different approaches to the collection of statistics (to the extent that statistics are collected at all). GA resolution A/RES67/189 (2012) requested that the UNODC continue "strengthening the regular collection, analysis and dissemination of accurate, reliable and comparable data and information, and strongly encouraged Member States to share such data and information" with the UNODC.

With a series of ECOSOC resolutions from 2012 to 2015 (ECOSOC resolutions 2012/18, 2013/37, and 2015/24), the UN Crime Commission together with the UN Statistical Commission endorsed the "International Classification of Crime for Statistical Purposes," to be used both as an international statistical standard for the collection of data and as an analytical tool. To help in this work, methodological tools and guidelines have been developed by UNODC, and training activities have been conducted by UNODC together with its two partners, the Center of Excellence in Statistical Information on Government, Crime, Victimization and Justice of the Mexican National Institute of Statistics and Geography (INEGI) in Mexico City, and the Centre of Excellence for Statistics on Crime and Criminal Justice of Statistics Korea (KOSTAT) in Asia and Pacific in Seoul (https://www.unodc.org/unodc/en/front-page/2021/May/unodc-inegi-center-of-excellence_-10-years-of-improving-crime-statistics-in-latin-america-and-the-caribbean.html and https://coeko-stat.unodc.org). The UNODC has also been working with Member States on request on the development of victimization surveys and, more broadly, on capacity building in the collection and analysis of data (https://www.unodc.org/unodc/en/data-and-analysis/capacity-building.html).

Although the UNODC does not engage in what can be called "basic" criminological research (for example, on the cause of crime), over the last two decades, particularly, it has increasingly engaged in the collection, analysis, and dissemination of data to assist Member States in planning and in the development of policy. A clear point of reference is the UN World Drug Reports, which have been produced on a regular basis since 1997.[9]

Since 2010, the UNODC has prepared a Global Report on Trafficking in Persons (https://www.unodc.org/unodc/en/data-and-analysis/tip.html) every two years. The reports are based on GA resolution A/RES/64/293, which contains the UN Plan of Action to Combat Trafficking in Persons. The data used in the reports are primarily official data submitted by Member States, but the series can well be said to have contributed to the development of research methodology and the analysis of the data from different sources, at a regional and international level.

Separate reports have subsequently been issued on homicide (2014 and 2019), the smuggling of migrants (2018), trafficking in wildlife (2016), trafficking in firearms (2020), and trafficking in cultural property (2022).[10]

In order to gather data to assess progress towards SDG target 16.4 on illicit financial flows, the UNODC is working together with the UN Conference on Trade and Development on two projects, one in Asia (Bangladesh, Kyrgyzstan, the Maldives, Nepal, Uzbekistan, and Vietnam) and one in Latin America (Colombia, Ecuador, Mexico, and Peru) (https://www.unodc.org/unodc/en/data-and-analysis/iff.html).

The UNODC also provides support for individual Member States in studying corruption (https://www.unodc.org/unodc/en/data-and-analysis/population-surveys.html).

Individual studies such as those just referred to deal with specific forms of, and markets in, transnational organized crime. The UNODC has also conducted regional studies that have taken the form of broader assessments of the threat of transnational organized crime in different regions (https://www.unodc.org/unodc/en/data-and-analysis/toc.html):

- Crime and Development in Africa (2005);
- Crime and Development in Central America: Caught in the Crossfire (2007);
- Crime, Violence and Development: Trends, Costs and Policy Options in the Caribbean (2007);
- Drug Trafficking as a Security Threat in West Africa (2007);
- Crime and Its Impact on the Balkans and Affected Countries (2008);
- Transnational Trafficking and the Rule of Law in West Africa: A Threat Assessment (2009);
- Transnational Organized Crime in East Asia and the Pacific: A Threat Assessment (2013) and Transnational Organized Crime in Southeast Asia: Evolution, Growth and Impact (2019);
- Organized Crime and Instability in Central Africa: A Threat Assessment (2011);
- Transnational Organized Crime in Central America and the Caribbean: A Threat Assessment (2012);
- Transnational Organized Crime in West Africa: A Threat Assessment (2013);
- Transnational Organized Crime in Eastern Africa: A Threat Assessment (2013); and
- Transnational Organized Crime in the Pacific: A Threat Assessment (2016);

and on the global level:

- The Globalization of Crime: A Transnational Organized Crime Threat Assessment (2010).

The creation of the PNIs provided a potential source of research capacity that can be harnessed for the purposes of the UN Crime Programme. As noted in Chapter 7, the PNIs have different mandates and capabilities. Out of the first "wave" of PNIs (the regional institutes and UNICRI), it was primarily ILANUD in Latin America and the Caribbean, HEUNI in Europe, and UNICRI that engaged in research from the outset, with UNAFRI, in Africa, and NAUSS, in the Arab region, providing regional perspectives to a lesser degree.

The expansion of the PNIs to include four national criminological institutes, the Australian Institute of Criminology, the National Institute of Justice (in Washington, D.C.), the Korean Institute of Criminology and Justice, and the Thailand Institute of Justice, marked a considerable improvement in research capacity, although it should be noted that the first three of these institutes have a largely national mandate.

Other PNIs provide a more focused contribution, often in the form of research: the Siracusa International Institute for Criminal Justice and Human Rights, the International Centre for the Prevention of Crime, the International Centre for Criminal Law Reform and Criminal Justice Policy, the Institute of Security Studies, the Raoul Wallenberg Institute of Human Rights and Humanitarian Law, the Basel Institute on Governance/ the International Centre for Asset Recovery, and the College for Criminal Law Science at the Beijing Normal University. Although it was established primarily as a coordinating body, the International Scientific and Professional Advisory Council (ISPAC) has produced valuable research on specific themes.

12.3 The UN Crime Programme, peacekeeping, and peacebuilding

A core activity of the UN is peacekeeping and peacebuilding, and the UN Crime Programme has an important role in this. Peacekeeping operations are deployed in order to support the implementation of a ceasefire or peace agreement. There have been over 70 peacekeeping operations since the UN was established in 1948, with twelve operations ongoing at the time of writing (https://peacekeeping.un.org/en/where-we-operate). Peacebuilding operations are intended to reduce the risk of lapsing or relapsing into conflict, by strengthening national capacities to manage the conflict and laying the foundation for sustainable peace and development.

The two main UN mechanisms involved in peacekeeping and peacebuilding are the UN Peacebuilding Commission (established in 2005), which provides strategic advice and harnesses expertise, and the UN Department of Peace Operations, which provides political and executive direction.

Restoring and rebuilding peace in post-conflict and crisis situations requires supporting development and reconstruction, the eradication of poverty, the provision of basic educational, health, social welfare, and other services, and the establishment of accountable institutions, good government, democracy, gender equality, the securing of rule of law, and respect for and protection of human rights and fundamental freedoms – a tall order.

A key part of this work is the establishment and development of a functioning justice system. The UN's long experience in peacekeeping has shown that the restoration and maintenance of order requires the strengthening of modern, accountable, and democratically oriented law enforcement in order to ensure that peace and stability can be sustained after the peacekeeping mission has ended. Similarly, the process of transitional justice[11] requires the development of legal aid services, victim and witness protection, and prosecutorial, judicial, and correctional services that are not only capable of dealing with accountability for crimes committed in the course of the conflict but can serve the community and society when peace is restored.[12]

Despite its limited resources, the UNODC has sought to provide expertise in the training of police, prosecutors, judges, and prison staff on UN standards and norms in their area of responsibility. The UNODC has, for example, assisted in operations in Angola, El Salvador, Kamputsea, Namibia, Northern Iraq, Somalia, South Africa, and former Yugoslavia in public service, justice reform, reconciliation policy, and the creation of a civilian police force (Neudek, 1993, p. 187, and Clark, 1994, p. 32 and fn. 42).[13]

A number of policy documents have been produced that deal with justice-related (particularly criminal justice-related) issues in peacekeeping and peacebuilding. These deal (https://peacekeeping.un.org/en/guidance) with:

- child protection;
- conflict-related sexual violence;
- gender-responsive UN peacekeeping operations;
- gender equality and women;
- justice support in UN peace operations;
- prison support;
- justice and corrections standing capacity;
- state authority in the justice and corrections areas;
- police capacity-building;
- police operations;
- police administration; and
- civil affairs.

Notes

1 Blaustein et al., 2022 pp. 28–29 note that UN technical assistance in general is largely funded by the global North, for the benefit of the global South. The amount in the UN General Purpose Fund has declined since the 1990s, making technical assistance largely dependent on donors.

2 There were no interregional advisors between 1974 and 1982.

3 On pp. 18–19, Vetere provides a list of the areas in which the UNODC provides technical assistance as of the mid-1990s. There has been little change in these areas since that time.

  See also Neudek, pp. 190–191. Neudek notes that, since 1986, the position of regional advisor for the Asian and Pacific region has been funded by the Japanese Government. The regional advisor is posted in Bangkok, at the Economic and Social Commission for Asia and the Pacific.

4 For an overview of the "lessons learned" in UNODC and PNI technical assistance projects, see Shaw.

5 The "One UN" initiative, formulated in 2006, seeks UN system-wide coherence so that the Organization can "Deliver as One" at the country level, with one leader, one programme, one budget and, where appropriate, one office. See https://www.un.org/en/ga/deliveringasone/index.shtml

6 Vetere provides a list of areas in which the UNODC has offered technical assistance to Member States on request.

7 For a critical assessment of the performance of the Global Focal Point, see Paige, 2018.

8 Criminal Justice Systems in Europe. Report of the Ad Hoc Expert Group on a cross-national study on trends in crime and information sources on criminal justice and crime prevention in Europe. HEUNI publication no. 5, 1985.

  Subsequent reports appeared at a roughly five-year intervals (publications 17, 25–26, 32–33, 40, and 55), culminating in publication no. 80, *European Sourcebook on Crime and Criminal Justice Statistics*, HEUNI, 2014.

9 The most recent report, published in 2023, is available at https://www.unodc.org/unodc/en/data-and-analysis/world-drug-report-2023.html

10 Homicide: https://www.unodc.org/unodc/en/data-and-analysis/global-study-on-homicide.html

  Migrant smuggling: https://www.unodc.org/unodc/en/data-and-analysis/som-observatory.html

  Trafficking in wildlife: https://www.unodc.org/unodc/en/data-and-analysis/wildlife.html

  Trafficking in firearms: https://www.unodc.org/unodc/en/firearms-protocol/firearms-study.html

  Trafficking in cultural property: https://www.unodc.org/documents/data-and-analysis/briefs/Trafficking_in_cultural_properties_brief.pdf

11 Transitional justice refers to the process through which a society recovers from a legacy of systemic or massive abuse. It seeks to provide redress to victims, establish accountability for the abuse, and deal with the root causes of the abuse.

12 GA resolution A/RES/70/262 (2018) on the review of the UN peacebuilding architecture, and the 2018 report of the Secretary General on Peacebuilding and sustaining peace (A/72/707–S/2018/43) emphasize the need for a comprehensive approach.

13 In connection with the operation in Kamputsea, a UNODC senior staff member served in effect as Governor of Phnom Penh, essentially overseeing civilian rule in the country.

References

Alper, Benedict S. and Jerry F. Boren (1972), *Crime: International Agenda, Concern and Action in the Prevention of Crime and Treatment of Offenders, 1846–1972*, Lexington Books

Alvazzi del Frate, Anna (2012): Statistical Analysis and the United Nations Crime Trends Surveys as Capacity-Building, in Slawomir Redo, *Blue Criminology. The Power of United Nations Ideas to Counter Crime Globally – A Monographic Study*, HEUNI publication no. 72, available at https://www.heuni.fi/en/index/publications/heunireports/reportseriesno.72.bluecriminologythepowerofunitednationsideastocountercrimeglobally-amonographicstudy.html pp. 163–167

Blaustein, Jarrett, Tom Chondor and Nathan W. Pino (2022), *Unravelling the Development – Crime Nexus*, Rowman & Littlefield

Clark, Roger S. (1994), *The United Nations Crime Prevention and Criminal Justice Program. Formulation of Standards and Efforts at Their Implementation.* University of Pennsylvania Press

David, Pedro (1985), The Interregional Adviser, in *Course on United Nations Criminal Justice Policy*. Report of the European course held in Helsinki, Finland, 25–29 March. HEUNI, pp. 66–78

Global Focal Point (n.d.), available at https://www.un.org/ruleoflaw/globalfocalpoint/#:~:text=The%20GFP%20arrangement%20provides%20country, crisis%20and%20conflict%2Daffected%20settings

Joutsen, Matti (1989), Assessment of the United Nations Crime and Criminal Justice Programme, Memorandum for the Subcommittee established by the United Nations Committee on Crime Prevention and Control, 20 March, unpublished paper (on file with the author)

López-Rey de Arroya, Manuel (1985) *A Guide to United Nations Criminal Policy*, Cambridge Studies in Criminology LIV

Neudek, Kurt (1993), United Nations Crime Prevention and Criminal Justice Programme, *European Journal of Crime, Criminal Law and Criminal Justice*, 1(2), 185–201

Paige, Arthur (2018), *Review of the Global Focal Point for Police, Justice and Corrections*, Center on International Cooperation, Folke Bernadotte Academy and the Norwegian Institute of International Affairs

Redo, Slawomir (2012), *Blue Criminology. The Power of United Nations Ideas to Counter Crime Globally – A Monographic Study*, HEUNI publication no. 72, available at https://www.heuni.fi/en/index/publications/heunireports/reportseriesno.72.bluecriminologythepowerofunitednationsideastocountercrimeglobally-amonographicstudy.html

Shaw, Margaret (2006), *Maximizing the Effectiveness of Technical Assistance Provided by Member States in Crime Prevention and Criminal Justice. Background Note for the PNI Workshop at the Fifteenth Session of the UN Crime Commission*, International Centre for the Prevention of Crime, 2006, available at https://cipc-icpc.org/wp-content/uploads/2019/08/Maximazing_effectiveness_of_technical_assistance_2006.pdf

Sokalski, Henryk J. (1989), The United Nations and Its Role in Development of International Co-operation in the Field of Crime Prevention and Criminal Justice, *UNAFEI Resource Materials Series*, vol. 35, April, UNAFEI, pp. 59–70

UNAFEI (1982), *Criminal Justice Systems in Asia*, UNAFEI

Vetere, Eduardo (1995), The Work of the United Nations in Crime Prevention and Criminal Justice, in M. Cherif Bassiouni (ed.), *The Contributions of Specialized Institutes and Non-Governmental Organizations to the United Nations Criminal Justice Programme. In Honour of Adolfo Beria di Argentine*, Brill Publishers, pp. 15–63

PART IV

Conclusions

13

CONCLUDING COMMENTS

13.1   How has the UN Crime Programme matched up to the original vision?

The UN Crime Programme was established on the basis of resolution 10(III)1948 of ECOSOC, which sought an effective structure "for studying on a wide international basis, the means of the prevention of crime and the treatment of offenders." A year later, ECOSOC adopted resolution 155(VII) C, which emphasized "the importance of the study, on an international basis, of the problem of the prevention of crime and treatment of offenders," and called on the UN to "assume leadership in promoting this activity, having regard to international and national organizations which have interests and competence in this field, and making the fullest use of their knowledge and experience."

That same ECOSOC resolution envisaged that the UN would devise and formulate "policies and programmes appropriate to (a) the study on an international basis of the problem of prevention of crime and the treatment of offenders; and (b) international action in this field."

Over 40 years later, in connection with the restructuring of the UN Crime Programme in 1991, the GA noted (A/RES/46/152, annex, preambular paras. 3 and 13) that it was

> convinced of the urgent need for more efficient international mechanisms to assist States and to facilitate joint strategies in the field of crime prevention and criminal justice, thus consolidating the role of the United Nations as the focal point in that field,

DOI: 10.4324/9781003480907-17

one that would:

(a) create the essential mechanisms for practical collaboration against common problems;
(b) provide a framework for inter-State cooperation and coordination to respond to the serious new forms and transnational aspects and dimensions of crime;
(c) establish information exchanges concerning the implementation and effectiveness of the United Nations norms and standards in crime prevention and criminal justice;
(d) provide means of assistance, particularly to developing countries, for more effective crime prevention and more humane justice; and
(e) establish an adequate resource base for a truly effective United Nations crime prevention and criminal justice programme.

Paras. 15 and 16 of the same GA resolution established the general goals of the UN Crime Programme for the first time. This Programme was to assist the international community in meeting its pressing needs in crime prevention and criminal justice and provide countries with timely and practical assistance in dealing with problems of both national and transnational crime, by contributing to:

(a) the prevention of crime within and among States;
(b) the control of crime both nationally and internationally;
(c) the strengthening of regional and international cooperation in crime prevention, criminal justice and the combating of transnational crime;
(d) the integration and consolidation of the efforts of Member States in preventing and combating transnational crime;
(e) more efficient and effective administration of justice, with due respect for the human rights of all those affected by crime and all those involved in the criminal justice system;
(f) the promotion of the highest standards of fairness, humanity, justice and professional conduct.

After 75 years, we can ask to what extent the original architects of the UN Crime Programme succeeded in creating a structure for the "international study of crime prevention and criminal justice, and international action in this field," and how well the stewards of the Programme have succeeded in adapting it to inevitably changing circumstances.

Chapters 2 and 3 of this book provide a historical record of the evolution of that Programme. Over the course of its 75-year existence, the UN Crime Programme has undergone three major transitions. The first was a transition from a forum for intellectual debate among primarily Western European and North American criminologists and practitioners to become a truly global programme, bringing in the global North and the global South (1950s–1960s). The second was a transition from an expert-driven programme to a government-driven programme (the 1990s). The third was a transition from a programme focused on "ordinary crime" and the formulation of standards and norms to a programme focused largely on transnational organized crime, and developing UN conventions on transnational organized crime and corruption (roughly the first decade of the new millennium). This book has sought to show that over the past ten years there has been a fourth transition, mainly through the adoption by the GA of the SDGs in 2015, the increase in UNODC and PNI research, and the expansion of the provision of technical assistance. This fourth transition has brought a greater balance in the work of the UN Crime Programme between ordinary crime and transnational organized crime.

Chapters 4–7 examine the main structures of the UN Crime Programme. The UN Secretariat unit responsible for the UN Crime Programme has remained quite small, although it has expanded over the past decade. The combining in 1997 of the units responsible for the UN Crime Programme and the UN Drug Control Programme to form the UNODC has allowed a much larger technical assistance footprint on the ground, through the network of UNODC regional and field offices. The footprint has been expanded further by the outreach and the depth of the work of the PNIs.

The UN Crime Commission, established in 1991, has served as an engine to increase the pace of negotiations. While the UN Crime Committee met every second year, the Commission meets annually not only for a regular session but also for a "reconvened" session as well as brief "intersessional" meetings throughout the year. Largely because of the increasingly crowded calendar of meetings, the discussions at the UN Crime Commission have tended to become increasingly dominated by diplomatic representatives, with fewer policy-makers and practitioners with substantive knowledge of crime prevention and criminal justice issues in attendance in Vienna.

New structural elements are the two Conferences of the States Parties to the UN Crime Conventions. Both Conventions now feature a mechanism for review of implementation. The work of these elements has been accompanied by an increasingly politicized discussion over the appropriateness of involving representatives of non-governmental organizations in the work.

Chapter 8 draws attention to how priorities in the UN Crime Programme, and the conceptual language used, have evolved over time.

Chapters 9–12 present the tools that are used in the UN Crime Programme. Chapter 9 examines the role of standards and norms in UN work. Although the amount of "soft law" being produced led to criticism that contributed to the restructuring of the UN Crime Programme in 1991–1992, more standards and norms continue to be produced, and they provide a framework for technical assistance.

The UN Crime Congresses (Chapter 10) provide a second tool, which offers a lens for examining changing views, priorities, and concerns in crime prevention and criminal justice. They have clearly fulfilled two of their main functions, which are the exchange of ideas and experiences, and the dissemination of these ideas and experiences globally.

Separately from the impact of the two UN Crime Conventions on the negotiating climate within the UN Crime Programme, the conventions (Chapter 11) have provided global structures for improved international cooperation, as well as a catalyst for developing domestic policy and practice in the prevention and control of transnational organized crime and corruption.

The two Crime Conventions and the standards and norms have featured in the extensive technical assistance provided by the UNODC and the PNIs to Member States on request (section 12.1). Similarly, UNODC and PNI research (section 12.2) has provided a more nuanced understanding of the prevalence and impact of crime and the operation of the criminal justice system.

To answer the question of how well the original architects of the UN Crime Programme, and the subsequent stewards of the Programme have succeeded, we can start by noting, as described in Chapter 1, that the Programme is part of what can be called an *international regime for crime prevention and criminal justice*. The UN, has arguably become the main actor in the *global governance of crime*.

Describing the UN Crime Programme as part of an international regime implies that the Programme is not the *only* international actor, or even the only global, actor. It is part of a broader constellation that is formed by a web of bilateral, regional, and global agreements, different intergovernmental structures, and international professional and academic organizations. The UN does not have the power, the resources, or the intention to coordinate these. The other actors will continue to operate in accordance with their own agendas, unless and until the UN Crime Programme (or another entity) can persuade them of the value of closer cooperation on specific issues. This was understood by ECOSOC at the outset; it stated the work to be carried out by the UN should have "regard to international and national organizations which have interests and competence in this field, and mak[e] the fullest use of their knowledge and experience." In restructuring the Programme, the GA called for "consolidating the role of the United Nations as the focal point," which also shows an awareness of the need to bring the different stakeholders together.

A second and related point is that this reference to "having regard to international and national organizations" clearly suggests that ECOSOC wanted the UN Crime Programme to be developed in close consultation with organizations that "have interests and competence in this field … making the fullest use of their knowledge and experience." This is an integral part of the emphasis in the UN in general on co-operating with intergovernmental and non-governmental organizations, as well as other relevant stakeholders. Responding to the challenges of crime prevention and criminal justice requires their "buy-in," their interest in contributing to the Programme, and their help in its implementation.

Initially ECOSOC was rather vague in describing what it sought: international study of the prevention of crime and the treatment of offenders and international action. Perhaps wisely, ECOSOC did not set goals, although it did establish a few priorities (which ECOSOC did not revisit in a comprehensive manner until 40 years later in connection with the restructuring of the UN Crime Programme).[1]

What was not and could not have been stated in the ECOSOC resolution is that, from the outset, the UN Crime Programme was not given the resources it needed to make any comprehensive international "study" of crime and undertake very meaningful action. The original complement was three(!) professional staff members. For almost 60 years, the number of professional staff members in the UN Secretariat unit assigned with the responsibility for studying crime prevention and criminal justice, developing standards and norms, servicing the meetings of the experts advising the Secretary-General, planning and organizing the quinquennial UN Crime Congresses (together with the preparatory meetings), and providing technical assistance to Member States on request remained about ten, although short-term staff have been provided by a few Member States (and at times by organizations), either through funding or secondments, generally in the run-up to Crime Congresses.

The UNODC representatives and the UN Crime Committee members were well aware of the paucity of resources and made repeated requests to ECOSOC, the Secretary-General, and donor Member States to provide the resources they regarded as necessary to carry out the work. These requests were almost always received with respectful understanding, but then largely treated with benign neglect. Other UN agencies were allowed to expand. For example, the UN Drug Control received considerable extra-budgetary funds (with the United States as one of the main contributors), but the UN Crime Programme remained under-resourced.[2]

The low status of the UN Secretariat unit responsible for the Programme was also reflected to some extent in the way that it was moved from the headquarters in New York to Vienna (as part of the Division for Social Development and Humanitarian Affairs) in 1980, and then, when the Division returned to New York in 1993, was detached to remain in Austria. According to the director of the unit at the time, Professor Gerhard Mueller, the move caused significant angst both among staff members and the members of the UN Crime Committee (Adler and Mueller, 1995, p. 11). The unit came to be considerably overshadowed by the Secretariat unit responsible for the UN Drug Control Programme. However, the combining of the two units in 1997, especially when more funds became available for review of implementation of UNCAC ten years or so later, has arguably provided the UN Crime Programme with synergy benefits.

It is against this background of a wide mandate but limited resources that an assessment can be attempted of what the UN Crime Programme has achieved, of what potential opportunities it has failed to seize, and of what changes could still be considered to further the work desired by ECOSOC and the GA.

13.2   What has the UN Crime Programme achieved?

Any assessment of successes and missed opportunities in the UN Crime Programme is coloured by personal preferences and idiosyncrasies. That said, based on a close observation of the inner work of the Programme for over half a century, I suggest that the following, listed more or less in chronological order, should feature among any list of successes (although perhaps hedged with some caveats).

1. *The continued organization of UN Crime Congresses.* These have provided an increasingly broad forum for exchanging information and experience among policy-makers, practitioners, researchers, non-governmental organizations, and other stakeholders and have contributed to the global dissemination of ideas. The Kyoto Congress Declaration in 2021 earns a special mention, as showing how a well-structured, coherent, and substantive statement of goals can be crafted on the basis of consensus of all UN Member States.
2. *The adoption of the Standard Minimum Rules on the Treatment of Prisoners in 1955, followed by continued work on UN standards and norms.* The standards and norms have provided a strong framework for technical assistance and the transmission of "promising practice."
3. *The establishment of the PNIs, starting with UNAFEI in 1962.* The PNIs have provided the UNODC with technical assistance and research outreach across the globe, and consequently offered a channel for bringing regional experience into the global UN Crime Programme.
4. *The restructuring of the UN Crime Programme in 1991.* This provided a necessary opportunity to reconsider what kind of global programme is wanted and needed, and how that programme should be structured. The government-orientation of the UN Crime Commission clearly generated increased and direct Member State interest in the Programme.
5. *The adoption of the two UN Crime Conventions in 2000 and 2003.* The two Conventions have established the minimum definition of key offences,

updated and expanded forms of procedural cooperation, and contributed to the forming of an international understanding of how to deal with transnational organized crime, trafficking in persons, the smuggling of migrants, trafficking in firearms, and corruption.

6. *The adoption of a peer-review based mechanism for the review of the implementation of UNCAC in 2009.* For the first time, a peer-review approach was taken in the review of the implementation of a UN convention – in any field. Moreover, the process of review of the implementation of UNCAC has identified many shortcomings in States Parties. The technical assistance services of the UNODC, as well as the training provided by the PNIs, have supported the national response to corruption.
7. *The strengthening of the UNODC research capacity and ability to prepare technical documents to be used in technical assistance missions and in training.*
8. *The integration of crime prevention and criminal justice concerns in the SDGs in 2015.* Although the number of crime and criminal justice related indicators established in the Agenda for 2030 are few and far between, the SDGs offer a cross-cutting paradigm for how to integrate the UN Crime Programme with other key areas of UN activities.

13.3   What has the UN Crime Programme failed to achieve?

A corresponding list of missed opportunities in the UN Crime Programme necessitates engaging in alternative history, an exercise in "what if" scenarios. There are understandable reasons why some initiatives did not go forward. Perhaps those making the proposals had not considered all the political aspects involved and had not anticipated from which quarters the resistance would come, and on what grounds. Possibly the proponents had not been able to explain sufficiently clearly why the initiatives should be supported. There may have been too many initiatives competing for the same resource base. The following list suggests some key missed opportunities.

1. *The continued under-resourcing of the UN Crime Programme, particularly the paucity of funding through the regular budget.* Although the Programme received a small increase in regular budgetary resources in connection with the review of implementation of UNCAC, the regular budget allocated to crime prevention and criminal justice cannot be regarded as being commensurate with the importance that the GA clearly accorded these issues when restructuring the Programme in 1991.
2. *The failure to reach agreement in 2009 on a more robust peer review mechanism for UNCAC, and the even weaker review mechanism adopted in 2018 for UNTOC.* Although peer review was accepted as a principle, the mechanism adopted in 2009 was weak. A stronger mechanism, based

on direct expert-to-expert consultations, would quite probably have generated more political will to implement a variety of needed changes in various Member States. It is worth noting that many elements of peer review that were accepted as part of the package on a voluntary basis (such as "country visits," broad consultation with non-governmental organizations and other stakeholders in connection with individual reviews and the publication of individual reports) have become common practice. It is understandable that the UNTOC review mechanism was more complex, and a more robust mechanism with country visits would have been much more expensive than was the case with UNCAC. Nonetheless, many of the features of the UNCAC review that could have been incorporated without significant additional work or expense were discarded when the UNTOC package was put together.

3. *The increasing politicization of the debate over the appropriateness of involving non-governmental organizations in the work of the UN Crime Programme.* From the outset the UN Crime Programme was designed to involve all the stakeholders: Member States, intergovernmental organizations, non-governmental organizations, researchers, individual experts, the private sector, religious communities, and so on. The debate over the involvement of NGOs arose specifically in the context of the review of UNCAC and the UNTOC, but then spread more widely in the UN Crime Programme.

4. *The lack of a coordinated method for reviewing implementation of the UN standards and norms.* Following criticism from a few Member States, the process of collecting information from Member States on the use and application of standards and norms has largely been abandoned (although the topic of their use and application has become a standing item on the agenda of the UN Crime Commission). While it is understandable that a reporting system that covered, on a regular basis, all the existing UN standards and norms would require considerable time and resources, it should be possible for the UN Crime Commission to devise a coordinated system that seeks to identify difficulties in the implementation of key provisions and provide technical assistance to Member States on request to overcome these difficulties.

5. *The waning involvement of "experts from the capitals" in the work of the UN Crime Commission.* As noted above, the crowded meeting calendar has led to a decrease in the number of policy-makers and practitioners attending meetings in Vienna. The input of such experts and diplomatic representatives is needed in crafting the proper mandates to be adopted by the Commission.

6. *The underutilization by the UN Crime Commission of the extensive reservoir of research and expertise that could be offered by the UNODC and the PNIs.* The UNODC regularly displays its impressive array of

publications at meetings of the UN Crime Commission and the Conferences of the States Parties to the two UN Crime Conventions, and reports by the Secretariat to these bodies often make reference to these publications. However, they are rarely mentioned in national statements nor are they reflected in the draft resolutions crafted by these bodies. The same is true of the very extensive amount of publications and other resources produced by the PNIs. UN Crime Congresses, the Commission, and the Conferences of the States Parties often note the importance of formulating policy on the basis of evidence. One would hope that these bodies could lead by example, by more clearly basing their conclusions on the evidence that has been placed at their disposal.

How can the UN Crime Programme be strengthened further?

The preceding description of how extensively the UN Crime Programme has evolved over the years shows that the Programme can be whatever the Member States want it to be. Nothing is set in stone: the GA, ECOSOC, and even the UN Crime Commission have considerable flexibility in establishing the priorities and in designing the process.

The successes of the UN Crime Programme definitely needs to be emphasized. While there have (arguably) been missed opportunities, as suggested above, an extensive amount of work has been and continues to be done, despite the limited resources.

What are referred to above as "missed opportunities" should not be understood as meaning that the issues in question could not be revisited, or at least the negative consequences alleviated.

The question of *expanding the regular budget*, however, is a critical one. A stronger UN Crime Programme would require more resources: more staff, more funds for technical assistance, more funds for the collection and analysis of data. The reality is that many demands are being made on the Secretary-General by the Member States, and there is no reason to doubt the need for increased spending on such issues as combating climate change, the response to the risk of global pandemics, alleviating absolute poverty, improving the status of women, or dealing with security threats.

One alternative that has been adopted is to rely increasingly on extrabudgetary funding (which is usually earmarked for projects desired by the donor). Another alternative is to make better use of the resources already available to the UN Crime Programme, and that includes the underutilized expertise of the UN research staff and of the PNIs.

The *weakness of peer review on the implementation of the UN Crime Conventions* seems to have become deeply entrenched in the work of the two Conferences of the States Parties, and there does not appear to be any realistic prospect of fundamentally revisiting the decisions made when the review mechanisms were set up. Nonetheless, as has been demonstrated in the review of implementation of UNCAC, a large part of the problem has been a lack of understanding on the part of some representatives as to how peer review works. Some of the elements of peer review can be adopted on a voluntary basis by individual States Parties to the two UN Crime Conventions, provided resources for this are made available. One obvious possibility is that, within the framework of review of implementation of UNTOC, direct contact between the governmental experts of the reviewing States Parties and the experts of the State Party under review could be arranged, in particular through video conferences.

The *sensitivity of the issue of the involvement of non-governmental organizations* has also become firmly entrenched in some aspects of the UN Crime Programme. This is unfortunate because as noted, the UN as an organization has been, and continues to be, very welcoming to non-governmental organizations as advocates and as providers of expertise. To some extent, the issue has spread because of an inability to make a distinction between, on the one hand, the general right of non-governmental organizations to participate in the work of the UN Crime Commission and the Conferences of the States Parties to the Conventions, and, on the other hand, the specific alleged right of non-governmental organizations to participate in the work, for example, of the UNCAC Implementation Review Group. As suggested in a UNCAC CoSP conference room paper prepared by the author (CAC/COSP/2015/CRP.3, pp. 20–24), the positive experience that the majority of States Parties have had with their engagement with non-governmental organizations in the review of implementation on the national level should be noted but the concerns of the critics should also be laid out and addressed more clearly.

The common ground between those advocating for greater non-governmental organization involvement in work on crime prevention and criminal justice and those advocating for limiting such involvement to "appropriate," "qualified," and "representative" non-governmental organizations would presumably be found around agreement on the right of civil society groups to act in a lawful manner to assist the authorities in crime prevention and criminal justice and on the right of sovereign States to determine what laws and regulations apply to such groups. In the context of the UN Crime Programme, clear procedures exist for granting non-governmental organizations consultative status with ECOSOC and for being invited to UN Crime Congresses.

A broadly scoped resuscitation of the reporting procedure for *reviewing the implementation of the standards and norms* (even in accordance with the cluster approach that has been already developed) would probably meet with considerable resistance by the UN Crime Commission and would be resource-intensive. Nonetheless, the Commission has the power to devise new procedures, such as by establishing special groups or appointing special rapporteurs. The fact that this possibility has never been utilized does not mean it could not be taken up in the future.

The number of policy-makers and practitioners – *experts from the capitals* – attending meetings in Vienna (and, to some extent, other UN Crime Programme meetings) has decreased for understandable reasons: the increasingly crowded meeting calendar, the many pressures on the time of the policy-makers and practitioners, the expense of travel, and then the impact of the Covid-19 pandemic. However, as noted, the input of both such experts and diplomatic representatives is a necessary part of crafting the proper mandates to be adopted by the Commission.

It is quite possible that the global pandemic, as tragic as it has been, has provided a learning opportunity. It has led to a considerable change in how UN Crime Programme meetings have been conducted. Online meetings and hybrid meetings have many advantages compared to in-person meetings (Joutsen, 2022). Despite the removal of travel and conference restrictions imposed during the pandemic, many meetings will continue to be held in a hybrid format. This offers an opportunity to reassess how the virtual environment can be harnessed to make UN Crime Programme meetings more representative and bring in more experts from the capitals as well as a broader range of views and concerns. There will undoubtedly be more information to process. However, a more inclusive and thorough exchange of views and experiences could lead to more productive meetings, a better outcome, and, ultimately, a UN Crime Programme that better serves Member States in improving crime prevention and reforming their criminal justice systems to be more effective, fair, and humane.

Given that the UN Crime Commission has so often emphasized the importance of evidence-based policy, it is unfortunate that the Commission has apparently *underutilized the extensive body of research and expertise* that is offered by the UNODC and the PNIs. Part of the reason for this may be the same disconnect between researchers, policy analysts, and policy-makers that is all too common at the local and national level: policy-makers want data, but they want a very specific type of data (for example, data that clarifies the costs and benefits of specific policy options), and they want it soon. Researchers and policy analysts, on the other hand, work with a longer time perspective. The researchers also tend to want to qualify their tentative conclusions, emphasizing the limitations on the data and on the drawing of conclusions from the data.

Policy-makers face a situation where they are confronted by a barrage of data, which may be offered by competing researchers and stakeholders, some of whom (in the view of the policy-makers) may have their own hidden agendas and possibly may selectively present the data and their conclusions.

Within the UN Crime Programme, several suggestions for improvement can be made.

The PNIs have already organized workshops related to the thematic debates at the annual session of the UN Crime Commission that have provided an opportunity to present the work that they have carried out on the issues in question. This practice should be continued, and the PNIs may wish to consider preparing short briefing notes on very specific issues that are otherwise coming up on the agenda from other sources, when one or more of the PNIs believe that they have material to contribute. This would be one way to achieve better integration of the input of the PNIs, as called for in GA resolution 46/152 of 1991, mentioned above.

In the reports of the Secretariat to the UN Crime Commission and other bodies, the UNODC usually includes references to the work that they have carried out. Frequently, however, these references are fairly brief (due to space limitations) and are often buried in the middle of documents, and therefore do not get the attention that this work would seem to deserve. Perhaps the UNODC could consider, along the same lines as suggested above, preparing short briefing notes highlighting how its work is relevant to the issue(s) at hand?

One further suggestion is to return to the practice, when requesting action by the UNODC in appropriate draft resolutions of the UN Crime Commission and the Conferences of the State Parties to the two UN Crime Conventions, of the reference being "requests the Secretary-General, in cooperation with the Programme Network Institutes ...."

Such a simple reference has largely been omitted in recent years, possibly because some of the original sponsors of these draft resolutions were unfamiliar with the work of the PNIs and with how they work in cooperation with the UNODC. Including such a reference would have two direct benefits. One would be to remind members of the UN Crime Commission and other UN Crime Programme bodies that there are such things as PNIs.[3] The second would be to provide individual PNIs with a mandate to offer assistance on request. Such an explicit mandate can be useful in securing financial support or in justifying to the management boards of the PNIs in question (where relevant) why such a project should be undertaken.

* * * * * * * * *

This book has attempted to show what the UN Crime Programme is, how it has evolved, how it operates, and what it has achieved. It has sought to provide an assessment of the role of the UN in developing crime prevention and criminal justice: its successes as well as its failures. The UN Crime Programme has reinvented itself over and over again in order to adapt to a constantly changing global environment: the expansion of the UN from a largely first-world forum for scholarly debate to a global and highly politicized forum for trying to balance national interests and concerns with the need to respond to what Member States regard as increasingly serious, and increasingly transnational, crime.

The global environment continues to change and new crime challenges continue to emerge. The UN Crime Programme continues to be needed as the focal point for international action, to the benefit of Member States, intergovernmental organizations, non-governmental organizations, practitioners, researchers, and, ultimately, the many people affected by crime. The Programme has provided much guidance and assistance. It has the potential to do much more.

Notes

1 The adoption of the Milan Plan of Action produced by the 1985 UN Crime Congress could arguably be considered a statement of priorities.
2 In its resolution 46/152 (1991) restructuring the Programme (annex, para. 10), the GA noted laconically that "it is a long-recognized fact that inadequate resources have been devoted to the implementation of the programme, which has in the past been inhibited from achieving its potential."
3 Awareness of the existence of the PNIs should not be taken for granted. The author has had to explain several times to new participants at UN Crime Programme meetings what PNIs are and why their work is relevant to the UN Crime Programme.

References

Adler, Freda and Gerhard Mueller (1995), A Very Personal and Family History of the United Nations Crime Prevention and Criminal Justice Branch, in M. Cherif Bassiouni (ed.), *The Contributions of Specialized Institutes and Non-Governmental Organizations to the United Nations Criminal Justice Programme. In Honour of Adolfo Beria di Argentine*, Brill Publishers, 3–13

Joutsen, Matti (2022), Staying Connected: The Impact of the Covid-19 Pandemic on United Nations Crime Programme Meetings, UN Crime Commission conference room paper, E/CN.15/2022a/CRP.5

Annex 1

GLOSSARY OF TERMS AND ABBREVIATIONS

ad hoc working group   an ad hoc working group is established for a specific purpose. Once this purpose is fulfilled, the working group is disbanded.

agreed language   a word or phrase that has been used in previous UN resolutions or other documents which all Member States have adopted by consensus. Since it has been the subject of negotiation, the implication is that all Member States understand what the word or phrase means in the context in question.

AIC   Australian Institute of Criminology, one of the UN Crime Programme Network Institutes. Based in Canberra, Australia.

ancillary event   in the UN Crime Programme, an informal meeting or other event organized by a Member State or other participants at a UN Crime Congress. (cf. *side event*)

Basel Institute   Basel Institute on Governance/International Centre for Asset Recovery, one of the UN Crime Programme Network Institutes. Based in Basel, Switzerland.

bureau   body consisting of the chairperson, the vice-chairpersons, and the rapporteur of a session. In the context of the UN Crime Programme, these positions usually rotate among the five regional groups: Africa, Asia-Pacific, Eastern Europe, Latin America and the Caribbean, and Western Europe and Others. The bureau deals with various practical organizational matters. The bureau may also meet in an "enlarged bureau" composition, which would also include representatives of the five regional groups as well as of the European Union and the Group of 77 + China.

CCLS   College for Criminal Law Science, one of the UN Crime Programme Network Institutes. Based in Beijing, China.

Committee of the Whole   body that allows for more relaxed debate on specific issues. The Committee of the Whole is used within the UN Crime Programme context largely to discuss draft resolutions, but the plenary may assign other matters to it for discussion.

COP   Conference of the Parties to the UN Convention against Transnational Organized Crime (cf.: *CoSP*).

CoSP   Conference of the States Parties to the UN Convention against Corruption (cf.: *COP*).

CPCJB   Crime Prevention and Criminal Justice Branch, the predecessor of the elements of the UNODC currently responsible for the UN Crime Programme

CRC   Committee on the Rights of the Child.

ECOSOC   Economic and Social Council.

equitable geographic representation   principle by which appointments and allocation of membership in UN bodies (including working groups) are allocated among the five regional groups (Africa, Asia, Eastern Europe, Latin America, and Western Europe and Others).

FINGOV   a standing open-ended intergovernmental working group on improving the governance and financial situation of the UN Office on Drugs and Crime. The working group was established in 2009 and meets several times throughout the year.

GA   General Assembly.

Group of 77 + China   coalition of developing countries, established in 1964. It currently has 134 Member States.

Grulac   Group of Latin American and Caribbean countries; one of the five regional groupings in the UN.

hard law   binding law, such as domestic law or an international instrument (cf.: *soft law*).

HEUNI   European Institute for Crime Prevention and Control, affiliated with the UN, one of the UN Crime Programme Network Institute. Based in Helsinki, Finland.

ICAO   International Civil Aviation Organization.

ICCLR & CJP   International Center for Criminal Law Reform and Criminal Justice Policy, one of the UN Crime Programme Network Institutes. Based in Vancouver, Canada.

ICPC   International Centre for the Prevention of Crime, one of the UN Crime Programme Network Institutes. Based in Montreal, Canada.

ILANUD   Latin American Institute for the Prevention of Crime and the Treatment of Offenders, one of the UN Crime Programme Network Institutes. Based in San José, Costa Rica.

INEGI   Mexican National Institute of Statistics and Geography.

informals   negotiations between representatives of Member States, generally to discuss problematic issues or to prepare proposals for formal meetings. One-day informals are often arranged before sessions of the UN Crime Commission and the opening of UN Crime Congresses to deal with procedural issues, such as nominations of members of the bureau. Informals are usually closed to representatives of other organizations, such as intergovernmental and non-governmental organizations.

intergovernmental working group a working group consisting of representatives of Member States. Opinions are currently divided in Vienna on whether representatives of intergovernmental or non-governmental organizations may attend as observers.

intersessional session held between the regular sessions of a deliberative body, in which no formal business is conducted. In the context of the UN Crime Programme, the UN Crime Commission may hold brief (often one-day) "intersessionals" to receive updates from the Secretariat, discuss developments, and prepare for the next formal session.

IPPC International Penal and Penitentiary Commission (predecessor of the IPPF).

IPPF International Penal and Penitentiary Foundation.

ISPAC International Scientific and Professional Advisory Council of the UN Crime Prevention and Criminal Justice Programme, one of the UN Crime Programme Network Institutes. Based in Milan, Italy.

ISS Institute for Security Studies, one of the UN Crime Programme Network Institutes. Based in Pretoria, South Africa.

KICJ Korean Institute of Criminology and Justice, one of the UN Crime Programme Network Institutes. Based in Seoul, Republic of Korea.

KOSTAT Statistics Korea.

MDGs Millennium Development Goals; adopted by the Millennium Summit in September 2000.

multilingualism the UN has six official languages, Arabic, Chinese, English, French, Russian, and Spanish. (Multilingualism at the UN was the subject of one of the very first General Assembly resolutions, resolution 2 (I) of 1 February 1946.) In principle, speakers of each official language are ensured full and equitable treatment, including written documentation and interpretation services at meetings.

NAUSS Naif Arab University for Security Sciences, one of the UN Crime Programme Network Institutes. Based in Riyadh, Saudi Arabia.

NIJ National Institute of Justice, one of the UN Crime Programme Network Institutes. A part of the Department of Justice, based in Washington, D.C., United States.

OHCHR Office of the High Commissioner on Human Rights.

open-ended intergovernmental working group a working group which can be attended by representatives of any Member State interested in participating in the work.

operative paragraph   in UN resolutions, a paragraph that lays out policy, establishes mandates, or requests action. Operative paragraphs form the essence of a resolution and carry more political weight than the preambular paragraphs (cf.: *preambular paragraph*).

preambular paragraph   in UN resolutions, a paragraph that gives context to the resolution (cf.: *operative paragraph*).

Programme Network Institute (PNIs)   institutes that have agreed to cooperate with the UNODC in implementing the UN Crime Programme. The PNIs consist of seventeen institutes and entities around the world, as well as the UNODC.

reconvened session   formal session held in addition to the regular session of a deliberative body. In the context of the UN Crime Programme, the UN Crime Commission has held reconvened sessions every year, in the first half of December.

RWI   Raoul Wallenberg Institute of Human Rights and Humanitarian Law, one of the UN Crime Programme Network Institutes. Based in Lund, Sweden.

SDGs   Sustainable Development Goals; approved by the UN General Assembly in December 2015.

side event   in the UN Crime Programme, an informal meeting or other event organized by a Member State or other participants at a session of the UN Crime Commission (cf.: *ancillary event*).

SII   Siracusa International Institute for Criminal Justice and Human Rights, one of the UN Crime Programme Network Institutes. Based in Siracusa, Italy.

soft law   instruments (such as declarations, proclamations, and resolutions) that do not have binding legal force (cf.: *hard law*).

South–South cooperation   technical cooperation between two or more developing States in the Global South.

"Spirit of Vienna"   principle according to which decisions at the UN headquarters in Vienna are made by consensus, without the need to vote. The principle has largely been respected in negotiations, and is often invoked in an attempt to reach consensus.

TIJ   the Thailand Institute of Justice, one of the UN Crime Programme Network Institutes. Based in Bangkok, Thailand.

transnational crime   criminological term used to refer to crime that has a point of contact with more than one State. For example, the offence can be directed at victims in more than one State (as with many cybercrimes), or the offender may cross national borders in the commission of the offence (as with much trafficking in persons and the smuggling of migrants). Distinct from international crime, which is a legal term used for a violation of international law (as with genocide or war crimes).

travaux préparatoires   official records of the negotiation of an international convention, often showing how the text evolved and what arguments were made for and against different options.

UNAFEI   United Nations Asia and Far East Institute for the Prevention of Crime and the Treatment of Offenders, one of the UN Crime Programme Network Institutes. Based in Tokyo, Japan.

UNAFRI   United Nations African Regional Institute for the Prevention of Crime and the Treatment of Offenders, one of the UN Crime Programme Network Institutes. Based in Kampala, Uganda.

UNCAC   United Nations Convention against Corruption.

UNDP   United Nations Development Programme.

UNICRI   United Nations Interregional Crime and Justice Research Institute, one of the UN Crime Programme Network Institutes. Based in Trento, Italy.

UNODC   United Nations Office on Drugs and Crime, the Secretariat unit responsible for servicing the UN Drugs Programme and the UN Crime Programme. The UNODC is based in Vienna and has an extensive network of regional and field offices around the world.

UNTOC   United Nations Convention against Transnational Organized Crime.

WEOG   a group of Western European and Other Countries; one of the five regional groupings in the UN.

Annex 2

INTERNATIONAL SENSITIVITIES IN THE UN CRIME PROGRAMME

Different Member States have different priorities, and there are often disagreements over what should be done. Some issues have been debated repeatedly within the scope of the UN Crime Programme, generally in the context of the drafting of resolutions.

Role of civil society

Issue: This topic (in addition to the current debate over the proposed UN convention against cybercrime) is arguably the cause of the greatest disagreement within the UN Crime Programme at present. It rose to prominence in connection with the negotiation of the UNCAC implementation review mechanism (2006–2011), and revolves around different understandings of the intergovernmental nature of the UN. Basically, some States are of the view that non-governmental organizations should not have a role in many international discussions on crime prevention and criminal justice within the UN framework, while other States are of the view that non-governmental organizations can strengthen the national and international response.

Appearance of the issue in practice:

- Within the framework of the UNCAC implementation review mechanism, non-governmental organizations may at present attend plenary sessions of the Conference of the States Parties but not sessions of the working groups or of the IRG. A one-day "briefing" is organized for duly accredited non-governmental organizations in connection with the annual main session of the IRG.
- The status quo is viewed by some States Parties as the result of a "final" decision, resting on a delicate balance, and therefore should not be

re-opened. Other States Parties are of the view that the status quo is a matter that should be kept under constant review in view of the "constructive dialogue" between the States Parties and the non-governmental organizations called for by the 2011 session of the Conference of States Parties.

- Within the framework of the UNTOC implementation review mechanism, non-governmental organizations may at present attend plenary sessions of the Conference of the Parties but not sessions of the working groups. A "constructive dialogue" is organized for duly accredited non-governmental organizations after the adoption of the report at sessions of the working groups.
- Within the work of the UN Crime Commission, earlier resolutions have included many references to the necessity for States to work together with non-governmental organizations also at the international level. Generally, the same States that have opposed non-governmental organization involvement on the international level in the review of the implementation of UNCAC and UNTOC also tend to object to references in draft resolutions to civil society in other connections.
- If references to non-governmental organizations in a draft resolution seem to have strong support, some objecting States may insist on language to the effect that the activity of such non-governmental organizations must be subject to the law of the State in question.
- A related point of contention has been the accreditation of non-governmental organizations to various meetings within the framework of the UN Crime Programme. The basic rule is that non-governmental organizations that have consultative status with ECOSOC may attend UN meetings, unless decided otherwise. Other non-governmental organizations may apply for permission to attend. The Secretariat drafts a list of such requests and circulates it among diplomatic missions in Vienna. Occasionally a State has objected to a specific non-governmental organization, in which case the matter is dealt with by the bureau of the meeting in question. If the bureau cannot reach agreement, the issue is decided by the plenary meeting itself. In such a case, the non-governmental organization is assumed to have the right to attend the meeting until and unless the meeting decides otherwise. (In the past such issues have been solved amicably before the start of the meeting in question. In recent years, however, the issue of the participation of specific non-governmental organization representatives has exceptionally led to procedural votes.)

Financing of activity, including technical assistance

Issue: which activities should be covered by the regular UN budget and which activities require "extrabudgetary funding." The UN Crime Commission cannot decide on the UN budget and therefore any draft resolution that may have financial implications (staff work by the Secretariat, organization of a meeting, and so on) requires a "statement of financial implications" from the Secretariat and an indication of how the funding would be obtained.

Appearance of the issue in practice:

- Major donors to the UN budget tend to oppose increases in the regular UN budget and require that any additional activities only be conducted if extrabudgetary funding is made available for this purpose. Those States that support the activity in question may argue that it is so important that it should be funded from the regular UN budget.
- If there are financial implications which cannot be covered by the regular UN budget, then the phrase "subject to the availability of extrabudgetary funds" (or something along those lines) is inserted in the draft. If it is not possible to identify the source of such funding, the relevant provisions of the resolution (if the resolution is adopted) will in practice not lead to any action.

Conditionality of technical assistance

Issue: Some States requesting technical assistance oppose requirements that, in order to receive such assistance, they must take certain steps (such as adopt certain legislation or certain policies). They generally argue that this constitutes interference in domestic matters. Donors, in turn, may be of the view that certain steps are necessary for the assistance to have the intended impact.

Appearance of the issue in practice:

- Some developing States are sensitive to phrasing in draft resolutions that would appear to imply that they must take certain action before they can receive any funding. Their principal argument is that it is only possible for the international community to respond successfully to crime if all States are able to take the requisite measures – and, therefore, (unconditional) technical assistance is required.

Multilingualism

Issue: the UN has six working languages: Arabic, Chinese, English, French, Russian, and Spanish. Member States have the right to participate in the work of the UN in their preferred language. Nevertheless, much of the work of the UN takes place in informal settings, in which case there is no allocation of funds for interpretation. In practice, most of the representatives based in Vienna are able to work in English, and these informal negotiations will generally be conducted in English.

Appearance of the issue in practice:

- Proposals for holding expert meetings or other meetings that do not specifically allow for interpretation may be opposed by those whose working language would not be made available.

- States may oppose expert meetings in general and require that the meetings be open-ended intergovernmental meetings which would implicitly require that all six UN working languages be used. This, in turn, increases the cost of the meetings and lessens the willingness of States to offer to host such meetings. It also raises the possibility that the participation of non-governmental organizations at such a meeting might be questioned, on the grounds that the meeting would be intergovernmental.
- If a meeting (even an informal meeting) is held in only one UN language, representatives of other language groups may argue that any decisions made, even provisionally, should be subjected to new debate, once the consideration proceeds to a forum where all six languages may be used. (In practice, interested governments have cooperated with the UNODC in the organization of monolingual expert meetings in order to prepare draft documents, which can then be submitted for the consideration of the UN Crime Commission.)
- If negotiations are being conducted on the basis of documentation (such as is the case with the adoption of a draft resolution or draft report), the consideration may be postponed until the documents are available in all six working languages.

Recovery of assets

Issue: Concern that some States do not take sufficiently effective action in tracing, freezing, seizing, and confiscating illegally obtained assets and in returning them to the State of origin.

Appearance of the issue in practice:

- Several developing States take the view that those States to which the proceeds of crime (for example, of corruption) have been transferred have an obligation under the two UN Crime Conventions (UNTOC and UNCAC) to be much more efficient in recovering and repatriating the proceeds of crime. The States to which the funds are transferred are generally of the view that the proper domestic legal procedure must be followed, and this, in turn, entails the provision of sufficient evidence that the assets in question are indeed the proceeds of crime and that the requesting State (and not any third party) is the legitimate owner.

Trafficking in cultural property

Issue: Concern that some States do not take sufficiently effective action in tracing, freezing, seizing, and confiscating trafficked cultural property and in returning them to the State of origin.

Appearance of the issue in practice:

- As with the debate over the recovery of assets, many developing States from which cultural artefacts have been taken are of the view that the States to which the artefacts have been taken are not sufficiently efficient in tracing, recovering, and returning the cultural property. The States to which the artefacts are transferred, may be of the view that the artefacts were legally taken out of the State of origin.
- In some cases, developing States call for the return of artefacts that have been taken from the State many years before, even though the records showing the provenance of the artefacts may in the interim have been destroyed, for example, in a war.

Use of peer review

Issue: UNCAC is the first UN convention for which national implementation has been subjected to peer review. At the time of negotiation, the concept of peer review was unfamiliar to the representatives of many Member States and there was concern, for example, that allowing foreign States to examine what action has been taken in a State Party constitutes intervention in domestic matters, which would be against the UN Charter.

Appearance of the issue in practice:

- Although there were considerable difficulties in the negotiation of the mechanism for the review of the implementation of UNCAC, and several States Parties were sceptical of the concept of peer review (in particular the necessity for the reviewers to visit the State Party in question – a "country visit" – which would allow discussions with a broad range of stakeholders), there are at present few, if any, State Parties that regard the UNCAC implementation review mechanism as intrusive. Country visits have been conducted in the vast majority of reviews.
- The major concern has to do with the expense of a multilingual review process, which may, in the case of an individual State Party under review, require the translation of hundreds of pages into one or two languages during the review process, followed by translation of the executive summary into all six working languages. The country visits also entail travel and other costs.
- A separate issue is that the UNCAC peer review mechanism is different from those used, for example, by the OECD or the Council of Europe. In particular, in the UNCAC process the State Party under review has control over what information is used and how the report is written; the IRG may not consider the situation in any individual State Party; and there is no rigid follow-up process.

"Ranking" of Member States

Issue: The issue of the ranking of Member States largely arose, in the framework of the UN Crime Programme, as a result of concern by several Member States that tables that purported to compare the level of crime in different States were not only misleading, but could be damaging to the reputation of States.

Appearance of the issue in practice:

- One of the principles on which the UNCAC and UNTOC implementation review mechanisms are based is that the reviews should not involve any ranking of States Parties. The UN thus avoids, for example, comparing the amount of corruption and specific forms of transnational crime in specific countries.
- Although the principle of avoiding any ranking has thus far been stipulated largely in the context of the review of implementation of UNCAC and UNTOC, the Secretariat has also become cautious when reporting more generally on the levels of reported crime or the operation of the criminal justice system. Tables listing, for example, the number of reported homicides or the number of prisoners per capita in different Member States tend to be avoided and may be replaced by charts or graphs comparing groups of countries.

"Questionnaire fatigue"

Issue: Some States are of the view that UNODC *notes verbale* that ask Member States for information may place an excessive burden on practitioners in the different States. For this reason, they would prefer to limit the number and scope of such requests.

Appearance of the issue in practice:

- The UN Crime Commission has considerably curtailed the number of requests for information on implementation of UN standards and norms.
- The scope of the UN crime trend surveys has been restricted.

Wording of resolutions: "shall," "should," "may consider" (and so on)

Issue: resolutions of UN bodies usually call for action. The degree to which the calls imply obligation varies and is usually indicated by phrases such as "States shall …," "States may…," and "States may consider …".

Appearance of the issue in practice:

- UN Crime Congress declarations and resolutions of sessions of the Conferences of the States Parties are much more likely than those of the UN Crime

Commission to include a mandatory phrase such as "States shall ..." (or, in the case of the Conferences of States Parties, "States Parties shall..."). The UN Crime Commission is generally not deemed to have the mandate to require that Member States act in a certain way or that they refrain from taking certain action. For this reason, softer formulations such as "States may consider..." or "States are urged to..." tend to be used.

- The references may be further qualified by phrases such as "subject to their constitutional principles," "subject to the basic principles of their legal system," or the like.
- In respect of intergovernmental and other bodies, a formulation such as "[IGO X] is invited to..." may be used.
- In respect of the UN Secretariat, the standard formulation is "the UNODC is requested to...".

Incorporation in draft resolutions of references to decisions or the work of other entities

Issue: different entities have different memberships, and different Member States may well have different views regarding their effectiveness or value.

Appearance of the issue in practice:

- Language that appears to endorse the work or decisions of other entities will often be weighed carefully. Such language may well be rejected, for example, with the argument that not all the Member States of the UN Crime Commission (or other UN Crime Programme body) are familiar with the work of the entity in question, and are therefore not in a position to endorse its work.
- Language referring to entities that have a restricted membership (such as regional organizations) may be rejected on the grounds that it is not the role of the UN body in question to comment on them or implicitly endorse their work.
- Language referring to a specific entity may be rejected as not representative of such entities in general. Alternatively, some States may require that many different entities, from different regions, are listed in the same connection.

Annex 3

THEMES, AGENDA ITEMS, AND WORKSHOP TOPICS OF THE UN CRIME CONGRESSES

(Note: the acronyms after the workshop topics refer to the PNIs that had responsibility for organizing the respective workshop)

First UN Crime Congress (Geneva; 22 August–3 September 1955)

Substantive agenda items:

- Standard Minimum Rules for the Treatment of Prisoners;
- Selection and training of personnel for penal and correctional institutions;
- Open penal and correctional institutions;
- Prison labour; and
- Prevention of juvenile delinquency.

Second UN Crime Congress (London; 8–19 August 1960)

Substantive agenda items:

- New forms of juvenile delinquency: their origin, prevention, and treatment;
- Special police services for the prevention of juvenile delinquency;
- Prevention of types of criminality resulting from social changes and accompanying economic development in less developed countries;
- Short-term imprisonment;
- The integration of prison labour with the national economy, including the remuneration of prisoners;
- Pre-release treatment and after-care, as well as assistance to dependants of prisoners.

Third UN Crime Congress (Stockholm; 9–18 August 1965)

"Prevention of criminality"
Substantive agenda items:

- Social change and criminality;
- Social forces and the prevention of criminality;
- Community preventive action;
- Measures to combat recidivism;
- Probation and other non-institutional measures;
- Special preventive and treatment measures for young adults.

Fourth UN Crime Congress (Kyoto; 17–26 August 1970)

"Crime and development"
Substantive agenda items:

- Social defence policies in relation to development planning;
- Participation of the public in the prevention and control of crime and delinquency;
- The Standard Minimum Rules for the Treatment of Prisoners in the light of recent developments in the correctional field;
- Organization of research for policy developments in social defence.

Fifth UN Crime Congress (Geneva; 1–12 September 1975)

"Crime prevention and control: the challenge of the last quarter of the century"
Substantive agenda items:

- Changes in forms and dimensions of criminality – transnational and national;
- Criminal legislation, judicial procedures, and other forms of social control in the prevention of crime;
- The emerging roles of the police and other law enforcement agencies, with special reference to changing expectations and minimum standards of performance;
- The treatment of offenders, in custody or in the community, with special reference to the implementation of the Standard Minimum Rules for the Treatment of Prisoners adopted by the United Nations;
- Economic and social consequences of crime: new challenges for research and planning.

Workshop

- Workshop on evaluative research (UNICRI).

Sixth UN Crime Congress (Caracas; 25 August–5 September 1980)

"Crime prevention and the quality of life"
Substantive agenda items:

- Crime trends and crime prevention strategies;
- Juvenile justice: before and after the onset of delinquency;
- Crime and the abuse of power: offences and offenders beyond the reach of the law;
- Deinstitutionalization of corrections and its implications for the residual prisoner;
- United Nations norms and guidelines in criminal justice: from standard-setting to implementation and capital punishment;
- New perspectives in crime prevention and criminal justice and development: the role of international cooperation.

Seventh UN Crime Congress (Milan; 26 August – 6 September 1985)

"Crime prevention for freedom, justice, peace, and development"
Substantive agenda items:

- New dimensions of criminality and crime prevention in the context of development: challenges for the future;
- Criminal justice processes and perspectives in a changing world;
- Victims of crime;
- Youth, crime, and justice;
- Formulation and application of United Nations standards and norms in criminal justice.

Workshop

- Research workshop on "Perspectives in action-oriented research: youth, crime, and juvenile justice" (UNICRI and HEUNI).

Eighth UN Crime Congress (Havana; 27 August–7 September 1990)

"International co-operation in crime prevention and criminal justice for the 21st century"
Substantive agenda items:

- Crime prevention and criminal justice in the context of development: realities and perspectives of international cooperation;
- Criminal justice policies in relation to problems of imprisonment, other penal sanctions, and alternative measures;

- Effective national and international action against: a) organized crime; b) terrorist criminal activities;
- Prevention of delinquency, juvenile justice, and the protection of the young: policy approaches and directives;
- United Nations norms and guidelines in crime prevention and criminal justice; implementation and priorities for further standard-setting.

Workshops

- Research workshop on "Alternatives to imprisonment" (UNICRI and HEUNI);
- Demonstration workshop on "Computerization of criminal justice administration" (HEUNI).

Ninth UN Crime Congress (Cairo; 28 April – 5 May 1995)

"Less crime, more justice: security for all"
Substantive agenda items:

- International cooperation and practical technical assistance for strengthening the rule of law: promoting the United Nations crime prevention and criminal justice programme;
- Action against national and transnational economic and organized crime, and the role of criminal law in the protection of the environment: national experiences and international cooperation;
- Criminal justice and police systems: management and improvement of police and other law-enforcement agencies, prosecution, courts, and corrections; and the role of lawyers;
- Crime prevention strategies, in particular as related to crimes in urban areas and juvenile and violent criminality, including the question of victims: assessment and new perspectives.

Workshops

- Extradition and international cooperation: exchange of national experience and implementation of relevant principles in national legislation (UNODC);
- Mass media and crime prevention (AIC, NAUSS, ICCLR&CJP, ICPC);
- Urban policy and crime prevention (ICPC, NAUSS);
- Prevention of violent crime (ICPC, AIC, ICCLR&CJP);
- Environmental protection at the national and international levels: potentials and limits of criminal justice (UNICRI, HEUNI, ILANUD, UNAFEI, AIC, and ICCLR&CJP);

- International cooperation and assistance in the management of the criminal justice system: computerization of criminal justice operation and the development, analysis, and policy use of criminal justice information (CP-CJB, HEUNI, UNICRI, and UNAFEI).

Tenth UN Crime Congress (Vienna; 10–17 April 2000)

"Crime and justice: meeting the challenges of the twenty-first century"
Substantive agenda items:

- The state of crime and criminal justice worldwide;
- International cooperation in combating transnational crime: new challenges in the twenty-first century;
- Promoting the rule of law and strengthening the criminal justice system;
- Effective crime prevention: keeping pace with new developments;
- Offenders and victims: accountability and fairness in the justice process.

Workshops

- Combating corruption (UNICRI);
- Women in the criminal justice system (HEUNI);
- Community involvement in crime prevention (ICPC);
- Crimes related to the computer network (UNAFEI).

Eleventh UN Crime Congress (Bangkok; 18–25 April 2005)

"Synergies and responses: strategic alliances in crime prevention and criminal justice"
Substantive agenda items:

- Effective measures to combat transnational organized crime;
- International cooperation against terrorism and links between terrorism and other criminal activities in the context of the work of the United Nations Office on Drugs and Crime;
- Corruption: threats and trends in the twenty-first century;
- Economic and financial crimes: challenges to sustainable development;
- Making standards work: fifty years of standard-setting in crime prevention and criminal justice.

Workshops

- Enhancing international law enforcement cooperation, including extradition measures (HEUNI);

- Enhancing criminal justice reform, including restorative justice (ICCLR&CJP);
- Strategies and best practices for crime prevention, in particular in relation to urban crime and youth at risk (ICPC);
- Measures to combat terrorism, with reference to the relevant international conventions and protocols (SII);
- Measures to combat economic crime, including money-laundering (UNAFEI);
- Measures to combat computer-related crime (KICJ).

Twelfth UN Crime Congress (Salvador; 12–19 April 2010)

"Comprehensive strategies for global challenges: crime prevention and criminal justice systems and their development in a changing world"
Substantive agenda items:

- Children, youth, and crime; and making the United Nations guidelines on crime prevention work;
- Provision of technical assistance to facilitate the ratification and implementation of the international instruments related to the prevention and suppression of terrorism;
- Criminal justice responses to the smuggling of migrants and trafficking in persons, and links to transnational organized crime; and crime prevention and criminal justice responses to violence against migrants, migrant workers, and their families;
- International cooperation to address money-laundering based on existing and relevant United Nations and other instruments; and practical approaches to strengthening international cooperation in fighting crime-related problems;
- Recent developments in the use of science and technology by offenders and by competent authorities in fighting crime, including the case of cybercrime.

Workshops

- International criminal justice education for the rule of law (UNODC, KICJ, RWI, HEUNI, SII);
- Survey of United Nations and other best practices in the treatment of prisoners in the criminal justice system (UNODC, HEUNI, ILANUD, ICCLR&CJP);
- Practical approaches to preventing urban crime (UNODC, ICPC);
- Links between drug trafficking and other forms of organized crime: international coordinated response (UNODC, UNICRI, NIJ);
- Strategies and best practices against overcrowding in correctional facilities (UNODC, UNAFEI, ICCLR&CJP).

Thirteenth UN Crime Congress (Doha; 12–19 April 2015)

"Integrating crime prevention and criminal justice into the wider United Nations agenda to address social and economic challenges and to promote the rule of law at the national and international levels, and public participation"
  Substantive agenda items:

- Successes and challenges in implementing comprehensive crime prevention and criminal justice policies and strategies to promote the rule of law at the national and international levels, and to support sustainable development;
- International cooperation, including at the regional level, to combat transnational organized crime;
- Comprehensive and balanced approaches to prevent and adequately respond to new and emerging forms of transnational crime;
- National approaches to public participation in strengthening crime prevention and criminal justice.

Workshops

- Role of the United Nations standards and norms in crime prevention and criminal justice in support of effective, fair, humane, and accountable criminal justice systems: experiences and lessons learned in meeting the unique needs of women and children, in particular the treatment and social reintegration of offenders (UNODC, RWI, UNAFEI, HEUNI, ILANUD, ICCLR&CJP, CCLS, TIJ);
- Trafficking in persons and smuggling of migrants: successes and challenges in criminalization, in mutual legal assistance and in effective protection of witnesses and trafficking victims (HEUNI);
- Strengthening crime prevention and criminal justice responses to evolving forms of crime such as cybercrime and trafficking in cultural property, including lessons learned and international cooperation (UNODC, NIJ, KICJ, ISPAC);
- Public contribution to crime prevention (UNODC, AIC).

Fourteenth UN Crime Congress (Kyoto; 7–12 March 2021)

"Advancing crime prevention, criminal justice and the rule of law: towards the achievement of the 2030 Agenda"
  Substantive agenda items:
- Comprehensive strategies for crime prevention towards social and economic development;
- Integrated approaches to challenges facing the criminal justice system;
- Multidimensional approaches by governments to promoting the rule of law by, *inter alia*, providing access to justice for all; building effective, accountable,

impartial, and inclusive institutions; and considering social, educational, and other relevant measures, including fostering a culture of lawfulness while respecting cultural identities, in line with the Doha Declaration;
- International cooperation and technical assistance to prevent and address all forms of crime: (a) Terrorism in all its forms and manifestations; (b) New and emerging forms of crime.

Workshops

- Evidence-based crime prevention: statistics, indicators, and evaluation in support of successful practices (ICPC);
- Reducing reoffending: identifying risks and developing solutions (UNAFEI);
- Education and youth engagement as key to making societies resilient to crime (UNICRI);
- Current crime trends, recent developments, and emerging solutions, in particular new technologies as means for and tools against crime (KICJ and NIJ).

Fifteenth UN Crime Congress (Abu Dhabi, 25–30 April 2026)

"Accelerating crime prevention, criminal justice and the rule of law: protecting people and planet and achieving the 2030 Agenda for sustainable development in the digital age"
Substantive agenda items:
- Advancing innovative and evidence-based crime prevention strategies towards social, economic, and environmental development;
- Promoting people-centred, inclusive, and responsive criminal justice systems in a world of continuous change;
- Addressing and countering crime – including organized crime and terrorism in all its forms and manifestations – in new, emerging, and evolving forms;
- Working better together to elevate cooperation and partnerships, including technical and material assistance and training, at the national, regional, and international levels, in crime prevention and criminal justice.

Workshops:

Building resilient societies, with a focus on protecting women, children, and youth: fostering engagement, education, and the culture of lawfulness (UNAFEI);

Ensuring equal access to justice for all: towards safe and secure societies while respecting the rule of law (ILANUD);

Getting ahead: strengthening data collection and analysis to better protect people and planet in times of new, emerging, and evolving forms of crime (TIJ);

Turning the digital age into an opportunity: promoting the responsible use of technologies in crime prevention and criminal justice (UNICRI and KICJ).

Annex 4

TEN RULES FOR SUCCESS IN NEGOTIATION AT UN CRIME PROGRAMME MEETINGS

As with so many negotiations, success at negotiations in UN Crime Programme meetings depends on preparation of one's own position, anticipation of the arguments that may be put forward to defend opposing positions, and an ability to influence the course of the negotiations. At times, the outcome may depend on misunderstood statements, seemingly trivial proposals for amendment, or chance events. In the experience of the author, the more influential and successful negotiators in UN Crime Programme meetings appear to be following a number of unwritten "rules."

Be polite (and never disrespect the chairperson)

Success in international diplomacy requires at least superficial respect for the views and concerns of the different stakeholders. One can succeed in negotiations only if one respects, and has the respect of, the other parties. Persons from different cultures have different negotiating styles, and the use of blunt language (especially when interpreted into the other five working UN languages) may unintentionally be regarded as impolite or offensive, taking attention away from the substance.

This politeness can be seen, for example, when participants in UN Crime Programme negotiations are referring to the interventions made by earlier speakers. No matter whether one agrees or disagrees with a statement, the rule is that speakers who want to refer to what someone said earlier should thank the "[distinguished] representative of X" for their statement and then go on to say if one supports it or, with great regret, cannot support it.

It is of particular importance to be polite to the chairperson. One of the key functions of the chairperson is to serve as the neutral arbitrator who ascertains the views of the participants, seeks to identify the points of conflict, and tries to piece together wording that would achieve consensus. If the chairperson's impartiality is questioned, this could endanger the success of the entire negotiations. Politeness is shown in that participants, when they are speaking for the first time at a session, almost invariably express sentiments along the lines of the following: "Thank you Mr./Madame Chairperson for giving me the floor. Since this is the first time that my delegation has the opportunity to speak at this meeting, I would like to convey to you, and through you to the other members of the bureau, our profound respect for the important work which you are doing."

Avoid pomposity

After attending a UN Crime Congress for the first time, the Norwegian criminologist Thomas Mathiesen wrote an article, published in the 1980s, in which he identified what he calls the "importance norm" and the "self-importance norm" at UN Crime Congresses.[1] Essentially, the "importance norm" requires that everyone respects the importance of the work being done. The "self-importance norm" is clearly linked to the one-upmanship that is so often evident in any social activity, both at work and at play. If a participant at a UN Crime Programme meeting is able to project an aura of importance (experience, or being knowledgeable), the other participants might pay closer attention to their views.

Examples of importance and self-importance, however, appear to be becoming more infrequent in UN Crime Programme negotiations. This is presumably related to the fact that most of the participants are representatives of the permanent missions based in Vienna and have generally worked with one another for many years.

Learn "the art of the deal"

The UN Crime Programme deals with a large variety of issues, on many of which there are considerable differences of opinion as to what exactly should be done: cybercrime, assisting victims, the role of civil society, and so on. Different individuals and different Member States have different experiences with crime prevention and criminal justice, and therefore have different priorities. Some States have a strong practical or political reason for addressing the issue of trafficking in cultural property; others do not. Some States want to involve non-governmental organizations more actively in the national and international response to crime; others do not.

The UN Crime Programme follows what is known as the "Spirit of Vienna," which calls for consensus on all issues, without taking a vote. The chairperson seeks throughout the process to ensure that all the delegations agree on the formulations used in draft resolutions or the report of the meeting. Because of the intense nature of the negotiations, and because a large proportion of the negotiators are career diplomats who do not have personal practical or academic experience in criminal justice or international cooperation, arguments based on criminology or criminal justice sometimes seem to have limited value, and more weight is placed on political and national priorities.[2]

That is not to say that no substantive arguments are made; indeed, they often are. The larger delegations, in particular, may have participants with extensive practical or academic experience who can readily explain why certain formulations suggested by others simply would not work in practice, or would have significant drawbacks. Yet other delegations may have participants who can quickly direct a logical mind at even the more obtuse questions and outline the key issues so that these can be better understood by all.

However, the stilted nature of the negotiations makes rational discourse difficult at times. With over 100 Member States attending some of the UN Crime Programme meetings, the floor needs to be given to each and all who have requested permission to speak. If the participant from Member State A happens to disagree with a participant from Member State B, it can often take many interventions before they can get the floor back and reply, by which time the focus of the discussion may already have shifted to something completely different.

As a result, the more successful negotiators include those who are good at "the art of the deal." Some of the tactics that the author has identified include the following.

Find out in advance who your main opponents might be, and find out what their interests and goals are. Sometimes it is necessary to find out the reason for the opposition to ideas, whether the opponents would be satisfied by a minor change of wording, or whether, for example, they might be brought on side by promising to support some of their initiatives.

Be careful of "blind-siders". With over 100 delegations in attendance, and with the constant turn-over in the participants, it is not enough to simply assume that certain delegations will be on your side, or at least will not speak out against your proposal. Opposition might arise from a completely unexpected source. Worse, when one delegation goes on record as being against your proposal, there is a strong likelihood that subsequent speakers (especially if they come from the same regional group) will say that they tend to agree with these critics.

Work the corridors. Sometimes, it is important to enlist as many speakers as possible to go on record as being in support of your proposal. This may encourage others to jump on the bandwagon of support.

Get the support of key delegations. If key delegations come out in your support, this can help considerably to win the field. Another tactic, which is especially important in matters with a political dimension, is to get the support of delegations from as many different regional groups as possible.

Set up extreme positions as bargaining chips and insist on them for as long as necessary. This is an unusual tactic, but it is occasionally used. By not showing your hand too early, it may be possible to appear to be satisfied with a compromise – and yet this "compromise" may be the position that you wanted to achieve from the outset. Since few negotiators would admit to their position being "extreme," it is difficult to know how often this tactic is used at UN Crime Programme meetings. However, towards the end of some negotiations over draft resolutions, there tend to be more and more examples of delegations stating that they want an entire paragraph or section deleted. Often, this leads to slight amendments of the text of these paragraphs "as a compromise," perhaps along the line that the delegations in question had wanted in the first place.

Be prepared

The old motto of "Be prepared" serves many delegations well in negotiations. For example, the drafting of resolutions may require familiarity with past or ongoing work in other parts of the UN system, for example, in Geneva or New York. The drafting of resolutions may also require familiarity with previous UN Crime Congress Declarations, with key ECOSOC or GA resolutions, or with resolutions adopted at a session of one of the Conferences of States Parties. When some delegations try to invent new refinements or terminology, or delete customary agreed wording, others may intervene to ask for justification for such changes.

"Being prepared" also applies to the giving of statements. It is helpful to work out in advance what points you want to make in a statement, how to make them, and how to justify your position. However, you should remain open to adjusting your remarks, depending on how the discussions go. One good method is to weave in points made by speakers before you. This can gratify those earlier speakers (making them more likely to support your own position) and it also conveys the impression to the audience that other Member State representatives think in the same way as you do.

Learn English

The UN has six working languages (Arabic, Chinese, English, French, Russian and Spanish). All official documentation has to be translated into these languages and the formal sessions at the UN benefit from excellent simultaneous interpretation. Multilingualism is an important, useful, and enshrined principle in the UN Crime Programme. Nonetheless, in practice, English is the dominant language. Most of the participants based in Vienna are able to read

English-language proposals and can discuss questions of drafting in English fluently. In addition, and with the exception of the Latin American and Caribbean regional group, where the dominant language is Spanish, most of the regional groups rely on English as their lingua franca. When informal negotiations are held or lobbying is carried out across regional divides, this tends to be done in English.

Most importantly, English dominates the drafting process. Although many representatives can speak several of the other UN working languages, discussions over a turn of phrase are almost inevitably in English.

Learn and use certain stock phrases and "agreed language"

In accordance with the "consensus norm" identified by Mathiesen, delegations which disagree on certain points tend to be pressured by the chairperson to find language acceptable to all. On the other hand, delegations applying the "my-country norm" identified by Mathiesen tend to try to avoid accepting any wording that would force them to make unwanted changes to their domestic law or practice or, more importantly, to go against their strong views on how international criminal policy should be conducted. If delegations in the minority fail to block wording with which they disagree, they may fall back on a set of defensive ploys, all of which involve inserting certain stock phrases that weaken the nature of the obligation, or even emasculate it entirely.

The first such ploy is to replace the phrase "States shall ..." (which implies an obligation) with the weaker "States may ..." or, even weaker, "States may consider ...." Other formulations along the same line include the exhortatory but non-binding "States are called upon ..." and "States are encouraged to ...." One more phrase, "States shall consider ..." may seem binding at first glance but ultimately all that it requires is that States consider something. What steps they actually take is left entirely to their discretion.

The second ploy is to insert a condition: States are required to undertake certain measures, but only, for example, those that "may be necessary, consistent with its legal principles" or "to the extent appropriate and consistent with its legal system." Even the insertion of the simple phrase "where appropriate" leaves each State with a margin of flexibility in deciding how to implement the resolution in question.

The third ploy is to subject everything to domestic law. It is, of course, understood that different legal systems require different measures for implementation. For example, in some States the police carry out measures which are carried out elsewhere by investigating magistrates, or the courts. Furthermore, Continental law countries rely primarily on statutory law, while common law countries continue to place considerable weight on court practice. Finally, different legal systems use different concepts. Consequently, a paragraph may sometimes be inserted in a draft resolution obliging States to do something "in conformity with fundamental principles of its domestic law."

In the drafting of resolutions in Vienna, a delegation may seek to insert a somewhat modified version of this phrase, "subject to the fundamental principles of its domestic law." At first glance the difference seems innocuous. However, when there is an obligation to do something "in conformity" with domestic law, the obligation to do something remains; domestic law only governs how it is done. However, if the obligation is to do something "subject" to domestic law, then, logically, the State is not required to do anything that would go against its domestic law.

Learn when form can be more important than substance

All words are not created equal. In the work of UN Crime Programme bodies, it is possible to identify four categories of words, from the most to the least important: words as such, words in an optional paragraph, words in brackets, and words in a footnote.

When words are left as such in the text of a draft resolution in informal negotiations, the assumption is that they reflect the general working consensus of the participants. They benefit from the rule of inertia: unless someone is later able to persuasively argue that these words should be amended or even deleted, they are allowed to stay in the text, all the way through to final adoption.

A second distinction is between the preambular and the operative part of a draft resolution. Contentious issues may be shifted from the operative to the preambular part, which is seen to carry less political weight.

If the representative of a State is not satisfied with a formulation in general, they may suggest a completely different formulation or an entirely new paragraph as an "option." Much of the work in informal negotiations involves trying to eliminate the options, so that just one text remains.

When brackets are used, they denote words or entire phrases that had been questioned by one or several delegations. These delegations may disagree with the entire purpose of the words or phrase, or they may simply feel uncomfortable with the wording. Again, considerable time can be spent on debating whether or not the brackets can be "lifted." (This phrase may give rise to confusion. At times, delegations may say that they want the brackets deleted. The chairperson will usually then have to ascertain whether it is only the brackets themselves that are to be deleted – in which case the words would remain in the text – or whether it is the words in the brackets that these delegations want to be deleted.)

Words in a footnote live an even more tenuous existence. (This category does not appear very often in practice.) Every now and then, a State or group of States may strongly disagree with the view of the majority. For them, it is often important to have their views clearly reflected in the drafting, even in a footnote, so that when the matter comes up again, the reason for their disagreement will be clear, and in the meantime, they may have succeeded in getting more allies. However, once words have been demoted to a footnote, it usually proves very difficult to get them back into the text.

Be prepared for lengthy and frequent informal negotiations

When a particularly difficult point arises, the chairperson might ask the key delegations to step outside and come back with an acceptable formulation. If the issue proves to be very vexatious, the chairperson might declare a break for informal negotiations, and the time is used – often quite successfully – to lobby for support for whatever proposals are on the floor.

In general, the pace of the negotiations in Vienna can be deceptively slow. Sessions usually do not begin on time, and fifteen-minute breaks may last half an hour or longer. Evenings tend to be free for most participants, but especially on the third and fourth day of one-week meetings, some informal negotiations continue well into the night. (The Secretariat usually has to work not only the hours during which the participants are meeting formally or informally but late into the night, checking and rechecking the texts and ensuring translation, editing, and dissemination for the next morning.)

Either bring colleagues or learn how to be in two places at the same time

Although the work at UN Crime Programme meetings formally takes place in one and the same room, delegations with only one participant may soon find themselves in difficulties. In addition to the formal meetings and the informal negotiations (several of which may be going on at the same time), many regional groups are convened throughout the meetings to review developments, discuss proposals, and plan strategy. The two-hour lunch breaks are often filled with drafting meetings or at least informal discussions.

Develop a sense of humour

The final lesson is an elective one, not a requirement. A sense of humour makes surviving meetings at the UN Crime Programme easier.

Humour can also be used deliberately at UN Crime Programme meetings. Humour may come in handy to defuse a tense atmosphere. Some of the more successful and respected chairpersons resort to it now and then, at times cajoling participants to agree, good-humouredly dangling the promise of a coffee break before them. One of the masters of this art is Ambassador Luigi Lauriola, who chaired the very difficult negotiations on the UNTOC

Convention with grace and patience. When told by a national representative that he seemed to have strong views on a sensitive issue at hand, he immediately replied that he may be strong, but had no views. At another tense time, he closed his statement by noting that he was "your obedient servant" – but then added in an almost inaudible stage whisper caught by the microphone, "almost."

Notes

1 Mathiesen, Thomas (1986), FN-kongress som kulturfenomen ("UN Congresses as cultural phenomena"), Nordisk Tidsskrift for Kriminalvidenskab, Oslo, vol. 73, no. 2 (April 1986), pp. 157 – 160.

   The other three norms he listed were the "politeness norm," the "consensus norm" (agreement is sought on all points) and the "my country norm" (in the experience of Mathiesen, each delegation seems to be trying to avoid any agreement that might result in the Member State it represents having to change its national policy and legislation).

2 This development can be seen to be related to the strengthening tendency to see crime and criminal justice as national security issues. While it is true that academics and practitioners represent a great variety of approaches, they can be said to have a greater tendency to see crime and criminal justice as social (or economic, or medical) issues.

   The tradition of seeking consensus may at times lead to strange results. At the 1993 session of the UN Crime Commission, the UNODC suggested that the Commission select four from among eight possible topics for the Workshops at the Ninth UN Crime Congress. Perhaps not surprisingly, all eight topics found some supporters, and in line with the tradition of consensus, ultimately all were included in the Congress agenda – leading to considerable logistical and substantive difficulties in trying to address all the topics within the scope of four workshops.

NOTES REGARDING SPELLING AND TERMINOLOGY

The spelling and style in this book primarily follow UN English usage. It has its own quirks which distinguish it from standard British English. For example, "Member States" and "States Parties" are capitalized (https://www.un.org/dgacm/en/content/editorial-manual).

UN English, however, can at times become so carefully couched and precise, and so weighed down with "agreed language,"[1] that it becomes somewhat stilted and well-nigh incomprehensible to outsiders. I have sought to ease the burden on the reader by simplifying the language where this can reasonably be done.

A glossary of UN Crime Programme terms and abbreviations is provided in Annex 1.

In the text and endnotes I generally provide only the signum of UN resolutions and documents, and not the full title and the date they were adopted, approved, or issued. That information can be readily obtained through an Internet search.

The structure of the signum of UN documents has changed from time to time, but now has become standardized through the UN system (https://research.un.org/en/docs/symbols).

The first component indicates the organ receiving or issuing the document, with A/- indicating the General Assembly, S/- the Security Council, E/- the Economic and Social Council, and ST/- the Secretariat.

The second (and in some cases third) component indicates subsidiary bodies, with for example -/CN.../- indicating a Commission (and -/CN.15/- the UN Crime Commission), -/CONF.../- a Conference, -/AC/.../- an ad hoc committee and -/WG.../- a working group.

A special component indicates the nature of the document, with for example -/RES/- indicating a resolution and -/CRP... indicating a conference room paper. Revised documents end with -/REV.

In 1976, the General Assembly began to include the number of the session in the signum of its document. (Earlier GA resolutions indicated the session with separate Roman numerals.) Thus, the signum A/RES/46/152 refers to a resolution adopted by the General Assembly at its 46th (1991) session. (It is this resolution that brought about the restructuring of the UN Crime Programme.)

Other UN organs followed suit, but instead of indicating the number of the session, the signum would generally include the calendar year. Thus, for example E/CN.15/2023/15 refers to the report (document -/15) of the UN Crime Commission (-/CN.15/-) in 2023 (-/2023/-).

Each of the Conferences of the States Parties to the two UN Crime Conventions have their own identifiers. Documents for the COP of the UN Convention against Transnational Organized Crime follow the format CTOC/COP/xxxx/yy, in which xxxx is the year of the session, and yy the number of the document.

Correspondingly, documents for the COSP of the UN Convention against Corruption follow the format CAC/COSP/xxxx/yy, in which xxxx is the year of the session, and yy the number of the document.

Note

1 In UN usage, "agreed language" refers to a word or phrase that has been used in previous UN resolutions or other documents which all Member States have adopted by consensus. Since it had been the subject of negotiation, the implication is that all Member States understand what the word or phrase means in the context in question.

   This, in turn, has given rise to a concept known in international diplomacy as "constructive ambiguity," a nicer way to refer to "fuzzy expressions" (on the latter expression, see, for example, Redo 2012, p. 45 and fn. 20). Two sides to a dispute, after objecting to language submitted by the other side, may find agreement on a word or phrase which is on a higher level of generality and which can therefore usefully be understood in two quite different ways, allowing each side to declare victory in advancing their political goals.

   Language evolves and political alignments may change. What was once agreed language may subsequently be disputed.

   Annex 2 provides some examples of words or phrases which at present tend to launch extensive debates at UN Crime Programme meetings.

INDEX

Note: Page numbers followed by "n" denote endnotes.

For Product Safety Concerns and Information please contact our EU
representative GPSR@taylorandfrancis.com Taylor & Francis Verlag GmbH,
Kaufingerstraße 24, 80331 München, Germany

Printed and bound by CPI Group (UK) Ltd, Croydon, CR0 4YY

08/06/2025

01897009-0011